CRIME BUSTERS

timewarner paperbacks

A TIME WARNER PAPERBACK

First published in Great Britain in 1976 by Verdict Press
Reprinted 1989 by Macdonald & Co (Publishers) Ltd under the Black Cat imprint

This edition published by Time Warner Paperbacks 2002

ISBN 0-7515-3361-0

Produced by Omnipress, Eastbourne
Printed in the EC

Time Warner Paperbacks
A Division of
Time Warner Books
Brettenham House
Lancaster Place
London WC2E 7EN

www.TimeWarnerBooks.co.uk

CONTENTS

Part 1: Enforcers of the Law

Part 2: Murderous Methods

Part 3: Forensic Evidence

Part 4: Cases of Scientific Deduction

PART ONE

ENFORCERS OF THE LAW

The FBI – Past and Present

On July 26, 1908, then-Attorney General Charles J. Bonaparte appointed an unnamed force of Special Agents to be the investigative force of the Department of Justice. The FBI evolved from this small group and is the principal investigative arm of the United States Department of Justice.

THE EARLY YEARS of the twentieth century in the United States were years of greed and corruption. Men were in imminent danger of losing confidence in one another and in many sectors of public life honesty had become a factor of small account. Industrial combines blatantly ignored the antitrust laws and government officials, charged with the stewardship on the nation's behalf of valuable land in the West, lined their pockets by private and illegal selling.

Theodore Roosevelt, who came to the White House in September 1901 after the assassination of President McKinley, was outraged by the moral chaos he saw around him and determined to press with all his energy for a campaign against the lawbreakers.

As his instrument for investigation Roosevelt chose the Treasury Department's secret service, formed in the years following the Civil War to stamp out a large-scale 'industry' devoted to counterfeiting United States currency. But this immediately excited the suspicions of Congressmen who, anxious to safeguard the rights of the individual and looking over their shoulders at some of Europe's more undemocratic practices, feared that a secret police force might soon arise.

They took swift action and Congress enacted a law prohibiting Treasury detectives from being employed by other government departments, including the Department of Justice.

Roosevelt was dismayed but not defeated. He therefore wrote an order to Attorney-General Charles J. Bonaparte – grand-nephew of Napoleon I of France – instructing him 'to create an investigative service within the Department of Justice subject to no other department or bureau and which will report to no one except the Attorney-General.'

This, too, caused a new wave of anger. 'If Anglo-Saxon civilization stands for anything,' thundered Congressman Sherley of Kentucky, 'it is for a government where the humblest citizen is safeguarded against the secret activities of the executive of the government . . . Not in vain did our forefathers read the history of Magna Carta and the Bill of Rights.'

This time, however, the President would not yield. If Congress obstructed his purpose, he warned, it would have to bear the responsibility of encouraging crime and comforting the criminal.

As a result, on July 26, 1908, there came into

being the Bureau of Investigation which, 27 years later, was to have the prefix 'Federal' added to its title and was to take its place in history as the FBI.

In the beginning the new Bureau's contribution to law-enforcement, under its first chief, Stanley W. Finch, was restricted to a limited fringe area – mainly concerned with violations of laws forbidding the inter-state shipment of obscene books, contraceptives, and prize-fight films, and the transporting of intoxicating liquors into 'dry' states.

Beating Vice Rings

But it was the White Slave Traffic Act, introduced in 1910 by Representative James Robert Mann, of Illinois, that gave the Bureau its first real opportunity to operate on a nationwide front and capture public attention.

The Mann Act, stopping prostitutes crossing state lines, arose from public anger over disclosures that, in ten years, a Chicago vice syndicate operated by Alphonse Daufaur and his wife, Eva, had imported 20,000 women and girls into the United States to 'stock' their brothels.

The first prominent personality to be arrested under the Act was Jack Johnson, the Negro heavyweight champion who won his laurels by knocking out Tommy Burns on Christmas Day, 1908, in Sydney, Australia. In 1912 he was convicted for persuading a girl, who later became his wife, to leave the brothel where she worked and go with him into another state.

Johnson, who was sentenced to one year – but

released on bond pending appeal – disguised himself as a member of a Negro baseball team, fled to Canada, then moved to Europe, and remained a fugitive for seven years. He returned home in 1920, surrendered to United States marshals and served his sentence.

America's entry into World War I, on April 6, 1917, brought new and larger-scale tasks to the Bureau, and necessitated the first major increase in the number of its agents – from the 300 of the pre-war years to 400. This small force was expected to keep watch on one million enemy aliens, protect top-security zones, including harbours, and pursue draft-evaders and army deserters.

It was not an era in which the Bureau covered itself in glory. Bureau chief Bruce Bielaski, who had succeeded Finch in 1912, accepted a Chicago businessman's suggestion that he should set up an organization of private citizen volunteers to aid the Bureau in its national security work.

Bielaski, however, found himself saddled with a giant that neither he, nor the government, were able totally to control. Within a few months this voluntary organization, the American Protective League, had recruited 250,000 members – many of whom took the law into their own hands in a mistaken sense of patriotism.

Encouraged by a hysterical spy mania, many League members who thought that they had acquired some kind of Federal status, turned their attention to the Industrial Workers of the World (IWW), whose leaders were opposed to the war.

They made illegal arrests, searched private

homes without authority, and in Butte, Montana, six masked men kidnapped Frank Little, an IWW leader, and hanged him from a railroad trestle set up as a makeshift gallows.

Such actions as those, and others by other vigilante groups, embarrassed the Bureau. Nevertheless, the situation was complicated by the fact that, whatever illegal action some groups might take, the Bureau was itself officially and legally obliged to move against the IWW and similar groups.

Much of its other activity was centred upon massive drives against draft dodgers and deserters whose numbers, by the last year of the war, totalled at least 308,000.

With the assistance of American Protective League members, roundups were launched in a series of major cities and thousands of innocent citizens were arrested and thrown into jail for periods of up to 24 hours. Although all men between the ages of 21 and 31 were required by law to carry their draft classification cards with them, they, and others of all ages were rounded-up first and asked their draft status afterwards.

One writer recalled: 'Some who were dragged into the Bureau's net were physically unfit, crippled, or hobbling on canes, like the 75-year-old man detained in a public square along with others held by the raiders for questioning . . .'

President Wilson called for a full report and Attorney-General Thomas W. Gregory agreed that the raids were contrary to law, and that some Bureau agents had 'acted out of an excess of zeal for the public good'.

However, the Bureau's record in World War I, when many people in European countries behaved with no less a degree of hysteria, was by no means all black. Agents, for example, learned that on their departure after the United States declaration of war, the German officials in New York City had left a cache of important documents in the Swiss consulate building on Broadway.

One afternoon, after the Swiss employees had left their work for the day, the agents broke through a wall into the consulate and found boxes and trunks containing around a ton of papers sealed with the Imperial German seal.

The senior agent afterwards reported: 'These records disclosed methods by which the enemy was enabled to secure information for delivering war materials and supplies by enemy ships under neutral flags. These papers also furnished the United States government with information as to the identity of methods of codes and enemy intelligence system activities in this country from the beginning of the war.'

Even before the United States was involved in the war, British intelligence had warned of the interception of a German General Staff secret message to Count von Bernstorff in Washington which, in preparing him for the likelihood of hostilities, read:

'In United States sabotage can reach to all kinds of factories for war deliveries; railroads, dams, bridges must not be touched. Under no circumstances compromise our embassy.'

In the early hours of July 30, 1916, an explosion

of two million pounds of dynamite wrecked Black Tom Island, the European shipment point and arsenal in New York Harbor.

Six months later a shell assembly plant in Kingsland, New Jersey, was blown up in a second sabotage attack and this, like the first, was financed out of the $150,000,000 budget provided by von Bernstorff for action inside the US.

Through some inexplicable ineptitude, details of the intercepted German sabotage signal to von Bernstorff had not been passed to the Bureau of Investigation – which, when the bombing attacks came, was unprepared.

Despite the sabotage, known so-called 'enemy aliens' were not as great a problem to the United States as had been expected. But war did add heavily to the Bureau's work.

John Lord O'Brian, a Republican from Buffalo, New York, was appointed as special assistant to the Attorney-General for war work. To head a unit in the enemy alien registration section, he chose a 22-year-old lawyer who had joined the Department of Justice on July 26, 1917.

This young man had received his Master's degree in law from the George Washington University Law School, and was a member of the District of Colombia Bar. His name was J. Edgar Hoover.

As yet the Bureau of Investigation was still very much in its formative stages, finding its way through the labyrinth of law-enforcement by trial and error. So far it had lacked a dominant personality at its head to guide it in positive directions and endow it with a true identity.

With the war's end its agents believed they might at last be free to concentrate upon domestic crime. While the United States had been absorbed in helping to secure the downfall of Kaiser's German Empire, new problems had arisen. In 1919 prohibition was introduced. The illegal manufacture and sale of alcoholic drink became a highly organized business, bringing gangsterism and protection rackets.

Advancement of the FBI

As the FBI moved into the early 1970s it was faced with new dimensions of criminology. The top ranks of the international criminal fraternity had concentrated on highly organized plans for developing such attractively lucrative 'business' as drug trafficking. At the lower end of the scale violent crime – most often perpetrated by small-time amateur hoodlums or drug-taking delinquents – had escalated alarmingly. This had its effects on the social pattern of life, and had gone far to restricting that personal freedom which is rightly regarded as a vital part of United States citizenship. In many cities men and women became increasingly afraid of returning to downtown or other inner-city areas late at night. The Judas-hole in the apartment door, the front hall door whose lock could be released only when occupants were satisfied about the identities of callers, became standard equipment.

In the single, five-year period of 1966 to 1971,

the FBI index of crimes increased by 83 per cent. Within that index, crimes of violence rose by 90 per cent and crimes against property by 82 per cent. During those five years arrests for narcotic drug violations increased by the astonishing figure of 469 per cent, and the enormous worldwide extent of drug-trafficking was demonstrated by the continuing and ingenious efforts to smuggle narcotics into the United States.

Such incidents as the attempts to set up a chain of drug 'imports' flowing through European ports into America, and illustrated in the *French Connection* type of operation, using reconstructed automobiles as containers, added to the FBI's always-rising workload.

Skyjacking became another new menace and, largely because of Middle East conflicts, grew into a worldwide problem. The FBI first experienced this phenomenon in August 1961 when Leon Bearden, an habitué of American penitentiaries, hijacked a Continental Airlines *Boeing 707* over New Mexico. With the help of his sixteen-year-old son, Cody, he ordered the $5 5$^1/_2$ million jet to be flown to Cuba – he was tired, he said, of life in the United States, and wanted to spend the rest of his days abroad.

To El Paso, where the aircraft had to land for refuelling, J. Edgar Hoover sent his special agents with a clear directive: 'Hijackers are to be informed that the government is not going to allow any aircraft to depart if they are in it. We are going to make no promises of any kind to them.

Legitimate Journey

'Tell them all the facts that will be given to the prosecuting authorities. Tell them their position is desperate, and that if anyone aboard the 'plane is harmed in any way they will be held responsible.'

Leon Bearden eventually allowed an FBI man on board the aircraft for a 'discussion'. While this was going on, other agents quietly boarded the aircraft. Just after Bearden had patiently explained that he could not afford to make a legitimate journey to Cuba 'because I've got less than 25 bucks to my name', the agents overpowered him and his son. Bearden was sent to jail for 20 years 'for obstructing interstate commerce by extortion'. Cody was also imprisoned, but paroled in 1963.

It was, by later standards, a bizarre and amateurish affair. But its importance lay in the lesson it taught the FBI and the United States. Any kind of individual could, and would, venture into the realms of skyjacking – whether he, or she, was a muddle-headed social misfit, or a highly sophisticated and brutally insensitive political fanatic.

To the public at large this kind of incident typified the work of the FBI, and helped to consolidate the romantic image that was conjured up by radio and, later, television. But, gradually and subtly, the Bureau was being called into question at a high, authoritative level. Hoover had long insisted that under his jurisdiction, the FBI would never be anything other than a fact-finding organization.

Then there came mutterings – and even outright

allegations – that the ageing Director was exceeding the bounds of his own self-imposed brief. He was frightened of those he considered too Left-wing, and compiled secret dossiers on citizens who had neither been involved in, nor suspected of, criminal activities.

There were alleged to be numbered files – and some were cited in the press – on such radicals as movie stars Jane Fonda and Paul Newman, and the Negro leaders, the writer James Baldwin and Dr. Martin Luther King. In one of his most ill-advised pronouncements Hoover slated Dr. King as the 'most notorious liar in the country'.

It was said that Hoover ordered detailed reports to be compiled on the sex lives, drinking habits, and other personal affairs of various prominent people, and that copies of these were passed to President Lyndon B. Johnson – who devoured them as bedtime reading. There was no doubt that some of these allegations were embroidered by opponents of the FBI. But it was equally clear that there were doubts about the Bureau which would have been considered as being unthinkable in earlier years.

Black and White Boss

As the gossip increased, one Bureau agent said of Hoover: 'He was never as good as his admirers think he is, nor as bad as his enemies say he is. He is just a very uncomplicated man who sees everything in black and white. He has been the boss so long he can tolerate no criticism. Any criticism of the FBI he sees as a direct attack on him.'

Merely to have that kind of thing said publicly, illustrated the vast gap which had opened since the days when a newspaper columnist wrote: 'There are three things in this country above criticism – Hoover, motherhood, and the flag.'

Many of Hoover's problems arose from the fact that he had begun to feud with politicians. When the late Robert Kennedy served as Attorney General Hoover refused to speak to him (although he was nominally his chief). He did not hide his irritation with those members of Congress whom he regarded as too 'Red' in their views. He was angered by the Warren Commission's strictures on the FBI over the assassination of President John F. Kennedy.

In March 1971 a self-styled Citizens' Commission to Investigate the FBI stole some 1200 documents from the local Bureau office in Media, Pennsylvania. The documents were used to bolster charges that the FBI was compiling archives on persons to whom the Director had developed personal dislike. Many people, including President Richard Nixon, believed that the time had come for Hoover to retire.

The Director, however, had no intention of doing so, and continued in his own, eccentric way of life. He lived alone in a Georgian house on the edge of a Washington park, within 15 minutes' drive from his office. In accordance with his lifelong habit, he neither smoked nor drank. He had never married, nor shown any interest in women as far as anyone knew, and his only close companion was his 71-year-old deputy director, Clyde Tolson. His only recorded hobbies, long since abandoned by the 1970s, had been occasional nightclub visits and bets on the horses, which always stopped when he had lost $10.

Behind Closed Doors

It was undoubtedly a sagging period for the FBI. Hoover, who had once been so open-minded and available to all his men, refused to allow certain aides into his private office, and shouted his orders from behind half-closed doors. At night he was driven home with his hat placed conspicuously on the rear window ledge of his limousine as a decoy for the assassins whom he was convinced were lying in wait for him.

His final and most consuming interest centred upon the $150 million new FBI headquarters being built seven blocks down on Washington's Pennsylvania Avenue. He personally photographed each stage of the construction.

J. Edgar Hoover, certainly one of the most colourful and enigmatic figures in modern American history, died in his sleep at the age of 77, on May 2, 1972, from a high blood pressure ailment. He had lived well, and in addition to his salary had earned some $250,000 from three books which were published under his name – although there were those who alleged that they had been written by FBI associates assigned to comb through bureau files. President Nixon headed the mourners at the public funeral on May 4.

As so often happens, once the architect of a great and powerful idea has departed it is difficult to find a replacement of a comparable calibre. The first man to take on Hoover's role ended his spell in office ingloriously. Patrick Gray, aged 56, a formal naval officer and lawyer, was appointed as acting director and immediately set about introducing reforms – some of which were welcomed by the FBI's staff.

Rules are Relaxed

Hoover had always insisted that agents should keep their hair cut short, should wear white shirts and always, after duty, return their Bureau cars to their office car pools, and make their way home on foot, or by bus or taxi.

Gray relaxed the rules on hair styles and white shirts and, for the first time FBI men began to assume 'outside' fashions in more colourful dress. A new broom seemed to be sweeping clean, but it had little time to penetrate into many corners. For, on April 27, 1973, Gray resigned, himself swept away by the tide of the Watergate affair.

Following the unhappy episode of the burglary of the Democratic National Committee headquarters in Washington, DC, Gray was alleged to have destroyed files that recorded a ludicrous attempt to discredit the Kennedy family. Patrick Gray himself insisted that he had put the folders into an FBI 'burn bag', for incineration, without examining them.

On June 27, 1972, the US Senate confirmed the

appointment of Police Chief Clarence Kelley as FBI Director, of Kansas City. Kelley had been an FBI agent for 21 years before joining the Kansas City police department – which he cleansed of its epidemic of corruption. He had earned the nickname of Dick Tracy, because of the electronics innovations he had introduced into police work, and FBI moral revived when he assured the Senate judiciary committee that he would not bow to political pressure from the White House or Department of Justice.

So the FBI prepared to grapple with the ever-new problems of crime and criminal investigation that were presented to it. The FBI laboratory and identification division, upon which Hoover laid his mark, had no equal anywhere in the world. The cooperation with local law enforcement agencies by which the former Director set so much store, continued to increase.

Each month of the year the FBI receives crime reports from more than 800 such agencies, and this material goes into computers which help to provide an exacting and detailed record of crimes and criminals. Individual records are available, to those who need them, in hours rather than in weeks, as was once the case.

More than 190,000,000 fingerprints are centrally filed – a far cry from the time when J. Edgar Hoover stumped the country in his campaign to persuade local law enforcement officers to help him compile a national collection. Over the years the Bureau's National Academy has supplied trained graduates for every State of the Union, for

Puerto Rico, and for foreign countries as well. Through them the latest techniques on crime prevention and crime detection have been disseminated to thousands of other police officers.

At the rest of local authorities the FBI co-operates in other police training schools, gives instruction in such matters as firearms, fingerprint classification, traffic control, and a host of other matters vital to the welfare of law-abiding citizens. At its annual conference with state and local law enforcement agencies the Bureau provides a forum at which common problems are discussed.

Daily, crime becomes ever more complex and the battle against it ever more technical. It calls for the kind of recruits whose brains and ingenuity can match those of the professional criminal. The qualifications required of FBI men necessarily remain high, with emphasis on legal or accountancy training and, above all else, personal integrity and good character.

Buggings, wire-tappings, personal dossiers, talk of political prejudice, the unwelcome events of Watergate – all these things washed against the Bureau's shores in the 1960s and 1970s. But the FBI, no less than any other American institution must come, from time to time, under close public scrutiny. The fact that it does, gives it its own special kind of strength in a democratic society.

ABSCAM was a controversial programme set up by the FBI that was designed to fight political corruption in the United States. During the investigation – which began in 1978 and ended in 1980 – FBI agents posed as representatives of a rich Arab sheik. They offered public officials bribes ranging from $10,000 to $100,000 in return for favours. Abscam took its name from the words Arab and scam (swindle).

The FBI offered the bribes from a number of locations, including a rented house in Washington, DC, hotel rooms in New Jersey and Pennsylvania, and a yacht in Florida. The agents used hidden cameras and special telephone listening devices to obtain evidence. The programme led to the conviction of 12 public officials, including seven members of Congress. However, a federal judge overturned one of the convictions on the grounds that the government had used 'outrageous' entrapment tactics in the investigation.

Critics of the Abscam investigation charged that its main aim was to encourage crime, whilst supporters argued that awareness of such a programme would help keep public officials honest.

Bringing the FBI into the 21st Century

The FBI, now under the leadership of Louis J. Freeh, has streamlined its operations in several ways. Cost-saving changes include reducing the number of field offices from 59 to 56; transferring Special Agents from assignments at FBI Headquarters to field operations; replacing Special Agents in administrative positions with Professional Support Personnel; and delegating authority and decision-making from FBI Headquarters to field office managers. The FBI also is involved in implementing the Government Performance and Results Act, which forces managers to focus on accountability and results rather than activities. Additionally, the FBI maintains an ongoing internal programme to inspect and evaluate its investigative, administrative and financial operations.

The Internet Fraud Complaint Center (IFCC) is a partnership between the Federal Bureau of Investigation (FBI) and the National White Collar Crime Center (NW3C).

IFCC's mission is to address fraud committed over the Internet. For victims of Internet fraud, IFCC provides a convenient and easy-to-use reporting mechanism that alerts authorities of a suspected criminal or civil violation. For law enforcement and regulatory agencies at all levels, IFCC offers a central repository for complaints related to Internet fraud, works to quantify fraud patterns, and provides timely statistical data of current fraud trends.

The FBI has taken a significant role following the fatal terrorist attack on the World Trade Center in New York City on September 11, 2001. The disaster occurred when two planes crashed into the upper floors of both World Trade Center towers minutes apart from each other. The FBI's role is to reduce the threat of terrorism in the United States and against American citizens and interests throughout the world. This is accomplished through professional investigation and coordinated efforts with local, state, federal, and foreign entities as appropriate.

Federal agents arrested Nabil Al-Marabh, who has been linked to an associate of Osama bin Laden, outside Chicago. The FBI also enlisted the aid of banks to follow the money trail in the September 11 attacks.

On the national level, U.S. Attorney General John Ashcroft expanded the investigation to enlist the help of US attorneys throughout the country, vowing to wage a 'concerted national assault'. Meanwhile, investigators began filling out clearer pictures of the terrorist attack suspects. Most of the suspects blended into their American communities and seemed completely ordinary, according to law enforcement sources.

Four people were arrested as material witnesses. About 115 other people were taken into government custody, questioned and in some cases investigated for possible immigration violations.

No review of the history of the FBI can leave anyone in any doubt, that without it, or something very much akin to it, law enforcement in the United States would be an ideal rather than a reality.

Special Agents of the FBI

Their deeds were glamorous in the eyes of Hollywood, but the men of the FBI worked with discipline and dedication . . . theirs was a scientific war against crime. One of their first battles was over fingerprints . . . and that victory is celebrated in a sign outside their headquarters.

THE FEDERAL GOVERNMENT maintains a high profile in many areas of law enforcement. FBI Special Agents are the Government's principal investigators, responsible for investigating violations of more than 260 statutes. Agents may conduct surveillance, monitor court-authorized wiretaps, examine business records to investigate white-collar crime, track the interstate movement of stolen property, collect evidence of espionage activities, or participate in sensitive undercover assignments.

In order to make its work fully effective an organization with such a wide range of operations as the FBI needs the support of modern science and technology. But the use of science as an aid is a comparatively recent development in law enforcement agencies. And it was not until the late 1920s that the Bureau began to develop one of the finest forensic laboratories in the world.

There were other key elements that contributed to the nucleus of the science and information branches of the service. As far back as 1896 the International Association of Chiefs of Police (IACP) had opened a bureau of criminal identification in Chicago, and subsequently moved it to Washington DC.

It provided a useful centre through which police departments could exchange information about criminals and their modes of operation. As the importance of fingerprints became increasingly recognized, however, the identification bureau found that it had very few prints.

The majority were held in prisons – the largest single collection at Leavenworth Penitentiary – and consequently there was no proper co-ordination.

In 1924, just after the close of a convention of the IACP, Hugh Harper, chief of Police of Colorado Springs, told Rush L. Holland, US Assistant Attorney General:

'Everything's at sixes and sevens over the fingerprint collection. Some of us think the government ought to take over the whole thing. The job is to make members of the Association a little more enthusiastic about turning over their prints.

'If you had someone who could talk to the Association, and show them all the advantages of a tie-up with the United States Government, it would help.'

Holland indeed had someone. 'We've got a young fellow here in Washington, who's got a marvellous record,' he told Harper. 'He knows more about fingerprinting than most experts. His name is J. Edgar Hoover and he's in line to be the next head of the Bureau of Investigation. Suppose I ask him to talk to you?'

The invitation was instantly accepted and a few weeks later young Hoover – who shortly afterwards did become the Bureau's acting head – addressed a meeting of the IACP urging the need for a centralized fingerprint collection.

After that speech, and others in which he sought to win further allies, Hoover achieved his first notable success. The custodians of fingerprints, including the IACP, passed their files over to the Bureau of Investigation. One of Hoover's first tasks, as Acting Chief, was to order the sorting and organizing of nearly one million prints into a properly functioning identification system.

It was a most important start but, despite Hoover's personal efforts, it was not until June 1930 that Congress approved a permanent Division of Identification and Information within the Bureau.

Complacency

Even after that many major cities exhibited either reluctance or complacency about cooperating with the Bureau's identification system. Until 1932, for example, only a trickle of prints reached the Bureau from its own 'home' city of Washington,

DC – even though there was a very high local rate of crime, especially of murder and gang warfare.

In 1929 two wealthy private individuals, a rug manufacturer, and an executive of a soap company, had set up a laboratory at Northwestern University to provide crime detection facilities for the Chicago police. This establishment was among the 'inspirations' for the FBI's own laboratory, which officially came into operation on November 24, 1932.

It was quickly appreciated that almost nothing, from a single human hair to the pieces of fluff in a suspect's pocket, could be disregarded in criminal investigation.

A physics and chemistry section was created dealing, among a variety of other things, with the examination of blood, poisons, fibres and metals. Handwriting, inks, watermarks in paper, shoe and tyre prints, and examples of forged cheques were studied and most of these items photographed and filed.

As time went on there were very few techniques or materials used in the commission of crime with which the FBI was not familiar.

Firearm Collection

As part of its general research facilities, the FBI also laid the foundation for its collection of every type of firearm. Criminals quickly learned that a bullet fired from a gun carries its own identification marks as unique as fingerprints, and just as incriminating.

For a time, therefore, crooked gun dealers did a brisk business in supplying the underworld with weapons which had interchangeable parts. It was not long before the FBI had the measure of those dealers and their handiwork.

The investigation of 'gunprints' is now so routine in law enforcement that it is taken for granted. But in 1936, as this science was still developing towards its high modern technical level, the FBI laboratory proved that it could – as it often has in later years – protect the innocent as well as help to convict the guilty.

In Alaska a prospector was murdered by a shot through the head and his money stolen from his log cabin. Initial inquiries centred upon an ex-convict who was seen by a US Marshal to be wearing bloodstained socks.

'Yes, it is blood,' the man agreed. 'I shot a reindeer and some of the blood dripped on to my socks while I was dragging it home.'

The ex-convict was unable to produce the reindeer's carcass and, as the Marshal found, his rifle had recently been fired. It seemed certain that he was guilty of murder. In earlier years, and on the evidence available, he might well have been convicted. The gun, socks, and murder bullet were sent to the FBI laboratory. So, too, was a rifle belonging to an Eskimo who had subsequently come under the microscope, to match perfectly the bullet that killed the prospector. The ex-convict went free and the Eskimo was sentenced to twenty years.

In the early 1930s, specialized and scientific

training for policemen was practically nonexistent. But Hoover, always consumed with the need for constantly improving efficiency and extending the range of Bureau services, began to devise ideas for a properly founded training scheme.

Jointly, he and the Attorney General, Homer S. Cummings, agreed upon the establishment of a police training college – the FBI's National Academy opened its doors on July 29, 1935, with a 12 weeks study course for a first batch of 23 police officers.

From that day on there emerged a steady stream of Academy graduates – men carefully chosen by their local police departments not only for a high sense of personal responsibility, but for an obvious capacity to impart the essentials of their training to fellow crime busters.

Apart from the Academy, the FBI also developed intensive specialized training for its own Special Agents – agents who were, increasingly, men of notable ability. Lawyers, accountants, teachers, and others with good educational backgrounds formed a large proportion of Bureau employees.

Their rigorous training involved a broad curriculum from weaponry to a general study of the many Federal statutes with whose violation the FBI was concerned.

Among those laws were some which the FBI had known from its earliest days – including the White Slave Traffic Act and the Antitrust Act – with many more being added as the years passed. Following the kidnapping and murder of Colonel

Charles Lindbergh's infant son, in 1932, abduction across a State line became a federal offence, and the FBI was given authority for immediate participation in kidnapping cases.

On the firing ranges the FBI recruits were given exhaustive instructions in the handling and firing of weapons from pistols to the Thompson submachine gun, or 'Tommy gun'. The minimum score on target was 60 per cent, and those who failed to reach that level were told that their services as special agents would not be required.

The remaining recruits were given written and oral examinations – some of the latter being sprung upon them without warning in order to test their degrees of alertness and observation. As a peak exercise just before the final examination, each man was assigned to take part in an actual investigation.

Important Theme

Hoover himself met each class of trainees and talked to them personally about the Bureau, invariably underlining the theme so important to him that the FBI was neither a national police force nor a political arm of the US government.

Discipline was then, and has remained, severe. Men who joined even in the earlier years found that their personal lives had to be sacrificed to the demands of duty. Hoover was an ardent believer in the principle that all agents must be able to rely upon each other totally, and that this kind of 'brotherhood' could be welded together only by discipline.

The fact that the Director himself worked long hours, took a direct interest in major investigations, and made the Bureau his life, made the rigorously applied standards acceptable.

Every aspect of training, and the general atmosphere of the Bureau, made it clear that life in the FBI was far removed from the glamour with which the Press, and later the motion picture industry, were to endow Special Agents.

FBI men were subject to being moved to new territory – often at a few hours' notice.

Behind the scenes, FBI work entailed many hours of drudgery, of patiently wading through mountains of evidence to seek out the one or two decisive facts.

The gold eagled badge with its insignia, 'Federal Bureau of Investigation, US Department of Justice', became a symbol to its bearers that they had exchanged personal lives for service to the nation.

Wire-tapping Order

One of the most heated of the early legal debates raged around wire-tapping (the interception of telephone calls) – a technique in which FBI men were not then instructed.

Even though it was approved of in 1928 by the Supreme Court – which ruled that wiretap evidence was admissible in federal courts – Hoover refused to make use of it, or include it in his training programmes. He was forced to relent in 1931 when Attorney General William D. Mitchell issued an order for the use of FBI wiretaps with the proviso that:

'Telephone or telegraph wires shall not be tapped unless prior authorization of the Director of the Bureau has been secured.'

Hoover's first authorization was not issued until a year later – when a series of kidnappings made it essential to intercept telephoned demands for ransom payments. From that time on increasing attention was paid in the FBI laboratory and training courses to the new and rapidly growing field of electronics.

Nuclear Physics

By the time the United States had emerged from World War II, every kind of scientific and technological aid – including nuclear physics – was being employed.

It had become possible to detect even the most 'perfect' crime through the assembling by experts of a host of minor and apparently irrelevant factors. Every day the FBI laboratory was looking more closely at clues invisible to the human eye.

The application of science brought new men into the Bureau in ever growing numbers; men who lived among isotopes and photographic processes; men who used chemical and biological techniques to examine worlds that were undetected by the old-fashioned microscopes.

Behind the men who went out to collect the facts that would bring the criminal to justice, stood powerful reinforcements who would evaluate those facts in new and mysterious ways.

Thousands of dedicated professionals work together to fulfill the mission of the FBI. Highly trained Special Agents are responsible for enforcing the federal statutes. Scientists, computer specialists, and other speciality personnel at the Forensic Laboratory, Engineering Research Facility, and the Criminal Justice Information Services Division provide expert assistance in developing cases. All these people are supported by other professional employees who efficiently maintain the day-to-day operations.

Scotland Yard

Scotland Yard's Flying Squad has developed over the years as a highly mobilized 'swoop' force whose task is to move quickly onto scenes of crime at a moment's notice. One of the most important advances in the Squad's efficiency was the introduction of a standard telephone link with the public, in case of trouble . . . 999.

IN 1850 CHARLES Dickens captured the attention of the readers of his *Household Words* with an article headed 'The Modern Science of Thief-taking', based on his own interviews with the handful of officers who then comprised the staff of Scotland Yard's 'detective office'.

Dickens was intrigued by the wiliness of 19th-century criminals, and fascinated by the clinical yet imaginative minds of the men appointed to search them out and bring them to justice.

Today the detective office is still a focal point of the Yard, the centre of the Criminal Investigation Department, but its work has moved light-years beyond simple thief-taking. The CID has grown as crime has grown, and its complexities have increased in step with the complexities of law breaking so that now it employs a multitude of specialist squads.

Murder, bank robbery, and housebreaking remain

the basic ingredients of Scotland Yard's routine. But to those have been added such other criminal activities as forgery, fraud, vice, drug trafficking, subversion and, in the latest period, bombings in large cities by political groups – including the Provisional wing of the Irish Republican Army.

The Flying Squad

Few Scotland Yard specialist squads have been endowed with such fiction writers' glamour as the Flying Squad. The original mobile unit was launched immediately after World War I to swoop quickly on scenes of crime. Yet there were certain ironic touches about its formation. The first main targets of the squad were groups of disillusioned front-line veterans who, overnight, found themselves transformed from national heroes into unwanted, workless spectres – and who took to crime with the same dedication they had shown in the trenches.

They launched housebreaking raids throughout the better-off suburbs of London and other large cities. They descended on banks and post offices like a bandit plague, 'worked' the London Underground as pickpockets, and emptied dockside warehouses. They hurled bricks through shop windows in main streets in broad daylight, made off with as much of the contents as they could scoop up in a few seconds, and added a new phrase to the language of crime – smash-and-grab.

At first, the Yard's new mobile police squad was given a horse-drawn covered van in which a dozen detectives crouched out of sight while observing the passing scene through peepholes. As suspects were spied the officers would leap from the back of the van, one by one, and pursue their quarry on foot. Crude as it now seems, the system worked, and very soon horse and van were replaced by two Crossley tenders – powerful motor vehicles used successfully in the war.

Increasingly, ordinary cars were added and, for a time, became known as Q-cars after the wartime fighting 'Q' ships disguised as merchantmen. It was the newspapers that dubbed the fast-growing mobile unit the 'Flying Squad', and noted the break-up of marauding smash-and-grab gangs as the squad developed in speed and technique.

Despite its speed of movement, what the squad initially lacked was speed of communication with its base. But that drawback began to disappear from the day, in 1922, when patrol cars were fitted with radio and headquarters' messages were broadcast over the London 2LO transmitter of the newly-founded British Broadcasting Company.

Indeed, the two most important additional arms provided for the police in general, and the Flying Squad in particular, were radio and the introduction of the 999 telephone link by which members of the public could pass information directly to the Yard or to local police.

A 999 Call

It was a 999 call, received in Scotland Yard's information room one October afternoon in 1955, that launched the Flying Squad on one of its most spectacular pursuits. It came from a young woman who had seen two armed men run from a jeweller's shop in West London's Earl's Court and speed away in a Rover car driven by a third man.

Sensibly, she had carefully noted the car licence number, and while some of the information room staff were alerting patrol units in the holdup area, others checked the stolen-car list and found that the Rover was on it.

Among those who heard the radioed alarm call were the three crew members of a Flying Squad car cruising sedately through Hyde Park on a routine patrol – Detective-Sergeants Albert Chambers and Ernest Cooke, and Police Constable Donald Cameron. At the very instant in which they acknowledged the Yard's message they saw the 'wanted' car, travelling fast through the park and sweeping past them in the opposite direction. PC Cameron, the crew's driver, brought the squad car around in a frantic U-turn and throttled to full power on the tail of the Rover.

Strollers, out to observe the autumn leaves in London's most famous park, gaped at the sight of two cars plunging at nearly 80 miles an hour over the Serpentine Bridge, and at the two men who leaned out of the Rover's rear windows firing bursts of pistol shots at the careering squad car.

At the park exits on the busy Bayswater Road the surge of traffic forced the gunmen's car to stop and, even before the Flying Squad car had slithered to a halt behind it, Sergeant Cooke leaped out and was battling to drag the Rover's driver from his seat. However, before he could complete the capture, a blow from one of the men sent him spinning to the ground, and the Rover sprang forward into a temporary gap in the traffic.

The chase continued down Park Lane – where another of the gunmen's shots shattered the squad car windscreen and destroyed all visibility as PC Cameron fought his own nerve-stretching duel with double-decker buses and taxis. With his bare fist, and apparently oblivious of the blood-letting lacerations, Cameron beat out the obscuring glass and sped after the getaway car along Mayfair's Curzon Street. There the Rover slammed into a parked car, ricocheted from that into another, and slid unevenly across the street to a final stop.

The holdup men ran from the wreckage, pursued on foot by the three Flying Squad men. Sergeant Chambers was shot in the forearm but, despite his wound, managed to leap on to the back of one of the escaping men and pin him to the ground. Another officer, PC Evan Wood, who had joined the hunt in Curzon Street, was hit in the stomach and in the general confusion the other two gunmen vanished.

Within hours one of the two was found in a hotel in Tottenham Court Road and two days later the third member of the trio was captured, asleep in bed, in a house in South London. To the surprise and relief of the Flying Squad men, who were prepared for a final shoot-out, his only comment was the tired old cliché 'I'll come quietly'.

The three men subsequently received sentences totalling 42 years and Lord Goddard, the Lord

Chief Justice, told the Flying Squad officers: 'I give the thanks of the community for your gallant and devoted sense of duty.'

Dedicated Detective Work

As in all British police forces, such spectacular events are still comparatively rare, and most of the CID's energies are devoted to the long, complex and often wearying routine of detective work. But Scotland Yard's international reputation for patient and dogged investigation has been responsible for the arrest and conviction of criminals in countless cases where the prospects at first seemed discouraging.

There was a notable example of the rewards for that patience following the murder, in a Soho street in April 1947, of Alec d'Antiquis – a motorcyclist who was shot down as he attempted to block the escape of a car carrying two men who had just held up a pawnbroker.

Onlookers' descriptions of the men, whose faces were covered by scarves, differed widely. But an office boy told the police that within minutes of the murder two men had pushed past him and run into the block of offices where he worked. A short while later they had dashed out again and the boy noticed that one of the men had discarded the raincoat he was wearing earlier.

Two days later a painter working in the same office building reported the discovery of a raincoat hidden behind a disused counter on an upper floor. On examining it at Scotland Yard the detective in charge of the case saw that the coat's name tag had been removed. But when he ripped open the lining he found a makers' tag marked with indelible code numbers.

From a translation of the code the makers were able to show that the coat had been one of a batch delivered to three shops in the London area. Teams of detectives were sent to check the order books of the shops' managers, and then embarked on the tedious chore of calling upon all those people whose addresses had been noted in the sales records.

It seemed to be a fruitless search until finally one CID man knocked at the door of a flat in the riverside district of Deptford where, according to the sales sheets, lived a Mr Thomas Kemp who had bought such a coat.

There Kemp agreed that he was the owner and first insisted that he had lost the coat in a cinema. Later, however, he said his wife had loaned it to her brother, Charles Henry Jenkins. Jenkins was already 'known' to the police and was on their current list as a suspect in a recent £5,000 robbery. Eventually, Jenkins and two other men, Geraghty and Holt, were tried at the Old Bailey and convicted of murder. Jenkins and Geraghty were hanged on September 19, 1947. But Holt, who at 17 was too young for the death sentence, was sent to prison for an indefinite term.

The crudities of petty hoodlums, like Jenkins, are balanced in the modern fight against crime by the sophistication of those who have used the enormously increased complications of finance and business methods to make a 'killing' through fraud. Today while many of the CID's senior officers study the new techniques applied to 'traditional' crimes such as housebreaking and bank robbery, others spend their working lives searching among ledgers and balance sheets for the hidden clues that will lead them to the big-money swindlers.

The Fraud Squad came into being, as a branch of the CID in 1946. One of its most notable features was that, for the first time, it brought about a formal link between the Metropolitan Police and the City Police – the separate law enforcement agency which covers the square mile of the City of London, the capital's financial centre.

Highly Involved

Demarcations were so rigid at the time that City officers had no power to exercise their police authority outside their own area. To make the new squad operative, a group of City detectives were specially sworn in as Metropolitan policemen. For the squad, as a cohesive body, it was an irritating situation which was later ended by an Act of Parliament.

While patience is regarded as a major virtue in the CID as a whole, it amounts almost to sainthood in the Fraud Squad. Many of its cases are so highly involved that they may take two or three years to unravel and require the production of evidence of the most specialized character. Often only the experts (and the criminals themselves) can understand the nature of the fraud and the methods employed in it.

Automobile theft is as much a prime occupation for criminals in Britain as it is in any other industrialized nation. And, since the most professional practitioners have also become extremely knowledgeable about their trade, the Yard's CID has evolved its own counter measures through its stolen car branch.

At their own London workshop the detectives of this branch spend much of their time, covered to their elbows in grease, minutely studying pieces of automobile ranging from complete engine blocks to small sections of chassis.

A considerable amount of their detection work is concerned with unmasking 'ringers' – the car thieves, or their mechanics, who interchange parts between a series of stolen cars to destroy the identities of the original vehicles. Cars are easy to steal, easy and profitable to dispose of, and comparatively simple to disguise.

But in their detection work the men of the stolen car branch are concerned almost as much with criminal threats to life as with theft. For the work of the car ringer – on parts not visible to the innocent second-hand bargain hunter – is often sub-standard, and many 'doctored' cars with faulty welding have broken apart at speed, with fatal results.

In one of their biggest single hauls in the car ringing racket officers of the stolen car branch helped to bring to court one group of 28 men who, at the time of their arrests, had cars worth a total of £300,000 – or nearly a million dollars. Evidence against them was supplied by 300 witnesses, but none would have been found if the CID men had not spent long and tireless hours at their workshop detection bench.

It takes experts to catch experts, and as science and technology continue to tempt the criminal into new and promising fields, Scotland Yard will follow with improved skill.

The headquarters of Scotland Yard were moved in 1890 to premises on the Victoria Embankment designed by Richard Norman Shaw. At this time they became known as 'New Scotland Yard'. In 1967, because of the need for a larger and more modern headquarters, a further move took place to the present site at Broadway, London SW1, which is also known as 'New Scotland Yard'.

The Yard's Special Branch

The men of Scotland Yard's Special Branch have always had to combat acts of violence and sedition. So an Irish bomb attack is just another job.

THE SPECIAL IRISH Branch was formed in 1883 to combat the threat from the Fenian movement, whose aim was independence in Ireland and who had been responsible for a series of explosions in London. The Special Irish Branch later became known as the Special Branch and extended its work into Royalty protection with Queen Victoria's Jubilee. While the Special Branch is a division of the police force, in practice it coordinates closely with MI5. Its main areas of activity cover such offences as treason, sedition, breaches of the Official Secrets Act and rioting. It is also responsible for the protection of government ministers, visiting foreign dignitaries, and the general surveillance of non-British citizens entering the country.

The delicacy of its position in the law enforcement system arises from the fact that while its duty is to protect the state from external and domestic enemies, it has neither rights nor powers to behave in ways which characterize secret or political police in some other countries.

In most cases its work is confined to investigation – and the tasks of acting upon its information, of making arrests and charging subversives and others, devolve upon other branches of the police. Apart from occasions when direct action is called for against specific law breakers, the day-to-day routine of the Special Branch centres largely upon the build-up of detailed knowledge of how potentially threatening groups work, and who the principal planners are.

Undercover Work

All extremists, whether on the Left or Right of the political spectrum, are carefully observed and so are their associates. To many people in a democracy such surveillance sometimes appears distasteful. But in Britain there is general agreement on the need for protection against forms of extremism likely to move from mere expression of off-centre views to positive subversion or sabotage.

The law itself confers the same rights on the arrested spy as on the offending motorist, and there are no torture chambers at Scotland Yard, or in any other British police force.

In order to do their department's job some Special Branch men are required to infiltrate certain potentially dangerous organizations, to 'mingle' with workers in industrial plants engaged on secret government contracts, and even to march with apparent enthusiasm in the more excitable public demonstrations.

But the extent and nature of this undercover work is far less sinister than some police critics suggest – largely due to the fact that, despite their awareness of possible threats to their security, the British people are not given to hysterical reactions, and do not approve of such reactions in their public servants.

Life for the Special Branch, founded in dynamiting days, has come full circle in recent years with bombing attacks in London by activitists belonging to the Provisional wing of the Irish Republican Army, or one of its associated groups, and by an anarchist contingent calling itself the Angry Brigade. But although the attacks have been regarded as an unbelievable outrage by a new generation of Londoners, they are by no means the first the Special Branch have had to contend with in modern times.

A Young Bride

In August 1939 a young Edinburgh University lecturer, Donald Campbell, who had just returned with his wife from their Paris honeymoon, paid a visit to the luggage office on London's King's Cross station. As he stood talking to the attendant there came a streaking flash and a roar as a bomb, concealed in a suitcase beneath the office counter, exploded with a shattering effect.

Both Campbell's legs were blown off and he died within a few minutes in the ruins of the office. Among the 15 injured men and women scattered around his body lay his young bride.

This was the worst attack, up to that time, in a reign of bombing terror launched in Britain by the Irish Republican Army seven months before. It came in a week in which Parliament had accepted a Prevention of Violence Act which gave the Special Branch power – along with other Yard squads and police forces – to round up IRA suspects.

So dramatically intense was the swoop by Scotland Yard and its associates, that the day the law received the Royal Assent the Dublin boat train was increased by threefold, carrying worried Irishmen away from Britain.

It was the discovery by the Special Branch of a sabotage plan that led directly to the introduction of the Act. The plan had been drawn up by the IRA Chief of Staff and, in disclosing some of its contents to the House of Commons, Sir Samuel Hoare, the Home Secretary, said: 'It is a remarkable document. It is not the kind of irresponsible, melodramatic document that one sometimes discovers in searches. It is a very carefully worked out staff plan setting out the way in which an extensive campaign of sabotage could be successfully carried out against this country.'

Sabotage Plan

Britain was then only a few months away from war with Nazi Germany, and the plan had been designed to take advantage of the nation's preoccupation with the forthcoming conflict. Aircraft factories were to be attacked, radio stations destroyed, and public utilities – gas, electricity, railways, and sewage systems – were to be put out of action.

Although the campaign failed to achieve those objectives, people in London and other cities suffered death and injury until the Special Branch men and their colleagues scooped up the ring-leaders, and the courts consigned them to prison.

The war itself brought new and complex tasks to Scotland Yard, not only as the result of operations by criminals flourishing in the blacked-out streets, but by the German Luftwaffe air raids which came close to crippling London. The Yard doubled the strength of the Metropolitan force to nearly 46,000 men and women by recalling pensioners and bringing in reservists and special constables for full-time duty.

Policemen helped with the evacuation from London to safer country areas of thousands of children, and the Yard secured the lease of a large school near Wimbledon Common – a few miles beyond its riverside headquarters – in which to house its extra administrative staff.

During the heaviest of the Luftwaffe's attacks – between January and July 1941 – 67 Metropolitan policemen were killed and 389 badly injured. In May of that year a bomb fell on Scotland Yard itself, plunging through the southeast turret, wrecking 15 rooms, including that of the Commissioner, and scattering a million index cards among the rubble.

Invasion Threat

Incredibly, no one was hurt and the Commissioner, Sir Philip Game, was out on his regular rounds, visiting other bomb sites. At the same time as she was bearing up under such air raids, Britain also faced the threat of invasion. Accordingly, the traditionally unarmed Yard men ordered 25,000 revolvers and 300,000 rounds of ammunition from the United States under lend-lease arrangements.

The abandonment of Hitler's invasion plans, and the scourging of the Luftwaffe by the Royal Air Force, brought a brief lull to the Yard. But new problems arrived with the unleashing of flying bombs (the V-1) in July 1944, and by rockets (V-2) in the following September.

When the last rocket out of a total of 1,050 fell at Orpington, in Kent, in March 1945, the final wartime death toll of the Yard's men and women officers was 200, and another 2,000 had been wounded. To members of the force were awarded 150 medals for bravery – most of them earned in the rescue of bomb victims – and the Yard emerged from the war with its relations with the public much enhanced.

Different Enemy

In the final period of the war, and in the austere, shortage-ridden years that immediately followed, the men of the Yard found themselves battling with a different kind of domestic enemy – the black marketeers. These were a fresh breed of criminals – some of them petty operators known under the general title of 'spivs and drones' – and others more skilfully organized.

They created an industry out of the theft of ration books – books in which coupons were exchanged for food, clothing and petrol. They found no shortage of purchasers, even among normally respectable citizens whose greed and self-indulgence impelled them to seek more than their fair share of the meagre supplies.

Crime figures, which had fallen as the war reached its peak, soared alarmingly and reached a record level in 1945 – with 128,954 indictable offences in the Metropolitan Police District. Among those arrested were a motley collection of deserters on the run: others who had gone hopefully into the black market as a quick means of acquiring peacetime capital; and still others who, from their jobs in various forms of transport, supplied the 'dealers' with pilfered goods.

Later the crime rate fell, only to rise yet again as the post-war years advanced. One of Scotland Yard's continuing problems has been the shortage of sufficient manpower to meet all the demands made upon it. In its recruitment drives the Yard has suffered from the competitive pay and regular hours offered by industry and commerce. Many Yard men, particularly detectives, work long and irregular hours, and generally only those with a strong sense of dedication – and who are prepared to sacrifice their home and private lives – stay the course.

False Alibis

British criminals have also learned, long after their United States counterparts, the value of understanding the law and hiring good lawyers. Scotland Yard, while recognizing the need to protect the innocent citizen, has become increasingly frustrated in recent years by what it sees as the ability of some clearly guilty crooks legally to defeat the ends of justice.

In November 1973, in a controversial television lecture, Sir Robert Mark, Scotland Yard's Metropolitan Police Commissioner, accused a minority of criminal lawyers of being 'more harmful to society than the clients they represent'. In a television speech he told the BBC's viewers:

'We see the same lawyers producing, off the peg, the same kind of defence for different clients. Prosecution witnesses inexplicably change their minds. Defences are concocted far beyond the intellectual capacity of the accused.

'False alibis are put forward. Extraneous issues damaging to police credibility are introduced . . . If the prosecution evidence is strong the defence frequently resorts to attacks on prosecution witnesses, particularly if they are police.

'They will be accused, as a matter of routine, of perjury, planting evidence, intimidation, or violence. What defence is there, when found in possession of drugs, explosives, or firearms, than to say they were planted?

'Lies of this kind are a normal form of defence but they are sure to be given extensive publicity.'

Sir Robert gave an example of the kind of 'bent' legal trickery with which, he said, the police had to contend: a hardened criminal burgled a flat and seriously wounded one of the elderly occupants. He was arrested, denied the offences, and was remanded to prison. Later his solicitor said the man had a complete alibi – on the night of the break-in, he was playing bingo at a club, and his signature was plainly to be seen in the club's visitors' book.

When the Yard examined the book they found that the man had indeed signed the book, on the right date, at the foot of the page. But, unfortunately for him, a group of four other people had also individually signed in, writing their names one after another. The suspect's name appeared in the middle of that group of names, indicating that it must have been entered later.

The investigating detectives realized that there was only one place in which the man could have made that late entry: in prison. It was not possible to prove who had taken the visitors' book to the man behind bars. But as Sir Robert stated:

'The prison authorities pointed out drily that only a visit by a lawyer or his clerk would be unsupervised!'

Convict Turned Detective

Early in the 19th century a Frenchman, a one-time criminal himself, utilized his first-hand knowledge of France's underworld to create a whole new, formalized entity called 'criminal investigation'. In doing so, Eugène François Vidocq brought crime fighting to a higher plateau, up from a disorganized and often-negative environment and into a social science.

THE RESIDENTS of the Paris district paid no serious attention to the little old eccentric with the pigtail and three-cornered hat. Wrinkled and bearing a gold-knobbed cane he shuffled through the streets staring into doorways, peering through windows, looking into courtyards. He was regarded as a harmless crank – especially when he knocked on a tailoress's door and told the woman he was looking for his runaway wife. He described the man the wife had supposedly gone off with and asked if such a person had been seen in the vicinity. On learning that he had – and, what was more, had only just moved to a new address – the old man started to sob. Taking pity on him, the tailoress helped him to obtain the address and sent him gratefully on his way.

A few days later the 'crank' – minus his pigtail and now wearing the garb of a coalman – went to the house and loitered outside until the man he was looking for entered his apartment. The coalman waited until night fell. Then, together with a number of gendarmes, he burst into the upstairs apartment and surprised the man in bed with a woman. While the gendarmes secured and gagged the woman, the coalman grabbed the alleged lover and hurriedly tied him up. Once again, Eugène François Vidocq – a master of deception and disguise – had got his man. By posing as an eccentric and then a coalman, he had captured a notorious thief named Fossard, who had previously frustrated all attempts by the Paris police to arrest him. Not only that, he recovered jewellery and 18,000 francs hidden in the apartment and added to the growing legend of Vidocq – the detective who had been on the wrong side of the law himself, and still strayed across the narrow criminal borderline.

Vidocq believed in the infallibility of setting thieves to catch thieves, and wrote: 'During the twenty years I spent at the head of the *Sûreté* I hardly employed any but ex-convicts, often even escaped prisoners. I preferred to choose men whose bad record had given them a certain celebrity. I often gave these men the most delicate missions. They had considerable sums to deliver to the police or prison offices. They took part in operations in which they could easily have laid hands on large amounts. But not one of them, not a single one, betrayed my trust.'

But Vidocq was not, as he has so often been called, a reformed crook. He never *was* a crook in the strict sense of the word. Up to his middle thirties he had been a soldier in Napoleon's armies, a show man and puppeteer, a frequent dueller, and admittedly rather a swashbuckler – not to say a womanizer. In 1789 he severely beat up a man who had seduced one of his girlfriends, and was sent to prison for breach of the peace. He promptly began a series of spectacular prison escapes, each one leading to recapture and an increased sentence.

This irresponsible man was finally sentenced to eight years in the galleys, and his next escape accordingly took longer to arrange. But in 1799 he was free again, went to Paris and set up shop as a secondhand clothes dealer which he then ran successfully for years. Eventually the underworld found out who he was, and they mercilessly blackmailed him until at last he went to the police, declared himself, and offered them a bargain.

If they got the threat of recapture and longer imprisonment removed from his life, he would provide them with priceless information from his acquired knowledge of 'the criminal scene'. They agreed, because crime had broken all bounds and the back streets of Paris had become, since the revolution of 1789–95 inaccessible to any party of less than four or five men armed with swords or pistols. So Vidocq began his job as a 'police informer', and in his first year of operation he put more than 800 men behind bars.

The following year, 1810, he was made head of

the Paris *Sûreté.* To 'legalize' his position the authorities arrested him once more and then discharged him with a clean sheet. He set up his new organization on the then revolutionary principle that serious crime can best be fought by criminals. He employed 20 discharged convicts and developed them into the nucleus of a brand-new French Criminal Investigation Department. He planted his men in prisons by having them arrested on sham charges; and got them out again when they had learned enough from the current gossip inside, by pretended escapes or even by bogus deaths and burials. He was the greatest enemy the criminal classes have ever had, and probably the greatest and most methodical of all detectives. His files and archives were colossal and his memory unfailing, and the surviving mystery of his 23 years as head of the *Sûreté* is that he was never assassinated by his underworld rivals.

As it was he lived another 24 years, set up a private detective agency (the first in the world and the inspiration for many a writer of who-dun-its), and himself became a prolific author. He compiled a work of reference on the criminal classes of France, a book about the rehabilitation of criminals, and two immense but undistinguished novels about criminal life. There is a much quoted book called *The Memoirs of Vidocq,* which he did not write and which he utterly repudiated for its dishonesty. He became friendly with the novelist Honoré de Balzac, and supplied him with the material for countless stories, becoming himself in due course the basis of Balzac's famous detective

Vautrin in the *Comédie Humaine.* In his old age he became a counter-espionage agent to the Emperor Napoleon III. Napoleon III's destruction of the Republic and his reckless foreign adventures got the country into its disastrous war with Prussia in 1870.

By then Vidocq, who had shared the general worship of the power-drunk Emperor, had been dead for 13 years: he was perhaps lucky not to see his Emperor's downfall and execration. But in France his name is remembered as vividly as that of the fictitious Sherlock Holmes in Britain or the real life Alan Pinkerton in the United States.

Contempt and Hatred

Although he was a colourful character, he was accounted an honest man, and though he was drawn into the 'crime war' by an acquired contempt and hatred for the criminals he came to know, he was also the first to recognize that ex-prisoners are better able than anyone to bring about the reform of an ex-prisoner; a belief which has recently been revived both in the United States and in Britain, where ex-prisoners' organizations (such as Recidivists Anonymous, based in Maidstone Prison in Kent) maintain a rehabilitation service with considerable success.

No other country ever had anyone like Vidocq. A century earlier, an English highwayman and truly squalid crook, named Jonathan Wild, secret 'organizer' of the London underworld, was induced in 1715 by the available government rewards of his old accomplices to prison or the gallows. He was a dandy in his dress, always carried a gold-headed cane, and kept an office in London and an estate in the country, each with a big staff of servants. But the offenders he turned over to the authorities were those who refused to submit to his criminal organization, and in this respect he was the ancestor of the two London gangs headed by the Richardson brothers and the Kray brothers; the forerunner of the American gangster boss such as Al Capone; and the prototype for the present-day Mafia. In 1725 he was himself convicted and hanged for robbery, and his odious story is satirically told by the eighteenth-century author Henry Fielding in his *History of the Life of the Late Mr Jonathan Wild.* He had turned his knowledge of crime to good account – the reward for the conviction of a highwayman was £40 (worth about £2000 today) plus the man's horse, weapons and property.

Informers Available

While there was much about Vidocq that was flamboyant, there was nothing odious – although the *Sûreté* came to disown him, and subsequently played down the comparative lack of success achieved by the recruiting, from 1833 onwards, of none but respectable citizens as its new detectives, all of whom it called 'inspectors'.

From then onwards, however, in France, Britain, and the United States, the 'hidden force' of the police-minded thief was indispensable.

Each of those countries relied, and now all countries rely, on the availability of informers by the thousand, and sometimes they act as *agents provocateurs*; not always willing ones, certainly not always paid ones. The 'picking up' of ex-prisoners for questioning, moreover, is especially easy in France, where there is a long-established system of subjecting the discharged prisoner to an *interdit de séjour*, a document listing a number of cities and towns in which, for the next five years, he may not 'live or appear'. To be found in any of them means arrest and imprisonment without trial. But in all countries, an ex-prisoner needs to live a very careful life if he values his freedom, and he will certainly never again live a carefree one. In the growing number of countries operating a parole system – which often involves long post-prison periods under supervision and a freedom which is specially precarious – the supply of potential informers is not diminishing.

'In the United States the FBI relies on informants,' states William W. Turner, who was an FBI agent for ten years. 'Payments are made from confidential funds, the total being one of the FBI's best-kept secrets. By purchasing information rather than obtaining it through other investigative techniques, the FBI gains a measure of protection against embarrassment to the Bureau. Should a case backfire, the informant can be piously disowned.' In the United States, as in England, journalists have actually gone to prison rather than divulge their sources of information: but police officers, New Scotland Yard Special Branch men, and FBI agents are never pressed about it.

Sometimes the police in all countries will actually use an experienced and cooperative ex-crook in setting up a crime – a robbery, an assault, a break-in – by way of an ambush. He is arrested with his accomplices, 'offers' to give evidence for the prosecution, and is therefore himself acquitted. The English High Court Judges will have none of this, and if it comes to their notice the other men are also acquitted, and there is trouble for the police for using an *agent provocateur.*

To catch criminals it is not enough to know what an artful man would do in given circumstances. You must more often know what a stupid man would do. And to do this it is necessary, not so much to be naturally stupid as to be capable of stupidity. In setting a thief to catch a thief, the one you set should be chosen with this in mind. But the system has two built-in dangers, one of them old and recognized, the other new, growing and sinister.

The first is that the informer may be a liar, concerned either to pay off an old score or to distract police attention from something else; the second is that he can (and does) use bugging devices and phone tapping techniques not always accessible to the police, whom he will then feed with the results – in which event all the statutory safeguards are ignored.

In the long run, however, even this abuse of the law may be preferable to living in a country where police are hobbled by unrealistic rules and regulations, and where the villain is king.

Vidocq's factual successes inspired world-class authors who borrowed his brilliance to embody their fictional heroes. Doyle's Sherlock Holmes character is much based on Vidocq; so are both Jean Valjean and Inspector Javert in Hugo's *Les Miserables.* Dickens mentions Vidocq in *Great Expectations*; Melville cites him in *Moby Dick*; and Poe refers to Vidocq's methods in *Murders in the Rue Morgue.* And there are more beyond these.

Fugitive, undercover agent, chief of detectives, private investigator, author, inventor and humanitarian – all these personalities describe one of the most amazing men in the history of criminal pursuit.

'Just as his behaviour irritated the conventional police, his personal behaviour was frowned upon by the conventional people who did not have his sheer love of life,' writes Philip John Stead in *Vidocq, Picaroon of Crime.* 'He preferred the tumultuous life of danger to the contentment of security. His story is one long swashbuckling adventure as he breaks out of jails, pursues actresses, duels to the death, raids the hells of criminals and stalks the Paris night in a thousand disguises.'

Such was Vidocq – a rare talent, a rare man.

The Pinkerton Detective Agency

Allan Pinkerton was born in Scotland on August 25, 1819 on the 3rd floor of a tenement flat in one of the worst slums of Glasgow. At the age of 31, he started his own detective agency and hired what he believed to be honest men, but one of Pinkerton's main rules was – no drinking. He wanted his men sober and alert at all times and even hired a woman. He taught his detectives how to do investigative work and showed them how to dress in disguise. His office was filled with costumes and wigs.

FOR MONTHS officials and workers of the Philadelphia and Reading Railroad had been worried by the 'terrorist acts' of the Mollie Maguires – the secret society formed by Pennsylvania miners to protect their rights against the bosses. But like the original organization (founded in Ireland to intimidate absentee landlords, and so-called because the men had worn women's clothes while hiding from the police), the members had turned into brutal thugs.

In October, 1873 – in desperation – railroad executive Franklin B. Gowen called in the services of America's first and leading private eye: the Scottish-born Allan Pinkerton. He told the detective that the state police were helpless, and that the mines and railways were being 'put out of business' by the Maguires. Could Pinkerton break up the gang?

Pinkerton believed that he could, but on one condition – that he was able to infiltrate one of his own men into the society. He found the man he wanted on his return to Chicago, when he came across one of his former operatives working as a horsecar conductor. Twenty-nine-year-old James McParland was eager to return to sleuthing, no matter how dangerous or unorthodox the assignment. He knew that discovery would mean death, but he also realized that Pinkerton – who at one time had been Chicago's only full-time professional policeman – would use all his power to protect him.

Since opening the Pinkerton National Detective Agency in 1850 (with the motto: 'We Never Sleep'; and an open eye as a trademark) Pinkerton had achieved nationwide success and worldwide fame. His agency was known as 'America's Scotland Yard'; he was a master of disguise; and the first detective to use women on some of his toughest cases. He had foiled an attempted assassination of Abraham Lincoln; he had worked behind the Confederate lines as America's first-ever Secret Service agent. In addition to this, he had 'ridden shotgun' against the outlaw gangs of the Wild West – including those of the Reno Brothers and Frank and Jesse James – and believed that a wrongdoer's crime 'haunts him continually . . . [until] he must relieve himself of the terrible secret which is bearing down on him'.

With this in mind, McParland, dressed in tramp's clothing, took the name of James McKenna, and set off for the mining towns of Pennsylvania. For the next few weeks he wandered from Port Clinton, to Middle Creek, to Tower City, making free with his Irish accent and broadcasting his dislike of the 'tyrant railroad chiefs, the devilish mine-owners'. He noted down the descriptions of everyone he talked to, recorded their conversations, and posted his reports to Pinkerton.

One night in Pine Grove he was actually mistaken for a Mollie Maguire, and learnt that the society's password was: 'The boys who are true'. A short while later, in a saloon in Tower City, he got into a backroom fight over a game of euchre. He caught the dealer cheating, felled him, and then proposed a toast, 'To make English landlords tremble! And to bring confusion to the enemies of old Ireland!' He then moved to Shenandoah, where he met the bodymaster of the local branch of the Maguires, and posed as a pedlar of counterfeit money. He was near to penetrating the core of the society, and his reports came directly from the bodymaster's house, where he was a boarder.

Before long, as more and more mines closed down, and the Mollies faced long-term unemployment, there was a call for a new bodymaster – one who would deal even more severely with the bosses. By then McParland had been appointed secretary of the Shenandoah Lodge, and was a 'natural' for the even more important job. He had memorized all the society's toasts, passwords, codes, signs, and symbols, and was aware that –

even as secretary – his own room was searched on occasion. There was nothing there to betray him, and certainly nothing worth stealing. But his large supply of stamps would have aroused suspicion if discovered – so he hid them in the sheepskin lining of his one pair of boots.

As the dissatisfaction with the current bodymaster grew – he was 'too weak', 'too timid' – it appeared inevitable that McParland would be asked to take his place. This, however, meant that he would have to plot and carry out assassinations. His year among the miners had taught him that anyone who opposed the Mollies or stood in their path was liable to be killed. McParland could not be a party to this, and he wrote to Pinkerton telling him that he had decided to become a 'drunk'. Hour after hour, and for day after day, he consumed cheap, gut-rotting whisky. The unaccustomed liquor had such a bad effect upon him that his hair fell out and he was driven to his bed.

Eventually, he recovered enough to buy a wig and resume his duties as secretary. But it was obvious to the society members that he was too much the drunkard to ever be their bodymaster. In April 1875 – his file in Chicago bulging with intimate and damning details about the gang – he travelled to Philadelphia to meet Pinkerton and Gower.

The two men, the detective and the railroad chief, were delighted with the operative's efforts, and more agents were assigned to the case. Within a few weeks there wasn't a mining town in Pennsylvania that didn't have its own undercover Pinkerton detective working there. But not all of them were as inconspicuous as McParland.

Word soon spread that the society and its activities was being spied upon, and every member was suspected of being 'untrue'. One by one the Mollies were able to clear themselves, until only McParland was left. By now the Irishman was a physical and mental wreck. The crude, raw alcohol he was still consuming was turning him blind, and his nerves were splintering. Only his smooth and rapid tongue saved him from an execution squad, and he begged Pinkerton to have him 'arrested'. Before this could happen, however, he said that his sister in Chicago was dying and that he had to be with her. He arrived at Shenandoah railway station minutes ahead of a group of assassins, and safely made his escape.

Later, when the Mollie Maguires were rounded up and put on trial, McParland's evidence – and the months he had spent with the gang – proved vital. Despite the $30,000 raised by the members to pay for their defence (and to have McParland murdered), scores of Mollies were found guilty and sent to prison. Two Pinkerton marksmen guarded the former spy throughout the courtroom proceedings, and McParland was afterwards appointed head of the Agency's branch in Denver.

Jesse James

Pinkerton and the outlaw Jesse James had an intense dislike for one another. For years, the James gang had managed to outwit the Pinkertons. On

January 5, 1875, Pinkerton's men threw an iron torch inside the home of Jesse James's mother thinking James was inside. The attack resulted in blowing off Mrs. James's right arm. Now, the Pinkertons looked bad in the public's eyes and Jesse James set out for retaliation.

James went to Chicago for one reason. To kill Allan Pinkerton. For four months the outlaw walked the streets of Chicago with a loaded gun. Inside the gun was a bullet with the name Pinkerton written on it. But, the famous detective never knew James was in the city. The outlaw James, being frustrated and unable to get Pinkerton at the right time and the right place, returned home.

Following their various successes, railroad companies and banks hired the Pinkertons and also manufacturing companies to put down strikes. Allan Pinkerton started the first 'Rogues Gallery', a file of pictures and information on criminals. He shared his file with law groups to help catch the unlawful. Later, this same system would form the ID system of the FBI.

Pinkerton eventually retired, due to his failing health, to his Chicago mansion and wrote eighteen books. He died on July 1, 1884, at the age of 65, but his namesake will always be remembered in honour and excellence.

In Pursuit of the Nazis

From his office in Vienna a lone Jew spreads tentacles to the farthest quarters of the earth in tracking the former persecutors of his people. His name is Simon Wiesenthal, and his organization, the Federation of Jewish Victims of the Nazi Régime, exists to bring survivors of the notorious Gestapo to justice.

RUDOLPHPLATZ IS a secluded square of rather hum–drum buildings in Vienna's first district. Nothing remarkable distinguishes it from a hundred similar squares in the Austrian capital or elsewhere – except, that is, for the sparsely furnished offices on the fourth floor of number seven. The entrance to them is heralded by a small, discreet sign which reads 'Documentation Centre', followed by the letters BJVN (*Bund Jüdischer Verfolgter des Naziregimes*), Federation of Jewish Victims of the Nazi Régime.

The director of this unusual organization is perhaps the best known – and most feared – Nazi hunter to have emerged from the horrors of World War II. His name: Simon Wiesenthal. Born in Poland of Jewish parents, Wiesenthal was an obvious target for persecution when the Germans overran his native country, and he was hounded through more than a dozen concentration camps during the war. But while six million of his fellow Jews died in gas chambers, Wiesenthal miraculously survived, to become one of the most outspoken witnesses of the atrocities committed by the dreaded German SS, whose task it was to carry out Hitler's 'Final Solution of the Jewish Question' – the extermination of the entire race. When he was at last liberated by the allies in 1945, Wiesenthal immediately began work on what was to become a lifetime obsession – the pursuit of Nazi criminals.

Apparently Without Trace

It was an exceedingly difficult task. There was no money, after the war, to finance a professional investigative centre with full-time staff, so he started alone by collecting and collating all the information he could lay his hands on concerning the activities of former SS men. Gradually he developed a series of files and card indexes detailing names, crimes and possible witnesses. These were already of value to the Allies during the preparation of the Nuremburg trials, and they were used extensively by the American Military Court at Dachau during proceedings against SS concentration camp guards.

Wiesenthal, however, was not satisfied. He realized that many of the worst Nazi criminals had escaped Allied justice and disappeared, apparently without trace. Among these were Adolf

Eichmann, the man charged by Hitler to organize the Jewish extermination programme, Franz Stangl, former commandant of the notorious concentration camp at Treblinka, and the horrifying Dr Josef Mengele, whose 'mission' at his Auschwitz surgery was to perform genetic experiments on 'inferior' races.

As sympathizers learned more about Wiesenthal's work they began to send contributions – usually small sums of money but also useful information – and in 1947 he was able to establish a small Documentation Centre at Linz, in Austria. Lack of funds and interest forced it to close down in 1954, but later, in 1961, it reopened in Vienna, and still operates under the tireless direction of its creator.

The Odessa Trail

Wiesenthal understood immediately that the first task of the new centre was to discover, if possible, how the fugitive Nazis had escaped. A chance meeting with an expert on Nazi affairs gave him the answer: ODESSA. The word has since become a legend. This complex escape network had already been organized by the SS well before the end of the war, and financed with vast quantities of gold spirited out of Germany into foreign bank accounts by Nazis who had foreseen the defeat of their country.

Along ODESSA's carefully concealed highways some of history's greatest criminals have travelled in safety to Spain, the Middle East and South

America. Their documents were always in order, their identities brilliantly disguised. Most of them left Germany in the confusion after the war and then vanished into apparent obscurity. No one, any longer, seemed to know who they were, or where they were, or what they had done.

It was a dispiriting situation for Wiesenthal, but he stuck to his work, slowly compiling dossiers on SS fugitives and piecing together, thread by thread, the pattern of their escape routes along the ODESSA lines in the hope that one day the information would be useful. Sometimes it was, as the case of Franz Stangl amply proves.

Even by the gruesome standards of the SS, the record of the commandant of Treblinka was particularly horrific; at least 400,000 Jews were either shot or choked in gas ovens under his orders alone. Some estimates reckon the figure to be nearer double that number. And for this contribution to Hitler's extermination plans he had been awarded a special Cross of Merit for what was euphemistically known as 'causing psychological discomfort'. In Nazi terminology this meant 'special excellence in the technique of mass murder'.

Ghastly Inventory

In 1948 Wiesenthal came across a fascinating document. It was a list of items recovered from Jews at Treblinka – both before and after death. The sheer size alone is staggering:

25	goods vans of women's hair
248	goods vans of clothing
100	goods vans of shoes
22	goods vans of sundries
46	goods vans of drugs
254	goods vans of blankets and bedding
2,800,000	US dollars
12,000,000	Soviet rubles
400,000	pounds sterling
140,000,000	Polish zloties
400,000	gold watches
145,000	kilograms of gold wedding rings
4,000	carats of diamonds
120,000,000	zloties in gold coins and pearls

The goods were consigned to the Interior Ministry of the SS to be ploughed back into the war effort – or the emergency escape fund. But it was not so much the figures that captured Wiesenthal's attention as the signature which lay at the bottom of the list. It was Franz Stangl's. Here then was the irrefutable evidence of his involvement in the extermination programme; evidence which would stand up to the closest scrutiny in a court of law. But where was the killer?

Waiting and Watching

Wiesenthal learned that he had, in fact, been captured at the end of the war and automatically imprisoned by the Americans as a former SS lieutenant. He was given a routine investigation and acquitted himself well. No one imagined that he could be the notorious Treblinka commandant. Later, however, it was discovered that he had once worked at Castle Hartheim, the Nazi training school for scientific human extermination, and on these grounds the Austrian government made preparations to try him.

Their plans were suddenly cut short. On May 30, 1948, Stangl slipped away from a prison working party and vanished under cover of darkness. At the time it seemed relatively unimportant – he was just another insignificant war criminal – and as a result the news was not officially reported.

Months passed before Wiesenthal discovered the truth, by which time Stangl had been carried by the ODESSA network to the safety of the Middle East, from where it was unlikely that he would be extradited even if he were found. Soon afterwards his wife and three daughters disappeared in the same direction. There was nothing that Wiesenthal – or anyone else – could do about it except shelve the file and wait.

It was ten years before any further information came to light. One day, in 1959, a German journalist burst into Wiesenthal's office in a flurry of excitement.

'It's Stangl,' he blurted out breathlessly. 'I've seen him – in Damascus.'

Wiesenthal was cautious.

'How do you know it's him?' he asked.

'I've checked,' came the reply. 'It's him for sure.'

There was still nothing Wiesenthal could do directly, but it meant that the man could be watched in case he ever attempted to leave his country of refuge. In the following year, however, the picture changed dramatically. Adolf Eichmann was seized in Argentina and later extradited to Israel for trial – an event in which Wiesenthal played a significant role. Stangl took fright. Supposing the Israelis decided to send someone over the border to get him as well? He decided to make a break for it – and once again he succeeded in vanishing.

There was another long pause in the saga. Over five years passed without any further news of the Treblinka killer. Then, on February 20, 1964, Wiesenthal gave a routine press conference at which he listed a number of wanted Nazi criminals. Deliberately he singled out Franz Stangl for particular attention and gave a vivid account of some of the crimes which the latter had committed. One day later an Austrian woman arrived at Wiesenthal's office in floods of tears.

'Herr Wiesenthal, I feel so ashamed,' she sobbed. 'I had no idea my cousin Theresia was married to such a terrible man. I can't believe Franz is a mass murderer.'

A US Cent For Each Victim

'Where is your cousin now?' interrupted Wiesenthal casually.

'They all went to Brazil . . .'

With a start the woman realized she had revealed too much. She had come to check on the press stories, not to give the game away.

As it turned out, however, her evidence did not betray the whereabouts of her cousin's husband as effectively as Wiesenthal's next visitor. This was a shifty-eyed, nervous-looking character who had also read the press reports on Stangl. Wiesenthal noticed immediately that the man was unsteady on his feet and his breath smelled of alcohol. Motioned to a chair, he sat down heavily and mumbled for a few seconds incoherently. Then, suddenly, as if coming to a decision, he began to speak.

'I used to be in the Gestapo,' he blurted.

Wiesenthal waited and said nothing. The visitor watched anxiously for the reaction. Then, having ascertained that all was well, he went on.

'I didn't do anything bad. I was just the little fellow who got pushed around.'

Again there was silence.

'I read the story in the papers. About Franz Stangl. Because of men like him we little fellows have had nothing but trouble since the end of the war. The big men, the Eichmanns, the Stangls – they had all the help they needed. False papers, money, new jobs. But look at me. No one will give me a job because I've been in the Gestapo. I've got no money. Can't even afford a little drink.'

Wiesenthal hesitated between throwing the stranger out and listening a while longer. He chose the latter course.

'Look,' the man continued, 'I know where Stangl is. I can help you find him. He never gave me any help, so why should I cover up for him?'

Suddenly interested, Wiesenthal leaned forward.

'Where is he? Come on, man. Where is he?'

The stranger grinned.

'I can't tell you just like that. Information – good information – is worth a lot of money . . .'

The whole purpose of the visit was now clear.

'How much?' Wiesenthal snapped.

'Thirty thousand dollars.'

It was an absurd amount to demand from a man whose organization had always been run on a shoestring. Since there was no way to raise such a sum, the price would somehow have to be lowered. Sensing this, the visitor, now in his element, offered to accept less.

'Tell me,' he rasped. 'How many Jews do you think Stangl managed to exterminate?'

The reply came quickly: 'As many as 700,000.'

'Very well. I'll take one US cent for each victim. That makes 7000 dollars. A bargain!'

Wiesenthal half-rose from his seat, for an instant blinded with rage, and reached out to grab the man. Seconds later he controlled himself and sat down. The information was too important.

'I agree,' he muttered.

Immediately the man responded. 'He's a safety officer in the Volkswagen plant in São Paulo, Brazil.'

Hurriedly, Wiesenthal arranged for secret checks to be made before paying his informant; it was true. Stangl was in São Paulo. The problem which now remained was how to bring him to justice. Wiesenthal handed over all the details to the West German authorities so that arrest warrants could be prepared. But there were difficulties; the Brazilian government had to be persuaded to take action, firstly by having the criminal arrested and then by extraditing him back to West Germany.

Meanwhile the entire negotiations had to be kept secret in case ODESSA got wind of the discovery and enabled Stangl once more to elude his pursuers. At last, however, in February 1967, Franz Stangl was arrested by the Brazilian police. Subsequently, he was transported back to face trial in a German court and sentenced to life imprisonment, officially for the murder of 400,000 men, women and children. He died in a Düsseldorf jail on June 28, 1971. Painstaking effort and patience had forced him to end his life where he belonged – behind bars.

For Wiesenthal the capture of Stangl was an undoubted triumph. But he knows that the task he has set himself will only end with his own death. There are 22,000 names on his card indexes, and it is inconceivable that all these men should be found and brought to justice. Nevertheless, he believes his work is of value not just in terms of punishing the guilty but of periodically reminding the world of what took place during the terrible years of Nazi power, so that a repetition of those events can be avoided.

For this reason publicity is vital to Wiesenthal – which is why he once set about the seemingly impossible task of finding the SS officer who arrested Anne Frank, the young Jewish girl whose diary of her life under the Nazis, shocked the world. In this, too, he succeeded.

The officer himself turned out to be small fry and was officially exonerated of any criminal guilt for the girl's death. But the hunt still proved worthwhile; many people had claimed, before, that Anne Frank's story was pure invention designed to discredit the Germans, and that she hadn't existed at all. Now, thanks to Wiesenthal the Nazi-hunter, they know the truth.

During the period from 1959 to 1964, the area of the Treblinka camp was made into a Polish national monument, in the form of a cemetery. Hundreds of stones were set in the ground, inscribed with the names of the countries and places from which the victims had originated.

International Interpol

The name Interpol conjures up images of an International Police organization working with James Bond type characters, using the most modern means to track down the world's worst criminals. It is indeed an organization whose probing arms stretch round the whole world.

INTERPOL, AFTER Scotland Yard and the FBI, is the police organization most popular among film producers and fiction writers, and its cosmopolitan image has launched dozens of mystery movies and books. Yet, surprisingly, Interpol in its present form is less than thirty years old.

The International Criminal Police Commission – to give its full title – was originally launched at an international police congress in Monaco in 1914, but was reconstituted in 1946 when its headquarters were switched from Vienna to Paris.

The first article of the 'new' statutes reads:

'The purpose of the International Police Organization is to ensure and officially to promote the growth of the greatest possible mutual assistance between all criminal police authorities within the limits of the laws existing in the different States, to establish and develop all institutions likely to contribute to an efficient repression of Common Law crimes and offences to the strict exclusion of all matters having a political, religious or racial character.'

Three years later, in 1949, the Secretary-General, M. Ducloux, restated Interpol's official policy thus: 'To establish rapid liaison among all criminal investigation branches so as to speed up the identification, arrest and trial of delinquents who have sought refuge abroad, enlighten fully courts as to the true personality of professional criminals, and to provide legal experts, sociologists and scientific experts of all nations with the benefits of the discoveries made by the police through their direct contact with Common Law criminals.'

In 1951 Ducloux handed over to his successor as Secretary-General, the brilliant Sûreté detective, M. Marcel Sicot, a staff of forty detectives and the nucleus of a well-run organization. Nowadays, thanks to Sicot and to Richard Leofric Jackson, then head of Scotland Yard's CID, who was President in 1961, Interpol is now housed in impressive modern buildings in Paris suitable for its importance.

Today Interpol spans the world with a permanent staff of around 100 men and women, most of whom work at St. Cloud, on the outskirts of Paris. It does not employ – as is sometimes believed – thousands of top scientists and research workers, but it can and does avail itself of the discoveries made by university laboratories, industrial research groups and individual scientists of all categories consulted from time to time by a criminal investigation department, as well as the work of all forensic laboratories maintained by member States. Thus it can command a far wider pool of expertise than any one Ministry of the Interior.

Interpol's nerve centre is its radio station thirty miles outside Paris – its fantastic efficiency depends on the speed of its communications. Paperwork and time-wasting correspondence have to be cut to a bare minimum. The Paris staff are almost all former detectives of the Sûreté or Prefecture: women staff act as interpreters and make on-the-spot translations so that no time is lost in sending off messages. Interpol holds files on 200,000 people, but the policy is to file only the records of the top criminals.

These records are contained in two index systems – one phonetic, the other alphabetical. There are, however, also card indexes containing the names of ships in which drugs have been found, registration numbers of cars, the numbers of certain passports, reports on mysterious deaths and details of unidentified stolen property.

Like every other police organization in the world, Interpol relies for positive identification on fingerprints, but also employs one system which is unique in police work. This is the Portrait Parlé, or Speaking Likeness, developed to an astonishing pitch of perfection by M. Beaulieu, chief of Interpol's photographic and fingerprints section. He has devised a system of facial measurements which cannot be altered. In his files there are sometimes as many as twenty pictures of the same man who, to the untrained eye, looks like twenty different men, but not to the expert in Portrait Parlé.

If a man is suspect or under surveillance in a country 10,000 miles from Paris, Interpol can transmit all its pictures within an hour to facilitate his arrest. The system is based on a series of coloured tags, each corresponding to a factor in the description. Thus a synoptic index is built up based on information obtained from police forces which complete a descriptive Form S, a document which lists 177 different characteristics of the subject in the following seventeen groups:

1 Nationality
2 Place where committed
3 Probable race
4 Apparent height
5 Face
6 Complexion
7 Colouring
8 Teeth
9 Voice
10 Gait
11 General demeanour
12 Traits of character and vices
13 Visible scars
14 Moles and other marks
15 Tattoos
16 Deformities and amputations
17 Habits and peculiarities

Interpol uses three categories of 'circulation' – now an internationally recognized document – to further the ends of justice. The red-cornered circulation spells urgency or top priority and is a request to the police force of the country receiving one to seek out, hold and hand over the subject named in it. A blue-cornered circulation is a request for information or particulars, say, of a person's present whereabouts or his movements on a certain date, his mode of life, real name and aliases. The green-cornered circulation is a warning: 'Keep an eye on X'.

In the course of tracking down a wanted man, half-a-dozen countries may be involved, and the work in each is carried out by its Central Bureau who are representatives of Interpol but not on its permanent staff. These detectives are seconded from their own police force for this specialized task and are the field workers who make the arrests.

There are three official languages for Interpol – English, French and Spanish – but, because some countries have trouble in sending accurate messages, a filing system based on purely phonetic spelling has been adopted. All names are filed according to their French pronunciation, which avoids the danger of breakdown in communication through confusion.

Almost all original messages received and transmitted by Interpol pass through the radio station outside Paris, and the traffic reaches 80,000 a year, arriving at the member countries within minutes. Interpol insists on real evidence being provided before it sends out a circulation except when:

> the offence is a crime against common
> Law; a warrant has been issued for the

suspect's arrest; the country requesting an arrest produces evidence and seeks extradition as soon as the wanted man is detained.

Britain became a member of the reconstituted Interpol in 1946, and the office of Interpol, Great Britain was set up in June, 1949 and incorporated as a separate unit within Scotland Yard by Sir Ronald Howe, who for many years was Interpol's representative for England, Scotland, Wales and Northern Ireland. Interpol GB is sited on the third floor of the seven-storied white stone block overlooking the Thames Embankment which houses New Scotland Yard.

Here, with desks set at right angles to each other and the walls well charted with diagrams of Interpol's radio links and maps of member nations, sit two Yard officers, the office staff of Interpol GB. They deal with inquiries from all points of the compass that may involve, at any hour, a drug-runner of British nationality held in Los Angeles or a Briton on the run tracked down in Australia.

Indeed, any British citizen who is ever tempted to get up to mischief abroad might be interested to know what can go on concerning him behind the scenes. Local police report all troubles caused by a British national to Her Majesty's Consular officials in their area. If these cannot be cleared up by British representatives on the spot then full particulars are requested about the Briton concerned through the Foreign Office's Consular Service – and the inquiries often land on a desk at Interpol GB. What happens then should certainly act as a deterrent to all would-be mischief-makers in a foreign land.

Take the case of Rex Macclesfield, a British national who came to the notice of Interpol in Paris, where he was using a fraudulent passport in the name of Louis Max. He was apparently on a racketeering tour of Europe – he spoke French and German well and had a smattering of Scandinavian languages. He was arrested by the Oslo police for petty theft in July 1954, and his trail of trickery left traces in France, Germany, Denmark and Sweden. The Norwegian police decided to pack him off home and reported this decision to the British Consulate in Oslo, who contacted Interpol GB.

It was quickly established that he had a dossier in the Yard's Criminal Records Office with his true name and favourite aliases. Further, he was listed on the Yard's files as 'wanted' for petty thefts and frauds in Sheffield, Barrow and Stratford-on-Avon. He was returned to Newcastle-on-Tyne docks on July 26, 1954, where he found a police reception committee waiting to take him in hand. He was tried at Sheffield and sentenced to a year's jail – because of eight international police telegrams.

International Cooperation

It is doubtful if any villain has caused Interpol Great Britain more trouble than the totally conspicuous Arthur French, 6 foot 2 inches tall, scarecrow thin, with ears sticking out of his head like huge question marks. He had an American partner named Norman Krebs, another six-footer, and together they played the 'false cheque caper' under dozens of aliases. They were the subject of an Interpol circulation as wanted men as far afield as Curaçao, the Dutch possession in the Caribbean.

Hardly had Interpol GB filed this international circulation when they received the news that French planned to apply for a British passport from an address in Christchurch, Hants. It seems he had lost the passport originally issued to him. Now the British Home Office does not allow their police to arrest a man merely on receipt of an Interpol circulation – as do many other countries. He may, of course, be put under surveillance or even held if he is known to be a man of violence; otherwise a provisional arrest warrant must be obtained from a magistrate's court before he can be taken into custody. That procedure eats away time which is often precious. But it protects the suspect's right to know the charge against him.

The Bow Street magistrate to whom application was made for a provisional warrant of arrest for Albert French raised no objection. But French's antennae must have warned him that he was tempting fate by applying officially for anything – and particularly for passport renewal. He took to his heels.

Phoney Cheques

Detectives traced a girlfriend of French and tried, without success, to persuade her to talk. Then Interpol GB got wind of the arrival in England of

French's partner, Krebs. So both men, wanted by the police of the USA, Mexico, Venezuela, the Cuban Republic and the Dutch West Indies, were now in the Yard's territory. And Interpol GB got a break just when it badly needed one. Krebs was reported to have left Manchester Airport on May 28, bound for Paris – and at once Interpol GB radioed the information to International Bureau in Paris.

Now it was up to Interpol HQ to run Krebs to earth. But he moved fast – it seemed he spent only five hours in Paris, in and out of night clubs cashing phoney cheques like a man with four hands. The Sûreté picking up the complaints after him, totalled his proceeds at 450 dollars, and there must have been several clubs which, for diplomatic reasons, preferred not to report their losses.

In the money once more, Krebs flew to Lisbon. The Portuguese police missed him, for he stopped off at Lisbon for only ten minutes before flying on to Madrid. This time Interpol's radio message had the Spanish police waiting for him. They picked him up as he was trying to board a transatlantic airliner – he had a first-class ticket for New York in his wallet.

Missing Link

With the much-wanted Norman Krebs now languishing in a Spanish jail, Interpol Spain notified their Paris HQ, and later officials in several countries looked at their extradition treaties. Interpol GB was as relieved as all the others, but for them one important question remained unanswered:

where was his partner in crime, Arthur French? Seeking the missing link, one of the Yard's Interpol officers decided to revisit French's girlfriend. And this time he found her eager to talk! It seems the fickle French had ditched her for a new girlfriend – and she willingly supplied the Yard man with details.

The Yard man found the new girlfriend also willing enough to talk – because, she said, she had heard from him the previous day. He had written to her from prison – in Madrid. She produced his letter to prove it: French's handwriting, beyond doubt. Now Interpol GB had to forward all details of French, including fingerprints and pictures, to Interpol HQ, which then asked Interpol Spain to compare the fingerprints. The man was the Briton French, not the American Krebs!

Slender Clue

As French had used Krebs's identity to leave England, it was obvious that he had entered England in the same way. So Interpol GB had to go back to French's girlfriend number one to discuss his movements immediately after his arrival in England. She remembered that they had dinner together in a Strand hotel, and that he had left her for a short time to send off a telegram. It was to a country she had never heard of, and she could only remember that it began with 'An–'.

With the help of this slender clue and the hotel's efficient administration the Yard established that French had sent cablegrams from this hotel to an accommodation address in Antigua. He had sent them in the name of Krebs's – and that was how he had signed the hotel register.

Elusive Partner

It now seemed to the police that the telegraphic address used by French offered a clue to the real Krebs' hiding-place, so a further message was drafted to the International Bureau in Paris, in which it was suggested that the Antigua address should be investigated in the search for Arthur French's elusive partner. The chief of Interpol's Department of Police Documentation sent a cablegram in English to the Police Commissioner, Antigua, stating that, on information supplied by Scotland Yard, it seemed likely that Norman Krebs, for whom there was a warrant of arrest, was hiding on the island. He asked for Krebs to be arrested, if discovered.

No one could even feel confident that such a tiny island in the British West Indies had even heard of Interpol. Yet, 48 hours later, came an answering cablegram to report that the wanted man had been identified, arrested and was now held pending further orders. When all the evidence was collected it was found that the two swindlers had 1,000 false cheque forms manufactured for them at a counterfeiter's premises in Haiti!

Interpol GB were called in twice in three years to take over two remarkable cases involving youths of eighteen. The first was nothing less than the theft of an aircraft in the early 1950s when 'skyjacking' was an unknown word. It happened on an RAF airfield at Sywell, Northampton, where a boy of eighteen jumped into the cockpit of an Auster, got the plane in the air and headed for the south coast. He travelled in a series of hops, as the Auster carried no navigational instruments. So he had to land – and ask passers-by for his bearings.

Airborne

He landed first in a meadow off the Great North Road near Daventry and asked a lorry driver: 'Am I all right for London?' Then he took off again, crossed the Channel and put down near Dieppe. Here a farmer gave him food and water, and he was airborne once more until he ran out of petrol – the Auster was fuelled for 300 miles – and was able to land in one piece outside Orleans.

So far the plane was undamaged, but now, as he tried to taxi towards a clump of trees for shelter, he had the bad luck to hit a rabbit hole, and the Auster's nose dipped sharply, buckling the propeller tips. As soon as the plane was plotted across the Channel Interpol GB reported the theft to their International Bureau, and, unknown to him, the eighteen-year-old made police history by becoming the youngest-ever subject of an Interpol circulation.

Extradition Formalities

Not that he was difficult to trace, with the Auster stuck fast in a foreign field. The boy had the sense to give himself up at once to the French police. He was held for entering France illegally, and some weeks elapsed before extradition formalities were completed, but, on March 9, 1951, officers of Interpol GB called for him at the Santé prison in Paris.

On the drive back from Dover one of his police escorts, himself a former RAF pilot, was so astonished by the boy's grasp of aeronautical technicalities that he refused to believe he had had no training. In fact his previous flying experience was limited to one seaside hop. He had read all the flying manuals he could put his hands on and was clearly a 'natural', as he subsequently proved when taken on by a major aircraft company who were impressed by his enthusiasm and gave him a chance to make good.

The second case of a boy in trouble came in the summer of 1953. An eighteen-year-old Spaniard was alleged to have plundered the Chapel of the Virgin of the Kings in the Cathedral of Seville and removed precious stones and gold pieces valued at 700 million French francs – a fantastic haul. The boy's home was in the Calle de Julio Cesar, and he had become friendly with a verger in the cathedral in order to familiarize himself with the layout and routine. Then he bided his time until he saw the chance of hiding himself among the treasures in the chapel on the night of April 14.

Stolen Treasure

All doors were locked and the lights dimmed. Alone in the Holy Shrine, he wrenched gems from their sockets, defiling the Image of the Virgin. Then, in the morning, he sneaked unnoticed out of the cathedral, his pockets stuffed with sacred symbols worth at least half-a-million pounds – if they could be sold.

In the hue-and-cry that followed, the boy was never a suspect. Indeed, on May 7, he left Seville for Paris, travelling with a properly authorized passport. After spending some days in Paris he made for London. Meanwhile the Seville police, combing through all local jewellers and silversmiths in an urgent hunt for the stolen treasures, came on an expanding gold bracelet studded with seventeen diamonds, and another relic consisting of a single diamond mounted on gold.

The Spanish Chaplain-Royal and the Keeper of the Treasury identified these items as part of the stolen treasure, and the silversmith who had them in his shop said the boy had handed them over and asked him to sell them – the silversmith claimed the boy's mother confirmed that her son had bought the jewels at the government pawnshop.

Meanwhile Interpol GB learned from the International Bureau in Paris that the boy was thought to be in London. The Scotland Yard men who were put on the case found that he had made no attempt to hide himself, but was staying at an address in Regent's Park Terrace which he had left in Paris as a forwarding address for his mother.

Sacred Symbols

They called on him there, but he denied any part

in the robbery – and no gems were found in his possession or at his address. Again the extradition formalities took some weeks, but, in the end, he was sent back to Spain. As all the sacred symbols were found intact, he was sent to the Spanish equivalent of an approved school.

Finding Forgeries

There is one sure way of always having enough money – whenever you wish you just go ahead and print some. Of course you need a little skill and a good printing machine. And how could police ever find you out?

AS COUNTERFEITERS present a threat to the economies of all nations, countries cooperate much more readily in running down these criminal-technicians than in dealing with, say, drug-traffickers. Fortunately for law enforcement the illicit business of counterfeiting calls not only for exceptional skills but for a heavy capital outlay on printing presses. The whole process inevitably involves a team of conspirators who must meet from time to time before the coup is perfected, thus offering the men from Interpol a better chance of infiltrating and eavesdropping. Then such teams must be recruited from the ranks of habitual criminals, and most of their records are on file at Interpol HQ in Paris.

It must be emphasized that Interpol (International Criminal Police Commission) is *not*, despite glamorization by films and television, a world police *force*. It is a clearing-house of crime on behalf of its member-states, and it represents the federal police systems of those countries, coordinating their efforts and acting as an information centre and records office, with powers to transmit requests from one country to all countries, if need be, to run wanted law-breakers to ground.

As well as bank notes, counterfeiters may forge credit cards, travellers' cheques, Giro cheques, letters of credit, and similar documents. The problem is often that of realizing the fruit of their forgeries without attracting suspicion. Obviously it would be dangerous for a forger to pay a large number of brand new bank notes into his bank account, or to make a substantial purchase with a bundle of freshly printed notes. Usually he will release his forgeries through a number of distributors, who 'buy' a few notes at a time at a substantial discount. Through the uncovering of such a distribution network the chief forger is often arrested.

The counterfeiter, of course, is no respecter of nationalities – he switches from one country's paper money to another whenever he sees an opportunity for high profit. In recent years a Japanese ring was discovered at work in Brazil running off cruzeiros; in the West Indies another gang was caught in the act of flooding black markets in South America with fake 50-peso notes of Colombian currency.

So much of Interpol's daily business is taken up in dealing with this menace that the General Secretariat has sponsored a film, *False Money and its Repression*, to help national police forces understand how dangerous this crime can be to their country's economic health. The film drives home the point that, unless the police can raid the counterfeiters' secret press-room while printing is actually going on, thus seizing the plotters *and* the proofs of their conspiracy, then it is extremely difficult to collect strong enough evidence for a conviction.

Phoney banknotes, whatever the currency, often give themselves away by the very feel of the paper – and the trained eye is ever on the lookout for tiny imperfections, some false swirl or scroll or even a minute flaw in lettering. The expert can usually tell whether a gang has been at work or a solitary crank; the gangs prefer small denomination notes – the 20 Deutschmark or the five-dollar bill – whereas the crank will slave for months to copy a note of high value, feeling that the small ones degrade his art!

The craftsmanship of the counterfeiter is usually of an extremely high order, and he is often prepared to go to great lengths and expense to get as near perfection as possible. One gang even raided the State Bank of France, stole several reams of the specially processed 1,000-franc paper and then used it for counterfeiting 1,000-franc notes.

In another case the gang's master technician confessed to the police after capture how he had stripped a 50-dollar bill in two, using special liquids, and then studied the structure. With the front of the note separated from the back, he said, he was able to examine the arrangements of the red and green filaments, distinguishing each side, and he set himself the task of faithfully reproducing the colouring pattern.

The counterfeiters went to their work immediately after World War II and copied currency issued by the Allied military authorities. They followed this up by forging the banknotes of the 'hard' currencies – Swiss francs, dollars, pounds sterling, German marks in the Western Zone, Belgian francs and Spanish pesetas.

During the years 1947 and 1948 the International Bureau of Interpol at The Hague identified 127 different types of counterfeit, among which only 24 concerned coins. This is because the technical improvements in printing methods have made counterfeiting easier. No longer does the counterfeiter have to make use of cumbersome material, nor does he need the services of an expert engraver – photo-mechanical processes are as easily available to the criminal as to the honest man.

Interpol has been campaigning for many years now – discreetly, of course, for it has no power to coerce its member-governments – for more frequent currency changes, for designs and colours on notes to be made more intricate, and for a specialized type of paper – all of which would make the counterfeiters' job very much more difficult.

The United States suffers more than any other country at the skilled hands of these forgers. The Treasury Department of the US Government is mainly responsible for tracking them down, and the Secret Service is also involved in this tricky work.

Jet travel has opened up fast and easy avenues of communication and escape for the big-time criminals, but in a bid to counter such opportunities Interpol now operates 20 radio stations covering the main cities in Europe, the Middle East, Iran and the Americas. These stations are grouped around the central one outside Paris, and their coverage is being extended to equatorial Africa and the Far East. All messages are sent by Morse in the Interpol code which cuts down sending and receiving time.

However swift air travel becomes in the Space Age, it cannot match radio, and many a runaway criminal has been held thousands of miles away from the scene of his crime and only a few hours after he committed it. Murderers, bank robbers, gold and diamond smugglers, drug-runners and forgers all use jet travel either to escape or to find a market for their loot, and might well get away with their crimes were it not for Interpol's radio network which is now serving well over 70 countries who are subscribers to the police organization.

In the 1960s a gang stole a large number of travellers' cheques from New York's First National City Bank – the cheques were in transit from the US to Montevideo, Uruguay, when they disappeared. They were all blank worth 700,000 dollars when cashed.

Commissioner U. E. Baughman, then chief of the US Secret Service, radioed Interpol, which at once circulated the numbers and other details of the cheques to all affiliated police forces. Within days news came that some of the cheques had been cashed in Cologne, Düsseldorf, Bonn and Wiesbaden by a Robert Castille, holding a passport issued in El Salvador. Other cheques turned up in Monaco, cashed by Isaac Gutlieb, using an Argentinian passport. Then the trail switched to Milan, where a man giving the name of Helmuth Kender ran off, abandoning his German passport when the cashier became suspicious of the cheques. Another man in the name of Joseph Decker tried to cash some of the cheques in Paris, but he, too, ran off when challenged, leaving behind an Argentinian passport.

When the abandoned passports were scrutinized it became clear that they had been used by one or two people. An Interpol circular went out with all available information about the men involved. A month later a man named Fischer was arrested in Bad Naheim, Germany, trying to cash one of the stolen cheques. He turned out to be the one who had used the passports in the names of Kender and Decker.

Within a month another man was arrested 3,000 miles away in Buenos Aires – he was identified as the one who had used the passport in the name of Isaac Gutlieb. When the Argentine police checked his fingerprints with their files and those of the FBI, his real name was found to be Salem Karngalder who had been on Interpol's wanted list since 1948.

Every fake currency seizure sent to Interpol by any of its member-nations is passed to the Paris section which deals with the counterfeiting of banknotes and coins, cheques and forgeries. It is there that comparison is made with genuine notes. The detectives in this department, with wide experience of every type of forgery, can often tell the author at a glance – so many of them tend to repeat their mistakes. In this section are filed specimens of thousands of forged notes and hundreds of dud coins. Here, too, is stored the apparatus seized in raids on counterfeiters' dens.

More than 6,000 cases of currency forgery have been notified to Interpol since the end of World War II, with notes of almost every known denomination involved. Detection is an exact business – the men of that job have studied the composition of the inks used, types of paper and watermarks and all the intricacies of design and lettering.

These experts do much more than detect – they also prevent by producing Interpol's *Counterfeits and Forgeries Review* so that banks, insurance offices, hotels and travel agencies can be kept up-to-date with the activities of the known gangs. Scotland Yard reserves one corner of its notorious 'Black Museum' to immortalize the work of celebrated forgers. Here Adolf Hitler and Jim the Penman share a showcase – the £5 and £10 notes printed on German Treasury apparatus lie beside the notes made by London's most infamous counterfeiter.

Another case holds a bundle of Post Office savings books and car log-books, examples of the work of an extremely talented family. Mr and Mrs Arthur Pierce occupied a semi-detached house in Norwood, London, with their son Harold, aged 24, and their daughter Janet, 18. All did respectable jobs during the day, but at night Harold made ready forgery implements while father brought up the treadle-operated printing machine from the basement. Janet organized inks and chemicals and mother sat down to pedal the machine.

Every evening for four months the Pierce family printed Post Office savings books until they had a stock of hundreds. They burned any books which showed the slightest imperfection. They chose names from the telephone directories, entered them into the forged savings books, gave them a modest balance – between £20 and £30 – and embossed the books with a beautifully forged rubber stamp. This done, the family took a day off, raced from one Post Office to another withdrawing £2 from each of their books.

Eventually the family decided to make a final killing of around £1,000, but on the great day Janet got her savings bank books mixed and presented one with a man's name on it. When challenged, she panicked and ran back to the family car. Later all four Pierces were arrested – they had 170 forged bank books in their possession, and Mrs Pierce had £488 in her handbag. Mr Pierce got seven years, his wife eighteen months, son Harold twelve months, and Janet was bound over.

Handwriting Experts

Handwriting experts are often called upon to help with the intricacies of forgeries. The job of a handwriting expert is primarily to determine whether handwriting is authentic or forged, and to identify or eliminate the person who wrote a particular writing. They examine and identify signatures, handwriting, hand printing, initials, and numbers on all types of documents, such as:

- Forged, counterfeited and altered documents
- Wills, deeds, legal contracts, cheques
- Medical records (in medical malpractice cases)
- Insurance records
- Court documents
- Typewritten and computer printed documents
- Photocopied documents
- Latent impressions on documents
- Charred documents

Handwriting Experts are also called 'Questioned Document Examiners', or 'Forensic Document Analysts'. The word 'forensic' just means 'the application of science to law'. So in this case, handwriting experts develop evidence that can be used in both civil and in criminal courts. In government forensic laboratories, the forensic document handwriting experts work side by side with the fingerprint experts cooperating to determine who has handled or written on a document.

However, other issues are also explored by the handwriting examiners. Through forensic analysis using specialized equipment, they may also determine that different pens were used to write on a document, or what printing methods were employed to create the basic form of the document. For example, the imprinted graphics and text that are seen on personal and business cheques. These examinations can help determine whether or not a document was counterfeited.

Credit Cards

Counterfeited (plastic) payment cards have become 'big business' as more and more people now prefer this method of payment. Interpol stated that efforts must be made to ensure that everything possible is done to tackle any type of fraud with payment cards. In more concrete terms, the authorities must ensure that the legislation includes provisions that combat the counterfeiting of payment cards and/or the use of such cards.

Indeed, it is such a major problem that it was decided to convene a working group to look into the possibility of developing a classification system for counterfeit cards. This group was called the First International Working Group On Counterfeit Payment Cards. The public-private collaboration between Interpol and the world's biggest card companies was to be of paramount importance. The collaboration between Interpol, the private industry, and the public sector, can be regarded as a strategic step in stamping out credit card forgeries.

Dealing with Drugs

Perhaps the most lucrative of all 'business' is the dope trade. Hard drugs which find their way from the East to the United States can be sold for up to 200 times the original cost. For that kind of profit almost anyone might be tempted to run the risk – which means one big headache for narcotic squads.

FEW WOULD DENY that, war and pollution apart, the greatest menace to the health, wealth and happiness of mankind in the twenty-first century, is undoubtedly drug trafficking. The growth of this social evil over the past two decades has been so stupendous that there are grounds for the suspicion that certain countries are actively promoting it either as a political, or an economical, weapon against others.

Despite the lip service paid by many of the guilty countries to the ideals of the United Nations, Interpol finds itself fighting a losing battle against the worldwide gangs – including the Mafia – which are cashing in on the multi-million-dollar business of selling narcotics.

The third floor of Interpol's headquarters in Paris has a room well charted with the routes used by the traffickers. That room contains some revealing statistics. The invidious distinction of being the main supply source of opium goes to the Lebanon, followed by Kuwait, Turkey, India and Germany. For morphine – a derivative of opium – the Lebanon again heads the League of Shame with the favourite routes used by the dealers in human decay listed as: Lebanon–Italy–France–USA and Iran–Egypt–Italy–France–USA.

Obviously the United States is the prime target for illicit narcotics dealers since it offers the highest rewards for the dope and the widest market for its distribution. Drug addiction is now one of the major social problems in the USA. In tackling it, the US Bureau of Narcotics has had to develop a world strategy. Interpol's role – remembering that it is pledged to political neutrality – is to keep the Bureau posted with information and to alert all its member-nations with the names of the traffickers, the ships, and the aircraft they use and the routes of supply and distribution.

Heroin

Heroin, which fetches a very high price on the New York streets, has probably crossed the world to reach the addict. After the resin from poppies is collected in the spring it is smuggled from the country of origin and sold at highly inflated prices. It is then taken to secret laboratories to be processed into morphine which increases its value by one hundred per cent. But there is a further process to come which turns the morphine into heroin, and the price soars even higher. Even this fantastic profit is not enough for some drug traffickers, who mix the white drug with bicarbonate of soda and kitchen salt, in order to get an even greater rake-off.

Countries that used to be considered as transit countries of heroin traffic have become consumption areas. In most of these countries, heroin traffic leads to severe punishment and the law is strictly enforced. Despite these positive facts, the number of heroin trafficking attempts and heroin addict population have increased in the past few years. In East and South East Asia, China takes the lead in heroin seizures for the past few years (7.4 tonnes in 1998 and 4.2 tonnes in 1999), followed by Thailand, Vietnam and Malaysia. Bangkok International Airport is identified as one of the Asian airports most affected by heroin traffic. Multinational heroin couriers have been arrested in Asia and the seizures indicate that the international heroin traffic out of the source areas is often well organised.

Australia and New Zealand are two of the major countries seriously affected by the heroin traffic.The abuse of heroin among youth is a serious problem. Children as young as thirteen have been found involved in heroin abuse. According to statistics in 1999, heroin overdose has caused more deaths than traffic accidents.

Indian Hemp

An equally complex problem is created by drugs derived from the Indian hemp plant, Cannabis, which is grown in the Far East, Middle East, parts of Europe and South America. It is the most consumed drug in the world and therefore the subject of the most traffic. When the leaves and flowers of the hemp plant are dried, they are formed into a cigarette which can be bought easily in most major cities.

Hashish is another drug which comes from the resin of the same plant. This is generally smoked in a pipe known as a 'kif'. The traffickers in this drug make vast profits, and as they pay their agents well it is difficult for the police to find an informer – unless it is someone who has watched a friend or relative go down the slippery slope to the hard drugs from the softer cannabis.

Cannabis trafficking has been increasing in response to a high and rising demand. The indoor cultivation of cannabis continues to develop, especially in the Netherlands, Canada and the United States.

A further complication with Indian hemp is that many countries cultivate it as part of their economy, and sell it quite legitimately for medical supplies. In China, Burma, Laos and Thailand, where opium is in common use as a stimulant, peasants cultivate the poppy, so the authorities tend to turn a blind eye to any *extra* cultivation – and it is this, sold to the traffickers, which is creating the world's narcotics problem. Morphine is from six to ten times more addiction-forming than opium, and heroin is from 30 to 80 times more potent.

These two killer drugs – morphine and heroin – are in greatest demand in North America, where millions of dollars are spent annually by addicts, including many thousands of teenagers. Hashish claims many addicts in Egypt, while Iran has the same problem with opium addiction. Cocaine is most popular in South America, where it is produced – Indians chew the coca leaf, which is supposed to help them survive the rigours of the Andes.

'Ecstasy'

In recent years synthetic drugs have become readily available. They are artificially produced substances for the illicit market which are almost wholly manufactured from chemical compounds in illicit laboratories (for example, amphetamines and benzodiazepines). On the illicit drug market amphetamines have been sold in the form of powders, liquids, crystals, tablets and capsules. Today tablets are the most common form – and have become designated as 'ECSTASY'.

When the term 'Ecstasy' was first used in the early seventies it was an American street name for preparations containing the active agent known as MDMA (in those days commonly taking the form of powder).

Nowadays the term 'ecstasy' describes the phenomenon of using drugs and street products taking the form of tablets or capsules predominantly containing one or more, or a combination of, psychotropic active agents (for example amphetamine or methamphetamine).

Not much is known about the long term effects of taking Ecstasy, although there is some concern that it can cause liver problems. Also, Ecstasy is not conducive to regular and frequent use, because tolerance builds up to the positive effects of the drug, while negative effects increase with regular use. Since there have been several deaths due to this 'designer drug' it is safe to assume that Ecstasy is a highly dangerous substance.

Undercover Agents

Traffickers use every conceivable dodge for smuggling opium for refining. It has been packed into small tins and forced down the throats of camels which are given a purgative when they reach their destination. It has been concealed in fish or in snake-skins which are made to look alive. It has been picked up in bags by parachute at the required destination. But the vast majority of the supplies are sent by sea, the carriers being sailors who find it fairly easy to smuggle it ashore.

Italy and France were the countries most plagued by the evil men involved in this sickening trade, both as transit centres and for setting up the secret laboratories for processing opium, and naturally it is on these two countries that Interpol and the US Narcotics Bureau concentrated. Working together, Interpol officers and US agents have smoked out and closed down more than a dozen illicit drug laboratories. They have attacked heroin supply sources in Italy, France and Turkey. In one case illicit factories, closed down in Yugoslavia, moved to Istanbul, but – thanks to an

American undercover agent's intervention – an international gang thirty-strong was broken up and its clandestine laboratory demolished.

These undercover men, known in their dangerous profession as 'tightropers', must be ready for any situation. One of them, George White, a district supervisor at the Narcotics Bureau in the seventies, several times pulled off arrests by masquerading as one of the trafficking gang. His most embarrassing assignment was when having won the confidence of a drug-runner in Ecuador by the name of Manuel Jarrin White, with 'chauffeur', he drove up to Jarrin's sumptuous mountain hideout near Quito. He was posing as a big-time dope purchaser. Jarrin, 65, small and sly-looking, seemed satisfied that he was on to a good deal. 'Three pounds of raw opium for cash' was his offer – and he pulled a brown-paper package from a drawer. White opened the package, confirmed it was dope, then nodded to his 'chauffeur' who turned out to be chief of the National Police of Ecuador.

As they closed in on Jarrin he yelled for help. At once his powerfully built wife, a bunch of her women relatives and the servants poured into the room. It was useless to threaten them with guns. White carried a blackjack, and whenever the women grabbed at Jarrin he clouted their wrists with his cosh. Still he and Col. Guerra, the police chief, were having a bad time of it from the women when reinforcements arrived in the shape of the colonel's men, bundled the women out and restored the dignity of the law.

Jarrin's villa was a storehouse of narcotics – raw opium, heroin, morphine, cocaine and marijuana. Police also unearthed a secret laboratory used by chemists in Jarrin's pay to process the opium into morphine. All the supplies were destined for the US market.

White next crossed to Europe to another drug suppression trip and, on advice from the Sûreté, decided to smoke out traffickers in Marseilles. He played the part of a loud-mouthed American businessman with plenty of dollars in his pocket and wandered into an Indo-Chinese café in the Old Quarter. There he struck up a conversation with the proprietress 'Zizi' and arranged a further meeting to pass over the 'stuff' for good American dollars. Zizi eventually led White (backed up by the US Vice-Consul and a squad of French police) to her main supplier, and another major operator was stopped.

By patient investigation the French police traced and closed down a large-scale secret heroin factory at Montgeron, twenty miles south of Paris. They started out by shadowing the mistress of one of their suspects, Marie Poteau, who proved to be an expert driver and 'lost' her tail in the Paris traffic. One day, however, they managed to hang on to her slick Peugeot, and she led them to Montgeron, where she disappeared into an isolated villa standing in its own grounds.

Detectives set up an observation post in the small upper room of a railwayman's cottage. For six months they photographed and registered everyone who visited or left the villa. When they were sure they knew the identities of the gangsters they pounced on the villa. Every room, except for the kitchen and bedrooms, was packed with dope or manufacturing equipment. Even the garage had a plant for purifying morphine and converting it into heroin. They also picked up five automatic pistols and a load of Swiss watches.

Sometimes the whole network of law enforcement can be badly shaken by the discovery of corruption in areas of society that might be assumed to be above such evil practices. Such a case shook Italy and, indeed, the whole of western civilization, in the 1950s. It was found that a major chemical firm there had been responsible for an appalling leakage of heroin in a racket of global dimensions.

The company was licensed to sell substances containing drugs, and its technical director, a professor at an Italian university, proved to be the mastermind of the conspiracy to dispose illicitly of a ton of the deadliest dope. Most of this was shipped through the well-known routes to dope syndicates in the US, where it was ingeniously distributed under the guise of lawful medicine to the wretched addicts for whom it was always intended – at sky-high prices.

The unpalatable fact must be faced: until all member-states of Interpol display the same ruthless determination to stamp out this revolting traffic as do the US, Britain and France, the grisly business of getting the shot to the addict will remain what it is today – Interpol's number one problem. Having a membership of 178 countries places Interpol in a unique situation of knowing what is going on around the world in relation to drug trafficking.

It offers the possibility of making links between drug cases being conducted by national administrations which would otherwise seem unrelated. When it is clearly established that there is good potential for developing a substantial case, it is given an operational name. As the case is developed, a working meeting of the concerned countries can be organized to bring together all of the case officers concerned to discuss all aspects of the case and to devise future strategy. The case officers bring with them information such as fingerprints, photographs, identity documents, telephone numbers, addresses, criminal histories and any other information related to the case in which they are involved.

Tracking Down Tricksters

Confidence tricksters are most plausible and use many different ruses to gain trust and money. Tricksters have the appearance of goodness that enables them to take advantage of others, taking all they can get, legally or illegally. Interpol has files full of them.

THE FILES OF Interpol offer a rich variety of confidence tricksters, from the smooth, handsome rogues who batten onto wealthy widows, to the quicksilver swindlers who deceive dealers in precious gems. All have one thing in common – the gift of the gab. And usually one aim in common too – to live in idle luxury.

Edward Johnston-Noad had most of the advantages. Early in life he inherited £100,000; he became a successful solicitor; he was extremely popular with fashionable women; and he threw lavish parties at his home in Mayfair. He became known to his wide circle of friends as 'The Count'. He felt this title suited him so well, that he used it to further his career of fraud.

In the 1950s he launched his first swindle from a small office in Kensington. He advertised two flats for sale at a time when Londoners were suffering an acute accommodation problem. The

Count not only let the flats several times over, but sold the furniture to different people. He took deposits from the professional classes – barristers, doctors, civil servants – and in all tricked seventy people out of £20,000. Whenever an impatient depositor complained, Johnston-Noad immediately offered him his money back, mentioning that the choice flat would at once go to the next person on his list. So desperate were the people for decent accommodation, that the threat was usually enough to silence objectors.

Count's Luck Ran Out

The Count knew very well that he could not stall them for ever, so he had planned to retreat to Paris as soon as his victims called in the police. He talked himself into a job in the British Embassy in Paris just as Scotland Yard were called in to clear up the flat swindles. Chief Inspector James Callaghan, of the Fraud Squad, was assigned to the case, and when he had heard that his bird had flown he sent a 'Wanted' notice to Interpol.

Chief of Interpol's Central Bureau in Paris was a conscientious young detective, Roger Ravard, who put a small photograph of The Count in his wallet. He did not, of course, realize that the wanted man was, in fact, in the same city. But The Count's luck was right out – because Ravard's wife also worked at the British Embassy in Paris.

Even then he might have escaped notice had not Madame Ravard needed some money to pay a tradesman at her door while her husband was still asleep. Rather than waken him she opened his wallet to take out a note – and Johnston-Noad's photograph fell out. She recognized the man as another employee at the Embassy. But she was in a spot, for she knew that the man must be wanted by her husband, yet she was reluctant to tell him she had 'raided' his wallet. In the end duty overcame scruple, she told her husband, and the Count was arrested next morning.

Lightning Switch

Edward Johnston-Noad was sentenced to four months for possessing false papers, but the Yard's extradition proceedings took one year to complete. At last it was all clear for Chief Inspector Callaghan to go to Paris and bring his man back to London. The Count wound up in the dock at the Old Bailey and got ten years in jail for his flat frauds.

Prime targets for the slickest fraudsters are the jewellers and diamond merchants who, naturally, will go to all lengths to avoid offending a valued client, and thus lay themselves open to every kind of trickery. The usual ploy is for a buyer to spend a long time examining a selection of stones, choosing several and then asking the dealer if he minds if the chosen stones are sealed in an envelope and left with the jeweller overnight. The buyer promises to return the next day to make his final selection. If the jeweller agrees, an envelope is produced, and the stones are sealed and locked in the safe.

Only when the appointment is not kept does the jeweller realize he has been the victim of a lightning switch, and he has been left with worthless stones. There were so many variations on this switch technique that Interpol allocated a team of three to track down the international gang of jewel thieves who were clearly behind the rash of incidents. All the victims were interviewed and all paid tribute to the skills of the thieves – some did not even know how they had been robbed.

Worthless Diamonds

In Zurich one of the gang, calling himself Wyeder, got away with 30,000 Swiss francs by 'selling' a worthless packet of diamonds. Another, called Chande, paid 20,000 counterfeit dollars for jewels from a Lisbon merchant. Neither of these men appeared in the records of Interpol, but the 'method' was circulated.

Later the Israeli police arrested a Pedro Cambo and sent his detailed description to Interpol in Paris. It was found that Cambo was identical with Chazan, an international crook known to deal in forged bankers' orders and counterfeit. A full description of him was radioed, and the Portuguese recognized him as the Chande who had defrauded the Lisbon jeweller. He served a sentence in Israel, but after his release he teamed up with Wyeder, first in New York, where they got away with 4,000 dollars, then in Geneva, where they picked up nearly 9,000 francs' worth of jewels and watches; two months later they swindled three Paris jewellers; so to Amsterdam, where they took tea with their jeweller dupe and left fingerprints on the tea cups.

'Arrest Them'

These were sent to Interpol, where Chazan was quickly identified, but, as there were no prints of Wyeder, his were sent out on all-world photo-transmission. Several days later a cable arrived from the Federal Bureau of Investigation in Washington to say that Wyeder's prints were in their records under the name of Simonetti – he had once applied to the US Embassy in Mexico for a visa which involved leaving his 'dabs'.

Two months after that Interpol got a radio message from Pretoria, South Africa, to say that a Kimberley diamond merchant was the latest victim of the switch technique. His two swindlers had given the names of Benjamin Shapiro and John de Rabinovitch, but this time they were identified by photographs as Chazan and Wyeder. It was soon established that they had fled to Australia, and 'Arrest them' messages were sent off to all airports and seaports on route. As a result Chazan was picked up at the airport of Port Louis, Mauritius.

The hunt for the elusive Simonetti was now on, in a big way. It was learned that, instead of heading for Australia, he changed direction towards Europe. All flights were watched without success. But Interpol kept on the alert for a full year until at last the Central Bureau learned that their quarry was flying into Paris! He booked – with Interpol's knowledge, of course – into a fashionable hotel in the Avenue Pierre Premier Serbie near Christian Dior's salon.

Three detectives were waiting for him in the foyer as he emerged, dressed to kill, carnation in buttonhole, for a stroll on the boulevard. Instead he was taken for a drive in a police car to the Quai des Orfèvres, police headquarters. When they searched him they found four gems valued at 10 million francs and three diamond rings in his pockets. He also carried many sheets of plain paper cut to the size of US 100-dollar bills. Under questioning it was discovered that he was already in contact with a jeweller in the Rue de la Paix, who was obviously to be his next victim.

Simonetti proved to be Berl Fareas, Austrian-born, and the head of a gang far more widespread than even Interpol had realized. In the next two years they caught up with and arrested 49 frauds-men working the same racket.

Within recent years a new scientific technique has come to the aid of law enforcement – the laser beam, which can be used to cut through a diamond, perform eye surgery, match paint flakes and test the authenticity of a painting. Many art forgers are so brilliant that only the analysis of the paint itself will reveal whether or not the painting is a fake.

Selling 'Vermeers'

The greatest art forger of them all was surely Hans

van Meegeren of Amsterdam, whose astonishing career of selling 'Vermeers' which he had painted himself was exposed when the art treasures of the Nazi warlord, Hermann Goering, were captured in 1945. Among those paintings was a supposed *Vermeer, Christ and the Adulteress*, for which Goering had paid 1,650,000 guilder. The Dutch are deeply concerned to preserve their art heritage, and when the sale to Goering was traced back to van Meegeren he was suspected of collaborating with the enemy by selling them Dutch masters which, in Holland, amounts to treason. Van Meegeren broke down under police grilling and confessed that he had painted *Christ and the Adulteress* himself. What art-lover Goering had bought as a Vermeer was, in fact, a van Meegeren . . .

Sensation

At first the Dutch police regarded his confession as the desperate device of a cornered criminal to evade punishment. But van Meegeren made statements that sent art experts scurrying round the museums to re-examine a number of Vermeers. Scientists were experimenting with a new X-ray technique in this post-war period and this was tried on the suspect Vermeers. Sensation! Some of the precious paintings were exposed as forgeries – and Goering's prize was among them. The charge of treason against van Meegeren was reduced to swindling and forgery, and, instead of a life-sentence, he got one year in jail. Even that short sentence was too much for him, for he died in prison a few months after the trial. It is a sign of our times, perhaps, to record that today, over half a century after van Meegeren's death, the master forger's own work is fetching increasingly high prices.

The 1960s was the decade of the great art robberies. Goya's portrait of the Duke of Wellington was stolen from London's National Gallery in August 1961 and was not recovered until May 1965. But the Goya theft sparked off many others, until paintings were disappearing at a rate of a million dollars' worth a week. Even Russia was not immune – in 1964 Moscow police reported that 'rare and priceless articles' had been stolen from the city's Historical Museum.

Police forces of the world, finding themselves confronted by what was becoming an art-theft epidemic, had to reorganize their procedures for dealing with such crimes. Now, when a major art theft is reported, Interpol is called in at once to notify all its member-nations. The FBI has greatly intensified its efforts in the last decade to track down art thieves and has recovered thousands of works by Van Gogh, Klee, Cézanne and Picasso worth a total of many millions of dollars.

The FBI crime-records section in Washington now houses a dossier of art thefts throughout the world, regularly analyses any trends in this field and keeps in touch with the special investigator of art thefts, frauds and forgeries, an official who maintains contact with all the major directors, curators and galleries in New York.

The FBI is now under orders to intervene in

every case in which the value of the stolen art is 5,000 dollars or above. Most countries, the US included, abide by international agreements requiring the return of stolen goods. Thus, in countries which are parties to such agreements, the legitimate buyer of a stolen work of art never gets title to it.

Honour Disgraced

Surely the daddy of all art thieves remains the Italian, Vincenzo Perruggia, who, on August 21, 1911, walked out of the Louvre in Paris with Leonardo da Vinci's masterpiece, the *Mona Lisa.* He claimed, when caught, that his country's honour had been disgraced by France's possession of this greatest of all paintings. Perruggia was let off lightly with a seven-month prison sentence.

The statistics on art crimes are staggering, no matter which country you survey. For example, in France 5,569 works of art were reported stolen in 1997 and that figure rose to over 7,800 in 1998.

Interpol has maintained a listing of stolen art and cultural artifacts, ever since they published their first international list in 1947. The organization's Secretariat General publishes a special bi-annual bulletin, called *The Wanted Works of Art*, which is distributed to various international agencies and entities in their constant fight against art thefts and forgeries.

MI5

In March 1909, the Prime Minister, Mr Asquith, instructed the Committee of Imperial Defence to consider the dangers from German espionage to British naval ports.

THE ORIGINS OF MI5 can be traced back to 1909, when the British Government established the Secret Service Bureau. Its main task was to assess the risk posed by German espionage to British naval ports. Initially it was divided into two sections, one to deal with counter-espionage within Britain, and the other to deal with overseas matters. Vernon Kell was the man put in charge of the former unit, which was later to become known as MI5.

The success of the Secret Service Bureau was immediate and emphatic. Between 1909 and the outbreak of the First World War, more than thirty German spies were arrested, essentially destroying their spy network and making it virtually useless during the war. This feat is made spectacularly impressive when you consider that the group that Kell was the head of, consisted of only ten people.

In 1916 MI5 was an officially recognized section of the security services. Wartime duties focused mainly on counter-espionage, but also included duties such as advising munitions factories on security and vetting. They also spread their work to all areas of the British Empire, in an attempt to curtail the work of all enemy spies. By the end of the war another thirty-five German spies had been arrested. This was rather to be expected though as the staff of MI5 had now increased to 850.

After the war, MI5 had to find different uses for its resources. It mainly worked preventing communist subversion within the British armed forces, which was considered a very real threat at the time. In 1931 it became formally responsible for dealing with all threats to national security, with the exception of Irish terrorists and anarchists.

The number of staff in MI5 had gradually declined since the conclusion of the First World War. By the outbreak of the Second World War, the staff levels were nearly as low as when the organization had first started up. They were, however, extremely effective in their duties of counter-espionage, monitoring and surveillance of enemy foreigners. Indeed, by sifting through German records after the war, Britain was able to establish that all German agents had been arrested, bar one (who actually committed suicide before an arrest could be made). MI5 also persuaded some of these agents to misinform the Germans, a key reason why later Allied offences were so successful.

The main threat to national security in the 1950s came from the Soviet Union. There were a large number of communist party members living in Britain. It came as no surprise, that the Russians, through careful character selection, choosing those with a strong communist ideology, were able to turn several MI5 agents to work for them. Guy Burgess, Donald MacLean and Kim Philby had all fled to the safety of the Soviet Union before they had been identified as double agents. A vetting procedure was introduced in the mid-fifties, and this helped to reduce the number of potential double agents in MI5.

Weaknesses in the national security system were further exposed in the early 1960s. First was the Portland spy case, in which it became clear that a Soviet spy network, led by Gordon Lonsdale, had access to military top-secret information. Little over a year later came the Profumo Affair. The Secretary for War, John Profumo, had been using the services of two costly prostitutes, who were found to be associated with Eugene Ivanov, a Soviet spy. This type of bad publicity had to be explained by MI5, who then had to find new ways to tighten national security. In contrast, MI6 dealing with overseas affairs found that a stonewall silence was more than enough to explain their mistakes, away from the attention of the British media.

MI5 then turned its attention to the threat of terrorism, mainly from the Palestinians and the Irish, often helping to neutralise potential bombings and hostage situations.

The early 1990s saw an end to the Cold War, and the threat of communist subversion was virtually nil. MI5 continued to battle terrorism, but also began to diversify, the detection of organised crime being a prime example. They also attempted to become less mysterious in the public eye, through innovations such as posting jobs available in the service on the Internet, and advertising on television.

Ever since its formation MI5 has done sterling work, helping to protect national security in Britain. Although some of its shortcomings have been highlighted through the media, they have been far outweighed by the successes over the years.

The Profumo Affair

A big scandal broke in the sixties, when it was discovered that Minister of War, John Profumo, had been sharing a prostitute with the naval attaché at the Russian embassy. He had lied to the House of Commons about it, and he was consequently forced to resign. That, however, was not the end of the matter. The Prime Minister, who had been fatally damaged by the affair, was also forced to resign and the following year the Conservative government was swept from power.

The scandal centred around Christine Keeler who, at the age of fifteen, quit her home in the Buckinghamshire village of Wraysbury for the bright lights of London. It wasn't long before her self-confidence and good looks had taken her from being a waitress in a Greek restaurant to being a part-time model. She was also a topless dancer in Murray's Cabaret Club in Soho, where she earned £8.50 a week. It was there that fellow show-girl Mandy Rice-Davis, a perky 17-year-old from Birmingham, introduced her to Stephen Ward.

Ward was a thin and elegant man in his late forties. He earned his living as an osteopath but was also a talented artist. Among his clients were several high-ranking members of the establishment. These included Lord Astor, who let him a cottage in the grounds of his Cliveden estate for the peppercorn rent of £1 a year, Sir Colin Coote, Editor of *The Daily Telegraph*, who associated with the head of MI5, Sir Roger Hollis, and whom Peter Wright later named as the fifth man in the Cambridge spy ring.

Ward liked doing favours for people, drugs and the company of pretty women, including prostitutes. Christine Keeler and Mandy Rice-Davis moved in with him in his London flat in Wimpole Mews. They also accompanied him to Cliveden at weekends for parties in his cottage.

In June 1961, over lunch at The Garrick, Coote introduced Ward to the Soviet naval attaché, Yevgeny Ivanov. MI5 had singled out Ivanov as a man who might easily succumb to the temptations of the West. They thought that a weekend party with some of Ward's attractive young female friends might be just the thing to turn him. The defection of such a high-ranking Russian official would be quite a prize. Specifically, MI5 wanted Ward to use Christine Keeler as bait.

Ward invited Ivanov down to Cliveden on Sunday 9 July 1951. The night before the Astors were holding a dinner party, and this was when Ward bought Keeler to the house. Keeler wanted to go swimming and Ward dared her to go in the nude.

When she did, he stole her swimming costume.

Lord Astor and John Profumo were out in the gardens for an after-dinner stroll when they spotted the beautiful, naked 19-year-old in the swimming pool. Christine realized that they were coming and struck out for the edge of the pool. She emerged nude and grabbed a small towel to cover herself, moments before the two men caught up with her.

The two middle-aged men were fooling around with the near-naked girl when suddenly the floodlights were turned on. The rest of the guests – including Profumo's wife – came out into the garden, too. Christine was introduced, and later Profumo managed to give her a guided tour of the bedrooms at Cliveden.

Profumo was forty-six years old, and a rising Tory politician. The son of a successful barrister, he was independently wealthy and lived the life of a Tory squire. Educated at Harrow and Oxford, he served on the staff of General Alexander during World War II, rising to the rank of lieutenant-colonel. He was elected to Parliament for Stratford-upon-Avon in 1950 and joined the government in 1952. He rose to the position of Secretary for War in 1960 and in 1954 married the actress Valerie Hobson.

The day after Christine met Profumo, Ivanov turned up at Cliveden. Ward laid on a swimming party as a way of introducing him to Christine. She was attracted to Ivanov immediately. She told the *News of the World*: 'He was MAN. He was rugged with a hairy chest, strong and agile.'

However, when they decided to have a piggy-back fight in the pool, it was Jack Profumo's shoulders she clambered on to, not Ivanov's. That evening, Christine left with Ivanov, but not before Profumo had asked her for her phone number. Christine was extremely flattered and told him to contact Ward.

Christine and Ivanov demolished a bottle of vodka back at Ward's Wimpole Mews flat. Then the passion began.

'Before I knew what was happening, I was in his arms,' she said. 'We left serious discussion and I yielded to this wonderful huggy bear of a man . . . He was a wonderful lover.'

Profumo phoned two days later and came round. On his third visit, he began to kiss her and soon, 'I was returning his kisses with everything that I suddenly felt for him,' she said.

Profumo would always call first before he came round for what Keeler called a 'screw of convenience'. It was essential that they were discreet. She went out on the town with Ivanov, but Profumo could not risk being seen out with her in public. Sometimes though they went for a drive. As well as having sex at Ward's flat, they had it in Profumo's red mini and a black car he borrowed from the Minister of Labour, John Hare. And once, when his wife was away in Ireland, Profumo took Christine back to their house in Nash Terrace near Regents Park. It was late and the butler and staff were asleep. Profumo took her directly to the bedroom.

Profumo had no idea that he was sharing his

mistress with Ivanov. He was deeply attached to her, but she did not share his feelings. For her, sex 'had no more meaning than a handshake or a look across a crowded room,' she said. Meanwhile, Profumo showered her with expensive gifts and money – ostensibly to buy her mother a birthday present.

It took MI5 about a month to learn about Profumo's affair with Keeler. Fearing that it compromised their entrapment of Ivanov, Hollis asked the Cabinet Secretary, Sir Norman Brook, to warn Profumo. On 9 August 1961, in panic, John Profumo wrote a note to Christine Keeler:

Darling,
In great haste & because I can get no reply from your phone.
Alas something's blown up tomorrow night & I can't therefore make it. I'm terribly sorry especially as I leave the next day for various trips & then a holiday so won't be able to see you again until some time in September. Blast it. Please take care of yourself & don't run away.
Love J

It was this note that sealed his fate.

Profumo continued seeing Christine Keeler for another four months, despite the warning from MI5. He started to take amazing risks. One evening an army officer turned up at the flat looking for Ward. 'I had to introduce him to the War Minister,' said Keeler. 'The colonel couldn't believe it. Jack nearly died.'

Keeler refused to move out of Ward's flat and into a discreet love nest, so Profumo broke off the affair.

MI5 now began to lose interest in the plan to trap Ivanov, particularly as they were finding Ward increasingly unreliable. Keeler had moved on, too. Through Ward she had met West Indian jazz singer, Lucky Cordon, and, through him, another West Indian named Johnny Edgecombe, both of whom she had been sleeping with. This had led to a fight at a nightclub in Soho in October 1962, where Cordon got his face slashed. Keeler moved in with Edgecombe briefly, but when things did not work out, she moved back into Ward's flat. One night, Edgecombe came round to try and win her back. It was late and she would not let him in. He pulled a gun and blasted the front door. The police were called and Edgecombe was arrested and charged with attempted murder.

As a result of this incident, Ward asked Keeler to leave the flat. She turned to one of his patients, solicitor Michael Eddowes, for help. She told him that she and Ward had actually been spying for the Russians and that Ward had asked her to find out from Profumo about British plans to arm West Germany with nuclear weapons. She told the same story to former Labour MP, John Lewis, who had a personal dislike of Ward. He passed the information on to George Wigg, a Labour MP who had a dislike of Profumo. In January 1963, a journalist, Paul Mann, took Keeler to the *Sunday*

Pictorial. Keeler showed the *Pictorial* the note that Profumo had written and the paper offered her £1,000 for her story.

The newspaper trod very carefully. The previous year, the exposure of the spy John Vassall, an admiralty clerk who had been passing secrets to the Soviets, had led to a Tribunal of Inquiry. The Inquiry had investigated the involvement of the press in the affair. During the course of it, two journalists had been sent to prison for refusing to name their sources.

The *Pictorial* contacted Ward, who managed to convince the paper that Keeler's story was a pack of lies and publication was dropped. Keeler was so annoyed that she went to the police and told them that Ward procured call girls for his rich clients. A few days later, Profumo found himself being questioned by the Attorney General, Sir John Hobson, the Solicitor General, Peter Rawlinson and the Chief Whip, Martin Redmayne. He denied any improper associations with Keeler. They chose to accept what he was saying, though they were somewhat sceptical.

Prime Minister Harold Macmillan was briefed. Being a man of the world, he said that if Profumo had had an affair with Keeler he had been foolish. However, he felt that sleeping with a pretty young woman, even if she was alleged to be a prostitute, was hardly a sackable offence. Everyone hoped that that was the end of it. But on 8 March 1963, a small-circulation newsletter called *Westminster Confidential* ran a piece about the story that the *Pictorial* had dropped. It repeated the allegation that both the War Secretary and a Soviet military attaché, one Colonel Ivanov, were the clients of the same call girl.

On 10 March, George Wigg, who by this time had a bulging dossier on the liaison between Profumo and Keeler, took it to the Labour leader, Harold Wilson. Wilson urged caution, but events now had a momentum of their own.

On 14 March, Johnny Edgecombe came up for trial at the Old Bailey. Christine Keeler, the key witness in the case, was on holiday and it was rumoured that she had been whisked out of the country to keep a lid on the scandal.

The next day, the *Daily Express* ran the headline, 'War Minister Shock'. It claimed that John Profumo had tendered his resignation for 'personal reasons'. Down the page was a picture of Christine Keeler under the headline, 'Vanished'.

The *Express* later claimed that the two stories running parallel with one another was purely coincidental. But everyone put two and two together and came up with five!

On 19 March, during a debate on the Vassall case, George Wigg, under the protection of parliamentary privilege, raised the rumours circulating about the War Minister. He was supported by Barbara Castle and the Labour frontbencher Dick Crossman. The government was agitated to say the least. Henry Brooke, the Home Secretary, told the Labour critics that if they wanted to substantiate their accusations, they should use a different forum, one that was not shielded from the laws of libel by the cloak of privilege.

Profumo did have one supporter, however – backbench Labour MP, Reginald Paget.

'What do these rumours amount to?' Paget asked. 'They amount to the fact that a minister is said to be acquainted with an extremely pretty girl. As far as I am concerned, I should have thought that was matter for congratulation rather than an inquiry.'

Profumo was again interrogated by the Chief Whip, the Leader of the House, Iain Macleod and Bill Deedes, Minister without Portfolio and future editor of *The Daily Telegraph*. Profumo again insisted that he was innocent. He then made a parliamentary statement in which he admitted knowing Christine Keeler, but said he had not seen her since December 1961. He also said that he had met Stephen Ward and Yevgeny Ivanov. He denied that he was in any way responsible for her absence from the trial and stated categorically: 'There was no impropriety whatsoever in my acquaintanceship with Miss Keeler.' He threatened anyone who repeated the allegations outside the House with a writ.

A few days later, the newspapers caught up with Christine Keeler in Madrid. She confirmed what Profumo had said, but George Wigg would not leave it at that. He went on the *Panorama* TV programme and said that Ward and Ivanov were security risks. The next day, Ward met Wigg and tried to convince him that it was not true. He failed. Wigg believed, more than ever now, that Profumo had lied. He wrote a report of his meeting with Ward and gave it to Harold Wilson, who subsequently passed it on to Macmillan.

Although the Vassall case was keeping the British press subdued, there was no such restraint in the foreign papers. Profumo issued writs against *Paris Match* and *Il Tempo Illustrato*, both of whom had said that he had been 'bonking'. In an attempt to rescue the situation, the Home Secretary told the Metropolitan Police to try and find some scandal on Ward. This was highly irregular. The police are supposed to investigate crimes and find out who committed them, not investigate people on the off chance they have committed a crime.

Obvious to Ward's friends and clients that he was in serious trouble, they deserted him in droves. Mandy Rice-Davis was arrested on trumped-up charges and held in prison until she agreed to testify against Ward.

Ward desperately wrote to everyone he could think of, protesting his innocence. Harold Wilson showed his letter to the Prime Minister, who agreed to set up a committee of inquiry under Lord Dilhome. Profumo was away at the time, but on his return, he realized that the game was up. He could not face a committee of inquiry and lie again, so he went to see the Chief Whip and Macmillan's Parliamentary Private Secretary, told them that he had lied and resigned his post.

His letter of resignation and Macmillan's reply were published the next day.

'I misled you, and my colleagues, and the House,' Profumo wrote, but, he explained, 'I did this to protect my wife and family.'

Macmillan's terse reply said: 'I am sure you will

understand that in the circumstances I have no alternative but to advise the Queen to accept your resignation.'

On 5 June 1963, there was even more drama. Christine Keeler's other West Indian boyfriend, Lucky Cordon, appeared at court on the charge of assaulting her outside a friend's flat. Keeler turned up at court in a Rolls Royce. From the dock, Cordon accused her of giving him VD. She responded with an outburst from the public gallery. The newspapers lapped it up. Cordon was sent down for three years, which was overturned on appeal.

Ward appeared on television on 9 June and denied that he had encouraged Christine Keeler to have an affair with John Profumo because he had a friend in the Soviet Embassy. The following day he was arrested and charged with living on immoral earnings.

By this time, newspapers worldwide were running the scandal on the front page. Mandy Rice-Davis told the *Washington Star* about society orgies in London and mentioned that at one dinner party, a naked man wearing only a mask waited at the tables. The hunt for the masked man was on. Was it a senior judge, a cabinet minister or a member of the royal family?

Under the headline, 'Prince Philip and the Profumo Scandal', the *Daily Mirror* vehemently dismissed the 'foul rumour' that Prince Philip was involved. The Queen's Consort was a member of a gentleman's association called the Thursday Club, which also boasted Stephen Ward among its membership. Allegations flew thick and fast. Everyone in any position in society was now a target. The Bishop of Southwark, Mervyn Stockwood, appealed for calm.

Politically the question came down to: how had John Profumo managed to lie about his affair for so long? Macmillan was now in the firing line for taking such a lenient attitude to the matter. Colleagues began to sense that his tenure of office was coming to an end. Lord Hailsham quit his title to become a contender for the premiership. He threw his hat into the ring by appearing on television and condemning Profumo for lying. Again, Reginald Paget rallied to Profumo's defence. 'When self-indulgence has reduced a man to the shape of Lord Hailsham,' he said, 'sexual continence involves no more than a sense of the ridiculous'.

Adding more fuel to the fire, Mandy Rice-Davis told the *Sunday Mirror* that the Soviet military attaché and the War Minister had missed bumping into each other at Ward's flat by a matter of minutes on a number of occasions.

Michael Eddowes issued a press statement, saying that he had warned the Prime Minister of the security risk as early as 29 March. Meanwhile, Christine Keeler sold her 'confessions' to the *News of the World*, which began to make a serial out of them.

The Conservative government was attacked by *The Times* for its lack of moral leadership. To this, Lord Hailsham responded petulantly: '*The Times* is an anti-Conservative newspaper with an anti-Conservative editor.'

Even the *Washington Post* got in on the act, saying that 'a picture of widespread decadence beneath the glitter of a large segment of stiff-lipped society is emerging.'

Labour immediately started to defend itself. In a debate in the House of Commons on 19 June, Harold Wilson said that the Profumo scandal had 'shocked the moral conscience of the nation'. Pointing a finger at the Prime Minister, he said that for political reasons he was gambling with national security. Macmillan could not even count on the support of his own backbenchers. Conservative MP, Nigel Birch, stated the simple facts of the case.

'I must say that [Profumo] never struck me as a man at all like a cloister monk,' he told the House. 'And Miss Keeler is a professional prostitute. There seems to me to be a basic improbability that their relationship was purely platonic. What are whores about?'

Addressing the Prime Minister directly, he said: 'I myself feel that the time will come very soon when my Right Honourable Friend ought to make way for a much younger colleague.'

Macmillan came out of the debate severely battle-scarred. He announced an official inquiry under Lord Denning, four days later. It did not, however, save him. Macmillan resigned in the early autumn, shortly before the party conference. He was replaced by Sir Alec Douglas Home, but the Conservative government was tainted by the scandal and was swept from office the following year.

Although Lord Denning was supposed to look into possible breaches of security caused by the Profumo scandal, like Ken Starr, he concentrated on the obscene aspects. In fact when witnesses were cross-questioned, he often sent the official stenographer out of the room to save her, or perhaps his own, blushes.

When Ward went on trial at the Old Bailey, the world's media were there in force. Again, the salacious details were brought to the fore. In fact one newspaper in New Zealand was prosecuted for indecency for merely reporting the case. The star of the show was undoubtedly Mandy Rice-Davis, whom the judge mistakenly addressed as Marilyn Monroe. When it was put to her that Lord Astor had denied that he had met her at his house parties at Cliveden, she said: 'Well, he would, wouldn't he?' That remark is now in the Oxford Dictionary of Quotations.

In his summing up, the judge pointed out that none of Ward's highborn friends had come to testify on his behalf. 'One would have thought from the newspapers that this country has become a sink of iniquity,' he told the jury. 'But you and I know that the even tenor of family life over the overwhelming majority of the population goes quietly and decently on.'

He might as well have been putting the noose around the defendant's neck. The judge was implying that Ward was not just guilty of introducing rich and powerful people to a couple of attractive and available girls, but that he was responsible for the general loosening of moral standards that many people felt was engulfing the country. Ward knew that he was being made a scapegoat.

'This is a political trial,' he told a friend. 'Someone had to be sacrificed and that someone is me.'

On the night of 3 July 1963, Ward took an overdose of sleeping tablets. He left a suicide note saying that, after the judge's summing up, he had given up all hope. He asked that resuscitation be delayed as long as possible, adding, bizarrely, that 'the car needs oil in the gearbox'. With Ward unconscious in St Stephen's Hospital, the jury found him guilty on two counts of living on immoral earnings. He died on 3 August, without regaining consciousness.

There were only six mourners at Stephen Ward's funeral and only two wreaths. One came from his family and one from Kenneth Tynan, John Osbourne, Arnold Wesker, Joe Orton, Annie Ross, Dominick Elwes and Penelope Gilliatt. The card on it read: 'To Stephen Ward, victim of hypocrisy'.

When the Denning report was published in October 1963, it was an instant best-seller, selling over 4,000 copies in the first hour. It, too, laid the blame squarely at the door of Stephen Ward, who was in no position to answer back.

Profumo left political life and threw himself into charity work, for which he was awarded the CBE in 1975. He remained married to Valerie Hobson. Christine Keeler was jailed for six months for contempt of court for failing to appear at the trial of Johnny Edgecombe. Her autobiography *Scandal* was published in 1989 and was made into a successful movie.

Mandy Rice-Davis wrote a series of novels, became a film actress, opened two clubs in Israel and married a millionaire. George Wigg became chairman of the Horse Race Betting Levy Board and later pleaded guilty to soliciting for prostitutes in Soho.

The Cambridge Spies

The four spies Burgess, Blunt, Mclean and Philby were not characters out of a novel. They were real. All four were eventually exposed but – amazingly – never caught. The first, Burgess, was a flamboyant, alcoholic homosexual. The second, Blunt, was a discrete homosexual who rose to knighthood as the Royal Curator of Art. The third, Maclean, was a tense, insecure diplomat of ambiguous sexual persuasion. The fourth, Philby – and perhaps the most intriguing of the group – was a dedicated heterosexual who has been called, not inaccurately, the 'Spy of the Century'.

The story involving the defection of Guy Burgess and Donald Maclean, and the subsequent implication of Harold "Kim" Philby, is a fascinating one of code-breaking, detection and discovery. In 1949, Robert Lamphere, FBI agent in charge of Russian espionage, along with cryptanalysts, discovered that between 1944 and 1946 a member of the British Embassy was sending messages to the KGB. The code name of this official was 'Homer'. By a process of elimination, a short list of three or four men were identified as possible

Homers. One was Donald Maclean.

Shortly after Lamphere's investigation began, Philby was assigned to Washington, serving as Britain's CIA-FBI-NSA liaison. As such, he was privy to the decoding of the Russian material, and recognized that Maclean was very probably Homer. He confirmed this through his British KGB control. He was also aware that Lamphere and his colleagues had found that the encoded messages to the KGB had been sent from New York. Maclean had visited New York on a regular basis, on the pretext of visiting his wife and children, who at the time were living there with his in-laws.

The pressure on Philby now began to grow. If Maclean was unmasked as a Soviet agent, then, were he to confess, the trail might lead to the other Cambridge spies. Philby, now in a very important position in his ability to provide information to the Soviets, might be implicated, if for no other reason than his association with Maclean at Cambridge. Something had to be done.

It is astonishing that Burgess, more and more an unpredictable heavy drinker and indiscreet homosexual, was assigned to the British Embassy in Washington. Why MI6 thought that Burgess could function in the highly charged Cold War environment of Washington, DC is beyond comprehension. As he was ready to leave for his new post in America, Hector McNeil cautioned him to avoid three things: 'the race thing', contact with the radical element, and homosexual adventuring. 'Oh,' said the irrepressible Burgess, 'you mean I shouldn't make a pass at Paul Robeson?' Only the tactless Burgess would have suggested the unlikely prospect of seducing America's best known black Communist.

Burgess was now staying in a basement apartment with Philby and his family in Washington, and was up to his usual outrageously drunken and predatory homosexual patterns of behaviour. Philby thought that he could keep an eye on the unpredictable Burgess by having him live with him. Nonetheless, Burgess was irrepressible, even insulting the wife of a high CIA official at one of Philby's dinner parties. Concerned that Maclean would be positively identified, interrogated, and, in the process (because of his highly agitated nervous state) confess to MI5, Philby and Burgess concocted a scheme in which Burgess would return to London. Maclean was now the Foreign Service officer in charge of American affairs in London. Burgess would then warn Maclean of the impending unmasking. But how could Burgess be sent home to London to warn Maclean without arousing suspicion?

One way was to have Burgess sent home in disgrace, so that his trip to London would be the result of the action of the British Embassy. Whether or not the plan to have Burgess recalled by behaving badly was deliberate, Burgess managed to receive three speeding citations in a single day. He was driving with a companion from Washington, DC to South Carolina to attend a conference. Two of his speeding altercations resulted in a release after his declaring his diplomatic immunity, but the third resulted in an actual citation. He and his 'hitchhiker' were detained by the police for several hours, and then released. This last event was communicated to the Governor of Virginia, who informed the State Department, who then informed the British Embassy. Burgess was told that he would have to return to London. If Philby and Burgess had planned his recall, this part of the plan worked beautifully. Before Burgess left, Philby was explicit in his instructions to Burgess – he was not to defect with Maclean.

The Philby-Burgess plan was for Burgess to visit Maclean in his Foreign Office quarters, give him a note identifying a place where the two could meet – it was assumed that Maclean, now under suspicion and denied sensitive documents, had a bugged office – and Burgess would explain the situation. They met clandestinely to discuss Maclean's imminent exposure and necessary defection to Russia. Yuri Modin, the Cambridge spies' KGB controller, made arrangements for Maclean's defection. Maclean was in an extremely nervous state, and reluctant to leave alone. Modin was willing to serve as his guide, but KGB Central demanded that Burgess escort Maclean behind the Iron Curtain.

Meanwhile, MI5 had insisted that Maclean be questioned. They had decided that he would be confronted with the FBI and MI5 evidence on Monday, May 28, 1951.

On Maclean's birthday, May 25, the Friday before the Monday that he was to be interrogated,

Burgess and Maclean fled to the coast, boarded a ship to France, and disappeared. Was it possible Blunt had learned of the impending questioning of Maclean, and warned Burgess that the time had come? Blunt never admitted to that, and it is possible that Burgess and Maclean had selected Friday to flee whatever the current circumstances. Both Modin and Philby assumed that Burgess would deliver Maclean to a handler, and that he would return. For some reason, the Russians insisted that Burgess accompany Maclean the entire way. Perhaps Burgess was no longer useful to the KGB as a spy, but too valuable to fall into the hands of MI5.

Burgess in Moscow

After Burgess and Maclean were safely in Russia – but only after several weeks – the British government reluctantly admitted that the two men had been Soviet spies. The Soviets, however, refused to acknowledge their past services to the Russian cause, and reported that they were simply 'ideological defectors', unhappy with their imperialist native country. Burgess spent twelve indolent years in the care of the KGB, never learning Russian, indulged with a modest apartment, complete with state-sanctioned live-in lover.

Even in exile, Burgess remained the quintessential Englishman. He frequently expressed the desire to return to England because life in Russia was so confining and dull, but neither the Russians nor the English would support his repatriation.

Maclean in Moscow

Maclean, unlike the self-indulgent Burgess, integrated himself into the Soviet system, learning Russian, and eventually serving as a specialist on economic policy of the West.

In Washington, when Philby heard of Maclean's defection, he feigned surprise, although he was of course relieved. When he was informed that Burgess had fled as well, Philby's surprise was genuine. He had told Burgess that he (Philby) would be placed in jeopardy if he (Burgess) were to defect with Maclean, since the FBI and CIA were well aware that Burgess had been living with Philby and his family. From then on, Philby referred to Burgess as 'that bloody man', and they never spoke again. When Philby arrived in Russia in 1963, Burgess was dying and wished to see Philby, but Philby would have nothing to do with him. Nevertheless, Philby was Burgess's principal heir.

From the point of the Burgess-Maclean defection, Philby became 'The Third Man', the one who was suspected of having warned them to flee. Philby was sent back to London, accused of having been, at the least, indiscreet in his association with Burgess, and, at the most, having been himself a Soviet agent.

The Third Man

Now in London, Philby was questioned by MI5. He was able to withstand the grilling with his usual aplomb. Even James Skardon, the famed interrogator who had induced Klaus Fuchs the atom bomb spy to confess, was unable to shake him. He was, however, forced to resign from MI6 and given a severance pay. He was now unemployed, with a wife and four children. Many in MI6, an organization that was fiercely competitive with MI5, refused to abandon Philby and they eventually hired him back.

Soon, Philby was in desperate financial straits. Modin arranged to deliver a large sum of money from the Russians. He was to deliver it through Blunt. When Blunt appeared for his late night meeting with Modin, Philby appeared from the shadows. It was the only time, up to that point, that Philby had met his controller. The money was made available to Philby, and his money worries were temporarily addressed.

Philby remained under a cloud. Then, in 1955, a member of Parliament asked the government if it was true that 'Harold Philby' was the Third Man. After a time, Harold Macmillan, then the Foreign Secretary, cleared Philby of being the one who warned Maclean and Burgess, saying only that Philby had been dismissed from MI6 because of early Communist affiliations. Philby then held a press conference at his mother's apartment, and, without a stammer, announced that Macmillan's statement completely exonerated him.

It is ironic that, eight years later, Macmillan, then Prime Minister, would have his government brought down by a sex-scandal involving one of his cabinet, the infamous 'Profumo Affair'. It did not help that it was about the same time that Philby defected to Russia. Thus the man who had cleared Philby now had his government's credibility further diminished. He had not only a ministerial scandal to contend with, but also a major spy's defection.

Under the cover of his being a reporter for two English newspapers, Philby was contracted by M16 to be their agent in the Middle East, based in Lebanon, where his father, Sir John Philby, lived with his Arab wife and two children. For the next six years, Philby continued to provide information for MI6, but, more importantly, for the KGB. Russia had an intense interest in the Middle East, as it sought to expand its sphere of influence into the oil-producing regions.

Then, in 1963, after revelations from a Soviet who had defected to Australia, Philby was confronted by an MI6 colleague, an old friend, who had been sent to Beirut to question him. Philby confessed, but bought himself a few days in order to prepare for his return to London. It was then that he defected to Russia, some twelve years after Burgess and Maclean. There is some suspicion that the British, in order to avoid further embarrassment to an already weakened reputation of their intelligence establishment, actually warned Philby to flee.

After a period of debriefing by the KGB, Philby's third wife and his children from his second marriage joined him in Moscow. He was able to live comfortably under fairly controlled conditions, but eventually his wife and children returned to England. He carried on a brief affair with Mrs. Maclean – Donald Maclean had become a Russian scholar of Western economics – and after Mrs. Maclean contritely returned to her husband, and then to America (where she still lives), Philby married his fourth wife, a Russian citizen introduced to him by one of his KGB controllers. He spent the rest of his life in Russia as a KGB adviser, lecturer, and trainer of spies until his death in 1988.

The Fourth Man

Anthony Blunt had been suspected of being a member of the Burgess spy ring as early as 1951, but particularly after the defection of Philby. In 1964, Michael Straight, an American who had been at Cambridge with the Cambridge spies, confessed to the FBI and MI5 officer Arthur Martin that Blunt had recruited Straight while at Cambridge. Other than meeting with several mysterious figures who may or may not have been Soviet agents, Straight had not really been an active spy.

The admission of the 'Fifth Man', John Cairncross, that he had passed secret papers to the Soviets, and that he was an associate of Blunt, also fired Martin's determination to catch Blunt. However, the evidence against Blunt was not substantial, so Martin needed a signed confession from Blunt. Blunt gave no indication of being ready to crack, and MI5 did not want the Blunt case to become public. Sir Anthony Blunt was a member of the Establishment, and, in a sense, a member of the Royal Household.

The only way to obtain a confession from Blunt, and to protect the reputation of MI5, was to offer Blunt immunity from prosecution, which had been done for Cairncross. The Attorney General approved, providing that Blunt had not spied for the Soviets after the war. This was a meaningless provision, since Blunt had participated in the defection of Burgess and Maclean, and had undoubtedly maintained contact with Yuri Modin, his KGB controller, until at least 1953.

A meeting between Martin and Blunt was set up for April 23, 1964. Martin outlined the charges made by Straight, and, after informing Blunt that he had been authorized to give him immunity, Blunt admitted it was true. During the debriefings that followed, Blunt provided information about other spies that were either dead, or already known to MI5 and MI6. Blunt was then interrogated by Peter Wright, the so-called 'Spycatcher'. The only information that Blunt gave Wright was about British Soviet agents who could not be prosecuted, such as Burgess – now dead – and others who were, to one degree or another, invulnerable. By 1972, Blunt had identified twenty-one such spies, none of whom provided new leads or information. He gave conflicting accounts of when and how he was recruited by the KGB. In general, he remained elusive and deceptive until he died in 1983.

PART TWO

MURDEROUS METHODS

Poison

The 1850s was the era of the high-profile poisoner. A series of celebrated murder trials introduced an ever anxious public to the terrors of the slow, the sophisticated – indeed the scientific – poisoner, and to his nemesis, the intrepid poison hunter. With a fervid press watching every move, the fear of poison drove changes in both law and medicine.

WAS NAPOLEON I murdered by the British on the island of St. Helena to which he was exiled after his final defeat? Officially he died of cancer of the stomach – the diagnosis of an Italian doctor who conducted a post-mortem. But a remarkable new space-age technique known as Neutron Activation Analysis has recently been used to cast doubts on the 'natural causes' verdict.

Neutron activity is a by-product of modern atomic research and has now reached an advanced stage both in the United States and in Britain. It uses properties of radio-active decay to detect and measure accurately a trace of arsenic one thousand times smaller than can be detected by any known chemical test.

Napoleon's body lay for a score of years in a grave on St. Helena before it was moved, with due pomp and ceremony, to its present resting-place in Les Invalides in Paris. The French have always been uneasy about the circumstances of the death of their great warrior-genius, and when the fantastic possibilities of neutron activation analysis became known to them it was agreed that samples of hair taken from the head of Napoleon should be subjected to it – almost a century-and-a-half after his death.

The result of the neutron activation test was that Napoleon's hair was found to contain thirteen times the amount of arsenic normally contained in human hair. This discovery was quickly claimed as evidence that he was poisoned – especially by historians who reminded the world that Napoleon had written in his will: 'I am dying before my time, murdered by the English oligarchy and its hired assassin' – an obvious reference to the English Governor of St. Helena at that time, General Sir Hudson Lowe.

Arsenic as a Stimulant

There are, of course, other possible explanations for the discovery of such an amount of arsenic in the hair. Arsenic from the soil of St. Helena could have infiltrated into it during his long interment there. It is also possible that, during his years in exile, Napoleon could have taken small quantities of arsenic as a stimulant; so it is likely that the case of Napoleon's hair will remain one of those insoluble mysteries so favoured by authors of historical romances.

But the discovery of neutron activation analysis

does illustrate dramatically the capabilities of modern forensic science. By using this new technique it is possible to detect the most minute traces of certain metals in hair – gold, silver, lead or cadmium. When analysis shows that the percentages of these elements are identical in two hairs, the chances that both have come from the same person are clearly increased.

This breakthrough by the nuclear scientists has come at a time when the headlong growth of the pharmaceutical industry since the mid-twentieth century is threatening to overwhelm forensic toxicologists – they now have to cope with a host of new synthetic poisons and medicines which can kill as well as cure those who take them. The alarming fact has to be faced that technological progress is making scores of previously unheard-of poisons available to millions and thus supplying new means for murder, suicide and accidental death at a rate which is far outrunning the techniques of forensic detection.

Worldwide Craving

Take the barbiturates alone: alphenal, amytal, delvinal, evipan, nembutal and seconal are a few that have become household names. World War II, followed by the strains and tensions of the Atomic Age, produced a worldwide craving for drugs which would make life more bearable.

By 1954 the number of known suicides from barbiturates in England was twelve times the number in 1938. But it was not until 1955 that the death of a child taught England that barbiturates were not only an easy way out for suicides – they could also be an effective murder weapon.

The scene of the first murder by barbiturate poisoning was set in Gosport, near Portsmouth. John Armstrong, a 26-year-old nurse at a nearby naval hospital, and his wife Janet, 19, were a nondescript couple whose married life was punctuated by three children, a load of petty debts and a series of rows. At 1.20 p.m. on July 22, 1955, Armstrong called the family doctor, Bernard Johnson, to report that his five-month-old son Terence was very ill.

Dr. Johnson knew the family background – their oldest boy, Stephen, had died suddenly the previous year. He reached the Armstrong bungalow at 1.30 to find the baby already dead. Dr. Johnson did not suspect foul play, but as he could not establish the cause of death, he notified the Gosport coroner who at once sent two of his staff to the Armstrong bungalow. They took away the dead baby's bottle, the pillow he had vomited into the previous day, and had the little body removed to the mortuary.

That same afternoon Dr. Harold Miller, a pathologist, carried out an autopsy. Examining the larynx, he found a shrivelled red shell that reminded him of the skin of a daphne berry – and there were more of these shells in the child's stomach. Dr. Miller put the shell from the larynx in a bottle of formaldehyde, placed the stomach's contents in another bottle and stored both bottles in a refrigerator.

By now Dr. Miller suspected that death must be due to some form of food poisoning. The coroner's men went back to the Armstrongs' home to ask whether the child had access to daphne berries – and they were startled to find the couple watching television as if nothing untoward had happened. There was, in fact, a daphne tree in the garden, and it was fruiting. Armstrong remembered that the baby's pram had stood under the tree and its fruit could have fallen within reach. Daphne berries are highly poisonous.

When this was reported to Dr. Miller he thought his problem was solved, but when he opened the refrigerator the red berry shell in the bottle of formaldehyde had vanished – it had dissolved and coloured the formaldehyde red. The shells in the other bottle had also vanished overnight and deepened the red colouring of the stomach contents.

Unusual Substances

So Dr. Miller sent both bottles, as well as the pillow and the baby's feeding bottle, to a chemical laboratory which regularly performed investigations for the coroner. The laboratory report stated that there was no sign of any known poison and no trace of daphne berries. The only unusual substances in the stomach were a very small quantity of cornstarch and red dye, eosin. The cause of the baby's death was still unexplained.

At this point Inspector Gates, in charge of the inquiries for Gosport police, decided to have a last look round. He went to see the Armstrongs and asked a few questions. John Armstrong made such a bad impression on Inspector Gates that he was unwilling to close the case. Gates discussed the baby's death with Dr. Miller who, it turned out, had been giving some thought to the disappearing 'berry skins'. He now suggested they could have been coloured medical capsules – for instance, seconal. He experimented with seconal capsules in gastric juices and found a red discolouration similar to that in the baby's stomach. Gates asked about the effects of seconal and was told that a few grains would be enough to kill an infant, but there was no precedent for murder by barbiturate.

Gates now felt he was getting somewhere, and he reported his misgivings to his superior, who decided to call in Scotland Yard. Superintendent L. C. Nickolls, Director of the Metropolitan Police Laboratory, at once asked for all materials relevant to the baby's death. Gates was asked to collect them and found, to his annoyance, that the Gosport chemists had only remnants left after their analysis – the best preserved was the pillow stained with the child's vomit. But he took all he could to the Yard.

Nickolls spent five days on tests and at last found that the vomit traces on the pillow contained $^1/_{50}$th of a grain of seconal, and then he succeeded in isolating another $^1/_3$rd of a grain from the stomach contents. He now applied for an exhumation of the child's body which was granted on September 6. While Nickolls was carrying out a meticulous examination of the tiny body, Gates went to the naval hospital because, assuming the child had died of seconal poisoning, it was important to discover how Armstrong had obtained supplies of the drug. After the most painstaking inquiries he tracked down a nurse who had been in charge of the drugs on Armstrong's floor – and remembered a mysterious theft of fifty one-and-a-half grain seconal capsules from a cupboard to which Armstrong had access. Of course this was not proof that Armstrong was the thief, but at least Gates had his nose to a strong scent.

Blue in the Face

Now Inspector Gates, the indefatigable, looked into the death of the Armstrongs' firstborn, Stephen, in March 1954. He found that the death certificate had been made out by a doctor aged 82 who had never previously attended the family. Further, Gates learned that Stephen's symptoms were similar to those shown by the baby – blue in the face, drowsiness, difficulty in breathing, then sudden death. More striking still, the Armstrongs' daughter Pamela, then aged two, had been taken to hospital in May 1954. Symptoms: gasping for breath, discoloured face, and drowsiness. She made a swift recovery in hospital.

At last Nickolls delivered his long-awaited analysis to the Gosport police – he had extracted $^1/_{20}$th of a grain of seconal from the baby's organs, and he concluded that the child must have been given between three and five capsules for such a quantity to be left in the body: a fatal dose.

The police chiefs were now certain that the Armstrongs were guilty, but how to prove it? They got an order to exhume the body of the firstborn. John Armstrong had to go with Gates to the cemetery for this macabre procedure. At the gates he said to the inspector: 'After all, there won't be much left of him by this time, will there?' He was right. All his efforts to detect poison in Stephen's remains had been defeated by time.

Everything now hinged on the baby's death. But there was an added problem for the police. Gates was convinced that husband and wife had planned together to kill their baby and be free of a tiresome and expensive burden. But which of them had administered the fatal dose? Nickolls got down to work again, visiting the makers of seconal until he found one which had, for three years 'for commercial reasons', used a different type of material for its capsules, which were made of methyl cellulose dyed with eosin. In addition to the seconal, the capsules contained a small quantity of cornstarch. The methyl cellulose absorbed the stomach fluids, and when the fluids penetrated the interior of the capsules the cornstarch swelled, bursting the capsule into two parts, thus releasing seconal into the stomach. The halves of the capsule later dissolved and their colour disappeared.

Suddenly it became clear that the Gosport chemists had found cornstarch in the stomach of the dead baby. Nickolls now resumed his experiments with capsules made of methyl cellulose. He found that, in some cases, they opened swiftly, but in others they took as long as 90 minutes before the two parts separated. These findings, while confirming that the baby had been murdered, made it impossible to rule out either parent as the one who gave the child the capsules. The police knew, too, that they must prove the Armstrongs were in possession of seconal on the day of the murder – and strong suspicion was not proof.

Inspector Gates decided to play a waiting game and kept both John and Janet Armstrong under observation for a year. He was beginning to despair when, on July 24, 1956, Janet applied to the Gosport Magistrates' Court for a separation and maintenance order against her husband, alleging that he beat her up again and again. The court refused her the order, but Gates contrived a meeting with her and found that, at last, she was ready to talk. She admitted she had lied and said that her husband had brought many capsules of seconal from his hospital. Three days after the baby's death he had ordered her to throw all the capsules away. She claimed she asked him: 'Did you give baby any?' and said he replied: 'How do I know *you* haven't?' She had not told the police all this because she was afraid of what he would do to her.

Gates knew full well that the woman was acting out of spite, but, whatever the whole truth of the matter, he now had an admission that the Armstrongs had seconal in their possession on the day of the baby's death. Four months later, on

December 3, 1956, the Attorney-General of the day, Sir Reginald Manningham-Buller, QC, personally prosecuted both John and Janet Armstrong on the charge of jointly planning to commit murder by poisoning their own baby, Terence.

It was a sordid trial, with charges and countercharges between husband and wife in an atmosphere of lies and hatred. An astute defence, throwing doubts on the time it took seconal to discharge its poisonous content into the stomach, achieved an acquittal for the wife, but John Armstrong was found guilty of murder.

The importance to society of this, the first trial for murder by barbiturates, lay in the complexity of the problems set by new and rapidly proliferating poisons.

Lethal Drugs

A chemical element, arsenic was a component of other interesting products during the late 19th century. Women (including Florence Maybrick) sometimes used it as a cosmetics base and chemists used it in flypaper, among other things. Even Queen Elizabeth I used arsenic as part of the preparation that made her face appear white.

'HOMICIDE BY POISON is rare,' opined Keith Simpson when Professor of Forensic Medicine at the internationally-known Guy's Hospital, London, England. 'The Maybricks, Seddons, Crippens, and Merryfields are famous only because they are of rare interest. On the contrary, suicide by poison is more common than ever, and the rapid rise in the figures of the barbituric acid drugs makes one doubt the effectiveness of the regulations which were designed to control their sale; overworked doctors may too readily prescribe these drugs for the many psychosomatic disorders of "civilized" life . . .'

It is certainly true that homicide by poison is rare, and equally true that forensic pathologists and others in the world of toxicology have a high success-rate in the cases of poisoning which do come into the laboratory. Nearly 90 per cent of all homicides are committed by close relatives or friends of the victim, and as most incidents of poisoning necessitate elaborate preparation, forensic examination of the human aspects of the case as a whole usually pinpoints one or more immediate suspects.

Small Man's Weapon

The late Sir Bernard Spilsbury, who was responsible for a large number of triumphs in forensic toxicology, caused his biographers Douglas G. Browne and E. V. Tullett to comment: 'Poison would seem to be the small man's weapon – not only, perhaps, because small men are not given to violence, but also because they suffer from a sense of inferiority. The remote and generally prolonged action of poison gives them a feeling of power. They can sit back, like gods, and watch it work.'

Psychiatrists probing motives for poisoning may agree or disagree with legal findings. However, it is sometimes wise of prosecution counsel to accept not-guilty pleas 'with intent to cause grievous bodily harm', and therefore to hear a judge accept the lesser charges of 'administering poison with the intent of injuring, grieving or annoying'. This is a distinction now possible in English courts, but not in the United States.

This merciful provision enabled, for example, an eighteen-year-old boy to walk out of the Manchester (England) Crown Court in July 1973, after telling the judge, Sir William Morris, of his practical joke which could have killed an entire works staff.

As a boyish prank, he poured cyanide into the milk used for the cafeteria tea at a Lancashire factory. Before the tea was actually poured, a cafeteria worker stooped down and gave some of the milk to two kittens. They died in agony. Fortunately this prevented harm to the two immediate intended victims of the practical joke, the woman in charge of that section of the factory and a seventeen-year-old workmate.

Giving the boy a six-month prison sentence, suspended for two years, the judge said: 'It was a wicked thing you did, and you might have been standing here on a very serious charge of killing.'

This is typical of the foolish practical jests and complete misunderstanding of the seriousness of poisons, equalled perhaps only by another Lancashire case a few weeks later. Here a student nurse became critically ill and later died after a hospital party at the Wigan infirmary.

Again, no complex forensic examination was necessary, since others who had attended the hospital party gave evidence that a bowl of punch had been placed in the recreation room, and near it were bottles containing methanol, ethanol and surgical spirits. As the party progressed and the level in the punch bowl went down, the ethanol was added.

Ethanol Added

Commercial products such as Ethanol are misused in this way to lace drinks – chiefly because they are easy to obtain. This is why the various types of cyanide feature in a high proportion of poison attempts. Almost the only person to benefit is the pathologist, since the hydrocyanics can usually be detected at once by the smell of bitter almonds (although Dr H. J. Walls, B.Sc., once said that 20–30 per cent of people can *not* smell it), and the US oleum amygdalae amarae (oil of bitter almonds) can contain up to 10 per cent of hydrocyanic acid.

Would-be poisoners able to get access to it have been known to misuse the solid cyanide used to kill vermin and wasps; but when poison attempts are reported in factories, shops and among people with access to chemical stores, it is more usually the commercially-pure potassium cyanide which is administered. This is in common use – and therefore does not create immediate suspicion – in photographic laboratories, plating works and process engravers.

Graham Young, the poisoner who killed after being freed from Broadmoor, avoided suspicion for a time because he used thallium, an insecticide which was virtually unknown as a poison at that time.

Toxicologists always hasten to stress that while even five grains of cyanide constitute a fatal dose, it deteriorates when stored and is not necessarily a certain killer. Provided, of course, a doctor is called in time to carry out cleansing by stomach tube, and to administer a stimulant such as methyl amphetamine, plus a detoxicant of the sodium thiosulphate nature.

It was Professor Keith Simpson who first pointed

out that cyanide is more or less harmless until it comes into contact with the ionizing acid in the gastric juices, so its action in the body may be delayed by carbonic acid gas.

He deduced from this a surprising explanation to the events of the last hour of Grigori Rasputin, the Russian peasant monk who gained an evil influence over the court of the Czar Nicholas II. As the result of a conspiracy among a group of noblemen, Rasputin was assassinated, presumably with cyanide.

His death in 1916 was long delayed, however, causing the assassins to dread that in his dying ravings, Rasputin would be able to unmask his poisoners. 'Should the victim suffer from chronic gastritis as Rasputin probably did,' asserted the blunt Keith Simpson, 'he may swallow many times the fatal dose and escape the fate an ordinary subject would quickly meet . . .'

Another odd case of homicidal poisoning occurred some years later in New York State. The body of a woman who had apparently leapt to her death from an upper floor of an office building was taken away for a post-mortem. The Chief of Homicide and the Chief Medical Examiner arrived almost simultaneously, because what might have been a straight-forward case of suicide proved to be one of murder. A brief examination by the toxicologist disclosed that the woman was in the early stages of pregnancy, and that she had been doped with an anti-cholinesterase poison (in fact a systemic insecticide with a well-known trade name) before the body was thrown out of the window.

Just how low down in the Crime Index scale of the United States are poisoning cases? In any typical year, handguns are the weapons used in 51 per cent of cases, knives and similar cutting weapons in 20 per cent, shotguns in 8 per cent, rifles in 6 per cent, and personal weapons (such as 'putting the boot in') in 9 per cent. Poison is used in the smallest group of all, far less than 6 per cent.

In real life it is always easier to identify and bring a poisoner to trial than it is to get the bandit before a jury for the dollars stolen from a bank. Poisoning is usually a personal affair, with a motive like a shining beacon. This is why the clear-up rate for poisoners, indeed for murders in general, is far higher than with *any* other type of crime.

In any one typical year, from FBI Crime Index figures, the proportion of murders solved is 84 per cent – and this includes all poisoning cases – compared with only 19 per cent burglaries and 16 per cent car thefts.

Some of society's problems are concerned with the difficulty of isolating involatile organic poisons, and the metabolism (change of cell or organism structure) which some of these involatile poisons undergo in the body. Dr H. J. Walls, a former Director of the Metropolitan Police (New Scotland Yard) Forensic Science Laboratory warned: 'What is extracted post-mortem may not be what was taken.'

In addition to this, there are other factors, such as lack of international uniformity of drug names, which makes for hazards in a poison emergency. In European usage drugs ending in '-one' (for example, phenobarbitone) usually, but not always, correspond with similar American drugs with names ending in '-al' – such as Seconal (quinalbarbitone) and Nembutal (pentobarbitone).

Time of Death

When death occurs from taking a rapid-acting barbiturate, especially if the deceased had lived for some time after taking it, very little of the unchanged compound may be left in the body. Unfortunately we are still extremely ignorant of the reactions involved and compounds produced in these metabolic processes.

'Time of death' was important to Sherlock Holmes, Father Brown and Agatha Christie, and still more so to a chemist in the forensic poisons laboratory. The British doctor, A. S. Curry, carried out forensic work which helped in solving a number of barbiturate-poison problems where the time factor was critical. He found, to put it briefly, that the longer the poisoned victim lives after taking the barbiturate, the lower will be the blood/liver concentration rate when it comes to the post-mortem stage. The ratio may be anywhere from unity to five or six; if for example, it is greater than four, in all probability death occurred in under five hours.

Three workers in the United States, Umberger, Stolman and Schwartz, have greatly helped toxicologists the world over with their development of an alcohol-distillation system to test body slurry where poison is suspected. It operates on a distillation and recycling principle. Boiling alcohol is passed continuously through the body slurry which is mechanically agitated, compounds are recovered from the gaseous stream, and then the alcohol is recycled back to the boiler after condensation. Naturally the toxicologist has to consider not only the time of taking the poison, but also what constitutes a fatal dose in the particular circumstances.

It is common knowledge that alcohol consumed at about the same time as barbiturates acts as an accelerator, greatly increasing the effect of the poison. There have been many cases on both sides of the Atlantic where addicts have taken compounds such as Oblivon to achieve the same effect more economically and quicker than a slug of alcohol. Normally with barbiturate compounds the minimum lethal dose is about twenty times the therapeutic (or sedative) dose. But toxicologists become tired of cases where it is said on behalf of the victim that: 'Only a few tablets were taken, but of course that drugged her mind and she didn't then realize she was swallowing the rest of them.'

Popular Belief

Keith Simpson states firmly, 'It has become a popular belief that a state of partial narcosis from barbiturates introduces a liability, because of mental confusion, to the taking of another dose, so accounting for many deaths as 'accidents', or misadventures rather than suicides. The possibility clearly exists . . . but there is usually no evidence whatsoever to justify taking such a view. It is upon such conveniences that erroneous views may become accepted as common truths.'

An Early Case of Poisoning

Born in Burlington in 1824, Lydia Sherman (her final married name) was orphaned at the age of nine and raised by an uncle. She left town in 1840, and moved to New Brunswick, New Jersey, where she met her first husband, Edward Struck, a widower with six children. They moved to Manhattan, where Struck joined the police force, and had seven more children together. After eighteen years of marriage, Struck was discharged and became depressed. Lydia poisoned him with arsenic 'to put him out of the way'.

Finding herself unable to single-handedly support at least half-a-dozen young children, she poisoned baby William, four-year-old Edward and six-year-old Martha Ann, in a single day. When fourteen-year-old George became chronically ill, she laced his tea with arsenic, and when twelve-year-old Ann Eliza had recurrent chills and fevers one winter, Lydia poisoned her as well. Lydia's oldest daughter, eighteen-year-old Lydia, died of natural causes two months after the last of her siblings was poisoned.

Hired by a storekeeper to care for his invalid mother in Stratford, Connecticut, Lydia was recommended as a housekeeper to a wealthy farmer, Dennis Hurlburt. He hired her, married her within days, and was dead of poisoning within months, leaving her with $10,000.

Finally, widower Horatio Sherman came calling, wanting to hire Lydia as a housekeeper and nurse for his baby. When he proposed marriage, she accepted. After they were married, Horatio drank heavily, abused her, and wasted her ill-found inheritance. In an effort to gain his attention and affection, Lydia poisoned baby Frankie, then sixteen-year-old Ada. When Horatio remained unchanged, she put arsenic in his brandy bottle.

Having poisoned three husbands and seven children, Lydia Sherman went on trial in 1872 and was convicted of second-degree murder. She was dubbed the 'Modern Lucretia Borgia', 'Poison Fiend', 'Borgia of Connecticut' and the 'Queen Poisoner'. She spent the remainder of her life in prison.

Doctor Hawley Harvey Crippen

The case of Dr. Crippen has fascinated the public for many years since the disappearance of his wife Cora on January 31, 1910. Her remains were found buried in the cellar at their home, Hilltop Crescent, Camden, in north London. The case continues to be debated to this day and has made Crippen almost a household name.

Even back in 1910 at the time of the trial the case was fiercely discussed, the full facts never emerging and eventually dying with Crippen in

Pentonville prison. Augustus Pepper, a young Bernard Spilsbury, and William Willcox played the main roles at the trial, with medical evidence being the main proof.

Crippen was born in Michigan, USA in 1862. One of the lucky few to attend school, he later went to Cleveland Homeopathic hospital to study medicine. He became a doctor in 1885, specializing in ear, nose and throat. He got married in 1887 at the age of 25 and had one son. His wife died in 1891 and the son went to be brought up by the grandmother. Crippen moved to New York where he met an attractive blonde, Russian-Pole. A year later they were married and went to live in St. Louis. They then moved to London in 1900, when Crippen became manager of an advertising agency for homeopathic remedies. In 1902 Crippen returned to New York on business, during which time Cora, it is claimed, took up an association with Bruce Miller. He returned to America before Crippen came home, and Miller never saw Cora again. It is at about this time, Crippen claimed at his trial, that the marriage started to break down. Cora had become irritable, and 'impossible to live with as a wife'.

In 1905 they took a house in Hilltop Crescent, Camden. This was a large three bedroomed semi-detached house, and was really too big for the Crippens. This gave them an income opportunity, so they decided to rent to a lodger. In 1909 Crippen resigned his position with the advertising agency and took up a position with a dental surgeon in Albion House, New Oxford Street, where Crippen was to become the medical adviser.

Cora Crippen was an arrogant and flamboyant woman with no real interest in her husband, and she resented her role as the mistress of a lodging house. She hankered after an acting career, and with only a moderate singing voice, she joined the Music Hall Ladies Guild. She was then mixing with the acting and stage fraternity with whom she struck up a good friendship.

By 1909 Crippen's affections, now not on his wife, had drifted to a young typist, Ethel Le Neve. Also, Crippen's finances were in a bit of a state, mainly due to Cora's flamboyance. On January 31 the Crippen's friends Mr and Mrs Martinettii came to dinner, they left at 1:30 a.m., and Cora Crippen was never seen alive again. Cora, according to Crippen had gone back to America to look after a sick relative. The music hall, to which Cora belonged, got a letter saying that she would not be attending for a while. The letter was handwritten, but not apparently in Cora's handwriting. On February 9 Crippen pawned some of her jewellery, a brooch and some rings, for £115.

Crippen, like so many criminals, could have got away with his crime had he not been overconfident and careless. On September 20 he went to the Ladies Guild Music Hall dinner, the society to which Cora had been a member. He took young Ethel Le Neve, not only wearing some of Cora's rings, but also some of her clothes. This was not apparently the behaviour of a lonely husband. By March 12 Ethel was living at Hilltop Crescent, and around the same time Crippen gave three months notice to quit the property. Just before Easter Crippen broke the news to his wife's friends, the Martinettii's, that Cora had developed pneumonia. Two days later Crippen and Ethel departed to Dieppe for a holiday, and Crippen sent a telegram to the Martinettii's informing them that Cora had died in Los Angeles. But Crippen had not counted for a friend of Cora's, a Mr Nash, being on business in California in May. Nash enquired after Cora but could find no record of her, her illness, or her death, and on his return to England he went straight to the police.

On June 30 Chief Inspector Dew began an investigation into Cora Crippen's disappearance. When Dew visited Hilltop Crescent on June 6 he found Ethel Le Neve running the household. Crippen gladly and enthusiastically gave Dew a tour of the house, showing the inspector the wardrobe containing his wife's clothes. But his nerve failed him and he admitted that the story of his wife's death was a fabrication, saying that he had made it up to cover up for the embarrassment and scandal that she had left him to return to a former lover in America. As far as he was aware she may well still be alive. Crippen promised Dew that he would write a description of his wife to be published in the American press, to discover her whereabouts, but this was never done. When Dew returned the next day he found that Crippen and Ethel had gone. Dew conducted a detailed search of the house, and found loose bricks in the coal cellar. On further examination they found human remains, caked in soil and lime. The police circulated pictures of the couple and issued a warrant for their arrest. On Friday, July 29 the missing couple became headline news around the world when Captain Randall aboard the ship *SS Montrose* revealed their identity. Randall had been given details of the couple before the ship set sail from Antwerp bound for Quebec, Canada on July 20. Randall, a keen amateur detective, had his eye on his passengers. He noticed that 'Mr Robinson' and his son were unusually close, and also, that Randall was certain that Master Robinson, was in fact a girl, wearing trousers and short cut hair. Two days after setting sail he ordered his wireless operator to send a message back to England, to Scotland Yard, detailing his findings. The first time ever that wireless telegraphy had been used to catch a criminal. Inspector Dew wasted no time, he left Liverpool the very next day, on a faster ship, the *Laurentic*. They overtook the *SS Montrose*, on July 31, and the 'Robinsons' were subsequently arrested, officially extradited from Quebec and arrived back in England on August 28.

The remains found in Hilltop Crescent were sent for forensic tests. Augustus Pepper, and William Willcox (later Sir) conducted exhaustive examinations. A young Bernard Spilsbury, also helped in the investigation. They were told by police that Crippen had purchased five grains of Hyoscine on January 1, 1910, from William & Burroughs chemist in Oxford Street. The pathologists needed, however, to exclude the possibility of poison in the soil at Hilltop Crescent. Willcox visited the site, taking soil specimens. They were satisfied that there was no trace of alkaloids in the soil, meaning that poison found in Cora's liver and stomach must have been introduced prior to death.

The inquest was held at Holloway, the magistrates hearing at Bow Street. The inquest had originally opened on July 18, but Mr Thomas the coroner had died, and the inquest had to be restarted. Coroner Mr Walter Schroder reopened the inquest on August 16. Pepper and Willcox gave prolonged evidence, causing the inquest and magistrates proceedings to clash – the inquest actually ended after the magistrates court hearing. At the inquest it was claimed by forensics that the body had been buried for between four and eight months. The jury returned a verdict of willful murder against Crippen, but at the coroner's instruction were asked to leave Ethel out of the verdict. On August 29, Crippen was charged with willful murder, and Ethel with being an accessory after the fact. The magistrates trial lasted six days and was packed every day, quite often with notable people such as W. S. Gilbert of Gilbert and Sullivan fame.

At the trial at the Old Bailey, which started on October 18, there was so much public interest and request for seats, that half-day tickets were allocated. The trial lasted five days, heard by the Lord Chief Justice, Lord Alverstone. Trevor Humphries appeared for the prosecution and Arthur Newton for the defendants. Crippen was charged with the willful murder of Cora Crippen, to which he pleaded Not Guilty. Over the next five days many witnesses were called, including Bruce Miller who sailed from America, a long and expensive journey in those days.

After retiring for half an hour the jury found Crippen guilty at 2:45 p.m. on Saturday 22 October. At her trial, again at the Old Bailey, on October 25, Ethel was found not guilty and was acquitted.

Crippen appealed against his verdict, but he was unsuccessful and was executed at Pentonville at 8 a.m. on Wednesday November 23, 1910.

Cruel Strychnine

If a grim, rigid smile fixed the features of Betsy Frances as she drew her last breath, it betrayed nothing less than murder at the hands of her smooth-talking boyfriend George Hersey, whose choice of strychnine was as cruel as it was effective.

STRYCHNINE IS an alkaloid extracted from the seeds of the East Indian tree *Strychnos nux vomica.* It was discovered in 1818. It has an exceptionally bitter taste and is used in tonics and animal poisons. Whether given orally or by injection, strychnine rapidly enters the bloodstream. It affects the central nervous system and in medicinal doses acts as a stimulant. The senses are made more acute and mental powers are heightened – there is a general feeling of well being.

The *British Pharmacopoeia* contains several strychnine preparations, including Tincture of Nux Vomica and Easton's Syrup. These contain very small amounts of the drug and are used as tonics in cases of convalescence after weakening illnesses. Strychnine is also used by veterinary scientists for killing moles and seals. No strychnine preparations are listed in the *US Pharmacopoeia.*

Strychnine comes out of solution in an alkaline mixture and accumulates at the bottom of the medicine bottle, and failure to shake the medicine properly has resulted in cases of accidental overdosing, while suicidal use of the drug was common before the laws relating to poison were made stricter.

In overdoses there is a twitching of the muscles and difficulty with breathing within about five minutes. The chest feels tight, and as respiration is further affected there is a feeling of suffocation.

The victim is suddenly seized by violent convulsions. As the motor areas of the spinal cord react to the drug, the back arches dramatically. The muscles are stiff and rigid and only the head and heels of the feet touch the ground. This condition is known as opisthotonus. This violent contraction of the spine may also bend the body forward or laterally.

The chest is also fixed so that cyanosis results and the face becomes contorted. The muscles of the face contract in a tetanic spasm, clamping the jaw and producing a grinning effect; this grim 'smile' is called *risus sardonicus.* The pupils of the eyes dilate and the eyes have a wild staring look; the fingers are clenched tightly in the palms of the hands.

This spasm lasts for anything up to two minutes and then the body relaxes, leaving the victim gasping for breath. Then, within a few minutes, there is another convulsion; this may be triggered off by the slightest thing, such as touching the victim in an attempt to give assistance. During the convulsions the victim is conscious and suffers intense pain. In the relaxed period between convulsions he is calm but weak. The pattern of convulsions followed by relaxation may be repeated several times before death intervenes. Death may occur within an hour from respiratory paralysis or exhaustion.

Strychnine poisoning closely resembles the symptoms of tetanus or lockjaw. A distinguishing feature is that fixation of the chest does not occur in tetanus, whereas the clamping of the lower jaw is one of the earliest symptoms of tetanus, it is only part of the condition of strychnine poisoning and relaxes between spasms.

A Popular Poison

A fatal dose of strychnine is considered to be 100 mg by oral administration, but fatalities with doses as low as 30 mg have been recorded. Individual variation is wide, and symptoms of poisoning can result from absorption by external application of the drug. A small dose of 5 mg of strychnine in the eye has been reported to cause effects of poisoning within four minutes.

There are no typical post-mortem characteristics of strychnine poisoning, although the lungs, brain and spinal cord usually appear congested. The drug may be found in the tissues and fluids but only in very small quantities.

Chemical tests for strychnine are simple. Suspected residues, normally colourless crystals, are treated with a drop of sulphuric acid. The crystals go into solution, and the edge of the solution is touched with a yellow crystal of potassium chromate. In the presence of strychnine, a purple colour forms immediately and changes to crimson before fading completely.

Strychnine was a popular poison in the latter half of the nineteenth century, and two infamous exponents of this form of murder were Dr William Palmer and Dr Thomas Neill Cream. Because of its extremely bitter taste, strychnine has to be disguised. Palmer found the answer by administering the poison in brandy, but Cream preferred to 'doctor' real medicine with it.

Another problem confronting the strychnine poisoner is obtaining the poison itself. This posed little difficulty for the doctors, but others have gained access to it ostensibly for the killing of dogs and rats. Jean Pierre Vacquier, murderer of the landlord of the Blue Anchor Hotel in Byfleet, Surrey, in 1924, had a novel excuse. He bought his strychnine from a local pharmacy, explaining that he wanted it for wireless experiments; he subsequently disguised the poison in a hangover remedy which the landlord took with fatal results.

George Hersey was a young man who had had the misfortune to lose his wife early in their marriage. He lived and worked at South Weymouth, Massachusetts. In January, 1860, the young widower became engaged again, but his fiancée, Mary Tirrell, died soon after the announcement. The girl's parents, distressed by his grief, offered him a home. He accepted and soon became friendly with the eldest of the remaining daughters. Betsy Frances was 25 years old, plain and unmarried.

Just a Melancholy Girl

Betsy Frances looked after George, mending his shirts and caring for his appearance. George was morose and did not work for a while, but he studied chemistry and could talk knowledgeably about poisons. At about this time family friends thought that Betsy Frances's health was not what it should be for a young woman. Unmarried women of her age were subject to moods, and in the phraseology of the time, she was thought to be just melancholy.

Subsequent events showed that Betsy Frances's otherwise dreary life was lightened by sexual intercourse with George. The opportunity was afforded on occasions when the family were away visiting. Eventually George went back to work. He seemed to have a new lease of life, and in no time at all he was secretly engaged to a girl called Loretta Loud. He told her that he did not wish to upset Betsy Frances's parents, and he ventured the opinion that he did not think Betsy Frances would live long if she did not get better soon. Perhaps George moved too quickly for Loretta's liking. At any rate she broke off the engagement.

Meanwhile Betsy Frances's 'melancholy' got worse. George thought that she would not last long. It was a prophecy that he intended should be fulfilled. He went to Boston and bought some strychnine from a pharmacy. The chemist warned him about the dangers of the substance – George said he wanted it to put down a dog. On May 3,

1860, George took Betsy Frances out for a ride in a horse-carriage. They returned home about 8 p.m. and George went to bed immediately, complaining of a headache. Betsy Frances sat with her family for a while and read aloud to them from the evening paper before retiring for the night.

Betsy Frances went to the room which she shared with her twelve-year-old stepsister, Louisa. She spoke to the younger girl, undressed and got into bed. Half an hour later, Louisa called for her mother in a terrified voice. Betsy Frances was thrashing about on her bed. She was twitching and convulsing and screaming, 'I shall die. I shall die.' Her back was arched and she was in terrible pain.

George appeared and was sent to fetch the doctor. Her convulsions exhausted her, and her face was covered in blood where she had bitten through her lip. She was dead before the doctor reached the house. The family were frightened of food poisoning, and they decided to boil all their water. An autopsy was suggested, but George objected to the mutilation of a loved one. He was overruled by the family, whose belief in coincidence after three sudden deaths must have been wearing a little thin.

In spite of his professed horror at the thought of an autopsy, George asked if he could be present when the doctors made their examination of Betsy Frances's body. No objection was raised. He was therefore right on hand when the doctors discovered that the dead woman was three months pregnant. In answer to his questions, the doctors told George that they thought Betsy

Frances had been poisoned. They notified the coroner of their findings, and parts of the body removed for analysis revealed the presence of strychnine.

The revelation that Betsy Frances had been pregnant was too much for her parents, and they ordered George to leave their house at once. Meanwhile a search was made of the dead woman's room, and on a spoon – found in the fireplace – were traces of jam, which analysis showed to contain traces of strychnine.

George Hersey's arrest was not long delayed. He was put on trial on May 28, 1861 – he pleaded not guilty. A Boston doctor testified that George had approached him regarding an 'operation' for a woman friend who was pregnant. The doctor would not listen and also refused a request for some strychnine to kill a dog. A former room-mate remembered George producing a small vial and telling him, 'There is something to kill young ones'.

The Fatal Spoonful of Jam

The conclusion drawn was that on learning of Betsy Frances's condition, George decided to rectify the matter and 'help' the girl out of trouble. No doubt he told her that if she took the medicine which he would get for her, all would be well. On the fatal night Betsy Frances took the strychnine-loaded spoonful of jam in the hope of getting rid of her baby. She had probably been well primed to hide the spoon in the fireplace after swallowing its contents.

The defence argued that Betsy Frances committed suicide, but the shadows of George Hersey's wife and fiancée cast their sinister spell. The jury brought in a verdict of first-degree murder and Hersey was sentenced to death. Before meeting his end, he confessed to causing Betsy Frances's death but denied killing his wife and fiancée.

Death in Tuttletown

Another case which involved the forensic chemist's skills was the murder of Carroll Rablen in Tuttletown, California. Carroll Rablen was deaf, due to an injury received during World War I. His attractive second wife, Eva, liked dancing, and although her husband did not dance himself, Carroll took her to dances and stayed on the sidelines while she danced with other men.

On April 29, 1929, the Rablens attended the regular Friday night dance in the schoolhouse at Tuttletown. Eva wanted to dance, and Carroll unselfishly let her enjoy herself while he stayed outside in his car; about midnight Eva pushed through the crowd with a cup of coffee and some refreshments for him.

She handed the refreshments to her husband and then went back into the dance. Seconds after swallowing some of the coffee, Carroll was writhing on the floor of the car in great pain. His distressed cries brought people running to his aid; among them was his father. Carroll complained to him of the bitter taste of the coffee. A doctor was called, but Carroll was dead before he arrived.

Eva appeared heartbroken. Although the possibility of suicide was mentioned, the police had no real idea of what caused Rablen's death. The contents of his stomach were analyzed by a chemist from a neighbouring town, but no traces of any poison were found. There was a good deal of gossip, and a lot of the talk was uncomplimentary to Eva. Carroll's father told the police that he thought Eva had poisoned his son for the insurance money. There were two policies worth $3,000.

The police had already made a search of the schoolhouse area and found nothing of significance to their case. Their second attempt was more rewarding. Under a broken wooden stair a police officer found a bottle – its label bore the menacing word STRYCHNINE. The supplier, whose name was on the label, was a pharmacist in a nearby town. The pharmacist traced the poison sale in his register. It had been made on April 26 by a Mrs Joe Williams, who said she wanted the poison to kill gophers. Eva Rablen was later identified as Mrs Joe Williams, but she denied buying the strychnine and said the pharmacist must be mistaken. Protesting her innocence and claiming that her father-in-law was behind it, Eva was arrested.

The police case was weak by virtue of failure of analysis to show any poison in Carroll Rablen's stomach. But Dr Edward Heinrich, an eminent chemist and criminologist, was called in to help. With an experienced forensic expert on the case, the evidence began to turn against Eva Rablen.

Heinrich found traces of strychnine in the dead man's stomach, but, more importantly, he also found traces of the poison in the coffee cup. With excellent cooperation from the police, Heinrich was able to back up a hunch with forcible results. He reasoned that Eva, pushing her way through the dance crowd with some sandwiches in one hand and a cup of coffee in the other, might have spilled some of the coffee on the clothing of someone in the crowd. An appeal brought forward a woman who remembered bumping into Eva Rablen that night. Yes, some coffee was spilled on her dress. The stains contained traces of strychnine.

Fittingly, perhaps, Eva Rablen's trial was held in an open-air dance pavilion. Only by doing so was it possible to accommodate the throng of people who wanted to be present. Confronted with Heinrich's evidence, Eva Rablen changed her plea to guilty, and was consequently sentenced to life imprisonment.

Corrosive Poisons

Hideous disfigurement, an overpowering acrid smell, and the absence of a corpse . . . these are some of the effects of corrosive poison. But even the most corrosive substance leaves a trace – just as John Haigh learned to his cost.

THE SWALLOWING of corrosive poisons – acids, alkalis and metallic salts – causes a particularly unpleasant kind of death. These agents erode and destroy the tissues with which they come into contact. Death from corrosive poisoning is commonly the result of suicide or accident. The ready availability of compounds such as metal polishes, bleaches, toilet cleansers and disinfectants make them convenient agents for suicide. The widespread industrial use of corrosive materials also increases the dangers of accident.

The destructive nature of the mineral acids has led to their criminal use in disfigurement and in the disposal of bodies.

When a corrosive is swallowed the tissues in contact with it are to some degree destroyed; the victim feels a burning sensation in the mouth and throat, intense stomach pain, which is followed by vomiting of shreds of bloodstained material, accompanied by intense thirst. Choking is common, and the air passages will probably be congested.

There will be signs of corrosion around the mouth and lips – grey or brownish stains. Consciousness is usually maintained, but the victim is drained of colour as respiration breaks down. Death usually follows within a few hours of a fatal dose which results from a combination of shock, extensive tissue damage and respiratory failure. Post-mortem examination will show the destruction of those tissues affected by the corrosive. The extent and colouration of damage will identify the agent used if that is in doubt.

Hydrochloric/Sulphuric acid	Grey/black
Nitric acid	Red/brown
Caustic alkalis	Grey/white
Cresols	Brown
Mercury chloride	Blue/white

Some corrosive agents have a double effect – attacking the tissues directly and also acting on the central nervous system. Such poisons are carbolic acid and oxalic acid. Carbolic acid in its pure form is phenol, and is used as a component in many branded disinfectants. These agents have a corrosive action which is partly modified by their anaesthetic effect – vomiting is therefore uncommon. But they also have a depressant action, and death usually results within about three hours from respiratory or cardiac failure. A fatal dose may be as low as 4 ml, but recoveries have been recorded from much higher doses. Phenol may also be absorbed through the skin.

Sulphuric acid – oil of Vitriol – is one of the

strongest corrosive poisons. It is used extensively in its most concentrated form for industrial purposes and also in laboratory work, but battery acid (30 per cent sulphuric acid) is still sufficiently strong to cause corrosive poisoning. Sulphuric acid acts by extracting water from the tissues and, in the process, generates considerable heat. This has a charring and blackening effect. Perforation of the oesophagus and stomach is likely to follow this.

Hydrochloric and nitric acids give off irritant fumes and therefore involve the respiratory system. Their destructive effects are less severe than those of sulphuric acid.

The principal alkaline corrosive poison is ammonia. It has an intensely irritant vapour and usually involves the air passages. It is commonly used in suicide and is frequently taken by accident. Many cleaning fluids contain ammonia in large proportions. The choking fumes of concentrated ammonia may cause cardiac failure, and they are particularly dangerous when inhaled, as they dissolve in the mucous membranes, thereby prolonging their action.

Caustic soda and caustic potash have a similar effect to the mineral acids, but the damaged tissues are distinctive because of the large quantities of mucus present. The destroyed tissues are also slimy to the touch.

Staining of the Mouth

The appearance of corrosion stains on the face may be a guide to the nature of the fatality. The general nature of the vessel from which the poison was swallowed may be ascertained from the staining of lips and mouth. A cup, for instance, will leave areas of staining around the mouth whereas a bottle may cause a smaller, neater stain. Dribbling stains down the chin and throat are quite common. Accidental poisoning from supposed doses of medicine often leave no marks – a spoonful being put straight into the mouth.

The powerful action of the mineral acids has frequently been applied to the problem of disposing of a body. In 1933 a French lawyer, Maître Sarret, concocted a get-rich-quick plan with the help of two girls who were sisters, Katherine and Philomene Schmidt. Sarret was in debt, and he persuaded Katherine Schmidt, who was also his mistress, to help him in an insurance fraud. He set up an elaborate scheme in which a man who was known by him to be in the terminal stage of an illness was insured for 100,000 francs. As insurance companies are not in business to insure people on the point of death, the scheme involved Katherine marrying the sick man and arranging for another party to the fraud, a man called Chambon, to impersonate her husband and get the insurance.

Lured into a Trap

This was done successfully, and in due course the sick man died. Maître Sarret and his confederates thus collected 100,000 francs. In no time at all Chambon decided that his share of the spoils was insufficient, and he threatened blackmail. Sarret and the girls pretended to play along with this but lured Chambon and his mistress into a trap. They were shot by Sarret while the two sisters ran a motorcycle engine to absorb the gunshot.

The bodies were put into a bath, and Sarret poured over them 25 gallons of sulphuric acid which he had bought, and the corpses were soon reduced to sludge. The deadly trio tried to repeat these tactics, this time for a larger stake of 1,750,000 francs. But before they could pull it off, one of the sisters was caught; when they were brought to trial, Sarret was sentenced to death, but the two sisters were each given 10 years' imprisonment.

John George Haigh, the acid bath murderer, was the most celebrated user of acid as a means of disposing of the victim. The 39-year-old self-styled engineer was convicted in 1949 of the murder of Mrs Henrietta Durand-Deacon. His victim was a well-off widow who lived in the same South Kensington hotel. She had spoken to Haigh of her plans to market a cosmetic product. Haigh expressed interest and invited her to visit his 'factory'.

The factory, which was no more than a storeroom belonging to another building, was at Crawley in Sussex. On February 18, Haigh drove Mrs Durand-Deacon down to his factory premises. There he shot her in the back of the head, stripped her body of all valuables and tipped the corpse into a tank of sulphuric acid. The same day Haigh pawned the wristwatch he had taken from his victim.

Mrs Durand-Deacon was reported missing from the hotel, and Haigh was among the first to express concern. He went with another resident to Chelsea police station to report her as missing.

The police were suspicious of Haigh's glibness and checked up on him. They soon found that he had a record as a petty criminal. Further inquiries were made, and the Crawley factory was visited. There detectives found some of Mrs Durand-Deacon's clothes, traces of blood and a recently fired ·38 Webley revolver. Haigh was apprehended. In cocksure mood he told the police, 'Mrs Durand-Deacon no longer exists – I've destroyed her with acid. You can't prove murder without a body.' When charged with the murder he admitted to seven other killings, the bodies all being disposed of in drums of acid.

While the acid had reduced his last victim's body to sludge there were sufficient identifiable traces remaining to bring the murder home to Haigh. Twenty-eight pounds of body fat, various pieces of bone and an acrylic plastic denture were among the grisly remains. The denture was positively identified by a dentist as belonging to Mrs Durand-Deacon. Haigh was executed on August 6, 1949.

Nitric acid was used in 1962 by a doctor in an incredible disfigurement of his wife. Early in August, Dr Geza de Kaplany and his new bride, Hajna, moved into an apartment block in San José, California. About 9.00 p.m. on August 28, fellow residents heard the sound of running water and classical music played at high volume. These noises, which came from the de Kaplanys' apartment, seemed to disguise a kind of wailing sound.

At 10.18 the police arrived at the apartment block. The music stopped, and a disturbing human wail was distinctly audible. Ambulance men were called and shortly afterwards brought out a figure on a stretcher. Siren blaring, the ambulance drove off at full speed to Santa Clara Hospital. The curious onlookers thought they could smell acid fumes.

The patient, Hajna de Kaplany, was a 25-year-old model. She had been married to Dr de Kaplany for only five weeks. When admitted to hospital, the surgeons were shocked to find the appalling state she was in. She had third-degree corrosive burns covering 60 per cent of her body. Her eyes were so burned that the pupils could not be seen; her breasts and thighs in particular had been subjected to the terrible corrosive action of the acid. The woman was choking, and a tracheotomy had to be performed to sustain her breathing. She was not expected to live – the last rites were administered.

Torture Chamber

Police meanwhile searched the apartment where she had been found. Retching at the stench of acid hanging in the atmosphere, they took in an incredible scene. The three-roomed apartment had all the appearance of a torture chamber. In the bedroom there was a heap of yellow-stained bedclothes disintegrating into a mess of rags, and there was a large hole in the carpet. A pair of discarded rubber gloves were lying near a leather case containing three pint bottles of sulphuric, hydrochloric and nitric acid – the last one was two-thirds empty.

Other items included acid-sodden surgical swabs, rolls of adhesive tape, some electric flex and a note written on a medical prescription form. It read, 'If you want to live – do not shout; do what I tell you; or else you will die.'

Hajna de Kaplany did die, but only after 33 days of agonized suffering. Her husband, Geza, who was a 36-year-old refugee from Hungary and anaesthetist at a San José hospital, told the police that he had attacked his wife to take away her beauty and to warn her against adultery. He did not think she would die. The police reconstructed the doctor's lesson against adultery.

After a period of lovemaking, de Kaplany beat his wife and bound her naked body at wrists and ankles with electric flex. He taped her mouth so that she would not scream. Then he put on rubber gloves and applied nitric acid to her naked, unprotected body. Nine doctors fought to save Hajna's life. Her lungs were inflamed as a result of inhaling the acid fumes, and large areas of her body became infected. She was on large doses of pain-killing drugs and had to be fed intravenously. Her condition was so painful that she had to be held upright by two attendants in order to urinate.

The poor woman was put on sterile bedding in order to try to check the spread of infection, and warm air blowers were used to reduce the moisture which oozed from the burns. The skin on her face went hard and turned brown – her near sightless eyes stared out of an inhuman head. She was disfigured beyond belief and was conscious enough to realize it.

Mercifully, she did not survive her ordeal by acid – she died on October 1. Hajna's condition had been the subject of daily progress reports in the press. Horror and revulsion expressed the public's reaction. Dr Geza de Kaplany was charged with murder by torture. He recorded two pleas – not guilty and not guilty by reason of insanity. His trial began on January 7, 1963, before Superior Judge Raymond G Callaghan at San José.

Terrible Testimony

During the presentation of evidence by the prosecution, de Kaplany seemed cool and detached. But his calm was shattered when a photographic enlargement was introduced to the court. It showed Hajna's frightful condition soon after entering hospital. De Kaplany leapt to his feet, shouting, 'No, no, no! What did you do to her?' He had to be restrained and was then half-carried from the court.

When he returned, the horror story, fully illustrated with photographs, was continued. A procession of witnesses followed. Police officers, ambulance men – who had burned their hands when moving the victim – doctors and criminologists all added their terrible testimony.

Dr de Kaplany was taken to a special cell and kept under constant supervision for fear that he might take his own life. In court the following morning, his defence attorney announced a change of plea to guilty. Judge Callaghan asked the doctor if he fully understood that he pleaded guilty to murder in the first degree. De Kaplany nodded and explained, 'I am a doctor. I loved her. If I did this – as I must have done – then I'm guilty.'

The defence called psychiatric evidence to show that the doctor's love for his wife had been rejected. It also transpired that de Kaplany occasionally posed as Pierre la Roche, a French journalist. This *alter ego* was used to build up a picture of a split personality. One psychiatrist offered the opinion that de Kaplany already considered himself dead, and that whilst he knew what acid would do, his schizophrenia prevented him from understanding the social significance of his act.

On the thirty-fifth day of the trial and after fifty-five hours of deliberation, the jury reached its verdict. They found that Dr Geza de Kaplany 'shall be punished by imprisonment for life as prescribed by the law'. The verdict was greeted by a furious public reaction. The newspaper switchboards were jammed with calls from angry men and women, and some of the jurors were threatened.

Manacled and under escort to the van which would take him to the State prison. Dr de Kaplany said, 'I am dead'.

A Soothing Draught!

Catherine Wilson was born in 1842 and was a nurse by trade although no-one could say that her life was dedicated to making people better. Her method was to find a sick person of means and befriend them. She would then work on winning them over and try and persuade them to make out wills in her favour. Once this was done she would then feed them various poisons. For a while she lived with a man named Dixon but he began to drink heavily so she poisoned him, as well.

In 1862 she was looking after Mrs Sarah Carnell. As soon as Mrs Carnell had rewritten her will in Catherine's favour it was time to get rid of her. Shortly afterwards Sarah brought the sick woman a 'soothing draught'. Mrs Carnell took a mouthful and promptly spat it out, saying it had burnt her mouth. She called her husband who immediately noticed that what his wife had spat out had burnt a hole in the carpet. Catherine, realising the mistake she had made, fled.

She was arrested a couple of days later. The mixture she had given Mrs Carnell contained enough sulphuric acid to kill fifty people. Catherine was charged with attempted murder and held while the police continued with their investigations. She was cleared of the charge of attempted murder because her defence argued that the pharmacist had given her the wrong bottle and, as no-one could be sure, the charge was dropped. She may have breathed a sigh of relief but if so it was short-lived as when she was released she was promptly rearrested. Post-mortems carried out on people that she had nursed revealed that a variety of poisons had been found in seven of the bodies exhumed. She was tried and this time found guilty.

She may not have been all that popular before but when she was hanged a crowd of 20,000 turned out to see her last moments outside the Old Bailey on October 20, 1862.

The 'Big M'

The juice of the Indian poppy is a cocktail of narcotics – the most potent of these being morphine. Among those people who have access to the deadly drug are doctors everywhere . . . they have a ready-made weapon for homicide.

MORPHINE IS NOT readily available to the public, but every doctor carries it in his bag because it is used in the control of pain. Because he has rightful access to morphine and controls its use in treatment, the unscrupulous doctor thus has a ready-made murder weapon.

The dried juice of the white Indian poppy, *Papaver somniferum* produces opium, and opium contains several natural narcotics of which morphine is the most powerful. Narcotics are drugs which kill pain and reduce consciousness; they are also habit forming. The use of opium-derived drugs in Britain is controlled by the Dangerous Drugs Act (1965) and the Misuse of Drugs Act (1971).

Morphine can be given by mouth or by injection, and it is available under a number of pharmaceutical and trade names. Several well-known medicines used for sedation contain morphine, and overdoses of all these can cause morphine poisoning.

Death Within an Hour

As a pain killer, morphine is usually given by injection. A normal dose of hydromorphine hydrochloride is 2.0 mg. A great danger with giving morphine is that a patient quickly acquires 'tolerance' to the drug. Patients treated for painful terminal illnesses frequently require amounts far in excess of the normal dose in order to obtain relief. Battle casualties injected with morphine have a large letter 'M' painted on their foreheads to ensure that their treatment is clearly identified and controlled. Addicts have been known to take up to ten times the normal therapeutic dose.

Morphine poisoning causes a deep coma, and this is accompanied by slow respiration, sweating and reduced reflexes. A lethal dose of about 180 mg can cause death within an hour. The telltale sign of morphine poisoning is the pinpoint contraction of the pupils of the eyes, so that when foul play is suspected, the presence of pinpointing will always suggest an overdose of morphine to the forensic expert. When death has only recently occurred, opium may be smelled in the mouth, or in the stomach on post-mortem examination.

It is possible to detect morphine by simple chemical tests on drug-containers, syringes or residues found at the scene of death. These usually apply only in cases of suicide or accidental death. Morphine gives a blue colour with ferric chloride and dry residues instantly turn purple when treated with a solution containing equal parts of concentrated sulphuric acid and formaldehyde. Where homicide is suspected, the presence of morphine in the body will be determined at post-mortem by analysis of blood, urine and bile.

Doctor Robert Clements

A case which illustrated how the unscrupulous doctor can use his position of trust for criminal purposes was that of Dr Robert Clements. On the evening of May 26, 1947, Clements, a 57-year-old Fellow of the Royal College of Surgeons, called a doctor to his Southport home to attend his wife. The fourth Mrs Clements was unconscious. Two doctors, Brown and Homes, examined her and transferred her immediately to a nearby nursing home, where she died the following morning. Her husband said she had mycloid leukaemia, and that was entered on the certificate as cause of death.

A post-mortem was performed by a third doctor, Dr Houston. He confirmed that the dead woman had been suffering from mycloid leukaemia. Drs Brown and Homes voiced their suspicions of Mrs Clements' eyes, the pupils of which were pinpointed, though Dr Houston said he was satisfied with the cause of death. However, the other two doctors spoke to the Southport coroner, hinting that there might have been an overdose of morphine and enquiries were begun.

The police discovered that the matron of the nursing home to which Mrs Clements was admitted had remarked at the time about the patient's pinpoint pupils. Dr Clements was interviewed at his flat. He said simply that his wife died of mycloid leukaemia, which, he added, was incurable.

People who knew Dr Clements and his wife remarked that Mrs Clements had been subject to sudden bouts of unconsciousness; yet, strangely, her husband always seemed to know when these were likely to occur. Friends who had been in the habit of talking to Mrs Clements on the telephone suddenly found themselves unable to do so – Dr Clements had the instrument removed. This was surely a remarkable action for a doctor with a sick wife at home.

Heir to a Fortune

Slowly, the story began to take shape. Mrs Clements's health had deteriorated over a period of time – she was prone to vomiting, her complexion yellowed, and she was lethargic – all the signs of a morphine addict. Finally it was learned that Dr Clements had prescribed large doses of morphine for a patient who never received them. The conclusion was obvious. A second post-mortem on Mrs Clements was ordered.

The Home Office pathologist was surprised when he found that some of the body's internal organs were missing. He was told that after the first post-mortem Dr Houston said they could be destroyed. Nevertheless, the result of the second examination showed clearly that Mrs Clements had died from morphine poisoning.

Police officers called on Dr Clements, only to find that he was dead. He had committed suicide by taking his favourite drug – morphine. No doubt he knew the game was up. He left a note: 'To whom it may concern – I can no longer tolerate the diabolical insults to which I have recently been exposed.' Dr Houston was also found by the coroner to have died by his own hand. In his case, the fatal drug was cyanide. He, too, left a note in which he referred to mistakes he had made in his work.

Dr Clements was found to be the murderer of his fourth wife by a coroner's court. Mrs Clements was heir to a fortune which, in the event of her death, would have gone to her husband. All of Dr Clements's marriages had been for money. He had a liking for the good life and had the knack of attracting rich women.

His record is quite remarkable. In 1912 he married his first wife; she died in 1920 from sleeping sickness; in 1921 he married again; his second wife died of endocarditis in 1925. He took his third wife in 1928, and she died of cancer in 1939. In each case, he signed the death certificate.

Some suspicion was voiced about the death of his third wife, but by the time this reached official quarters she had been cremated. Dr Clements had cheated the gallows by taking his own life. It was not thought necessary to exhume the bodies of his first two wives.

Doctor Robert Buchanan

Another celebrated case involving murder by morphine was that of Dr Robert Buchanan in

New York. Buchanan qualified at Edinburgh and in 1886 went to New York with his wife, where he set up in general practice. He was a successful practitioner, but he had an appetite for the seamier side of life; at night he forsook his respectable medical background and spent his time in clubs and brothels.

He became friendly with a woman called Anna Sutherland, a brothel madame, who was also one of his patients. In November 1890, Dr Buchanan divorced his wife on the grounds of her adultery. Shortly afterwards he persuaded Anna Sutherland to make a will leaving her money to her husband, or, if she died unmarried, to her trusted friend and physician Dr Buchanan. Within weeks, the doctor married Anna Sutherland, who was twice his age, ensuring himself of inheriting her wealth.

The doctor continued to enhance his professional reputation, only to find that his wife's brothel madame's ways were a source of embarrassment; he was afraid of losing patients, and his wife was fast becoming a liability. Early in 1892, Dr Buchanan announced that he was travelling to Edinburgh for further study. It was his intention to leave his wife behind, but Mrs Buchanan thought otherwise and declared that unless she accompanied her husband she would cut him out of her will altogether. Despite this threat, Dr Buchanan bought a single ticket for a passage on April 25.

Four days before he was due to sail he cancelled his passage and told friends that Mrs Buchanan had been taken seriously ill. A Dr McIntyre was called in to attend her. She went into a coma and died within a matter of hours. Cause of death was certified as cerebral haemorrhage, and Dr Buchanan, showing few signs of grief, inherited $50,000.

A Disappointed Suitor

The following month, a man who had been the late Mrs Buchanan's partner and disappointed suitor visited the coroner. He declared that Dr Buchanan had murdered his wife in order to secure her money. The coroner was disinclined to take any action, but the *New York World* got hold of the story and started to ask questions.

The interest of New Yorkers had been aroused in 1891 by a case of morphine poisoning in which a medical student called Carlyle Harris was convicted of murdering his wife with the drug. The poisoning was diagnosed by the victim's characteristic pinpoint pupils.

Dr McIntyre was interviewed by the newspaper about Mrs Buchanan's death, but refused to consider the idea of morphine poisoning because the contraction of the pupils was entirely missing in this case. The newspaper persisted with its enquiries, and a reporter found out that Dr Buchanan had lied about the date on which he cancelled his transatlantic passage. The ticket was turned in ten days before his wife fell ill, not four days as he had said. But the real scoop was the discovery that 23 days after Mrs Buchanan's death the doctor remarried his former wife.

It was not long before pressure was brought to

bear on the coroner to set up an inquiry into Mrs Buchanan's death. An exhumation order was granted. Post-mortem examination showed no sign of cerebral haemorrhage, the certified cause of death, but Professor Witthaus, the eminent toxicologist, found 1/10th of a grain of morphine in her body which he estimated was the residue of a fatal dose of 5 or 6 grains. To the disappointment of the prosecutors, the universal indicator of morphine poisoning – pinpoint pupils – was absent.

Nevertheless there was sufficient evidence to arrest Dr Buchanan. He was put on trial in New York on March 20, 1893. Witnesses came forward for the prosecution who stated that at the time of the Harris case Dr Buchanan had called the medical student a 'stupid fool' and a 'bungling amateur'. He hinted that he knew how to disguise morphine poisoning with belladonna. The suggestion was that the doctor had put belladonna drops into his wife's eyes which counteracted the pinpointing of the pupils, and the dead woman's nurse confirmed that Buchanan had put some drops into his wife's eyes for no apparent reason.

To make their case, the prosecution killed a cat in court with morphine and put belladonna drops in its eyes. The drops completely disguised the pinpointing. There followed a battle of the experts. The defence showed that the colour reaction tests used to identify morphine in the organs of the dead woman were not infallible. Again with a dramatic court-room demonstration it was shown that the test which produced a red colour in the presence of morphine was not specific. The same test resulted in a red colour when morphine was not present.

With the case swinging in his favour, Dr Buchanan mistakenly insisted on going into the witness box, and the prosecution gave him a severe grilling. He failed to answer why he took such an unlikely person as his wife, and he could not convincingly explain away his lies nor his boast about knowing how to disguise morphine poisoning. Dr Buchanan was found guilty of murder in the first degree. After two years in Sing Sing prison while various appeals were heard, he died in the electric chair on July 2, 1895.

Modern toxicological methods are fortunately more precise than those available to Dr Buchanan's prosecutors. Drugs can be clearly identified by a variety of methods, and their presence determined down to amounts as small as 1/5000th of a grain. Methods commonly used by the forensic toxicologist include colour reactions, thin-layer chromatography and gas chromatography.

Is Too Much Morphine Murder?

In 1982, the Commonwealth *v.* Capute, a highly publicized murder trial in Fall River, Massachusetts, raised the question of whether a caregiver's use of drugs could betray an intent to kill. After five weeks of testimony, Anne Capute was acquitted of both a murder charge and a second charge, for illegally dispensing morphine. In 1990, the county attorney and the medical examiner in Hennepin County, Minnesota, accused five physicians of committing homicide in two separate cases. Both cases involved terminally ill patients who received large doses of morphine before they died. The county attorney chose not to carry the cases forward to a grand jury and, instead, he issued guidelines for treating end-of-life pain. Although the county attorney determined that the deaths were homicides, he believed that he had little chance of conviction because the elements of the crime could not be proved beyond a reasonable doubt.

Gas Inhalation

Accident, suicide . . . or murder? So stealthy is the slow, sleepy poison of gas that the victim rarely knows what hit him.

THE EVERYDAY domestic coal-gas supply is, in fact, something of a menace; it accounts for large numbers of accidental deaths and suicides and for a smaller number of murders. Murder dressed up to look like suicide by gassing is one of the ruses that the forensic pathologist has to be aware of.

The killing component of coal-gas is carbon monoxide, and death from coal gas is really carbon-monoxide poisoning. The proportion of carbon monoxide in coal-gas varies according to the nature of the supply but is usually within the range of 5 to 10 per cent. The introduction of natural gas, which contains little or no carbon monoxide, is a safeguard against suicide by this means. Some years ago, a major British university converted its gas supply to 'natural' and thus dramatically reduced suicide among its students.

Carbon monoxide is also produced by various forms of incomplete combustion. Paraffin heaters in unventilated conditions, for instance, can be lethal, and smouldering upholstery and furnishings in burning buildings also produce the poisonous gas. Another major source of carbon monoxide is car-exhaust fumes, both accidental and suicidal deaths are common.

Readily Absorbed

Carbon monoxide is odourless and non-irritant. For these reasons its action is often insidious. It is readily absorbed by the body and quickly accumulates, poisoning the bloodstream. Vital oxygen is normally carried to the body's tissues by haemoglobin in the blood. Haemoglobin is the blood's colouring material, and oxygen, brought in through the lungs, combines with it to form oxyhaemoglobin. But oxyhaemoglobin is unstable, and its oxygen is easily displaced by carbon monoxide.

Consequently, carbon monoxide, which has 300 times more affinity for haemoglobin than oxygen, forms carboxyhaemoglobin, which is stable. The effect is that less and less oxygen reaches the body tissues, and death results from oxygen starvation. Since nerve cells, especially, cannot long survive lack of oxygen – those in the brain begin to die after about eight minutes – deterioration is rapid.

Symptoms of poisoning vary according to the amount of carbon monoxide accumulated in the blood. There are seldom any symptoms at all until saturation has reached 20 per cent and then usually only when the subject is engaged in physical acts of exertion. The first signs are dizziness and difficulty with breathing. The symptoms then move progressively to unconsciousness and death as the level of carbon monoxide builds up in the blood.

10%	No symptoms. Heavy smokers can have as much as 9% COHb.
15%	Mild headache.
25%	Nausea and serious headache. Fairly quick recovery after treatment with oxygen and/or fresh air.
30%	Symptoms intensify. Potential for long term effects especially in the case of infants, children, the elderly, victims of heart disease and pregnant women.
45%	Unconsciousness.
50%+	Death.

The onset of symptoms is insidious. Muzziness leads to a feeling of weariness and a disinclination to make any exertion, then unconsciousness intervenes and death ensues. Even where there is a willingness to make the effort to escape or to open a window, the limbs are often too weak to respond.

A level of 1 per cent carbon monoxide can cause unconsciousness in 15 to 20 minutes. Coal-gas containing between 5 and 10 per cent carbon monoxide is likely to be lethal within 5 minutes. Exercise quickens the respiration and merely serves to speed up the poisoning process.

Even small proportions of carbon monoxide in inhaled air may prove fatal due to the steady accumulation of the gas in the blood. A person at rest inhaling 0–1 per cent carbon monoxide from the atmosphere may have a blood saturation level of 50 per cent in just over two hours. With exercise, this time would be halved. In general, conversion of more than 50 per cent of the haemoglobin to carboxyhaemoglobin will cause death.

Post mortem appearances of carbon monoxide poisoning are distinctive. The blood, which often fails to clot, has a bright cherry-pink colour. It colours the organs and muscles so that the face usually has a high pink colour. Post mortem lividity – when the blood sinks by gravitation to the lowest parts of the body – is also bright pink. Similar colouring can occur in cyanide poisoning and in bodies exposed to cold conditions.

Diagnosis of carbon-monoxide poisoning therefore should not be made on the basis of colour alone but should be backed up with chemical and spectroscopic tests of the blood. The lungs are usually congested and often contain quantities of frothy fluid. Pin-point capillary haemorrhages (petechiae) are seen in the lungs, brain and conjunctiva of the eye.

Saturation Level

Kunkel's tannic acid test is used to detect the presence of carbon monoxide in blood. A few drops of 3 per cent tannic acid are added to a sample of blood that has been diluted 1 to 10. A precipitate forms which ranges in colour from pink to dark brown, according to the saturation level of carbon monoxide.

Confirmation of carbon-monoxide poisoning is made by a standard spectroscopic test. The various compounds of haemoglobin have a typical spectrum which can be identified on an instrument called a Hartridge reversion spectroscope.

Blood affected by carbon monoxide contains oxyhaemoglobin and caroxyhaemoglobin in varying amounts, and these show up as dark absorption bands in the spectrum formed when light is passed through a solution of blood and then a prism.

The spectrum is displayed on a scaled screen, and the various absorption bands are designated A, B, C, D, E, F and G, starting from the red end. Oxyhaemoglobin and carboxyhaemoglobin each have two absorption bands, D and E. The carboxyhaemoglobin bands lie a little closer to the violet end of the spectrum than those of oxyhaemoglobin. This difference or 'shift' may be measured on the spectroscope and the saturation of carbon monoxide in the blood calculated. Values of 60 per cent or more are taken as clear evidence of carbon-monoxide poisoning – 20 to 30 per cent is considered sufficient in elderly persons.

Carbon-monoxide poisoning falls into the usual three categories of accident, suicide and murder, the domestic gas supply commonly being the source of death for many accidents and suicides. Leaks from supply pipes and appliances such as hot-water geysers, radiators and gas fires allied to inadequate ventilation have accounted for many deaths.

Weariness and Lethargy

Special hazards trap the elderly who allow pots to boil over and put out the flame on a gas cooker which, unless reignited, fills the air with lethal fumes. Again, elderly persons, and sometimes drunks, turn on the gas and forget to light it. With an impaired sense of smell, or stupefied by alcohol, the gas is undetected and is allowed to pour out its deadly poison; the subtle nature of carbon monoxide produces weariness, and its victims sleep on till death.

Examples of carbon monoxide producing devices commonly in use around the home include:

- Fuel fired furnaces (non-electric)
- Gas water heaters
- Fireplaces and woodstoves
- Gas cookers
- Gas hot-air dryers
- Charcoal grills
- Lawnmowers and other garden equipment
- Automobiles

Reduction of ventilation caused by blockage of air pipes with birds' nests has been known to cause accidental poisoning from hot-water geysers in bathrooms. Deliberate but foolish blocking of ventilation to conserve warmth in rooms and caravans heated with gas fires or paraffin heaters can also be lethal.

Accidental poisoning occasionally results from car-exhaust fumes which build up in a garage with doors and windows shut. In these circumstances the air is made lethal by exhaust from the car inside five minutes. Car exhaust contains between 1 and 7 per cent carbon monoxide. The person intending to commit suicide usually sits in the car, having fixed a tube to the exhaust pipe to bring the poisonous fumes into the vehicles.

The classic suicide by gassing has unmistakable signs of preparation. The doors and windows of the room are sealed and a note is left. A feature of self-destruction by this method is that the victim first makes him/herself comfortable. Cushions and pillows are placed so that they may conveniently put their head in or near the oven of a gas cooker. Suicides prefer to die in bed, and connect a tube to the gas outlet which they lead under the bedclothes, thus forming a kind of gas chamber. Another method is to place a plastic bag, into which a gas tube is introduced, over the head.

Accident and Suicide

The distinction between accident and suicide is sometimes complicated by other considerations. Such proved to be the case with Major James Dunning, a 59-year-old retired American army officer living in London. Dunning, who had financial interests in the City, lived in fine style in a house in Chelsea. He also had a farm in Sussex.

The Major owned a 1913 Rolls-Royce of which he was very proud. One of his pleasures was to carry out his own mechanical repairs on the vehicle. On February 17, 1931, he sent the car to a specialist garage for some major repairs that would take several days to complete, and on February 23 he set out by train for a business appointment in Birmingham. The next day he sent his wife a telegram saying that he would collect the car on his way home to London. He did not return to Chelsea where his wife was expecting him.

But he did collect the car. He drove it down to his farm in Sussex, and on arrival there he told the maid that he had run into some mechanical trouble and would be staying overnight. After dinner he told the servants that he was going to work on the car. This was about 10.35 p.m.

The maid and cook went to bed about 11.15 p.m. They heard the car engine running in the garage beneath their bedroom, and they smelled the fumes. They thought the engine stopped at 11.45 p.m.

Early the following morning, Major Dunning was found dead on the floor of the garage beside his car. Tools were scattered about, and the circumstances suggested that the dead man had been working on the car when he was overcome by exhaust fumes. The ignition was switched on, but the engine had stopped. The garage doors and windows were firmly shut, but the chauffeur explained that this was the standard practice during cold weather, as the garage was draughty.

Post mortem examination showed that Major

Dunning died of carbon-monoxide poisoning. The blood contained a high level of the gas. A verdict of death by misadventure was brought in. It appeared that the dead man's life had been heavily insured – one policy had amounted to £10,000. This was an accident policy which excluded death resulting from suicide, and the company refused to admit liability.

The case eventually came before the courts. The insurance company contended that there were suspicious circumstances attending Major Dunning's death. Apparently his financial position was in some jeopardy as a result of income tax difficulties, and this was suggested to be sufficient cause for suicide.

Medical experts, on the other hand, supported the original verdict of accidental death. It was calculated that the Rolls-Royce would emit about two cubic feet of carbon monoxide every minute. Taking into consideration the cubic capacity of the garage at the Sussex farm and the fact that the doors and windows were closed, 30 minutes' running of the car engine would result in a 2 per cent level of carbon monoxide.

This was ample to cause death. The fact that the car engine seemed to have stopped of its own accord could be accounted for by the reduction of oxygen in the closed atmosphere of the garage. Arbitration was given in favour of Major Dunning's widow.

Covering Up

In the aftermath of killing, some murderers try to

cover their tracks by 'gassing' – they arrange the body to simulate suicide. Evidence of a struggle and of injuries on the victim usually give the game away to the skilled forensic examiner. Gassing has featured in a number of murder cases, but, except in rare incidents, it is usually the killing stroke after the victim has been overpowered by physical violence or stupefied with drugs or alcohol. Blood samples taken from persons found dead in suspicious circumstances are always routinely checked for both drugs and alcohol.

The so-called Murder Trust Case in New York in 1932 was one in which the victim was first stupefied before being gassed. Michael Malloy, having survived various attempts on his life by a gang who wanted to secure the money for which he was insured, finally succumbed to coal-gas poisoning. Having been generously plied with alcohol, he had a rubber gas pipe held in his mouth until he stopped breathing and died.

Gassing was also part of John Christie's murder technique. Carbon monoxide was found in the blood of three of his victims, a phenomenon for which Christie provided an explanation at his trial. After he had got the women partially drunk, he persuaded them to sit in a deckchair of the type that had a sun canopy over the head. He then made them fall unconscious with coal-gas drawn from the domestic supply and brought to the lethal deckchair by a rubber pipe. In Christie's case this was a prelude to strangulation and rape.

The Mysterious Death of Thelma Todd

Thelma Todd was a popular actress of the late 1920s and early 1930s. Born in Lawrence, Massachusetts in 1905, Todd was a schoolteacher and model before beginning her career in films. Appearing in over forty movies between 1926 and 1935, she is best remembered for her comedy roles in films like Marx Brothers movies, *Monkey Business* and *Horse Feathers.* In the 1930s, she opened a restaurant, *Thelma Todd's Sidewalk Cafe,* and took up residence in a luxurious apartment above the cafe. Located near the ocean on the Roosevelt Highway at Catellammare, it became a popular meeting and eating place. It was in the garage of the Sidewalk Cafe on December 15, 1935, that she was found in her parked car, dead of carbon monoxide poisoning. But was it suicide or murder?

The Grand Jury investigation into her death yielded conflicting results. Spots of blood were found both on and in the car, and on Todd's mouth. This led to the theory that she might have been knocked out, then placed in the car by persons unknown. In support of this theory was the additional fact that her blood alcohol level was .13; enough, it was stated, to 'stupefy' her. To further this theory, Todd would have had to ascend a steep flight of outdoor stairs after leaving the cafe to reach the garage, and the shoes she was wearing when her body was discovered were high-heeled sandals and were free of any dirt. Additionally, an unidentified, smudged handprint was found on the door of her car.

If it was murder, who might have had a motive, and was there any supporting evidence? Todd had been the victim of an extortion attempt, and had also just come through a rather acrimonious divorce that involved charges of abuse. Investigators ultimately decided that neither of these occurrences were related to her death, and no other motives or suspects were revealed during the investigation.

The suicide theory was supported by the testimony of several witnesses at the Grand Jury investigation, who stated that Todd had been subject to depression, and often spoke of ending it all. It was also revealed that she was in trouble with the IRS, and on the verge of bankruptcy.

In the end, the Grand Jury ruled her death a suicide. But doubts remained, and the mystery lingers: What really happened to Thelma Todd on that December morning in 1935?

Carbon Monoxide Found in Paul's Blood

There is still a lot of mystery surrounding the fatal crash shortly after midnight, on August 30-31, 1997, involving Diana Princess of Wales, her companion Dodi Fayed, and their driver Henri Paul. The assertion that Paul was drunk and high on two prescription drugs is an ongoing investigation, by the French government and the British establishment, to cast the crash as nothing more than a case of reckless, drunk driving. The claim that Paul had blood alcohol levels three times the legal limit at the time of the crash, was based solely on tests conducted by French coroners within hours of the crash. Independent forensic experts, including Dr Peter Vanesis of the University of Glasgow, who reviewed the autopsy report, had harsh criticisms of the post mortem on numerous technical grounds.

A television report revealed that the forensic tests also showed a near-lethal level of carbon monoxide as well. A separate toxicological test on Paul's blood sample revealed a carbon monoxide level of more than 30 per cent at the time of the crash.

Yet, Dodi Fayed had no carbon monoxide in his blood. Is it possible that Paul could have had high levels of alcohol, traces of two prescription drugs, and toxic levels of carbon monoxide in his blood at the moment of the crash, and yet Fayed had no carbon monoxide present? This would not be possible if the carbon monoxide was inside the passenger cabin of the Mercedes.

Furthermore, if Paul had been somehow poisoned with carbon monoxide sometime prior to getting behind the wheel of the Mercedes, experts interviewed later said he would have shown obvious signs, such as dizziness, loss of balance, loss of depth perception, and an unbearable, throbbing pain in his temple. Security camera video footage of Paul, taken in the lobby of the Ritz Hotel between 9 p.m. and midnight, clearly showed that Paul had none of the tell-tale signs of being drunk or suffering from the effects of carbon monoxide.

In a live television interview the documentary's

host, Nicholas Owen, stated that he believed that the blood sample used in the post mortem was probably not taken from Paul. There were a dozen other corpses in the Paris city morgue at the time that Paul was brought in. This startling conclusion by Owen, adds further weight that there has been a vicious cover-up of the events surrounding the crash.

The television documentary also cited several eyewitness accounts that a powerful burst of light inside the tunnel, seconds before the crash, may have blinded Paul. Owen showed a commercially produced anti-personnel laser, that he purchased in a Paris shop for $300, to buttress the possibility that such a device was used in the vehicular attack.

In a move that promises to raise even more questions about what happened in the Paris tunnel on that fateful night, Magistrate Stephan convened an extraordinary group interrogation, or 'confrontation,' on June 5 2001, at the Justice Ministry in Paris. Mohammed Al Fayed, Dodi's father and a civil party to the case, was invited to participate, as were a dozen eyewitnesses to the crash. The nine paparazzi who stood to be prosecuted for manslaughter and interference in the rescue effort, were also interrogated by Stephan.

Knife Wounds

Few names in history are as instantly recognizable as Jack the Ripper. Fewer still evoke such vivid images: noisome courts and alleys, hansom cabs and gaslights, swirling fog, prostitutes decked out in the tawdriest of finery, the shrill cry of newsboys. The silent, cruel death personified in the cape-shrouded figure of a faceless prowler of the night, armed with a long knife and carrying a black Gladstone bag.

IN EVERY CASE where a dead body is found to have knife wounds, one of the first questions asked is: 'Are the wounds suicidal or homicidal?' Injuries made with a knife fall into two basic classes – incised wounds or cuts and stab wounds. Because cuts are made with a sweeping movement they are usually found on unprotected parts of the body such as the hands and face. The injury most frequently requiring expert opinion – murderous attack or self-inflicted – is the throat wound.

In general, suicide throat-cutting has a clean and deliberate appearance, whereas the homicidal cut-throat is normally crude and suggests a death struggle. Since a suicide usually extends the head before making the cut, the line of the wound is frequently transverse. This stretching action causes the carotid arteries to slip back, thus escaping the knife and reducing the loss of blood.

A right-handed person cuts the throat from left to right. Considerable pressure on the knife at the beginning of the cut makes the wound deep at first but this becomes shallow as the knife is drawn across the throat and slopes slightly up towards the chin. In addition, there may be a few tentative shallow cuts on the throat – sizing up the stroke before making the lethal incision. As many as twelve of these tentative cuts have been noted on a suicide victim.

In a murderous wounding of the throat, the injury lacks the precision of the suicide. There may by several cuts from different directions, depending on the positions of the victim and assailant. The wild struggle of the victim and the desperation of the attacker combine to make gross wounds, and a key factor is the presence of defensive injuries on the victim. Protecting hands trying to force away the knife are usually heavily slashed across the palms or between the fingers. The classic 'ear-to-ear' cut severs the neck muscles, blood vessels and windpipe down to the spine. The wounding may be eight inches long with a gape of three inches.

Neville Heath inflicted such a wound on Doreen Marshall, whose body was found in some bushes at Branksome Dene Chine, Bournemouth, on July 8, 1946. The particular savagery of this killing was indicated by signs of a violent struggle. These included severe cuts on the victim's hands where she had attempted to fend off the knife.

Jack the Ripper

The Grand Master of the cut-throat murder was, of course, Jack the Ripper.

When Charles Cross walked through Whitechapel's Buck's Row just before four in the morning on Friday, August 31, 1888, it was dark and seemingly deserted. It was chilly and damp, not unusual for London even in the summer, especially before dawn. He saw something that looked like a tarpaulin lying on the ground before the entrance to a stable yard.

As he walked closer, he saw it was a woman lying on her back, her skirts lifted almost to her waist. He saw another man walking the same way. 'Come and look over here,' he asked the man, assuming that the woman was either drunk or the victim of an assault. As they tried to help her in the darkened street, neither of the two men saw the awful wounds that had nearly decapitated her. They fixed her skirt for modesty's sake and went to look for a policeman.

A few minutes later, Police Constable John Neil happened by the body while he was walking his beat. From the light of his lantern, he could see that blood was oozing from her throat which had been slashed from ear to ear. Her eyes were wide open and staring. Even though her hands and wrists were cold, Neil felt warmth in her arms. He called to another policeman who summoned a doctor and an ambulance.

Neil woke some of the residences in the respectable neighbourhood to find out if they had heard anything suspicious, but to no avail. Soon, Dr Rees Llewellyn arrived on the scene and examined the woman. The wounds to her throat had been fatal, he told them. Since parts of her body were still warm, the doctor felt that she had been dead no longer than a half-hour, perhaps minutes after Neil had completed his earlier walk around that area.

Her neck had been slashed twice, which had cut through her windpipe and oesophagus. She had been killed where she was found, even though there was very little blood on the ground. Most of the lost blood had soaked into her clothing. The body was taken to the mortuary on Old Montague Street, which was part of the workhouse there. While the body was being stripped, Inspector Spratling discovered that her abdomen had been wounded and mutilated. He called Dr Llewellyn back for a more detailed examination.

The doctor determined that the woman had been bruised on the lower left jaw. The abdomen exhibited a long, deep jagged knife wound, along with several other cuts from the same instrument running downward. The doctor guessed that a left-handed person could have inflicted these wounds very quickly with a long-bladed knife. Later, the doctor was not so sure about the killer being left-handed.

There have been several theories about how the wounds were inflicted. Philip Sugden makes a persuasive case:

If (the victim's) throat were cut while she

> was erect and alive, a strong jet of blood would have spurted from the wound and probably deluged the front of her clothing. But in fact there was no blood at all on her breast or the corresponding part of her clothes. Some of the flow from the throat formed a small pool on the pavement beneath her neck and the rest was absorbed by the backs of the dress bodice and ulster. The blood from the abdominal wound largely collected in the loose tissues. Such a pattern proves that her injuries were inflicted when she was lying on her back and suggests that she may have already been dead.

Identification would not be easy. All she had on her was a comb, broken mirror and a handkerchief. The Lambeth Workhouse mark was on her petticoats. There were no identifying marks on her other inexpensive and well-worn clothes. She had a black straw hat with black velvet trim.

The woman was approximately five feet two inches tall with brown greying hair, brown eyes and several missing front teeth. But later, as news of the murder spread around Whitechapel, the police learned of a woman named 'Polly', who lived in a lodging house at 18 Thrawl Street. Eventually a woman from the Lambeth Workhouse identified her as Mary Ann Nichols, age 42. The next day her father and her husband identified her body.

Polly had been the daughter of a locksmith and

married William Nichols, a printer's machinist. They had five children, but her drinking had caused their marriage to break up. For the most part, Polly had been living off her meagre earnings as a prostitute. She still had a very serious drinking problem. Every so often she would try to get her life back together, but it never worked out. She was a sad, destitute woman, but one that most people liked and pitied.

The inspector in charge of the investigation was a police veteran named Frederick George Abberline who had been on the force 25 years, most of which had been spent in the Whitechapel area.

The murderer of Polly Nichols left nothing behind in the way of witnesses, weapon or any other type of clue. None of the residents nearby heard any kind of disturbance nor did any of the workmen in the area notice anything unusual. Even though Polly had been found very shortly after her death, no vehicle or person was seen escaping the scene of the crime. At one point, suspicion focused upon three horse slaughterers who worked nearby, but it was proven that they were working while the murder occurred.

At the time of Polly Nichols's death, the inhabitants of London's Whitechapel area had already heard about a number of attacks on women in that neighbourhood. Whether or not one or more of these attacks was perpetrated by the man who later became known as Jack the Ripper is controversial. However, in the minds of the people of Whitechapel, most of these crimes were linked indisputably.

Identifying Wounds

In some cases of cut-throat wounds the injured person does not fall at the place where the wound was inflicted, but collapses at some distance from it. Sir Bernard Spilsbury, the eminent pathologist, recorded an example of a suicide who not only replaced the knife in his jacket pocket but walked nearly a hundred yards before collapsing and dying.

Apart from observing that a sharp cutting knife has been used, there is not much that the forensic expert can deduce about the nature of a weapon used to cut a throat. His main objective is to note the direction and dimensions of the wound and to examine the victim's hands for blood stains, defensive injuries, hairs and pieces of torn clothing.

Stab wounds are characterized by their penetration into the body. Their points of entry are usually fairly small slits which look relatively trivial, and frequently there is little external bleeding. For these reasons the seriousness of such wounds can be underestimated. In reality a single entry wound may be of great penetration causing internal haemorrhage and death.

The weapon used in stabbing is most commonly the knife but stab wounds are caused by all manner of pointed instruments including bayonets, scissors and even hat-pins; unlike cut-throats, examination of stab wounds can give an indication of the weapon used. Most stab entries are elliptical but the ends of the wound may suggest whether the knife was single- or double-edged.

Main points of comparison between suicidal and homicidal cut-throats

SUICIDAL

Incised and careful

Hands injured
(suicidal slashes may be present)

Tentative cuts

Cut slopes upwards

HOMICIDAL

Slashed and gross

Severe defensive cuts on hands

No tentative cuts

Cut slopes downwards

STAB ENTRY WOUNDS

Double-edged knife:
wound is sharp at both ends

Single-edged knife:
wound is rounded at one end,
sharp at the other

In a case of multiple stabbing it is likely that some of the entries will be torn as the victim struggles under the assault or as the knife is twisted in the body. The least torn wound will be the best indicator of the type of weapon used, and because the knife may not have penetrated to its hilt, the deepest wound will only indicate the minimum length of the blade.

Suicide or Homicide

The length of the entry wound is a guide to the width of the knife but it is only an approximation, for allowance has to be made for the elasticity of the skin under the impact of the knife thrust. Roughening or bruising around the edge of the entry would indicate that a blunt instrument such as a poker or a pair of closed scissors was used. The sharper the weapon, the cleaner the wound will be.

Like cut throats, stab wounds may be either suicidal or homicidal, although self-inflicted stabbing is thought to be less common than throat cutting. Homicidal stabbing, on the other hand, is frequently encountered by the forensic expert, and such wounds are usually found in the neck, chest, abdomen and back. The chest is the area usually selected for murderous use of the knife, presumably because it contains the heart. Penetrating wounds of the chest frequently pierce the heart or large blood vessels and lead to serious internal bleeding. Loss of blood varies widely but the effusion of as much as two or three pints in the chest cavity has been known. Wounds in the neck often damage the carotid and jugular blood vessels.

The distinction between suicide and homicide is fairly easy in the case of stab wounds. Persons bent on suicide select a 'target area' – usually the region of the heart. Because suicides are deliberate, the 'target area' is often narrowed even further to the epigastric region. It is here that the average person feels the heart beat most strongly and the area is also free of obstacles such as ribs. The clothing is sometimes lifted in order to make the knife thrust easier, and the wound is usually a single or, at the most, it may be a double thrust with no tentative or trial efforts.

Wounds outside the general target area of the heart are regarded with suspicion, especially if they have been made through the clothing. The suicidal wound naturally must be in an accessible part of the body – the stab in the back obviously being homicidal. A further distinguishing feature is the likelihood of finding defensive wounds on the hands of the victim of a murderous attack.

The angle of a knife wound in the body is also important in helping to establish whether or not a stabbing has been self-inflicted. Expert examination of this aspect of knife wounds enabled Sir Bernard Spilsbury to advise the police about the death of Patrick Swift at Stockton-on-Tees. Swift was found dead in the kitchen of his house – the fatal wound was a single knife thrust. His wife told the police that he had stabbed himself following a drunken quarrel.

There were no witnesses, and although the police suspected Mrs Swift they could not disprove her story – not, at least, without Spilsbury's help. The pathologist demonstrated that the single downward thrust of the knife in the chest which killed Patrick Swift could not have been self-inflicted, for Swift was right-handed and the angle of the wound was such that he could not have stabbed himself with that hand, nor was it possible for him to have used his left hand to produce the fatal thrust. Therefore, it was a case of murder and not suicide.

Dismembering

The knife is not only an instrument of death. Its use in a number of celebrated dismembering cases testifies to other needs. John White Webster, a 57-year-old professor at Massachusetts Medical College, was certainly adept with the knife. The first count of his indictment for the murder of Dr George Parkman read that he '. . . feloniously, wilfully and of his malice aforethought did strike, cut and stab . . . giving . . . one mortal wound . . . of the depth of three inches'. This was Webster's way of settling his inability to repay money owed to his elderly colleague. But, having killed Dr Parkman, he was faced with the problem of disposing of the body. With a doctor's skill he dismembered the body and put it in the cellar beneath his laboratory. Webster was subsequently sentenced to death, and hanged in August 1850.

A famous case involving dismembered bodies was that of Fred and Rosemary West. 1973 was a year for the Wests to celebrate. They walked away from Caroline Owens's rape and abduction charge with only a fine and they murdered Lynda Gough with no police repercussions at all. Then in August, their first son, Stephen, was born.

Emboldened by their success, they abducted fifteen-year-old Carol Ann Cooper in November and amused themselves with her sexually – that is, until she outlived her entertainment value and was killed by strangulation or suffocation, dismembered and buried. She joined the growing city of the dead at 25 Cromwell Street.

Industrious Fred, persistent in his home improvements, had enlarged the cellar and was demolishing the garage to build an extension to the main house. No matter that these improvements were done at very strange hours.

A little over a month later, university student Lucy Partington had gone home to her mother's house to spend the Christmas holiday. On December 27, she went to visit her disabled friend and left to catch a bus shortly after 10 p.m. She had the misfortune to meet up with Fred and Rose, who probably knocked her out and abducted her. Like Carol Ann Cooper, she was tortured for approximately a week and then murdered, dismembered and buried in Fred's construction projects. He cut himself while dismembering Lucy and had to go to the hospital for stitches on January 3, 1974.

Lucy, like Carol Ann Cooper, was reported missing, but there was nothing to tie the two girls to the Wests.

Between April of 1974 and April of 1975, three young women – Therese Siegenthaler, 21, Shirley Hubbard, 15, and Juanita Mott, 18, met the same fate as Carol Ann Cooper and Lucy Partington. Their tortured and dismembered bodies were buried under the cellar floor of the Wests's house.

Incredibly enough even with all the bodies in his cellar, Fred continued to attract the police with continuous thefts and fencing stolen goods. It was necessary for Fred to keep stealing to pay for his home improvement projects. His home improvement projects were necessary to keep the monstrous habits of his wife and himself covered up with layers of concrete.

In 1977, the upstairs of the house had been remodelled to allow for a number of lodgers. One of them was Shirley Robinson, 18, a former prostitute with bisexual inclinations. Shirley developed relationships with both Fred and Rose. Shirley became pregnant with Fred's child after Rose was pregnant with the child of one of her black clients.

While Fred was pleased that Rose was carrying a mixed child, Rose was not comfortable with Shirley carrying Fred's child. Shirley foolishly thought that she could displace Rose in Fred's life and, in the process, jeopardized her own existence. Rose made it clear that Shirley had to go.

And go she did, seven months after Rose gave birth to Tara in December of 1977, Shirley joined the rest of the girls buried in Cromwell Street. The cellar being full, Shirley was put in the rear garden along with her unborn child. This time, Fred dismembered Shirley and their unborn baby.

In November of 1978, Rose and Fred had yet another daughter who they named Louise, making a total of six children in the bizarre and unwholesome household.

In May of 1979, Rose's father died of a lung ailment. Several months later, the Wests were up to their old tricks and murdered a troubled teenager named Alison Chambers after they raped and tortured her. Like Shirley, Alison was buried in the 'overflow' cemetery in the rear garden.

The Wests' children were aware of some of the goings-on in the home. They knew that Rose was a prostitute and that Anna Marie was being raped by her father. When Anna Marie moved out to live with her boyfriend, Fred focused his sexual advances on Heather and Mae. Heather resisted her father and was beaten for it.

In June of 1980, Rose gave birth to Barry, Fred's second son. Then again, in April of 1982, Rose gave birth to Rosemary Junior, who was not Fred's child. In July of 1983, Rose gave birth to another daughter who they named Lucyanna. She was half-black, like Tara and Rosemary Junior. Rose became increasingly irrational and beat the children without provocation. The stress of so many children in the household took its toll on Rose's already bad temper.

The Wests probably continued to carry on their sexual abductions, but did not bury any of these new victims at 25 Cromwell Street.

In 1986, the wall of filial silence that had protected the Wests was broken. Heather told her girlfriend about her father's advances, her mother's affairs and the beatings she received. The girlfriend told her parents, who were friends of the Wests, and Heather's life was in jeopardy.

After her parents murdered her, they told the children that she left home. Fred asked his son Stephen to help him dig a hole in the rear garden, where Fred buried Heather's dismembered body.

Rose built up her prostitution business by advertising in special magazines. She and Fred were on the lookout for women who they could get to participate in their various perversions as well as to prostitute themselves under Rose's direction. One such woman, Katherine Halliday, became a fixture in the West household and saw first hand the black bondage suits and masks that they had collected, plus the whips and chains. With good reason, Katherine became alarmed and quickly broke off her relationship with them.

As time went on, Fred and Rosemary became increasingly concerned about creating a minimum façade of respectability, not because they cared what people thought of them, but because they were concerned that knowledge of what had gone on in their house would jeopardize their freedom.

The Wests' long run of luck was coming to an end. One of the very young girls that Fred had raped with Rose's assistance told her girlfriend what happened. The girlfriend went to the police and the case was assigned to a very talented and persistent Detective Constable named Hazel Savage. Hazel knew Fred from the days when he was involved with a pretty 16-year-old named Catherine Bernadette Costello, or 'Rena'. Rena had been in trouble with the police since early childhood, and by the time she met Fred she was an accomplished and experienced thief. They became lovers almost immediately, but the affair ended when she went back home a few months later to Scotland. Hazel remembered the stories that Rena had told her about Fred's sexual perversions.

On August 6, 1992, police arrived at 25 Cromwell Street with a search warrant to look for pornography and evidence of child abuse. They found mountains of pornography and arrested Rose for assisting in the rape of a minor. Fred was arrested for rape and sodomy of a minor.

The younger children were taken from Rose and put into government care. With Fred in jail and the police closing in on her, Rose took an overdose of pills and attempted suicide. Her son Stephen found her and saved her life. Later, she escaped from her loneliness by stuffing herself with candy and watching Disney videos.

Fred didn't do much better in prison. He was very depressed and sorry for himself. Actually, his luck was holding – for the time being. The case against the Wests collapsed when two key witnesses decided not to testify against them. But the seeds of their discovery had been sown

Finally a warrant to search the Cromwell Street house and garden was signed. Fred finally confessed to killing his daughter after human bones, other than Heather's, were found in the garden. When Rose was informed of Fred's confession, she claimed that Fred had sent her out of the house the day Heather disappeared and had no knowledge of Heather's death. As Fred chatted about his murders, the police tried to grapple with the evidence. Lining up bodies with names was not an easy task. Nine sets of bones were discovered in the cellar and the police did not know whose they were. Fred was not much help since he could not remember the names and details of some of the women he had picked up. Considering the many women who go missing every year, extensive work had to be done to match up 'missing person' reports with the remains. As the case developed, Rose abandoned Fred to save herself. She tried to position herself as the victim of a murderous man, but she was not particularly convincing. Police worked continuously to tie her in to the crimes. At their joint hearing, Fred attempted to console Rose, but she avoided his touch. She told the police he made her sick. The great partnership in crime was over.

Disposal of the Body

As dead bodies are difficult to transport, many murderers have sought to ease the problem by cutting them into smaller parts – five or six pieces being the general rule. The fragments may then be disposed of by burning, burying, treating with chemicals, or by a variety of other means. In 1949, Donald Hume, for example, stabbed Stanley Setty to death in London with a German SS dagger. Then he cut the body up and made it into three parcels which he dropped into the English Channel from an aircraft.

Dismembering a corpse is not an easy task and the results usually reflect the skill or otherwise of the perpetrator. Cartilage and bone are remarkably tough but yield easily to disarticulation with a sharp knife in the right hands. The unskilled and unknowing merely hack with brute force and desperation.

Charles Avinmain in Paris in 1867 deposited portions of his dismembered murder victims in the River Seine. Some of these were washed up and their most notable feature was that the severing cuts were clean and even. A surgeon advising the police suggested that the murderer was probably a man who had worked in a hospital and either watched or assisted with surgical operations. Avinmain had indeed worked in a hospital and had attended many post-mortems. When arrested he told the police, 'I do not wish it to be said that I dismembered my victims . . . I dissected them in a decent and proper manner. I am not a bungler.'

The same could be said of Patrick Mahon, whose spectacular fragmentation of his victim horrified England in 1924. Mahon, a 33-year-old salesman, was in the habit of leaving his wife at weekends. He failed to give very convincing reasons for these absences so Mrs Mahon decided to find out for herself.

Her first thought was to search through her husband's clothes. She turned up a railway left luggage ticket in the pocket of a suit, issued at Waterloo Station. She asked a friend to find out what had been deposited, and he exchanged the ticket for a Gladstone bag. Though locked, the bag was prised open sufficiently to reveal some bloodstained clothes and a knife, and the discovery was immediately reported to Scotland Yard.

Mahon was quickly apprehended. He said the bag had been used for carrying dog meat. The fact that the blood on the clothing in the bag was shown to be human left him with a good deal to explain. A tennis holdall with the initials E.B.K. was also found in the Gladstone bag. Mahon admitted that the initials stood for Emily Beilby Kaye, a young woman who was his mistress, and a sinister story began.

Mahon mentioned an old coastguard house on a lonely stretch of beach at the Crumbles, on the Sussex coast near Eastbourne. He had taken Emily Kaye there for the weekend on April 12. A quarrel had taken place and a struggle ensued during which he claimed that Emily fell and hit her head on the coal scuttle, fatally injuring herself.

Detective officers accompanied by Sir Bernard Spilsbury visited the house, and even the great pathologist was appalled by what he found there. Pieces of flesh and organs, many of which had been boiled, were discovered in a variety of containers – a hat box, a fibre trunk and a biscuit tin. A carpet was sodden with blood and blood-stained female clothing was strewn about. In the fireplace and elsewhere were ashes containing human bone splinters. In the kitchen there were saucepans and other receptacles containing unmistakable evidence of having been used for boiling human flesh. A rusty saw with bits of flesh on it also told its story.

The pathologist collected together the hundreds of human fragments and returned with them to St Bartholomews Hospital, London. In the post-mortem preparation room he began a painstaking reconstruction of the body to which they had once belonged. It was a feat of brilliance. He identified all the pieces as human and corresponding to a single adult female body. The head was never found. From bruises on a portion of one shoulder Spilsbury was able to show that a heavy blow had been struck before death.

'One of the Foulest Crimes'

He could not say exactly how Emily Kaye had died but knew enough to smash Mahon's lies. The cook's knife and saw were said by Mahon to have been bought after Emily Kaye was dead, but the proprietor of a Sussex ironmongery shop produced receipts showing that they had been bought on April 12 – the day Mahon travelled down to the bungalow. Mahon denied using the cook's knife to dismember the body, saying that instead he used an ordinary carving knife from the bungalow's kitchen. But Spilsbury unmasked this pretence, for the carving knife was not keen enough to cut through skin. The cook's knife, however, was designed to cut raw flesh.

Patrick Mahon was found guilty and hanged without lamentation on September 9, 1924. Spilsbury's remarkable care and skill in this case won wide admiration. The Direction of Public Prosecutions referred to Mahon's killing of Emily Kaye and subsequent dismemberment of the body as '. . . one of the foulest crimes'.

Gunshots

A criminal detective examining a fatal gunshot wound on a dead body may be able to determine from the entrance wound the type of weapon used and the range from which it was fired – the exit wound may indicate the direction of the shot.

FORENSIC BALLISTICS is the study of guns and ammunition. It is a highly developed subject falling within the province of the firearms expert, though examination of gunshot wounds is part of the forensic pathologist's work. The starting point for an understanding of gunshot wounds is the weapons that cause them. Firearms in crimes of violence can be divided into smooth-bore weapons and rifled weapons.

The smooth-bore class of weapon is characterized by the shot gun, the inside of the gun barrel being smooth throughout. Guns of this type are designed for sporting purposes and they fire a mass of tiny lead pellets or shot, accurate to a range of about 50 years. Smooth-bore guns have one or two long barrels which take hand-loaded cartridges, and the empty cases are retained in the gun after the shot has been fired.

The calibre of shot guns is usually expressed as the 'bore' – the term '12-bore' is well known. This is the traditional method of expressing calibre and refers to the number of lead pellets exactly fitting the barrel which can be made from a pound of lead. It is common nowadays to give the calibre of all types of gun as the inside diameter of the barrel expressed either in decimals of an inch or in metric units. Hence the 12-bore shot gun has a calibre of 0.729 inch.

Shot-gun cartridges consist of a cardboard cylinder with a rimmed brass base. In the centre of the base is a priming charge or detonator. At the top of the cartridge is a quantity of lead shot held in place with discs of cardboard. Separating the shot from the explosive powder at the bottom of the cartridge is a thick cardboard disc called the wad which drives the shot before it and out of the gun's barrel when the weapon is fired. The principle of the firing action is the same for most guns. When the trigger is pulled a hammer snaps down on the detonator at the base of the cartridge; this in turn ignites the main explosive charge and expels the shot or bullet.

The shot leaves the gun as a solid mass at a velocity of around 1,100 feet (335 metres) per second. Up to about 3 feet (0.914 metres) the effect is of a single shot, but beyond that the lead pellets spread out and the effect is projected for several feet before falling to the ground. The end of the barrel is often restricted or 'choked', in order to hold the shot together over longer distances.

Rifled weapons are distinguished by a spiral grooving, or 'rifling', on the inside of the barrel. This spins the bullet, making it more stable in flight and giving greater accuracy. Rifled weapons may be either long-barrelled rifles (2 to 3 feet/

0.611 to 0.914 metres), or short-barrelled pistols (1 to 12 inches/2.540 to 30.5 cm). The long barrel of the rifle makes it accurate for ranges up to 3,000 yards (2,743 metres) and the weapon has a high muzzle velocity of 1,000 to 4,000 feet (304.800 to 1,219.600 metres) per second. Pistols with their short barrels and low muzzle velocity (600 to 1,000 feet/182.880 to 304.800 metres per second) are intended for shooting at close range and bullets carry only 400 to 600 yards (365.80 to 548.50 metres).

Pistols form two classes – revolvers and automatics. The revolver is the classic six-shooter of cowboy fame. It has a revolving chamber which brings each cartridge into position after the previous one has been fired. Spent cartridge cases remain in the chamber and usually have to be removed by hand. Revolver chambers commonly hold five or six rounds of ammunition. The automatic is a self-loading pistol with ammunition stored in a magazine, usually in the butt. Each round is fed into the barrel by a spring mechanism and spent cartridges are ejected automatically from the weapon.

The calibre of rifled weapons is expressed as the internal diameter of the barrel in either inches or millimetres, the measurement being taken between the raised parts of the rifling are known as 'lands', and not between the grooves.

Ammunition for rifled weapons consists of a brass cartridge case filled with explosive powder and a solid metal bullet at its tip. Bullets are made of hardened lead or a lead core covered with cupro-nickel coated steel. The bullet is held in the end of the cartridge case by a grooved indentation known as a cannelure. The base of the cartridge has a detonator at its centre which ignites the explosive powder when the weapon is fired. All rifled weapon ammunition, except that for automatic pistols, has a rimmed base which retains the spent case in the firing chamber after the bullet has been fired. Spent rounds are then ejected manually. Automatic weapon ammunition is tapered at the base with a groove for the automatic ejector.

Bullets fired from rifled weapons spin at 2,000 to 3,000 revolutions a second, but over the first few yards of trajectory – distance varies with the weapon – their flight is slightly unstable. The end of the projectile wobbles before it picks up a smooth flight path. This phenomenon is known as 'tailwag' and is of considerable importance in evaluating gunshot wounds. A bullet with 'tailwag' does not strike its target cleanly.

There are three basic kinds of gunshot wounds distinguished by the proximity of the weapon causing them:

1. Contact (gun muzzle pressed against, or within an inch or two of the body)
2. Close discharge (6 in/15.240 m to 2 ft/0.611 m)
3. Distant discharge (over 2 to 3 ft/0.611 to 0.914 m).

Wounds are always considered from two points of view – the point of entry of the bullet and its exit. The entrance wound in particular may have special features which will assist the crime investigator in determining the range and type of weapon used. The exit wound examined in relation to the point of entry will also help to decide the direction of a shot. Differentiation between entry and exit wounds is essential in judging between suicide and homicide.

Unlike bullet wounds inflicted by a rifled weapon, a shot gun discharge rarely produces an exit wound in the trunk of the body. Shot has little penetrating power and is easily arrested by tough tissue, especially bone, but contact wounds in the head or mouth, such as those met within the suicidal use of a shot gun, result in massive destruction.

Where a shot gun is discharged in contact with the body (or within a few inches) the shot does not scatter but enters as a solid mass. The hot gases and flame emitted from the gun's muzzle will tear the tissues and there will be evidence of burning on the skin. Powder particles are likely to be forced into the skin giving rise to a tattoo effect. The wad may also be forced into the wound and if this is the case, it's extraction may prove a useful guide to the type of cartridge used. A contact wound in the trunk will make a round hole with a narrow rim of soot blackening. Bruising near the wound is often caused by the recoil of the gun.

At close range, from 1 to 3 feet (0.305 to 0.914 metres), a more or less irregular wound of about 2 in (5.108 cm) in diameter will be produced. There will be evidence of scorching and tattooing, also singeing of hair by flame, unless the weapon was fired through the clothing. Beyond a range of 3 feet (0.914 metres), the shot begins to spread out and at 4 feet (1.219 metres) the wound will appear as a central hole with small perforations around it. There will be no powder deposits visible to the naked eye although a swab taken from around the wound may reveal traces. The wad is often found in such a wound.

At ranges of over 4 feet (1.219 metres) the shot continues to spread out and produces a mass of small perforations with no central wound. An approximation of the range can be obtained by measuring in inches (metres) the diameter of the wound (including the outermost perforations), subtracting one, thus arriving at the range in yards. Of course the exact range depends on the choke of the weapon and only test firing can give an accurate answer.

Bullet wounds are produced by projectiles fired from a rifled weapon and are the same for revolver and automatic. Entry wounds are generally clean, round holes slightly smaller than the bullets which caused them. As the bullet travels through the body it produces a shock wave which damages the tissues around its path. This is known as 'tissue quake'. The bullet will be slowed by its passage through the body and its exit will leave an irregular hole. If the bullet exits nose-on, the wound will be smaller than the entry, but if it leaves the body at an irregular angle, or takes pieces of bone with it, the exit wound will be ragged. Should the bullet meet a bone and be deflected inside the body, its change of direction may cause considerable internal damage, and the bullet may even fragment, again causing severe injury.

Contact wounding with the muzzle pressed against the skin will produce not a round entry but a star-shaped hole with lacerated edges. If there is underlying bone – the skull for example – gases produced by the explosion of the cartridge may enter with the bullet and be forced back through the skin causing laceration. The tissue at the margin of the wound may contain soot and powder particles and show a degree of burning, and the skin will be tattooed. At close range, exit wounds are generally smaller than entries, but this is reversed at increased range.

At close range, between 6 inches (15.240 cm) and 2 feet (0.611 m), a different effect is noted. The wound is more or less circular and corresponds to the size of the bullet. Discharge gases do not enter the wound and tattooing may be absent. Injuries of this kind have been confused with penetrating stab wounds. If the bullet was 'tail-wagging', the entry would not be as clean as for a nose-on hit.

Guns fired at ranges over 2 feet (0.611 m) are too distant to leave traces of the explosion at the wound site. The entry will conform to the size of the bullet, appearing as a round hole with an abraded margin. The edge of the wound will also exhibit a ring of grease wiped from the spinning surface of the bullet as it enters the body. The exit wound at distant ranges will be the same as the entry, and in some cases the only point of differentiation will be the grease or 'soiling' ring around the entry wound. If the bullet has been deflected in the body the point of exit may be lacerated, and may be misinterpreted as being caused by a blunt instrument.

The characteristics of entry remain virtually the same at distances over 2 feet (0.611 m), and it is therefore not possible to tell at what range a distant shot was fired. Evidence of direction may be obtained where a bullet has passed through bone, as the exit side is bevelled as a result of the destructive force of the impact.

Advances in Ballistics

The development of high-speed photography and of the 'stroboscope', by the American engineer Harold Eugene Edgerton and others, has led to greater understanding in all branches of ballistics. By means of such devices any projectile can be photographed in flight, thus permitting accurate studies, not only of its velocity but also of its position (to determine the degree of wobble) and even of the shock waves it produces.

The most important recent development in ballistics is the use of computers. The calculations of exterior ballistics generally involves sets of different equations. Solving such a set of equations typically involves hundreds of thousands of computations. To find the position of the projectile at various points along the trajectory, dozens of such solutions are required. For example, for each of the various elevations of the gun, the entire process must be repeated. Even with the aid of slide rules and ordinary calculating machines, such an operation would take a mathematician an inordinate amount of time. Electronic computers compile complete solutions within a few seconds.

Technology That Solves Firearm Crime

Integrated Ballistics Identification System (IBIS) is the advanced tool law enforcement needs to help with the problems of increased workloads, shortages of firearm examiners and shrinking budgets. Using the power of leading-edge technology, IBIS assists the firearm examiner in comparing the mounting volume of firearm evidence.

IBIS digitally captures the images of bullets and cartridge cases, stores them in a database, performs automatic computer-based comparisons of the images and ranks them according to the likelihood of a match. The firearm examiners are then able to employ their specialized skills in performing microscopic comparisons of high-confidence candidates.

IBIS's major contribution to crime solving is its unprecedented ability to automatically search a database for potential matches from thousands of previously entered pieces of evidence. This analysis can be done locally, nationally, or internationally, opening up tremendous possibilities to link previously unlinkable crimes. IBIS brings firearms identification into the computer age.

JFK Assassination

Ballistic analysis played a major role in one of the world's most baffling assassinations, that of John F. Kennedy. By comparing the markings on the three largest fragments of bullets found in the limousine and at Parkland Hospital with various other rifles, FBI investigators were able to determine that they had all been fired from Oswald's rifle. Similar results were found for the three cartridge cases found on the sixth floor of the Texas School Book Depository.

The physicians who examined the bullet wounds to Kennedy tried to categorize them as entrance or exit wounds from their properties. They got most of them right. The team at Parkland, however, misidentified the tiny hole in the throat as an entrance wound. They were right that it looked like an entrance wound, although it was really the exit wound from the body shot that entered Kennedy's upper back/lower neck region. The Parkland personnel were handicapped because (a) they did not know of the back wound, and (b) they soon destroyed the wound by using it as a starting point for their tracheotomy.

The motions of Kennedy's head and body after the fatal bullet hit his head are recorded on film. When analyzed carefully in terms of conservation of momentum and energy, the number of bullets hitting his head and their general direction of origin can be determined nearly conclusively. The JFK assassination controversy is huge and is now into its fourth decade.

Strangulation

In India, a cult of silent assassins, the Thuggee, has for centuries practised the ancient and highly secret art of strangulation.

THE VERY WORD 'strangler' has a brutal ring to it. It conveys the idea of physical violence, and in fact most stranglers have been violent and brutal men. The act of strangling suggests a deliberate savagery. A man who kills with a gun wants to get it over with as quickly as possible, whereas the strangler seems to take pleasure in close contact with his victim.

The Boston Strangler

Between June 14, 1962 and January 4, 1964, thirteen single women in the Boston area were victims of either a single serial killer or possibly several killers. At least eleven of these murders were popularly known as the victims of the 'Boston Strangler'. While the police did not see all of these murders as the work of a single individual, the public did. All of these women were murdered in their apartments, had been sexually molested, and were strangled with articles of clothing. With no signs of forced entry, the women apparently knew their assailant or, at least, voluntarily let him into their homes. These were respectable women who for the most part led quiet, modest lives.

Even though nobody has ever officially been on trial as the Boston Strangler, the public believed that Albert DeSalvo, who confessed in detail to each of the eleven 'official' Strangler murders, as well as two others, was the murderer. However, at the time that DeSalvo confessed, most people who knew him personally did not believe him capable of the vicious crimes and today there is a persuasive case to be made that DeSalvo wasn't the killer after all.

Death of Isadora Duncan

Isadora Duncan, one of the world's most famous dancers, died on September 14, 1927 by accidental strangulation caused by a vehicle. Sitting on the front passenger's seat, Duncan's scarf became tangled in the spokes of the rear wheel of a Bugatti. The driver, Duncan's friend Ivan Falchetto, could not see Duncan while looking forward but immediately stopped after 20 metres. Duncan died at the scene. In the hospital, fractures of the nose, the spinal column and the larynx were observed; furthermore, carotids were torn.

The Hillside Stranglers

Murder is a common occurrence in a city the size of Los Angeles, but when three women were found strangled and dumped naked on hillsides northeast of the city between October and early November of 1977, a couple of sharp homicide detectives got nervous that this was just the start.

Everything changed in Thanksgiving week when five more young women and girls were found on hillsides in the Glendale-Highland Park area. These five young women – one of whom was twelve, another only fourteen – were not prostitutes, but 'nice girls' who had been abducted from their middle-class neighbourhoods.

Until Thanksgiving week, only Frank Salerno of the LA Sheriff's Department had known that a serial killer was at work. After Thanksgiving week, it was the top priority for the entire law enforcement community of Los Angeles. Eight victims in the space of two months. The investigation went into high gear, but the killer or killers took a couple of weeks off.

Unfortunately, nothing much came from their leads and the police did not make any immediate arrests. Things became quiet for a while – there were no more victims in December or January. Then in mid-February, there was another victim. On Thursday, February 16, an attractive young woman named Cindy Hudspeth was murdered. Her strangled, violated body was put into the trunk of her Datsun and was pushed off a cliff on Angeles Crest.

The next day when the police investigated, it was clear from the ligature marks that the Hillside Strangler was at work once again. Police focused on the details of Cindy's life in the hopes that they could determine who was with her when she disappeared.

It was a known fact that relationships between the LAPD and the LA Sheriff's Department had been notoriously bad for many years. However, in this particular case, the two key investigators – Frank Salerno of the Sheriff's department and Bob Grogan of LAPD – worked well together and made a point of ensuring that information was shared between both large law enforcement organizations. But still the investigation was going nowhere. The few clues they had produced no good suspects. One unusual twist to the investigation was the arrival in LA of a psychic from Berlin. Grogan was polite, but unenthusiastic when the psychic wrote in German what they should be looking for:

Two Italians
Brothers
Aged about thirty-five

Months passed and the Hillside Strangler seemed to have retired. The activities of the task force wound down and detectives began to work on other cases.

On January 12, 1979, the police in Bellingham, Washington were told that two Western Washington University students were missing. The two women roommates, Karen Mandic and Diane Wilder, were not the type of people to take off irresponsibly without telling anyone. When Karen didn't show up for work, her boss became worried. He remembered that she had accepted a house-sitting job in a very wealthy Bayside neighbourhood from a security guard friend of hers.

Bellingham police contacted the security firm,

who in turn called the security guard to ask him about the supposed house-sitting job for one of the company's clients. The security guard claimed he knew nothing about it and had never heard of the two missing women. The security guard told his employer that he had been at a Sheriff's Reserve meeting the night the two women disappeared.

When police found out that the security guard was not at the Sheriff's Reserve meeting as he had told his employer, they decided to contact the security guard directly. They found him to be a friendly young man who had skipped the Sheriff's meeting because it was on first aid, which he already knew.

The police had no indication that the two women had met with foul play. It was very possible that they had just gone away for the weekend and had forgotten to tell Karen's employer. However, Terry Mangan, the former priest who was the new Bellingham police chief, was not comfortable with that explanation. When he visited the girls' home, he found a hungry cat – an unusual situation for an otherwise very pampered pet. In their home, he found the address of the Bayside home where the two of them were to house-sit. A close look at the records of the security firm brought up the name of that same security guard in conjunction with the address in which the girls were to house-sit.

Also, police learned that the security guard had used a company truck the night the women disappeared, supposedly taking it into the shop for repair. However, the guard never took the truck in for servicing. Chief Mangan was becoming increasingly concerned about the safety of the two missing women. He asked the Highway Patrol to check on sites that might be used to dump bodies or abandon cars.

The next step was for the police to search the Bayside address where the girls were supposed to house-sit. They found a wet footprint in the kitchen that had been left a few hours earlier, but there was no sign of the girls or Karen Mandic's car. Police found a neighbour who had been contacted by a security guard and asked to check on the house each day except for the night that the girls disappeared. That night, the guard told her, there was special work being done to the alarm system and he didn't want her to be taken as an intruder.

Next, Chief Mangan enlisted the help of the news media, requesting that they describe the missing women and car to their audiences. Shortly thereafter, a woman called about a car that had been abandoned near her home in a heavily wooded area. Inside the car were the bodies of Karen Mandic and Diane Wilder. Both had been strangled. Other bruises suggested that they had been subjected to other injuries as well.

While the missing women were sent to the morgue, Chief Mangan ordered that the security guard be picked up for questioning. They needed to proceed cautiously since this suspect was a trained security officer. As it turned out, the security guard gave them no trouble whatsoever when they picked him up. He was a handsome, friendly, intelligent and articulate husband and father by the name of Kenneth Bianchi.

The Bellingham police mounted a first class investigation of all the forensic evidence. Meanwhile, the police wanted to keep Kenny under lock and key. This was made easier when they found stolen goods in his home – items stolen from job sites he had been managing. Chief Mangan remembered the Hillside Strangler case in Los Angeles. Since Kenny had lived in LA before he had come to Bellingham, Mangan had calls placed to the police in LA and Glendale and to the LA Sheriff's Office.

Detective Frank Salerno responded to the Bellingham police call. Suddenly everything made sense to Salerno. The addresses of Cindy Hudspeth and Kristina Weckler on East Garfield and the client Kimberly Martin visited on Tamarind matched Kenny's places of residence during the times of the murders. He lost no time getting to Bellingham to assist the police there in the investigation. He left his partner, Peter Finnigan, to work with Grogan and others on uncovering Bianchi's activities when he lived in LA

Piece by piece, the evidence mounted that Kenny Bianchi was at least one of the Hillside Stranglers. The jewellery that was found in Bianchi's home matched the description of jewellery that was worn by two of the victims: Kimberly Martin's ramshorn necklace and Yolanda Washington's turquoise ring. And hair and fibre evidence further substantiated his guilt.

The second hillside strangler was later

discovered to be Angelo Buono who was born in Rochester, New York, on October 5, 1934. He was an ugly man physically, emotionally and intellectually. He was coarse, vulgar, selfish, ignorant and sadistic. He was also a big hit with the ladies and called himself the 'Italian Stallion'. He had been married several times and had a number of children, all of whom he abused at least physically and sometimes sexually.

Angelo Buono was sent to Folsom Prison, where he stayed in his cell, fearing injury from other inmates. Kenneth Bianchi was sent to Walla Walla prison in Washington.

PART THREE

FORENSIC EVIDENCE

The Start of Forensic Science

Modern forensic science has a broad range of applications. It uses highly developed technologies to uncover scientific evidence in a variety of fields – including the investigation of criminal cases involving a victim, such as assault, robbery, kidnapping, rape, or murder.

ONE OF THE most effective weapons in society's battle against crime is science. With the pace of advance in modern science, the battle becomes increasingly sophisticated, but the idea is hardly a new one. Indeed, it goes back to the days of the Old Testament. It was in 930 BC when Solomon, the third king of Israel, was confronted with the two women who had just had babies. One baby had died, its mother had secretly changed it for the live one (while the second mother slept), and Solomon had to decide which of the two shouting women was the live one's mother. 'Bring me a sword!' he said. 'Cut the living child in two; give half to one, half to the other.' The women's demeanour instantly decided which was the true mother and the surviving baby was spared. There is reason to believe that the basis of this story is much older than Solomon or Israel, but it can be taken as marking the arrival in the courts, whenever it was, of forensic evidence in the form of experimental psychology. Today it would be called forensic psychiatry and it would all be done by doctors.

At a more practical level, the early development of forensic science was less dramatic. It was many centuries before this method of crime-fighting gained pace.

In 1786 a Scottish crofter and his wife came home to their cottage after a day in the fields and found their teenage daughter murdered. Suspicion fell upon a young man named Richardson; but for some time there was no evidence on which he could be arrested. Even when there was judged to be enough, he promptly produced what seemed to be a perfect alibi. Then, rather belatedly it must seem today, the police took plaster-casts of some footprints near the cottage, and found that the pattern of the hobnails was exactly the same as that on Richardson's boots. Then further and similar 'forensic' evidence began to accumulate. Stains on the stockings he had worn on the day of the murder were found to be bloodstains (though they could not, in those days, be identified as belonging to any particular blood-group). Mud and sand on the stockings *could*, however, be proved to be mud and sand from the cottage garden. It was largely on this evidence that Richardson was convicted at Dumfries in 1787.

The Richardson case thus offers all the classic features of a prosecution founded on forensic science: identification of the suspect (by footprints), identification of the clues (the blood and, more exactly, the sand and the mud), and association of all the clues with the man Richardson.

But that, in 1787, was about the extent of what could be called forensic science, and so it officially remained for the next 100 years. However, outstanding members of the 'Bow Street Runners' and the original 'Peelers' (so called after Sir Robert Peel, the Home Secretary, who, in the 1820s, created the London police), were given extraordinary personal licence and developed some ingenious stratagems of their own.

Man-measurement

In 1879 Alphonse Bertillon, of the French Department of Criminal Police, began to develop a system of classified 'anthropometry' – which simply means man-measurement. It was not Bertillon's invention, but he was the first to persevere with it, in the face of universal ridicule, and finally gain reluctant official approval. No two people have the same measurements *in combination*: the circumference of the head and chest, the length of the ears, nose, fingers, arms, legs, feet and so on. List all these against one criminal's name, argued Bertillon, and you can always identify him whatever he does about his name, his beard, his hair, his walk, or his clothing.

And Bertillon was right. His system was slow and laborious but it was just about infallible. If you recorded the measurements of fourteen parts of a man's body, the odds against any other man having the same combination of measurements were 286,435,456 to one. Nevertheless for six years he was derided as a crank (which in some ways he was), rebuked for wasting his time, and ordered by successive Prefects of Police under whom he served to stop romancing and get on with his clerical duties.

Meanwhile, however, the science of identification by fingerprinting – which was probably of great antiquity – had been revived, developed and applied to criminology by an official in the Indian Civil Service named William Hershel. Both in Bengal and in England he had to meet exactly the same kind of ridicule, fight the same kind of battles, as Bertillon was doing. It was soon established, of course, that the odds against two men having identical fingerprints ran into meaningless billions – that, in fact, there existed no such possibility. But unlike Bertillon, Hershel allowed himself to be discouraged by official hostility or stupidity, and fell back on the use of fingerprints for his own administrative purposes. For example, getting the thumbprint 'signatures' of Indian labourers unable to write when drawing their pay. He had been doing it for twenty years before he made his futile attempt to interest the authorities.

These two systems, anthropometry and fingerprinting, became almost battle slogans. Anthropometry had reached the United States, which had (and still has) about 40,000 separate police forces. Between them they spent so much money installing the measuring apparatus, the filing systems and the clerks that the usual 'vested interest' barrier to further progress was quickly established. It is worth remembering that one of the most scornful critics of fingerprint identification was Bertillon himself. He allowed himself to believe, at the time of the Dreyfus case in France, that he was a handwriting expert as well as an anthropometrist. (He 'identified' Dreyfus's handwriting, quite wrongly, and stuck to his confident and stupid opinion even when it was proved, five years later – while Dreyfus was on Devil's Island – that he was wrong and Dreyfus innocent.) From 1880 onwards a Scottish medical missionary in Japan, Henry Faulds, was urging the infallibility of fingerprints for identifying the absent criminal who had left his prints at the scene of the crime. And Sir Francis Galton, the illustrious founder of the science of eugenics, or 'fine' breeding, began to urge upon the Home Office in 1894 that fingerprinting was an exact science of identification. Even in 1892 he had calculated that the chances against error were 64,000,000,000 to one.

Sherlock Holmes

It was a Buenos Aires police officer, Juan Vucetich, who finally convinced world criminologists about the great superiority of fingerprints, both in the simplicity and speed of operation. And it was Vucetich whose initiative and energy hastened the inevitable change, expensive as it was for everyone. Anthropometry had been used in England only from 1894 until 1900.

And it was in the 20th century that other forms of forensic science came into their own. This was encouraged, to an appreciable extent, by the ingenuity of Sherlock Holmes stories and by Conan Doyle's friendly contacts with senior police officers. Not enough acknowledgement has ever been accorded to the effect of the imaginative detective fiction of that period on the climate of public opinion, and the creation of an ideal sleuth beside whom the real-life policeman could be made to seem ineffectual – sometimes even in his own eyes. The Bordet blood test could already distinguish animal from human blood. Today we can prove that human blood belongs to a group of individuals, though not (as yet) that it is the blood of anyone in particular.

Spectacular Advances

In America the famous Crime Detection Laboratory in the Northwestern University at Chicago has advanced the boundaries of forensic science at a speed that is almost spectacular. It is still the model for most police and university crime laboratories, and the man who put it on the map was Dr Calvin H. Goddard, universally known for his work on the linking of firearms and bullets. But of almost equal importance in that story is the name of Charles E. Waite of the New York State Prosecutor's Office – a man who 'solved crimes as a hobby' and became involved, in 1916, in the investigation of a gun murder in Orleans County, New York. It was the case of Charles E. Stielow, a farm labourer accused of shooting the farmer and his housekeeper. It was one of those American cliff-hangers in which the convicted man is actually strapped in the electric chair when the reprieve comes through. Stielow's case is known to criminologists throughout the world as the one which established the new science of forensic ballistics, by which any bullet, so long as it is not seriously distorted by impact, can be proved to have come from a particular gun. Waite proved by microphotography that the murder bullets could never have been fired from Stielow's revolver. In doing so he established not only forensic ballistics but also the probability that many a man, in that gun-ridden land, had been executed for a crime he did not commit. It wasn't long before ballistic experts were able to prove not merely that a bullet could *not* have been fired from gun No. 1, but that a bullet could *only* have been fired from gun No. 2.

There are also peculiarities of individual type-writers – faults in spacing, type alignments, changes in type face through wear and tear. No two machines are alike. Similarly it has long been common knowledge and experience that no two people have identical *handwriting*. This leaves us a long way from being able to prove that one man must have written two separate documents or signatures; and yet this is what handwriting experts are sometimes expected (and will sometimes even profess) to be able to 'prove'. Handwriting experts, in their capacity to establish the falsity or even the genuineness of 'questioned documents', are often witnesses of great value; but they have limitations which the genuine experts willingly recognize, while the quacks and charlatans (e.g. those who read 'character' and fortunes) recognize none.

Contradictory Evidence

The trouble about expert witnesses, even scientific ones, is that they have so often been able to discredit the name of 'science' by giving evidence in total opposition to each other. This gave juries – and the general public – the feeling that the best forensic science was available to the highest bidder, whether prosecution or defence; and because the prosecutor is usually the State, it has the most money. The truth is that evidence which is genuinely scientific, *exactly* provable, cannot be refuted by science itself. In Britain, before the passing of the Road Safety Act 1967 and the introduction of breathalyzers and blood-alcohol tests, eminent physicians often gave evidence flatly contradicting each other about a motorist's fitness to drive. Not any more. They can't argue with a blood-alcohol reading unless they can prove (or believe they can) that it was rigged.

Thus the many forms which murder takes, the many motives behind it, have generally nourished the development of forensic science: jealousy, greed, sexual excitement, fear, misery, compassion, superstition, political idealism, bravado. Each of them is likely to involve methods of aggression, and of concealment, which the scientific investigator is now more and more likely to discover or defeat. From 1910, when Hawley Harvey Crippen was arrested mid-Atlantic as a result of a police radio message – the very first use of wireless telegraphy in a criminal case – until the modern use of microscopy, tape-recorded 'voice-prints', the analysis of poisons, etc., the swift progress of modern technology has gone on increasing the greatest of all deterrents to murder: the growing certainty of detection.

Within the broad area of forensic science, there are many subspecialities, including pathology (the examination of body tissues and fluids), toxicology (the study of poisons, including drugs), odontology (the study of teeth), psychiatry, anthropology (the study of human beings), biology, chemistry and physics.

Forensic science as practised today is a high-technology field using electron microscopes, lasers, ultraviolet and infrared light, advanced analytical chemical techniques, and computerized databanks to analyze and research evidence.

Techniques of Forensic Science

Modern forensic science uses sophisticated laboratory techniques to detect the presence of substances in the victim, in the suspected criminal, or at the crime scene. For example, in determining whether alcohol was involved in a crime, the amount of alcohol in the blood can be measured in two ways. One is to measure the amount of alcohol exhaled in the breath of an individual, which reveals the concentration of alcohol in the person's blood. Recent advances in technology have produced alcohol breath-testing instruments so accurate that their results are capable of providing evidence in court. Blood-alcohol level can also be determined by actual blood tests, usually through gas chromatography. In this method, the blood sample is vaporized by high temperature, and the gas is then sent through a column that separates the various chemical compounds present in the blood. Gas chromatography permits the detection not only of alcohol but also of other drugs, such as barbiturates, cocaine, amphetamines and heroin.

When a body is discovered in water and the lungs are found to be filled with water, the medical examiner must determine if the drowning occurred where the body was found or elsewhere. A standard microscope that can magnify objects to 1,500 times their actual size is used to look for the presence or absence of diatoms, single-celled algae that are found in all natural bodies of water. The absence of diatoms raises the possibility that the drowning took place in a sink or bathtub, not where the body was found, since diatoms are filtered from household water during treatment.

A scanning electron microscope that can magnify objects 100,000 times is used to detect the minute gunpowder particles present on the hand of a person who has recently fired a gun. These particles can also be chemically analyzed to identify their origin from a particular type of bullet.

Forensic examination of substances found at a crime scene can often establish the presence of the suspect at the scene. One of the oldest techniques of forensic science is dusting the scene of a crime for fingerprints, impressions of the fingertips left on surfaces touched bare-handed. In one method of obtaining a fingerprint, a technician spreads fine powder over a surface with a brush or magnetic wand. The powder sticks to proteins secreted by the sweat glands on the skin ridges of the fingertips. When the excess powder is removed, an outline of the contours of the ridges remains. In other methods, the print may be chemically treated to reveal the contours. Because no two fingerprints are the same, fingerprinting provides a positive means of identification. Computer technology now allows law-enforcement officers to record fingerprints digitally and to transmit and receive fingerprint information electronically for rapid identification.

Other evidence present at a crime scene may include blood, hair, skin or semen. Recent developments in technology now allow scientists to examine the deoxyribonucleic acid (DNA), or genetic material, of these substances to establish whether they belong to the victim or to a suspected assailant. By means of a high-technology method known as the polymerase chain reaction (PCR), a laboratory can rapidly clone, or multiply, the DNA from a tiny sample of any of these substances. This process produces enough DNA to compare with a sample of DNA taken from a suspected criminal. The use of DNA for such identification purposes is commonly referred to as DNA fingerprinting.

Human bite marks can also serve as circumstantial evidence. Such bites may be found upon the body of a homicide victim or within pieces of food or other objects, such as chewing gum, found at the crime scene. A forensic scientist can fill the impressions caused by these bites with liquid plastic. Upon hardening, the cast formed is an extremely accurate replica of the assailant's teeth, which can be compared with a cast made from the teeth of the suspect.

Bloodstains

When police have a strong suspect in a murder case, the temptation is to leave it at that, to close down the search for a killer. But a few blood samples submitted to tests in the forensic laboratory can change the entire case!

GOOD BLOOD cannot lie, they say. Nor can bad. As the distinguished forensic expert Alistair R. Brownlie (Solicitor Supreme Courts, Edinburgh, Scotland) put it to Britain's Forensic Science Society: 'Since Cain slew Abel, spilt blood has borne its mute testimony in crimes of violence. Stains of blood and body fluids still play an important part in crime *detection*, a lesser but increasing part in the proof of *guilt* . . .' And not only the nature and grouping of stains, but their position at the scene of the crime can be revealing and is now recognized as a vital piece of evidence in itself.

On June 15, 1965, a forensic episode, in which a victim's good blood cleared a suspect, occurred in a small Norwegian community in the village of East Hartland, in the Connecticut tobacco country, Litchfield County, USA. On that day, book-keeper Arnfin Thompsen returned home to find his wife lying dead. 'Her face and head were crushed, the jaw appeared to be broken, the left temple was smashed in. Her face was heavily caked with blood.

'It looked like she had been murdered in the kitchen and dragged through onto the porch. On the kitchen floor there was a big pool of blood, and then there was a single path of blood – maybe ten or twelve inches wide – like something had been dragged from the kitchen out . . . In a corner of the dining area the ironing board stood in the place where Dottie usually ironed; on it a partially-pressed white shirt, spattered with blood. The trail of blood angled past it to the sliding glass doors . . .'

Brown Bloodstain

A blood scene, indeed. The prime suspect was Dottie's mother-in-law who shared their white-board and grey-brick cottage – Agnes Thompsen, a religious fanatic with a failing mind, who had spent ten months in the Connecticut Valley Hospital for the mentally ill. Her opening words to the detectives were: 'Is she dead yet?' Then police chief Captain O'Brien found a bloodstained dress in the clothes dryer in Dorothy Thompsen's kitchen.

'Teams of men combed the house,' reported Mildred Savage in her classic book on the case. 'They emptied the contents of wastebaskets and garbage pails into plastic bags. They probed into plumbing fixtures and took water from sink traps' (where blood had been detected) 'and then took the traps themselves . . . Dr Abraham Stolman, chief toxicologist for the state of Connecticut, arrived to do on-the-spot testing . . .'

During the probe, a brown bloodstain was found on a step leading up to Agnes Thompsen's apartment. Some attempt had been made to sand or scrub it clean. So the whole stair was taken to the forensic laboratory. There, in an ordinary test by routine methods of serology, the prime suspect was eliminated. It was almost certainly her own blood and could not have been that of the murder victim since the two women had different blood groups. Later a neighbour of the Thompsens was sent to Connecticut State Jail for the crime and released after serving only eight months.

Petty Theft

Blood is not the only body product which can be of use to the forensic blood grouper. The word serology comes from the ancient Sanskrit *sara*, meaning 'to flow'. Today it is known that every fluid which flows in the human body can be identified: sometimes to prove the guilt of a suspected person, but also very often to protect the innocent.

A different sort of innocent victim was discovered in the English Midlands, when a police officer reported the case of a young child thought to have been attacked and raped in bed. Specimens were rushed to the forensic laboratory – where a simple test startled the serologists. The 'bloodstains' were those of a piece of plum tart the child had stolen from the kitchen. Her distress was due solely to the fear of the police officer calling and discovering her petty theft.

Bloodstains, types and grades usually remain constant, but sometimes they do not. One problem concerning antigens – substances introduced into the blood to stimulate production of health-protecting antibodies, as in blood plasma – is that in recent years scientists have realized that the red cells can actually acquire an antigen of the B-type. This is caused by certain bacteria (proteus and clostridium are examples) which produce substances similar to A, B and other blood-group substances, and thus may result in false grouping.

Haematology and Forensic Medicine was inspired by the serologist Pierre Moureau who, in 1963, was called in to examine the body of a child which had been in water for quite some time. The police had reason to suspect the mother. But tests showed that she had Group-O blood, while Moureau's absorption-inhibition tests at first showed the presence of A and B antigens in the dead child. An O-group mother, of course, cannot have an AB-group child.

Then Moureau repeated his tests. Gastric mucin at autopsy (active for Group-A only) and cultures of blood showing bacteria and a B-activity led to the discovery that the B-antigen had been acquired . . . In laymen's terms, the blood group had changed after death.

In their research in the 1970s, the London Hospital Medical College team was later asked to solve a query about the dismembered body of a woman found in the river Thames, London.

'The first part to be recovered,' the team reported, 'was the thoracic region, and from this it was possible to obtain a limited quantity of intact red cells, which were found to be Group-O Rh positive. From the pelvis, which remained in the water for a longer period, no red cells were recovered, but muscle tissue gave reactions of Group-B. The blood groups, therefore, did not support the conclusion that the (previous discovered) thorax and the (later found) pelvis were from one and the same individual.

Blood Groups

'However, the shape of the cut surfaces proved beyond a shadow of doubt that the two parts belonged to each other, and this raised the suspicion that the B reaction might be of bacteriological origin. Further work confirmed this . . .'

Essentially, forensic serology is based upon facts known vaguely since the dawn of time, and with much more certainty since in 1628 the English physician William Harvey discovered the circulation of blood. Christopher Wren is said to have experimented with transfusion, and in his diary Samuel Pepys recorded that a donor was paid a sum of 20 shillings as well as speculating what would happen 'were the blood of a Quaker to be let into an Archbishop'. For centuries the English aristocracy were genuinely believed to be born with blue blood, and boasts such as 'the blood of an Englishman' were taken seriously.

Then in 1930 the Viennese doctor Karl Landsteiner received a Nobel Prize award for his research into serology. He had announced to the scientific world that all human blood can be grouped into four main types. His work stimulated other biologists. Today for convenience the groups are known as O, A, B and AB.

Independent System

Landsteiner, in conjunction with Levine, was able to set up an entirely independent system of M and N groups. In 1940 he and his colleague Dr Wiener experimented with animal blood, injecting into rabbits and guinea pigs the blood of an Indian rhesus monkey. A hitherto undetected antigen was discovered, and for convenience this was given the title Rhesus (Rh). It was observed that the animals produced an anti-Rhesus antibody which also agglutinated human cells and by which the human population could be divided into two phenotypes, Rh positive and Rh negative.

In criminology scientists do concern themselves with medical matters such as agglutination, but primarily the vital question involves whether or not a sample *is* blood. A minute sample in the laboratory is extracted from the stained material kept in a saline solution, and a tiny drop of the extract is mixed with a solution containing phenolphthlein and potassium hydroxide, powered zinc and hydrogen peroxide. If this test is negative (meaning no change), the sample cannot be blood. If the mixture shows a clear pink colour, it *is* blood.

Blood Test

Biologists sometimes use a different test, in which glacial acid is added to a solution of hydrogen peroxide and benzidine – a drop of this being added to the test sample, which immediately turns a deep blue if there is blood present. The next step is to use an antiserum prepared in an animal which will react specifically with human blood, thus demonstrating whether the sample is of human origin.

The frequencies of the various genes within different blood group systems may, however, vary from race to race and could possibly provide important evidence. Blood group systems in general have acquired names such as Kidd, Duffy and Kell after the patients in whom the antibodies were first discovered, and all of them, of course, allow scientists to narrow down the field. At the extreme of the blood groups is a certain LU (a– b–) factor, which many serologists believe to be so rare than an estimated total of only about ten people in the world can have it. However, researchers may be only on the threshold of discoveries in investigation of body fluids. It is now nearly 100 years since serologists put blood samples under the microscope and found the elements which are freely suspended in the plasma. Essentially, these are the erythrocytes (red corpuscles), leucocytes (white corpuscles) and the blood platelets (egg-shaped and circular bodies suspended in the straw-plasma more commonly known as the 'serum').

But there is much more to serology than that. In many instances it is now possible to determine sex from examination of the leucocytes. This was demonstrated in Britain in a forensically interesting case of alleged sexual attack. The girl and the suspect volunteered for blood-group tests, when it was found that both people had the same blood group. A specimen for the test came from a mackintosh lining, on which it was alleged the man had wiped his blood stained penis.

The serologist engaged in the examination knew that when the white cells of female blood are inspected under the microscope, they show minute, drumstick-shaped marks. Although the girl's blood was the same group as that of the suspect, the stain from the mackintosh produced cells of feminine identification. Expert evidence on this was unsuccessfully challenged in court. It was obvious the male attacker had been in contact with female blood.

While it should be remembered that it is never possible to say 'this bloodstain originated from this person', nevertheless it may be possible to conclude that 'this bloodstain *cannot* have originated from that person'. A defence case may depend on this crucial fact. One striking example came to light early in September 1961, when a 24-year-old army private at Aldershot was cleared of sexual attack on a 38-year-old mother walking on a local racecourse.

'I can't remember exactly what happened,' the woman said to the police. 'He jumped on me and got hold of my shoulders. I screamed as hard as I could . . . Then somehow I found I was at the bottom of a steep bank, and my little daughter was crying. The man had pulled off my blouse, but I gave up the struggle because he twice threatened to hurt my child . . .'

False Identification

The doctor who examined the woman later confirmed there had been an attack. A soldier was picked out at an identification parade, and charged with rape. Bryan Culliford, from the New Scotland Yard Laboratory, demonstrated that the tests proved the suspect was in Group-B, while the stains on the unfortunate woman were Group-A. 'We find there is no case to answer,' announced the chairman of the court.

In her distressed state, the woman had picked out the wrong man at the identification parade. But for serology and its forensic application an innocent man could have been sent to jail.

Computers Aid in Detection

When conducting a crime scene investigation, and the use of bloodstain pattern interpretation is needed, deciding what tools to use can be of vital importance. When determining the point of origin of bloodstain patterns, a decision must be made to utilize the computer or manually string a bloody crime scene. Each has its time and place.

The crime scene is located at an apartment complex with the scene located outside next to

J. Edgar Hoover focused all of his energies on making the FBI Bureau the model of good organization and efficiency.

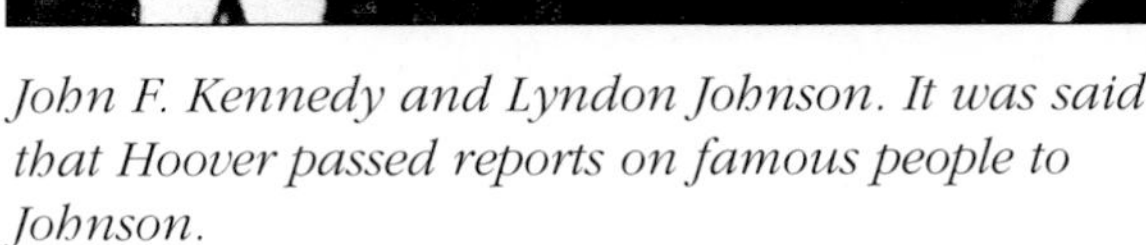

John F. Kennedy and Lyndon Johnson. It was said that Hoover passed reports on famous people to Johnson.

The only way to prove beyond doubt that a crime bullet was fired from a particular gun is to test fire the gun and compare the groove marks.

To improve police mobility, this 1938 police car was equipped with a radio.

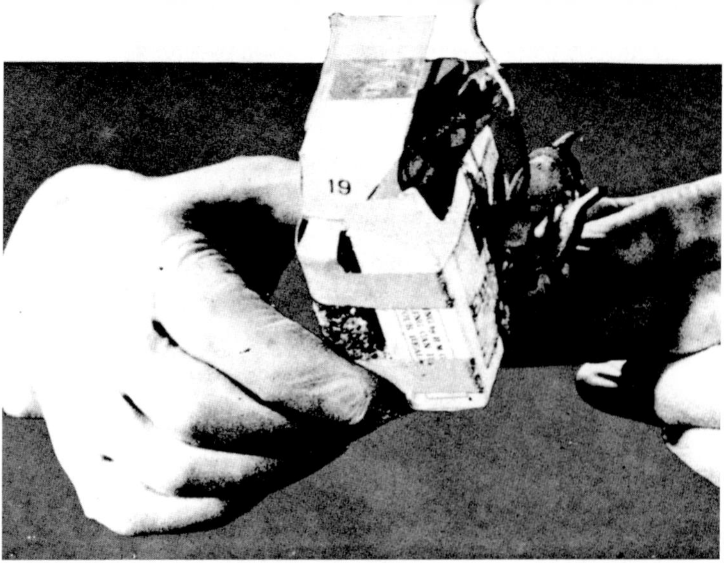

The Provisional IRA was formed in late 1969, when it split from the Marxist-inclined Official IRA. Some of the horrific weapons they have used include: pocket bombs, letter bombs, bombs in Bibles and shopping bags.

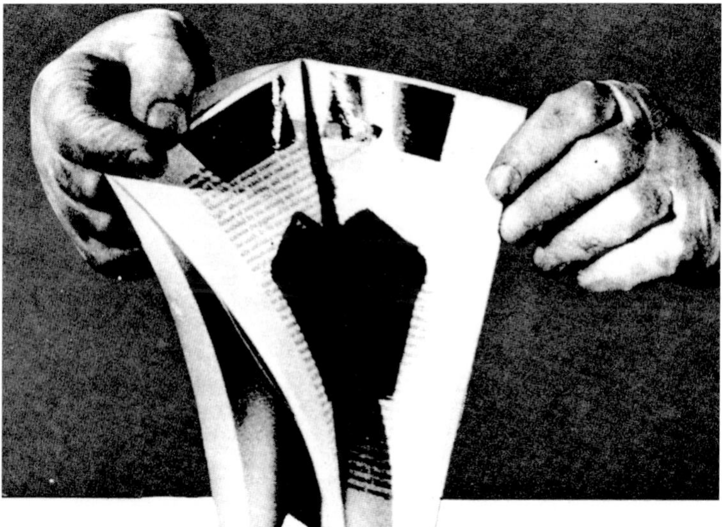

Eugène Vidocq's factual successes inspired world-class authors who borrowed his brilliance to embody their fictional heroes. Doyle's Sherlock Holmes character is much based on Vidocq; so are both Jean Valjean and Inspector Javert in Hugo's Les Miserables. *Dickens mentions Vidocq in* Great Expectations; *Melville cites him in* Moby Dick; *and Poe refers to Vidocq's methods in* Murders in the Rue Morgue. *And there are more beyond these . . .*

ROYAL COBURG THEATRE,

UNDER THE SOLE MANAGEMENT OF MR. DAVIDGE.

First Night of New and most peculiar Drama, which has been many Weeks in Preparation, giving a comprehensive glance at the Crimes, Police, and Manners of the French Metropolis.

FIFTH WEEK of that Unequalled Display of Splendour, the LORD of the MAELSTROM!!!

MONDAY, JULY 6th, 1829, and During the Week,

At Half-past 6 precisely will be presented, an entirely New Melo-Drama, in Three Acts, of peculiar interest, written by Mr. J. B. Buckstone, founded upon Incidents in the Life of *Eugene François Vidocq*, the Secret Agent of the French Police, and which will be produced, with entirely New Music, Scenery, Machinery, Dresses and Decorations, to be called,

Vidocq, the French Thief-Taker!

Music by Mr. T. Hughes.—Scenery by Mr. Dennes & Assistants.—Properties by Mr. Kellett.—Machinery by Mr. Durson.—Dresses by Mr. Saunders & Mrs. Follett.

Act 1.—Scene 1.—Mountainous View — ROMAN's BAND. — EXTERIOR OF A RUDE HUT. — DISTANT VIEW OF LYONS, with MILITARY ENCAMPMENT! — THE CAMP NEAR LYONS. — VIDOCQ DENOUNCED AS AN ESCAPED GALLEY SLAVE.

Act 2.—Scene 1.—Interior of a Prison. — SECOND ESCAPE OF VIDOCQ. — THE ENVIRONS OF PARIS. — AN APARTMENT. — THE ROBBERY! — ROOM AT ANNETTE's — THIRD ESCAPE OF VIDOCQ.

Act 3.—Scene 1.—A SQUARE IN PARIS. REJOICINGS FOR THE *Victory of Marengo!* — THE BRASS-WORKER's GARRET. — THE BATTLE OF THE WOODEN LEG — POLICE OFFICE. — *The Secret Agent of the French Police.* — 7.—A LANDSCAPE. — EXTENSIVE VIEW of the COUNTRY, WITH THE Ceremony of a Military Execution! — *Death of the Thief Fossard, & Triumph of Vidocq.*

LORD of the MAELSTROM!

Or, The Elfin Sprite of the Norwegian Seas.

Asgard, - *the Elfin Sprite of the Norwegian Seas,* - Mynheer Von Klishnig,

Act 1.—GRAND VESTIBULE OF THE PALACE OF THE KINGS OF NORWAY AT SANDAAL.
Tremendous Ravine in the Rocks by Moonlight, with Falling Stream of Real Water.

Act 2—STUPENDOUS CATARACT of the Maelstrom, formed by REAL WATER!

Act 3—The Temple of Fifty Fountains in the Mystic Regions of Valhallah!

The whole of the Magnificent Effects in this Scene produced by Real Water.

Doors open at Half-past Five. Second Price at Half-past Eight. Romney, Printer, Lambeth.

Biographer, Sigmund A. Lavine writes of Allan Pinkerton: 'A man of great power of observation and courage, prevented an assassination attempt on Abraham Lincoln; organized the first official Secret Service for duty behind Confederate lines during the war between the States; and rode with lawmen along the Old Frontier, hunting down members of Jesse James's gang, the Reno brothers and other desperadoes.'

Anne Frank was one of the Jewish victims of Nazi persecution during WWII. During a period in hiding Anne Frank kept a diary. In it she described daily life, the isolation and the fear of discovery.

Interpol's criminal records office as it was in the 1970s. It was the most comprehensive international documentation centre ever set up to help the fight against crime.

A million dollars was in these small bundles in the form of 50 pounds of raw opium. The three Chinese seamen were seized as they tried to smuggle the drug from Baltimore docks.

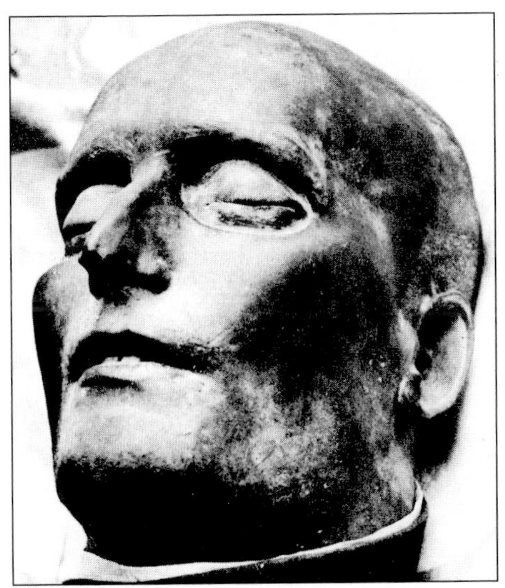

Always uneasy about how their great warrior-genius died, the French subjected hairs embedded in Napoleon's death mask to neutron activation analysis.

In January 2000 Harold Shipman, a general practitioner in Hyde, Greater Manchester was convicted of murdering 15 of his patients and of forging the will of one. These terrible crimes, tragedies for the patients and families concerned, led to widespread feelings of horror and outrage amongst the British public and within the medical profession itself.

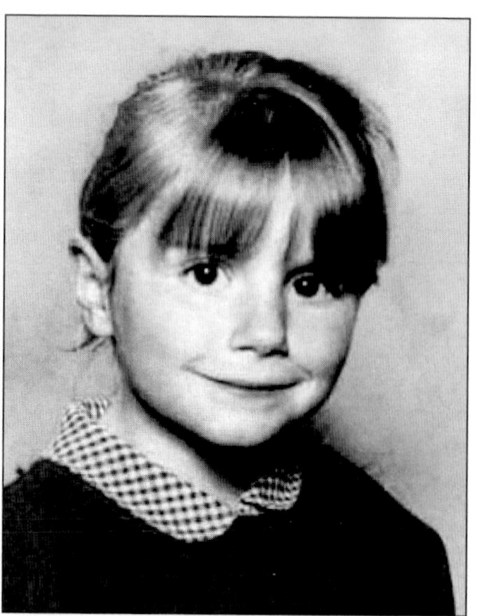

Sarah Payne vanished seconds after playing with her sister and brothers in a cornfield. Within days, the girl in the photograph was familiar to the entire country. Sarah Payne had become the victim of a crime that haunts every parent.

one of the apartment buildings. The deceased, a white female, was found on the ground with a single gunshot wound into the mouth and exiting the top rear area of the head. Located against the wall/doors next to the deceased were multiple bloodstain patterns.

After evaluating the crime scene, an attempt to string the bloodstains was made. This immediately became difficult and it was obvious that too many directions and locations within a small area would make the visualization confusing. A computer was used to display several different points of origin, all within a relatively small area, where the strings appeared to be disorganized. Viewing the computer displays, bloodstains with the same points of origin were visible and easy to view. The case was ultimately ruled a suicide by the Medical Examiner's Office, yet a serious event occurred at or near the time of the suicide.

Drops of Blood

Derry Police Sgt. Vincent J. Byron has been 'reading' bloodstains to reconstruct violent crimes since 1993. A recent murder in Derry, showed that the victim had been struck repeatedly with a wrench as he cowered on the bedroom floor. Blood splatters at the scene of the crime say so.

Sgt. Byron is one of four experts in New Hampshire trained in bloodstain-pattern analysis, a scientific technique in which the size, shape and location of bloodstains are used to determine everything from how many times the killer struck his victim to the type of weapon used. He is called to the scene of a bloody crime or suicide to read the writing on the walls, floors and ceilings, so to speak. Blood tells him how the crime was committed and sometimes confirms 'whodunit'.

He conducted his first bloodstain analysis in 1993 in a suicide case that police initially thought might have been a murder. It involved a 25-year-old Derry man shot in the head with a shotgun in his home while a friend was visiting. Sgt. Byron's analysis showed that there had been no murder. The man had shot himself inside his bathroom, and he was alone at the time, according to the blood patterns inside that room.

Since 1996, Sgt. Byron has used the technique eight separate times, including the murder of a woman inside a trailer at Whispering Pines Mobile Home Village last April. He began reconstructing that crime by examining the splatters of blood on the trailer's ceiling, walls and even the stove and refrigerator. His work started in the afternoon and finished by 11.00 that night.

The bloodstains showed that the woman had been struck repeatedly by her estranged husband with two separate baseball bats in the trailer's kitchen. The length and width of the stains indicated where the victim was when she was attacked. The shape of the stains showed the types of strokes her attacker used to kill her.

Sgt. Byron's interest in this type of analysis started eighteen years ago, two years after he joined the Derry police force in 1978.

In 1980, he began studying and reading everything he could find on the subject, including a book written by Herbert MacDonell, a noted forensic scientist who testified in the O.J. Simpson double murder trial. He also learned from Sgt. David Goldstein, a member of the New Hampshire State Police Major Crimes Unit. He spent much of his own time learning the technique and now passes this knowledge on to others through teaching courses.

Fingerprints

Pre-historic picture writing of a hand with ridge patterns was discovered in Nova Scotia. In ancient Babylon, fingerprints were used on clay tablets for business transactions, while in ancient China, thumb prints were found on clay seals.

FINGERPRINTS OFFER an infallible means of personal identification. Other personal characteristics change – fingerprints do not.

In earlier civilizations, branding and even maiming were used to mark the criminal for what he was. The thief was deprived of the hand which committed the thievery. The Romans employed the tattoo needle to identify and prevent desertion of mercenary soldiers.

More recently, law enforcement officers with extraordinary visual memories, so-called 'camera eyes', identified old offenders by sight. Photography lessened the burden on memory but was not the answer to the criminal identification problem, because personal appearances can change.

Around 1870 a French anthropologist devised a system to measure and record the dimensions of certain bony parts of the body. These measurements were reduced to a formula which, theoretically, would apply only to one person and would not change during his/her adult life.

This Bertillon System, named after its inventor, Alphonse Bertillon, was generally accepted for thirty years. But it never recovered from the events of 1903, when a man named Will West was sentenced to the U.S. Penitentiary at Leavenworth, Kansas. You see, there was already a prisoner at the penitentiary at the time, whose Bertillon measurements were nearly exact, and his name was William West.

Upon an investigation, there were indeed two men. They looked exactly alike, but were allegedly not related. Their names were Will and William West respectively. Their Bertillon measurements were close enough to identify them as the same person. However, a fingerprint comparison quickly and correctly identified them as two different people. The West men were apparently identical twin brothers as discovered later in prison records, showing correspondence from the same immediate family relatives.

How Fingerprints are Made

It was Dr Nehemiah Grew, a physician and microscopist born in Warwickshire in 1641, who discovered the ridge patterns on his fingertips. The friction ridges contain rows of sweat pores. Sweat mixed with other body oils and dirt produces fingerprints on smooth surfaces. Fingerprint experts use powders and chemicals to make such prints visible. The visibility of a set of prints depends on the surface from which they are lifted. However, with the help of computer enhancement techniques that can extrapolate a complete pattern from mere fragments, and laser technology that can read otherwise invisible markings, fingerprint experts increasingly can retrieve identifiable prints from most surfaces.

The age of a set of fingerprints is almost impossible to determine. Therefore, defendants often try to explain away evidence that their fingerprints were found at crime scenes by testifying that they were at the scene and left the prints at a time other than the time of a crime.

Sir William Hershel

The English first began using fingerprints in July of 1858, when Sir William Herschel, Chief Magistrate of the Hooghly district in Jungipoor, India, used fingerprints on native contracts. On a whim, and with no thought toward personal identification, Herschel had Rajyadhar Konai, a local businessman, impress his hand print on the back of a contract.

The idea was merely '. . . to frighten [him] out of all thought of repudiating his signature'. The native was suitably impressed, and Herschel made a habit of requiring palm prints – and later, simply the prints of the right Index and Middle fingers – on every contract made with the locals. Personal contact with the document, they believed, made the contract more binding than if they simply signed it. Thus, the first wide-scale, modern-day use of fingerprints was attributed to, not scientific evidence, but upon superstitious beliefs.

As his fingerprint collection grew, however, Herschel began to note that the inked impressions could, indeed, prove or disprove identity. While his experience with fingerprinting was admittedly limited, Sir Herschel's private conviction that all fingerprints were unique to the individual, as well as permanent throughout that individual's life, inspired him to expand their use.

Sir Francis Galton

Sir Francis Galton, a British anthropologist and a cousin of Charles Darwin, began his observations of fingerprints as a means of identification in the 1880s. In 1892, he published his book, *Fingerprints*, establishing the individuality and permanence of fingerprints. The book included the first classification system for fingerprints.

Galton's primary interest in fingerprints was as an aid in determining heredity and racial background. While he soon discovered that fingerprints offered no firm clues to an individual's intelligence or genetic history, he was able to scientifically prove what Herschel and Faulds already suspected: that fingerprints do not change over the course of an individual's lifetime, and that no two fingerprints are exactly the same. According to his calculations, the odds of two individual fingerprints being the same were 1 in 64 billion.

Galton identified the characteristics by which fingerprints can be identified. These same characteristics are basically still in use today, and are often referred to as 'Galton's Details'.

John Vucetich

Vucetich was a Croat, born on an island off the coast of Dalmatia in 1858. His background was middle-class, and he proved to be a good scholar with a knack for acquiring languages.

The police system in Lesina was modest and not called upon to deal with more than the general run of sins. It jogged along without even the rudimentary knowledge of police science which then existed on the mainland of Europe. Vucetich, however, became a civil servant in the police employ, and acquired some knowledge of the profession that was to be his future. In 1884 he emigrated to the Americas, but chose Argentina as more appealing to him than the United States. His final destination was La Plata, where he had a relative, and in his 26th year he joined the provincial police. He took to Argentinian life with all the great enthusiasm that was natural to him, even changing his christian name to the Spanish 'Juan'.

With a natural bent for mathematics, a considerable knowledge of theoretic police work and forensic science such as it was, Juan Vucetich's progress was rapid. His Croat forthrightness, his hard-headed ability, and his enormous energy drove him rapidly ahead of his more casual Spanish-American colleagues.

By 1891 Vucetich was head of the Statistical

Bureau of the police, where he worked quietly, reading of Britain's excitements of the 'Jack the Ripper' case and the French jubilation about the work of the great Alphonse Bertillon. As a result of Bertillon's successes, Vucetich was ordered to set up an Identification Bureau on the Bertillon principle, which was, very broadly, a system of measurements of the adult human body by which identity could be proved. The Chief of La Plata's police, Nuñez, presented Vucetich with various publications intended to guide him in forming the new Bureau.

As an afterthought he added a French publication of that year, the *Revue Scientifique*, containing an article by a Henri de Varigny on the work of Francis Galton, the English scientist and criminologist, who, along with Sir Edward Henry, set up the 'Galton-Henry' fingerprint system.

Vucetich, the shrewd mathematician, was not overwhelmed by *berillonage*. He distrusted a system of measurements which, he was to argue, could depend to some extent on the abilities of the technician concerned. But he was under orders to create a system of anthropometry, as the Bertillon method was named, and he put it in hand. La Plata police headquarters acquired its own Bertillon department, headed by a chief who kept his views to himself.

State of Hysteria

What actually set his imagination on fire was the fingerprint system or, as it was known, dactyloscopy. Vucetich realized the value of the system. He acquired such elementary material as was available. He studied the prints of the living and, in the local mortuary, of the dead. He recalled Faulds's communications to *Nature* and learned about Sir William Herschel of the Indian Civil Service, who had taken his own hand impressions at intervals of 28 years, qualifying the permanence of the lines. By the next year, 1892, Vucetich had, in his own time and with his own money, quietly worked out a fingerprint system which, though he did not know it, roughly followed the lines thought out by Galton.

Vucetich itemized four basic types of prints:

1 arches
2 those with a triangle on the right side
3 those with a triangle on the left side
4 on both sides

He used the first four letters of the alphabet to qualify his four categories in referring to the thumbs, and numbers for the fingers. This enabled him to use a simple formula which might begin, for example, with a letter B for a thumb – triangle on the right – followed by numbers indicating the marks on four fingers such as 2 – also triangle on the right – for the first finger with the next fingers listed accordingly.

An imaginary formula for both hands could be expressed thus: B2131/D2213, which permitted immediate classification. This was capable of enormous variations since there were four classifications for each finger which meant something like a good million possible combinations.

Exact classification was easy with a simple linked filing system which enabled new prints to be checked quickly with the files. Obviously sub-classifications would be needed with large expansion, but this Vucetich was to anticipate by counting so many papillary lines over an area of given measurement. This method foresaw something that, in later years, the great Dr Edmond Locard of France was to use when he devised poroscopy, the system of counting the number of pore orifices, sweat gland mouths, over a given space in a fingerprint.

Juan Vucetich managed to interest one or two of his colleagues, among them Inspector Carlos Alvarez, of La Plata Headquarters. It was a form of bread upon the waters which was to return tenfold, for though Vucetich's superiors were quite unimpressed by his spare-time work on fingerprints he was suddenly and impressively vindicated.

In Necochea, a small seaside town some 200 miles south of La Plata, a tragedy happened. On a hot summer night an attractive 25-year-old woman, a casual worker named Francisca Rohas, summoned her nearest neighbour and, in a state of hysteria, explained that her two illegitimate children had been brutally murdered. They were found, a boy of five and a girl of four, in bed with their heads smashed in.

Rohas accused a man named Velasquez, a labourer on a nearby *estancia*, of the crime. He was known to be in love with her, but also known to be quite devoted to the children. Rohas stated she had seen him rushing from her hut when she came home, immediately before she found the children.

The police did not worry much about examining the scene of the crime, but cross-examined Rohas, who admitted that Velasquez was madly in love with her but that she loved another man. On her evidence Velasquez, a pleasant, if somewhat simple, man, was arrested and admitted his devotion to Rohas and the children. This the police would not accept, treating the unlucky suspect with great brutality, thrashing him to extract a confession and, when this failed, binding him to the bodies of the children to force the truth out of him. Other melodramatic methods were tried when he said nothing, and even Rohas was subjected to tricks in case she were the guilty one.

In the end help was sought from La Plata; Inspector Alvarez was sent and achieved results in record time. First, he found that Velasquez had an unbreakable and provable alibi for the whole period of the murders – he had not mentioned it 'because nobody asked' him! Then Alvarez did what nobody else had bothered to do; he examined the scene of the crime with care.

Shopkeeper Murder

In his search he found a bloody thumbprint on the hut door. This he cut out and took with him to the local police station, had Rohas brought in and, with an ink pad, took impressions of both her thumbs. Even with his elementary knowledge, Alvarez was able to show clearly that the bloody print came from her right thumb.

Under questioning she confessed, admitting that her secret lover wanted her but not her children. She had battered them to death and put the blame on Velasquez. The case became a police and a press sensation; Vucetich's name, and his personal work on fingerprints, were quickly known all over South America. Then, soon after this, a man was accused of murdering a shopkeeper in La Plata itself, and the police proved his guilt when they found his prints on the shop counter.

Juan Vucetich and his system were on the way up. He paid for the printing of a book on his work, and wrote study after study for his superiors to show how fingerprints proved case after case with which he had worked, but that *bertillonage* was not nearly so successful. Despite this, Vucetich's progress was impeded by his superiors. Then in 1894, under Captain Lozano, a new and enlightened Chief of Police, the whole province of Buenos Aires adopted the Vucetich system.

Argentina thus became the first country in the world to adopt fingerprinting as a method of police identification. At a South American scientific congress Vucetich explained his methods and criticized the Bertillon system, for which Bertillon never forgave him.

As the years went by he was to see country after country in South America adopt his system; experts today suggest that if universal fingerprinting were to come then the system most suitable for it would be that of Vucetich, there being a difference between the Henry (British) system and that of Vucetich, and the variations on both systems used in other lands.

But Juan Vucetich's fame was confined to his continent, for though western European ideas reached Argentina, that part of the world was quite uninterested in the Argentine, and Europeans tended to ignore the Vucetich system.

Viciously Snubbed

Nevertheless, Vucetich's views on *bertillonage* had not gone unnoticed, and when he managed to convert his police pension into an immediate lump sum, he achieved a great ambition by setting out to travel the world, studying fingerprint systems, and meeting policemen. Bertillon snubbed him viciously in Paris, but in 1913 Vucetich discovered that his name had at last reached the outer world through the partisanship of far-seeing police officers in other lands. His name was honoured, he was given decorations, and he realized that the Vucetich system was widely appreciated.

However, the bureaucrats had not finished with him. Just as the Argentine government was poised to fingerprint the whole population – Vucetich's dream – the enemies of the idea intimated that people would not want to be fingerprinted like criminals. The Latin temperament took over from there. Riots broke out, there were arrests and the building intended for fingerprint registration records was badly damaged by the rioters.

In 1917 the whole project was cancelled, and Vucetich was banished to another city, his records and files sequestered, his work destroyed. Embittered and defeated, a mentally and physically sick man, Vucetich rested for a time with an English friend, Edward Lomax, who bred horses on an up-country *estancia.* There Vucetich told of his defeat and tragedy, but he also prophesied the future triumphs for the fingerprint system.

Vucetich was never a physically strong man, and in his last years was afflicted with both tuberculosis and cancer of the stomach. In 1925, the year of his death, he wrote to Edward Lomax: 'I shall not see this year out, I fear. My work is destroyed and perhaps will be forgotten . . . nobody will ever remember me . . .'

He was wrong. Today, the name of Juan Vucetich is honoured by criminologists throughout the world.

Dr Henry Faulds

During the 1870s, Dr. Henry Faulds, the British Surgeon-Superintendent of Tsukiji Hospital in Tokyo, Japan, took up the study of 'skin-furrows' after noticing finger marks on specimens of 'prehistoric' pottery. A learned and industrious man, Dr. Faulds not only recognized the importance of fingerprints as a means of identification, but devised a method of classification as well.

In 1880, Faulds forwarded an explanation of his classification system and a sample of the forms he had designed for recording inked impressions, to

Sir Charles Darwin. Darwin, in advanced age and ill health, informed Dr. Faulds that he could be of no assistance to him, but promised to pass the materials on to his cousin, Francis Galton.

Also in 1880, Dr. Faulds published an article in the Scientific Journal, *Nature* (nature). He discussed fingerprints as a means of personal identification, and the use of printers' ink as a method for obtaining such fingerprints. He is also credited with the first fingerprint identification of a greasy fingerprint left on an alcohol bottle.

Faulds died in March 1930, at the age of 86, but it wasn't until 1987 that his reputation was finally secured, when two researchers accidentally stumbled across his grave in Stoke-on-Trent. The British Fingerprint Society officially recognized Faulds's contribution, and now they pay for the upkeep of his grave.

A Case That Made History

On the morning of May 23, 1905, two brothers Albert and Alfred Stratton were taken to the gallows and blindfolded by the hangman. Witnesses said that Albert's death was instantaneous, his body becoming limp straight after the drop through the trapdoor. In Alfred's case there seemed to be some muscular movement afterwards. These were indeed gruesome deaths, but not compared with the savage butchery that the brothers had inflicted on others, only three weeks earlier.

One Monday morning, a sales assistant called William Jones, had turned up to start work at a

London paint suppliers, only to find the street door locked. The shop's elderly manager, Thomas Farrow, would normally have opened up the shop a couple of hours earlier. Jones was puzzled and broke into the shop, only to find a grisly scene. Farrow was lying face down, his body crumpled in a bloody pile, and his skull staved in by a crowbar. His wife Ann lay dying upstairs, her wounds also the result of a sustained bludgeoning with a metal implement.

Later that morning, when Scotland Yard's assistant commissioner Melville Macnaghten joined the policemen in the shop, he noticed a greasy smudge on the shop's empty cash box. He had this immediately sent to the Yard's Fingerprint Branch. A witness, Ellen Stanton, informed the police that she had seen Alfred Stratton, a well-known petty criminal, and another man making a high-speed getaway from the shop. The Stratton brothers were arrested and Detective Inspector Charles Collins of the Fingerprint Branch, subsequently discovered that the print on the cash box matched that on Alfred's righthand thumb.

Though fingerprints had never been used before as evidence in a murder trial, Macnaghten decided to commit the case to prosecution. Forensic evidence was still widely mistrusted, and until then convictions for murder had relied on sworn statements from the witness box that placed the accused at the scene of the crime. But in fact no one had seen the Strattons commit murder, they had merely been spotted near the scene of the crime.

It took the jury just two hours of deliberation to find the brothers guilty, and in fact to change legal history for ever. The Strattons became the first men to be hanged for murder on the evidence of a fingerprint.

Detailed Police Records

Detailed records of convicted criminals – their fingerprints and the way in which they work – are an essential to any police force, and more information is added every day.

INFORMATION, CAREFULLY recorded and stored, is the lifeblood of any police force. Every day more and more is pumped into Scotland Yard's Criminal Record Office, the national registry of crime. Within its millions of neatly docketed files are the complete records of every person convicted of serious crime throughout Britain. Each file records the name, age and personal description of the person, together with a photograph and a list of their convictions and prison sentences. Whenever a suspect is held, anywhere in the country, a message is sent to the Yard asking if 'anything is known' about the man or woman.

As sub-divisions of the main collection there are further records showing details of the way in which known criminals work, their so-called *modus operandi*. There is also an alphabetical index of the types of crime committed – running from Abduction, Arson and Burglary, down to Treason and Warehouse break-ins.

Even the pseudo-respectable roles adopted by criminals are listed in A to Z files, from Actor and Architect to Wealthy Person (posing as). Every type of detected fraud is meticulously noted so that the Yard has been able to pinpoint the true identity of some con-men simply from the literary style of letters written to potential victims.

One of the latest measures taken by the Yard to add to its storehouse if information, is the development of a Criminal Intelligence branch. Detectives keep close watch on full-time professional criminals in the London area, and pool the results of their observations. Continually updated records present a detailed profile of the criminal – where he eats, the public houses he frequents, descriptions of his wife or girlfriend, names and backgrounds of people with whom he associates. A sudden deviation from a man's regular routine, his mysterious absence from his usual haunts, can be an indication to the Yard men that a new 'caper' is about to be launched.

Vital Analysts

However, some Scotland Yard men and women, who play an important part in criminal detection, have never been to a scene of crime nor, sometimes, ever knowingly spoken to a criminal in their lives. They are, among others, chemists, physicists, toxicologists, biologists, handwriting and ballistics experts. They are the forensic scientists, many of them working in the Yard's own laboratory, seeking out half-hidden clues which help to bring the guilty to justice and punishment. The most minute scrap of evidence rarely escapes their expert analysis, and it is true to say that, in the days when capital punishment applied in Britain, some murderers were hanged not only by a rope but by tiny scraps of cotton thread that connected them positively to their victims.

Daniel Raven, a young Londoner who, in 1949, beat his parents-in-law to death with the base of a television antenna, thought himself safe when he burned a heavily bloodstained suit in his kitchen boiler. But a tiny fragment of unburned cloth was retrieved by a quick-witted detective and sent to the Yard's laboratory. There the scientists found that the cloth bore minute blood spots and these, when analyzed, matched the blood group of the murdered couple.

Other traces of blood on Raven's shoes and in his car, which had survived despite frantic washing, also matched. all these pieces of evidence, painstakingly assembled in the laboratory, helped to send Raven to the gallows.

In recent years much of the laboratory's work has been concerned with tests on clothing and other articles for traces of narcotics. Indeed, nearly 70 per cent of the chemists' examinations arise from drugs, drink or sex crimes. A notorious West End prostitute, suspected of trafficking in dangerous drugs, was several times searched by the police but always found to be 'clean'. Finally, her handbag was delivered to the laboratory and its contents scoured, down to the smallest piece of fluff, by a vacuum cleaner. When the little heap of debris was subjected to exhaustive tests it produced positive reactions for morphine and its derivatives.

It is now common knowledge that a fired bullet carries the imprint of gun-barrel markings that are almost as unique to any one gun as fingerprints are to each person's hands. But forensic ballistics is a comparatively modern science, and it was not until 1928 that evidence based upon it was first offered in a British criminal trial. It led to the conviction and execution of two men, Frederick Browne and William Kennedy, for the murder of Police Constable Gutteridge, attached to the Essex County Constabulary.

In 1946, a Miss Elizabeth McLindon, housekeeper in a Belgravia, London, mansion rented by the late King George of Greece, was found shot dead in her room. On the carpet was an empty ·32 Browning automatic. A ballistics expert, who examined the spent shell case in the housekeeper's room and another found on Boyce, was able to prove conclusively from identical markings that Boyce's gun had fired the fatal shot. Boyce made the dreaded journey to the Old Bailey, and from there to a rope's end.

Establishing Identity

At every crime scene experienced police officers are careful not to disturb anything on the ground or the premises, since every mark, every particle of material, may hold vital clues waiting only for the specialist to unravel them. Even a quite small impression of a tyre tread may be enough for the expert to identify the make of the tyre, and – where there are indications of wear – to match it precisely to the actual tyre itself. From such a mark a skilled examiner can prove the direction in which the vehicle was moving.

Like motor tyres, scattered fragments of glass often have their own story to tell. In one typical case, the clothing of two men suspected of having broken into a London store by smashing the glass panel of a door was taken to the laboratory for close examination. Tiny shards of glass found on the clothes were compared with sweepings of the shattered door panel gathered by detectives. The scientists were able to show that both samples of glass exhibited exactly the same manufacturing characteristics. Each suspect had his own explanation for the glass on the clothing. One said the fragments had come from a public house beer glass which he had accidentally smashed, while the other claimed that he had been removing a broken window in his house.

Both incidents were found to be true, and the police obtained surviving pieces of the beer glass and the broken window. But they still did not prevent the conviction and jailing of the two men. The laboratory experts compared the glass fragments with the scatterings from the store, and proved the structure and peculiarities of the two groups to be different.

There are times when the Yard's forensic pathologists are asked to establish the identity of corpses, and even to piece together the outline of a once-living body from a few, dismembered remains. This happened in 1948 when two small boys, playing by a pond on the edge of a golf course at Potters Bar, fifteen miles north of London, pulled a human hand and forearm out of the water.

The police drained the pond and brought in a mechanical excavator to scoop out the foul-smelling mud and slime into which stomach-heaving detectives delved and searched. Finally, they had gathered together many other portions of human remains which – when put together with the original hand and forearm – were re-assembled in the local mortuary and built up into the almost complete body of a man.

An initial examination showed that the man had been between 35 and 45 years of age, had been dead for between four and eight months, and that the body had been crudely dismembered, probably with an ordinary carpenter's saw. The front of the skull was broken and it was certain that the man had died from a violent head blow. The body's fingertips were so far advanced in composition that it was impossible to obtain fingerprints.

From their checks on men reported missing from the area the police found that all were accounted for except one – a 45-year-old railway-man named Albert William Welch who had disappeared from his Potters Bar home, not far from the golf course, on November 17, 1947. Detectives were almost certain that the remains were those of Welch, but they asked the Yard laboratory to make a positive identification.

The laboratory's forensic pathologists copied a photograph of Welch in the form of a transparency and superimposed it on a similar transparency, of exactly the same dimensions, of the skull found in the pond. The two fitted absolutely. From Welch's former workmates Superintendent Colin MacDougal, in charge of the investigations, learned that the dead man had complained of toothache shortly before his disappearance, and the laboratory found a jaw cavity which showed signs of having harboured a root abscess.

In the final and most important step of their investigation the laboratory men obtained from Welch's widow a pair of the dead man's boots. They then made a cast of the inside of each boot, using a mixture of plaster of Paris and gelatine. The casts, carrying clear impressions of Welch's feet, were photographed and scientifically matched with X-ray photographs of the feet taken from the pond. Once again, the match was perfect – even to the slightly enlarged big-toe joints. Despite all this patient effort, Welch's killer was never found. But by its work the laboratory was able to prove the victim's identity to the complete satisfaction of a coroner's jury.

DNA Records

Our system of criminal justice is best described as a search for the truth. Increasingly, the forensic use of DNA technology is an important ally in that search. The development of DNA technology furthers the search for truth by helping police and prosecutors in the fight against violent crime. Through the use of DNA evidence, prosecutors are often able to conclusively establish the guilt of a defendant. Moreover, DNA evidence – like fingerprint evidence – offers prosecutors important new tools for the identification and apprehension of some of the most violent perpetrators, particularly in cases of sexual assault.

The introduction of DNA profiling has revolutionized forensic science and the criminal justice system. DNA technology has given police and the courts a means of identifying the perpetrators of rapes and murders with a very high degree of confidence. As recently as the late 1960s, the only methods available for genetic marker analysis of blood and other body fluids were the Lattes test, the absorption-elution test, and the absorption-inhibition test. For a variety of reasons, DNA profiling has significantly advanced the analysis of biological stain evidence.

An unforeseen consequence of the introduction of DNA profiling has been the reopening of old cases. Persons convicted of murder and rape before DNA profiling became available have sought to have the evidence in their cases re-evaluated using this new technology. In some cases, DNA test results have exonerated those convicted of the offences and resulted in their release from prison.

Perhaps some day a complete DNA record of all known criminals will be stored on police databases for future use.

'Pictures' of Sound

Edison recorded sounds on wax cylinders. Modern forensic scientists can also produce 'pictures' of sound. These voiceprints can be as valuable as fingerprints in trapping crooks.

IN A SMALL and cramped workshop near Detroit is one of the pioneer launch pads of that latest forensic tool, the voiceprint. It is not in the FBI laboratory or any other forensic research centre as might be supposed, but in what is part of the Edison Institute complex at Henry Ford's fantastic Greenfield Village history-of-America centre.

When he had made his first million and was inspired by his American grass-roots origin, Ford began to gather around him all that he loved in the world. The Wright Brothers' cycle shop where the aeroplane was born, the Logan County Court where Abraham Lincoln practised law, the church where his mother worshipped, the house where he himself was born, the little shop where Mr Heinz prepared the first of the 57 varieties, and the house where Webster compiled his dictionary.

Ford had them all transported to Deaborn, Michigan, and re-erected there. He even had the surrounding soil brought, to maintain a correct atmosphere. In all the 260 acres of this treasure-store of Americana, one of the outstanding buildings is the workshop from Menlo Park where Ford had worked once as a lad, assisting Edison in his inventions.

There, as a century ago, one can sit at the table where the first satisfactory electric-light bulb glowed through the night, and at the bench where Edison hand-turned his first drum-type phonograph.

In 1877, on this machine which still exists, Thomas Alva Edison produced the first voiceprint, traced by a stylus point on tinfoil wrapped around the cylinder – for it was left to others (notably Charles Tainter and Dr Chichester Bell) to develop the wax cylinder that enabled a satisfactory *reproducing* photograph to be manufactured.

Edison quickly patented his system in 1877 for *sound* reproduction, but one of the other early pioneers was Leo Scott, an inventor who in 1856 had devised a system of voiceprinting by a light stylus and membrane at the end of a trumpet. This drew a wavy pattern across a smoke-blackened cylinder.

Scott could not reproduce from this voiceprint, and in these early nineteenth-century years when battles were being waged between Edison and Alexander Graham Bell, Edison hastily patented his device with audio recording in mind. Neither he nor Bell foresaw voiceprint possibilities in other directions.

It was therefore a happy coincidence that some ninety years after the innovation of the Bell telephone, L. G. Kersta of the Bell Telephone Laboratories (where, also, the transistor was born) proposed the voiceprint as a new forensic method of identification.

His system went much further than merely presenting a single audio waveform in physical means. He had solid-state amplifiers at his disposal, and the laboratory oscilloscope with its television-like cathode-ray tube to present a screen pattern of what he termed his spectrograms or 'sonograms'.

The essence of the system was to produce not merely an audio waveform (which today every television engineer does as a matter of routine when setting up his camera channels), but a pattern which is uniquely characteristic of the speaker. That there *is* such a characteristic was realized years before our present pitch of electronics.

'It was your voice that gave you away' is commonplace. So, too, the telephone booth trick so often used in motion pictures and television scenes, where the caller puts a handkerchief over the handpiece of the microphone to disguise his voice.

It must be said that Lawrence Kersta's work originally was not directed towards helping criminalistics, but as a general branch of the science of acoustics applied to aerodynamics and medicine.

Many voice-display systems were built – in the Bell Telephone Laboratories, at the RCA Research Center and elsewhere – in connection with vibration and shock waves of missiles, and uniquely in the analysis of throat sounds as an aid to diagnosis of lung and throat illnesses and defects.

What are known as the 'articulators' – tongue, palate, teeth and lips – are just one factor controlling the tonal quality of speech. Mouth, nose and throat cavities also have a decisive effect. But the overriding factor is the subconscious muscular control of all these, which produce speech patterns of varying frequencies and of characteristic timbre.

Women generally have a more limited and naturally higher vocal range than males. Because of resonant nasal cavities, actors and others who have voice training, speak and sing with a noticeably different tone colour and resonance.

In developing voiceprint techniques, Lawrence Kersta, David Ellis and others realized that some of these factors were purely physical. For example, the characteristics are partly due to the two strap-like membranes across the larynx, known as the vocal cords. The medial (central) part of the cords vibrates in the air stream produced by speaking. From the very first moment a baby cries, there is developed the subconscious control of these two membranes.

Pitch of the Voice

Very shortly after birth the natural pitch of the voice is developed by individual control of the vocal cords; and, like everything else in audiophysics, the pitch is controlled by the frequency of vibration.

Women's cords are usually shorter than men's, although both men and women have a fairly limited control range so that for short intervals either can speak with an affected 'deep' or 'high' voice. This does not always affect the natural timbre (on which the success or failure of the voiceprint depends), but is controlled also by the trachea, lungs, and diaphragm – all of which are usually also of different size in the female. Thus, the range of a soprano is approximately from top-treble A to the A below middle-C on the piano. The male base range is from D above middle-C to the F an octave and a half below.

If forensic voiceprinting were concerned with only range, there would be little difficulty. The real breakthrough came with Lawrence Kersta's work when it was realized that an electronic sound analyzer could detect and record frequency characteristics and harmonics – all uniquely individual – due to fundamentals of the voice cavities, and the subconscious control in every individual of his own articulators.

Unhappily the first time a Bell Telephone voiceprinter was demonstrated in court, there was an inconclusive ending to the experiment. This was in the United States in April 1966. A subsequent use of the voiceprint technique (by a British team of physicists) in an English court in November 1967 was successful, and resulted in a conviction.

To Kersta's credit, he was not downcast by the difficulties of the April 1966 case, and he decided to set up his own voiceprint company, manufacturing equipment for it and operating under licence from the Bell Telephone group, which still controls the patent rights.

This initial 1966 hurdle happened in the Westchester County Court (at county court level) when a new Rochell police officer was on trial for an unusual perjury. It was alleged that the police officer had warned a professional gambler of a planned police raid. The question of a tip-off had already been brought to official notice, so a phone-tap was arranged and Lawrence Kersta's staff were allowed to record voiceprints.

Later, with the suspect's permission, these prints were compared with open-microphone prints. In the opinion of Kersta and the DA's office, these were identical.

Because of the novelty of the forensic evidence, Kersta was subjected to vigorous cross-examination. The defence challenged the legal (not, of course, the technical) competency of the witness, but the judge ruled that this was for the jury to decide. On the stand Lawrence Kersta showed how his recorder produced bar spectrographs, the amplitude information of a number of successive frequency bands being marked on sensitized paper. He gave details of some 50,000 preceding tests on other voices.

It is possible some members of the Westchester County jury did not understand this forensic milestone. They disagreed, and were discharged. A re-trial was requested, but through the complex intricacies of the US legal system, a case was stated to the United States Supreme Court who promptly ruled that the New York State law which allowed the phonetap (*not* the voiceprinting itself) was unconstitutional. Since this meant that none of the telephone evidence could be given at the re-trial, whether frequency-analyzed or not, the case against the police officer was dropped.

In Britain the technique was more successful at its introduction. At the Winchester petty-sessional court in November 1967 a man was charged with making malicious telephone calls. Here there was no shred of doubt about the legality of the police tapping and recording the conversations, so recordings were made on hi-band audio tape. These were frequency-analyzed at Leeds University. Spectro-analysis disclosed a number of distinct similarities which convinced the magistrates. The defendant was convicted and fined. Perhaps because of the novelty and uncertainty of it all, the case failed to make national headlines.

Seen by Millions

Voiceprints made by Kersta from a TV news interview at the time of the Los Angeles Watts riot, certainly hit the front pages. They put the technique right on the map so far as forensic science in the United States is concerned. Indeed, part of the proceedings were seen by many millions of television viewers overseas.

Bill Stout, a TV interviewer with the Columbia Broadcasting System, interviewed a group of coloured youths immediately after the Watts riots. One of them turned his face away from the camera while admitting that he had been involved in burning some shops in LA. Stout's first duty was to his CBS-TV public, and, only after the video-tape recording, was it possible for the police to intervene. Without much difficulty they tracked down an eighteen-year-old youth, Edward Lee King.

Everything depended on the weight of the forensic evidence, and whether the jury would accept voiceprint evidence from Kersta. As it turned out, they did. The arson trial took nearly seven weeks. The police had been able to get a second set of voiceprints while King was in jail on a narcotics charge, and these were found to tally with those recorded at Watts. King was convicted and jailed.

In the United States two vital features now arose, since lawyers defending a suspect where voiceprint evidence might be given were concerned about self-incrimination, and also the rights of a defendant to refuse to make a print for comparison.

Both these questions were determined in the United States in 1967, and it is likely that the legal luminaries in other nations will follow this example.

State v. McKenna 226 A 2d 757 stands as the State of New Jersey Superior Court ruling that a defendant has no right to refuse taping or voice-printing. And *US v Wade*, June 1967, is a US Supreme Court ruling that the traditional American ruling (privilege against self-incrimination) does not apply to a defendant asked to record or voice-print so that he may be identified.

While the first courtroom appearances of voice-prints were with audio-tape recordings made at 7½ inches/second, research is continuing at Polaroid Corporation (Cambridge, Mass.) and elsewhere on photo-recording at different speeds, with other frequency ranges, and with systems of securing permanent photoprints off the television-like screens of dual trace oscilloscopes.

Photoprints now being researched by forensic workers using Polaroid Land PolaScope techniques are designed to show on the one print (for simple inspection by members of a jury) the specimen and control voiceprints.

Waveforms from the two separate audio tracks are fed to the two amplifiers of a dual-trace oscilloscope. Here on a 5-inch screen two separate timebases swing independent cathode-ray beams across the fluorescent tube screen. Any frequency differences or similarities between the voice of the defendant or suspect can be seen by comparison – then instantly photographed.

Ordinary amateur-camera film has an American Standards Association speed of around 25, and high-speed Kodak Ektachrome is 160 ASA. By contrast, the Polaroid Land stock used for oscilloscopes is 10,000 ASA-equivalent.

Separate Research

It is therefore easily possible to photograph at a maximum trace writing-rate of 3,500 centimetres per microsecond – fast enough to show up differences in an audio waveform.

All this research is entirely separate from the forensic work being done currently by the Kersta company, Voiceprint Laboratories.

But the strangest aspect of all is that although Leo Scott produced his carbon-film voiceprints in 1856, and the Danish inventor Valdemar Poulson had his

Telegraphone (the world's first magnetic-wire audio-recording system) working in Paris in 1900, it has taken society so long to realize that voices have fundamental differences. And that these can be recorded and *compared* – forensically.

The Voiceprint of a Killer

The year was 1971. Neil LaFeve, an amiable but law-abiding game warden in Wisconsin, was found murdered on September 24, on his 32nd birthday. That afternoon, he had been out in the woods posting signs and had planned to finish long before the party that his wife had organized for him. When he failed to show up, his wife grew worried and phoned his boss. They discussed it together, but there was no reason they could think of that Neil might still be out in the woods.

LaFeve's boss went out to look for him. He noticed that all the signs had been posted, so when darkness came and there was still no indication that LaFeve was returning, he called the police. They searched through the night, but gave up without finding the missing warden.

In the morning, the search party came across LaFeve's truck. It was empty and the door was ajar. Things looked bad and only got worse when they found a large amount of blood not far away. Another searcher picked up some broken sunglasses and two spent shells from a .22 rifle. From there, more signs of a wounded man formed a trail: human body matter, a tooth, blood and bone fragments. They felt certain they would not find him alive. Finally the search party reached a spot that looked like it had been recently dug up. The police got shovels and soon they had located Neil LaFeve – without his head. Another freshly dug spot nearby, though much smaller, yielded his head. It had been hacked off with a blunt instrument – a shovel or spade – and two bullets were imbedded in the skull. The coroner also found several bullets in the corpse.

The first step was to determine if LaFeve had any enemies. The officers in charge of the investigation looked through a list of men that LaFeve had arrested for poaching, as possibly these men could have a vendetta. The brutality of the attack indicated rage or revenge, not just a random killing. All of the men who had been convicted of hunting illegally on those grounds were located and interviewed on tape, and a few were asked to submit to polygraph exams. However, there was one man who refused to cooperate – 21-year-old Brian Hussong. LaFeve had arrested him several times, yet he had continued to poach. Hussong had no alibi for September 24 and he resisted all attempts to clear up the murder mystery. He seemed a likely suspect.

Sergeant Marvin Gerlikovski was in charge, so he got a rare court order that allowed him to put a wiretap on Hussong's house. He took the extra precaution of recording everything that was said, which paid off in a way he didn't expect.

It wasn't long before Hussong got on the phone to get his grandmother to hide his guns and give him an alibi. She appeared to cooperate, so Gerlikovski sent detectives to her house. Flustered, she led them straight to the hiding place. Ballistics experts confirmed a match between the .22 rifle and the bullets found in LaFeve's body, which was enough evidence to place Hussong under arrest.

Gerlikovski then sent the tapes he had made to Michigan's Voice Identification Unit – at that time the best in the world for this type of procedure. The leading experts in voiceprint analysis had trained these officers. Ernest Nash examined the tapes, gave his opinion, and ended up serving as an expert witness during Hussong's trial. However, it was not Hussong's voice that he testified about, but that of Hussong's grandmother. She had denied saying that she had hidden the guns, so Nash explained how he could match her voice to that of the voice on the tape. He then used his laboratory results to affirm that she was definitely the person speaking to her grandson on the tape.

The jury listened to the tapes again, and after less than four hours of deliberation, they returned a guilty verdict of first-degree murder that gave Hussong a life term in prison.

Voiceprint Analysis Expertise

To be qualified as experts in voiceprint analysis, technicians must:

1. Complete a course of study on spectrographic analysis that generally runs from two to four weeks
2. Complete one hundred voice comparison

cases under intense personal supervision by a known expert

3. Be examined by a board of experts in the field

Since courts generally contest the methods of interpretation, not the actual accuracy or reliability of the spectrographic instrument, it is important that any spectrograph technician who testifies in court be highly qualified. The less training and experience the technician has, the more such testimony becomes vulnerable to serious questions by the judge and jury.

All of the studies that have been done on spectrographic accuracy, including a 1986 FBI survey, show that those people who have been properly trained and who use standard aural and visual procedures get highly accurate results. Bringing such studies to the attention of the courts could help determine who is indeed an expert and could minimize some of the controversy and confusion that comes from misperception.

Those who do the recordings for analysis must also be competent to operate the recording device, because the quality of the tape has great bearing on the interpreter's results.

Anyone who talks on a phone or tape recorder is fair game for voice analysis, especially if they have criminal intent. Increasingly, more law enforcement officers are getting trained in voiceprint analysis, and with the development of computer and digital spectrogram technology, the procedure is becoming widely used. In all likelihood, voiceprints will continue to play a key role in any investigation that involves voice evidence. As such, they will become part of the evidence brought into court. Like other technologies that once were resisted but are now fully admissible, voiceprints may soon have their day.

The Lie Detector

Your heart pounds. Your throat constricts. Your eyes glaze, and you can feel the orbital muscles begin to twitch. No good trying to bluff – your every movement is recorded, and the mild-mannered questioner facing you is trained in every physical symptom of deceit . . . you might just as well confess!

THE LIE DETECTOR has a firm place in crime fiction writing as a magic machine which strikes fear into the hearts of hardened criminals. It is not quite like that, for although the lie detector is widely used in crime investigation in the USA, information gained by its use is not generally accepted as direct evidence in the courts.

An English heart specialist, Sir James MacKenzie, invented the 'ink polarograph' in 1908. This was a heart recorder and was the forerunner of the lie detector used in criminal detection. It has long been observed that persons telling lies are subject to involuntary physiological reactions. A pounding heart, an impulse to swallow and a twitching eye are all signs of deception. The principle of the lie detector is to record and interpret these reactions.

Early detectors recorded blood pressure, pulse and respiration changes – later developments added muscle movements and galvanic skin reaction. The modern lie detector is a mechanical device which uses well-tried instruments for recording individual reactions. For instance, blood pressure is measured with the pneumatic arm cuff apparatus common to the doctor's surgery.

Respiration is a most difficult activity to control consciously and tell-tale changes take place under the stress of telling lies. This is an important function to monitor. Fluctuations in respiration are measured by means of a flexible rubber tube fastened across the subject's chest. This expands and contracts with respiration and the movements are transferred to pen recorders.

In addition to changes in blood pressure and respiration, the act of deception leads to an increase in perspiration. This can be measured by electrodes attached to the palmar and dorsal surfaces of the hand which record changes in the activity of the sweat glands. This is the galvanic skin reaction (GSR) or electrodermal response. GSR, together with the other responses, are transferred by pen recorders to moving graph paper. A permanent record of an examination is thus obtained.

Agencies using lie detectors have developed their own codes of practice to make the testing procedure completely objective. The integrity of the examiner is highly stressed. Examination is carried out in a private room free from noise and interruption. The only persons present are the examiner and the test subject. Some agencies use a two-way mirror which allows another examiner to observe the test subject without being seen.

Detached and Unemotional

The examiner is fully briefed about the events on which a subject is to be examined. He must have a full understanding in order to ask perceptive and unambiguous questions. It is essential that he remains detached and unemotional. Once the subject is hooked up to the lie detector, the examiner begins a sequence of questioning which is usually divided into four clear parts.

1. The examiner helps the subject to acquaint himself with the equipment. From general questioning the examiner seeks to form an opinion as to the character of the subject. A subject giving untruthful answers may be expected to delay his replies, to fidget in his chair and not to look the examiner straight in the eye. It is made clear that the lie detector is also a truth detector.

2. Questions relevant to the crime under investigation are asked. Replies are marked on the recording chart.

3. The card test. The subject is shown a series of cards placed face down on the table. He is told that each card bears a number and he is asked to select one and take note of the number. He is not to say what the number is. The examiner collects the cards, shuffles them and tells the subject to answer 'No' to each question. In this way the subject tells a lie about the identity of the numbered card he has selected.

The card test is a kind of calibration. By looking at the recorded trace, the examiner will be able to tell the subject which card he selected.

This is a convincing test of the lie detector's efficiency.

4. The subject is asked if he wishes to make any corrections or admissions regarding the truthfulness of the answers given in 2. If the answer is 'No', the question routine is repeated. If 'Yes', suitably modified questions are asked.

Where the results to this sequence of questions are inconclusive, further tests are made. These involve changing the order and wording of the earlier questions.

Interpreting the recordings made of a subject's replies to a question sequence is a matter for the skilled and experienced examiner, but the visible evidence of a lie is often quite dramatic.

Three or four lie detector test records are usually considered sufficient for analysis. Evidence of deception must be recorded on at least two separate tests for it to carry weight. When properly used, the technique has a high degree of accuracy and is a widely used investigative aid.

Deep Suspicion and Fear

Since 1923, advocates of the lie detector have fought a long battle to have information obtained by the apparatus recognized by the courts. Many of the decisions refusing recognition have implied that the method has insufficient scientific validity. In some quarters there is deep suspicion, even fear, of the machine which, though it may trap the criminal, is thought capable of ensnaring the innocent too. Some States prohibit the use of the lie detector altogether. On the other hand, various Federal and local government agencies use the technique as a matter of course for screening job applicants. The appointment of police officers in some cities is also conditional on passing a lie detector examination.

Many police departments ask suspects voluntarily to submit to the lie detector and a convincing number of confessions has resulted. The mere threat of the lie test is often sufficient to make a criminal confess. Confessions obtained as a consequence of a voluntary lie test, but not as part of it, have been admitted in the courts. Apart from mistrust of justice dispensed with the aid of a machine, the main anxiety over the lie detector concerns the examiner. He must obviously be trained to a high standard and be answerable to professional discipline in the way that doctors are. Another factor which prevents ready acceptance of the lie detector is the possibility of disputes arising out of an individual's privilege against self-incrimination.

A celebrated case in which the lie detector featured at a late stage was the Sheppard murder. On July 10, 1954, Dr Sam Sheppard was questioned by the Cuyahoga County Police about the murder of his wife, six days previously. Sam, youngest of three doctor brothers, worked in the Cleveland osteopathic clinic run by the Sheppard family. When questioned by the police he had obvious facial injuries and his neck was in a medical collar. According to Sheppard he had been injured when grappling with an intruder at his house on the shore of Lake Erie.

Sheppard told the police that he and his wife had dinner at home with friends on the evening of July 3. The friends left after midnight. He was dozing on the couch in the living-room – his wife went upstairs to bed. His next recollection was of hearing his wife cry out. He ran upstairs. In the bedroom he grappled with an intruder who knocked him unconscious.

When he came to, Sheppard had a hazy memory of seeing his wife lying on the bed. He thought the intruder was still in the house. He went downstairs and chased a person out of the house, there was a struggle and again Sheppard was knocked out. Recovering consciousness for the second time, Sheppard found himself lying shirtless in shallow water at the lake's edge. He staggered to his feet and went into the house, immediately going up to the bedroom. In a dazed condition, he took his wife's pulse – he realized then that she was dead. He telephoned a neighbour. 'My God, Spence, get over here quick. I think they've killed Marilyn.'

The police were called to the scene and Dr Sheppard's brothers also arrived at the house. His brothers were concerned at Sam's injuries – he had a fractured neck vertebra – and they took him off to hospital. It happened that the nearest hospital was also the family clinic. The family's action in taking Sheppard away from the house caused a great deal of subsequent controversy.

The main bedroom of the Sheppard house contained twin beds. On one of them, lying on her back, was Marilyn Sheppard. Her head had been terribly battered and the sheets were soaked in blood. Blood was spattered on all four walls, though not on the ceiling, and there were spots on Sam's bed, which was undisturbed. There was no trace of the murder weapon.

A Search of the Grounds

Sam's study was in disarray. Desk drawers had been turned out and the contents of the doctor's medical bag lay strewn on the floor. A strange feature of the case was that the T-shirt worn by Sheppard on the night of the murder was missing. A search of the grounds around the house revealed a cloth bag belonging to Sheppard, which contained the doctor's wristwatch with the hands stopped at 4.15. Blood on the watch proved to be that of his wife.

The police concluded that Sheppard had killed his wife in a fit of anger and tried to cover it up by feigning a burglary. The missing T-shirt they presumed had been destroyed because it was blood-stained. Sam said that blood must have got on his wristwatch when he took his wife's pulse. The discovery that Sheppard had been having an adulterous affair with another woman did nothing to placate public opinion. His guilt was widely assumed in the Cleveland area and rumours abounded of debauchery and a cover-up. When the inquest on Marilyn Sheppard's death opened on July 21, the public were openly hostile to Sam and on July 30 he was arrested.

The case of the State of Ohio versus Sam

Sheppard opened on October 18. The prosecution made much of the lack of fingerprints in the Sheppard's house – only one identifiable fingerprint was found. That was a print of Sam's thumb on the headboard of his wife's bed. This was thought to be odd, as a few hours before the murder there had been four adults and two children in the house. There was a strong suggestion that furniture had been wiped clean of fingerprints.

Blood on the Pillow

The scientific evidence was confusing. There were arguments about blood spots found on the stairs and about a bloody imprint on a pillow.

The jury deliberated for three days. They found Sheppard guilty of second degree murder, and concluded that he had tried to fake a burglary, had inflicted injuries on himself and had hidden the murder weapon and blood-stained T-shirt. They could find no evidence of premeditation. Sam Sheppard was sentenced to life imprisonment.

Sheppard's lawyers went through all the appeal procedures in an effort to introduce new evidence and get a retrial. Finally, in October 1956, the US Supreme Court refused to set aside the conviction. But in July of the following year, a 26-year-old Florida convict named Wedler told prison authorities that he had murdered a woman in Cleveland in 1954. There had already been a number of confessions to the Sheppard murder but none worth considering seriously. However, Donald Wedler's story sparked off a concerted attempt to prove Sam Sheppard's innocence.

Wedler said that he had stolen a car in Cleveland and broken into a lake-side house intent on theft. His attempts at burglary awakened a woman whom he silenced by beating with an iron pipe. He used the same weapon to knock out a man who tackled him on the stairs. Wedler did not mention the name but the similarities made it possible that it was Marilyn Sheppard he killed.

The Cleveland police were reluctant to take any action but interest was quickly roused when the story appeared in the press. Erle Stanley Gardner, a highly successful crime writer and also a practising lawyer, suggested that Wedler be given a lie test. Gardner wanted this carried out under the auspices of the Court of Last Resort, a non-profit making organization which gave professional services in cases of injustice. The Sheppard family had already appealed.

Put Through Their Paces

Sam Sheppard's brothers and their wives were the first to undergo lie tests. An impressive array of lie-detector experts was assembled and the Sheppards were put through their paces. On July 15 the newsstands sold copies of *Argosy* magazine carrying an article by Erle Stanley Gardner – its title was 'Are the Sheppards telling the truth?' It was the view of the lie-detector experts that they were. The examiners were satisfied that the Sheppards were sincere in their view that Sam did not kill his wife and that the family were in no way connected in any attempt to conceal evidence.

Next, Wedler was subjected to the lie test. He spent three and a half hours hooked up to the detector. The examiners' conclusion was that he too was telling the truth or, as they modified their statement to the press, '. . . what he believes to be the truth.' Wedler was subsequently interviewed by reporters who seemed satisfied with his story.

The Court of Last Resort now won approval from the Ohio State Governor to give a lie test to Sam Sheppard in the Ohio Penitentiary. Arrangements were made to carry out the test although critics were quick to point out that Sheppard's lawyers had earlier refused to let him submit to the lie detector. Opposition to the lie testing of the convicted man mounted and the trial judge objected to the Court of Last Resort setting itself above the United States Supreme Court.

The Ohio Governor's permission to allow the lie test to be given was withdrawn. It was a bitter disappointment to Gardner and to the advocates of lie detector examination, and it was a blow also to public interest in justice. The results of lie testing the Sheppard family and Donald Wedler seemed to merit the final step of examining Sam Sheppard himself. While the possible outcome of such a test can only be speculated upon, both Sam Sheppard and the lie detector were denied final vindication. Sam Sheppard was finally acquitted at a second trial in 1966 when celebrity lawyer F. Lee Bailey conducted his defence. Sheppard died four years later, but this case inspired the TV show and the movie *The Fugitive.*

FBI to Test Their Employees

The FBI made all of its employees undergo random polygraph tests as from February 2001. This policy change came about because Robert Hanssen, accused of selling US classified information to the Russians, never had a polygraph test during his 25-year FBI career.

Hanssen was arrested at a park near his Vienna, Virginia, home while allegedly dropping classified materials into a secret location for pickup by Russian agents. He was charged in a federal court with two counts of espionage activities from the 1980s. As a result of this the FBI's computer systems were also redesigned. The redesign included updating audit abilities and flagging mechanisms. For example, even though Hanssen searched his name several times to see if he was under investigation, the computer system did not raise any red flags. The search for the $600,000 Hanssen allegedly was paid for offering secrets to the Russians continues to this day.

Scraps of Evidence

It was a saying of the French criminologist, Professor Edmond Locard, one of the greatest forensic scientists of the twentieth century, that 'Wherever he steps, whatever he touches, whatever he leaves, even unconsciously, will serve as a silent witness against him.'

WHEN A MAN tries to cover up the traces of evidence deliberately, he is almost certainly in trouble. Not only his fingerprints or his footprints, but his hair, the fibres from his clothes, the glass he breaks, the tool mark he leaves, the paint he scratches, the blood or semen he deposits or collects, and so on . . .

All of these things and more, bear silent witness against the criminal. This is evidence that does not forget. But of course this evidence has to be found, studied, and understood before we can know its true value in solving a crime.

Documents are so much the basis of modern life that they are obviously often involved in crimes. Documentary evidence does not mean forgery alone. The document examiner covers, both figuratively and literally, a large amount of territory.

Paper, the root of most of his work, is, to be briefly technical, an aqueous deposit of any vegetable fibre in sheet form. The name, as most people know, comes from the Latin *papyrus*, which in the hands of the early Egyptians, its first known users, comprised the pith of a sedge-like plant which was sliced into layers and beaten or pressed into sheets.

But, as so often happens, the Chinese were ahead of everybody and nearly 2,000 years ago were using paper made by hand. This paper was fashioned by processes used all over the world until not long ago – though paper, as such, did not appear in Europe until about the eleventh century. In Britain paper first came from a paper mill erected around 1490. Its products, in fact, were used for an edition of Chaucer's *Canterbury Tales*.

The forger, in his efforts to defeat science, has tried his hand at artificially aging paper. For example, the general discolouration due to age is a process of oxidation, which is easily confirmed by the expert examiner. The faker tries to imitate this, using liquids like tea or coffee, woodfire smoke, extract of tobacco, and even permanganate of potash to achieve that vital faint brown effect.

Age is also attempted by pressing a false document into folds and rubbing these folds along a carpet or an old wall to simulate an ancient fold. The microscope, however, will pick out in seconds the rubbing or dirt grains along a bogus fold.

Watermarks, another weapon of forgers, began in Italy about the thirteenth century. They are made when paper is a wet pulp. A dandy roll, a woven wire gauze-covered skeleton roll, has the watermark device soldered on to it. The impression of the roll on the wet pulp causes a thinning of fibres which, when the paper is finished, is the familiar watermark.

A faker's trick is to process finished paper by imprinting with his own dandy roll, using some sort of oily substance as a watermark – this looks genuine to the casual eye. But test it with a damp cloth or a petrol soaked paintbrush and the watermark will vanish.

One of the problems which frustrates the examiner of documents is what experts call 'sample'. A document cannot always be cut, marked, or touched with reagents – chemicals which act in certain ways on materials. Suppose it is desired to find out if a paper contains linen and cotton, important in dating it. It can be touched with something called zinc-chloriodine. The marked spot will turn wine red, unthinkable on a perhaps valuable document.

Then the microscope steps in. Dates of paper origins are generally well authenticated and if an old type of paper is examined, say, one made from rags, the linen or cotton fibres in it show distinctive features which are absolutely different from modern wood pulp papers. But – and here is the exception – many high grade modern papers are still made from linen or cotton.

There was the case of a questioned document, brilliantly forged, as it turned out. It was supposed to be 400 years old. The false writing was almost foolproof; the forger had found some old paper of the right age; the ink used was genuine carbon ink which goes back, according to the great Egyptologist, Professor Flinders Petrie, to Egypt 5,000 years ago.

The expert working on this document saw hours of investigation ahead to produce evidence that would stand up in court about something he only 'felt' was wrong. Then, through his microscope ocular, he saw something incredible. Embedded in the ink of a letter was an almost invisible particle that looked metallic. Elaborate examination showed that there were minute particles embedded in that ink – aluminium.

This modern metal was the giveaway, for the police were later able to show that the forger's brother, working in the same room during the actual writing, was filing an aluminium casing. Aluminium dust, floating invisible in the air, settled in that carefully processed carbon ink writing until the microscope found the answer.

Inks, next to paper, are usually the expert's friend. When a letter is written in ordinary ink, and not blotted, it seems natural to the naked eye. A simple hand-lens or magnifying glass, will reveal clues. The writer paused for a second to think of a word and then hyphenated it. The lens shows the faintest difference in ink shading, or perhaps the pen is lifted in the middle of a letter and then it carries on; the lens shows that, too.

Ink itself will 'talk'. One notable forensic chemist in the 1920s, claimed that ink in ancient times was made from soot taken from cooking vessels, which accounts for its almost indefinite life. Iron gall ink (a mixture of ferrous sulphate with an infusion of nuts, galls and gum) came in about the first century of the Christian era. The Romans generally used an iron compound ink, the one, for example, used in the *Codex Sinaiticus*, which dates from the fourth century AD.

So the dating goes on – iron gall ink had logwood put into it in the middle of the eighteenth century to improve its colour. A hundred years later they were using logwood with potassium chromate, and no iron, for writing purposes. All this and more means reasonably accurate dating.

The first modern ink, aniline dye ink, came in a blue form in 1861, a fairly impermanent writing fluid. This was followed by a famous advertisement for blue-black ink which showed a large blot, dark in the centre and light at the edges. Indeed it was incorrect, for in practice the reverse order would have been the case.

In current years that well-known enemy of all who love good handwriting, the ballpoint pen, contains a so-called 'solid' ink which is, in fact, a thick suspension of dye in a drying oil. Its stable companion, the fibre-tipped pen is one that, unluckily, does present problems in forensic document examination.

Traces of metal, usually iron, can be found when ordinary pen marks have been erased or bleached out. Ultraviolet light will reveal these interferences. Pencils or ballpoint pens often leave no residue which can be picked up after erasure, but embossing occurs in the paper used. Fibres are disturbed in the paper as well, and these will answer to the expert.

The fibre-tipped pen, as it is usually called, is so

light in its effect that it leaves behind no clue after erasure – other than disturbed sizing on the paper. But where additions or amendments have been made on a fibre-pen written whole, then all is reasonably well – close examination soon reveals the differences in ink quality, shading and such.

The copying pencil, the one which leaves mauve marks on the tongue when it is accidentally licked, can be a godsend to the document examiner. In the Southampton garage murder in England in 1930 a man named Messiter was found killed. There were no apparent clues until a sharp-eyed detective picked up a dirty little scrap of paper. The back was a lodging house receipt, the front also seemed to bear words – but they were invisible under tread marks, dirt, and oil.

Words Bleached Out

A simple method worked this time. The paper was very delicately 'washed' in benzene and there, under the dirt, was the name 'F. Thomas' written in copying pencil. A letter was found in the victim's files bearing this name, later proved to be an alias of a man named Podmore. It was not long before evidence was found to support a charge of murder. Podmore was duly convicted, the scrap of paper becoming vital court evidence.

Erasures have been mentioned and these continually arise in document examination. Erasures are, simply, the removal of words, bleaching out before substitution; such partial interference with documents being a not uncommon crime.

A first test is to hold the suspect document on an angle before a good light. The eye, or a hand-lens, often reveals interference – chemical erasures tend to 'stand out', particularly those on paper with a high finish.

Suppose a word has been bleached out and another put in its place. The original word can generally be read by using ultraviolet light with the correct plate and filter. This method shows up the original disturbed fibres of the paper, assuming an ordinary pen has been used, and a 'shadow' of the word is revealed.

One of the most delicate and adroit recovery methods is one used by the late Paul Kirk, a leading American documentary expert. To recover erasures, obliterations, or indented ('ghost') writing he used plastic casts, a process so exacting and so difficult that an ordinary man would not have patience to try it. Kirk, however, achieved some excellent results.

Burning a document is not always a successful evasion. One man in a crime burned a vital cheque in a grate, and broke up the ashes with a poker. Experts worked for hours, spraying the fragments with diluted lacquer until they were strong enough to be touched.

Then the bits were reassembled until they were almost complete. Strong oblique light showed up the inked writing, which had carbonized, and the case was solved. The point of these examples is that the expert is a trained man who never neglects anything, no matter how trivial or even silly it may seem, and who possesses patience so limitless that it appears unearthly.

Another facet of document examination is graphology. This is a suspect word, for it suggests people who profess to read character from handwriting. To some extent this may be possible, but it is seldom taken seriously.

Once, at a court hearing, the writer of a letter was designated by a 'graphologist' (not a handwriting expert) as 'French, middle-class, and young'. When the man in question was called as a witness he turned out to be the English son of an Armenian father, educated in the United States and well over fifty at the time of the hearing.

But handwriting can turn out to be dangerous when the expert deals with it. Writing, after all, is the conditioned reflex of a person using a writing instrument, and to disguise one's natural self in *such* circumstances is extremely difficult.

For example, in 1970 a great controversy raged when a British journal, *The Criminologist*, published an article which indicated that the Duke of Clarence, Queen Victoria's grandson and until his death, heir to the English throne, might have been 'Jack the Ripper' – the sex murderer who terrorized London's East end in the autumn of 1888.

The journal itself later put an end to all this excitement by asking Professor C. L. Wilson, an important document examiner in government service, to study the handwriting of the Duke and the handwritings ascribed to the 'Ripper'.

Professor Wilson wrote: 'To sum up, on the basis of the handwriting, all the evidence is against identification of Jack the Ripper with the

Duke of Clarence.'

Nor is the typewriter proof against the expert. The wear, the defects, the individualities of each machine all 'talk' to the expert, who, given a sample, can produce all sorts of vital facts. The hand-lens, the microscope, and measuring devices play their part in studying wear, defects, accidentals (dirt, damaged letters, and so on).

The slant of the characters, angles, alignment, and footing are important – footing being that a letter may strike heavier on its right, its left, or its bottom.

Every typewriter is peculiar to itself, after a little use. Similarity in all details in two machines may be ignored (the chance of two machines being identical is estimated to be one in 3,000,000,000,000).

Last comes forgery, and in this field, free writing is one of the most skilful forms. It means the forger practises endlessly from the subject's handwritten models until it can be copied without an original. In time and place it can be successful, but it does not stand up when the expert examines the *corpus delicti* (which does not mean corpse but 'the sum or aggregate of the ingredients which make a given fact a breach of given law').

Counterfeit Chaos

Banknotes, postage stamps, and insurance stamps are fair game for forgers. But the false banknote is often marked by indifferent or incomplete work – these poor examples the forger usually passes in crowded in shops or presses on busy, overworked cashiers.

Forgery on a massive scale is not always successful. During World War II the Hitler government produced numerous £5 banknotes as a weapon against Britain – intending that the counterfeit money would find its way to England and cause chaos in the businesses and banks.

The full technical resources of German experts were used, and with what result? Ultraviolet light showed that the ink was different. There was a fault visible to the naked eye just above the B in the *Bank of England* watermark; the watermark also had three lines too many on one sample, and two lines lacking in the second.

A forged note and a real one were given to an ordinary bank cashier, who was blindfolded. He indicated the forgery immediately – it did not 'feel' right.

Car Crimes

Forensic investigation of car crimes has become more and more sophisticated – rust and paint fragments, motor body fillers, pieces of glass, skid marks etc.

WITH A SCREAM of tyres a hit-and-run driver swung across a boulevard in Berkeley, California, colliding with another automobile then careering off into the darkness. It seemed a grim eternity before the police came, and reports were being made under the staccato flashes of official cameras recording the scene for forensic examination . . . because, as is so often the case with hit-and-run, there were no effective witnesses.

Electron Beams

Yet within hours the police came upon a suspect vehicle, and the incident at Berkeley made forensic history as the first occasion on which the SEM (scanning electron microscope) was used to nail down an offender – when every other crime-laboratory method had failed.

The experts concerned in the examination were J. I. Thornton and G. T. Mitosinka of the School of Criminology, and T. L. Hayes of the Donner Laboratory, all at the University of

California, Berkeley, USA.

It was in 1963 that the first scanning electron microscopes became available to forensic workers, and five years passed before they were demonstrated at a forensic symposium before the American Chemical Society at Atlantic City in 1968.

They were greatly needed – for even with the best glass lenses the limit of magnification of an optical microscope is 1300x (that is 1,300 times the size of the specimen), whereas by scanning the specimen with television-like electron beams – as in a TV picture-tube – workers can get magnifications in excess of 25,000x. Something that is just as important when studying small forensic samples, is a depth of focus of around 100 microns. (One micron is a thousandth of a millimetre.)

From the case-history of Thornton, Mitosinka and Hayes it was shown how effective this proved in the Berkeley hit-and-run offence.

Metal Helix

'An alert police officer at the scene recovered, in addition to glass and paint evidence, an exceedingly minute metal helix, all that remained of a car headlight filament. The piece was some 1-mm in length, and the problem was to match it with a portion of tungsten filament still attached to the filament-post of the suspect car.'

An initial check was made with a stereoscopic binocular optical 'comparison' microscope, which suggested the possibility of striae (minute lines of furrows and scratches, capable of being matched) along the tungsten wire surface. Filaments are made by drawing fine tungsten wire through steel dies, so the score-marks are similar along the entire length.

Same Die

The Berkeley team, with the help of the Donner Laboratory and facilities of the United States Atomic Energy Commission, took but thirty minutes to photograph the two samples of hair-like filament in a scanning electron microscope. Taking picture after picture, they were able to keep the 200-micron-diameter wire fragments in focus.

'Examination of the filaments,' the team reported, 'indicated that the striae persisted throughout the length of the helix, indicating that the two fragments had been drawn through the same die. But presumably there could be other filaments with essentially identical draw marks . . .'

This is as far as the forensic scientist can go. It is then left to the police and the District Attorney to show that the possibility of the damaged automobile *not* being involved in the hit-and-run incident would be several million to one?

While the SEM is among the latest sophisticated forensic tools, some years went by – and doubtless many criminals escaped identification – until a basically simple device was adopted by forensic workers. An auxiliary steering-wheel was introduced so that a suspect car could be driven by police to the crime laboratory without destroying fingerprints or other material evidence.

Not until 1954 when a detachable steering wheel was devised by Superintendent Fred Cherrill (then head of the New Scotland Yard Fingerprint Bureau, responsible for indexing the Yard's first ten-million dabs) was it possible to handle an abandoned or 'crime' car without risk. Until then, all dabs had to be dusted or sprayed and photographed on the spot.

The Cherrill auxiliary wheel fitted the type of symmetrical-spoked steering wheel then in vogue, but it could not be bolted to the more modern American and European wheels.

Then, in 1968, Mr D. D. F. Hardinge of the Department of Scientific and Industrial Research, Lower Hutt, New Zealand, devised a new auxiliary wheel for the New Zealand Police Department. This clamps on with rubber pads to almost every style of wheel, and is currently becoming a universal piece of police forensic equipment.

Next, from a neighbouring crime laboratory, at Private Bay, Petone, New Zealand, came another forensic aid to auto investigation.

Almost every report of a car chase includes details not only of debris such as rust and paint, but of motor body fillers. The complex body pressings of modern cars are given a crack-free and seam-free surface with plastic or other fillers. So, when there is an impact, identification of the filler may prove evidential.

In 1967 research on this was started by Mr B. Cleverley of the DSIR Chemistry Division at Petone – who built up a file of infra-red spectra, so that a suspect filler sample could be matched against a known control. With a Perkin-Elmer model-21 spectro-photometer, he put pellet after pellet of filler into the optical system, and brought it to incandescence. The resultant light was viewed through a prism and lens system, splitting it up not only into the colours of the rainbow, but disclosing identifying dark bars or bands between the colours.

To get an absolute standard, pellets 13-mm in diameter were prepared in the laboratory, ground up with potassium bromide in a few drops of tetrachloroethane, blended and dried.

Depending upon the resins in the car-body fillers (epoxy and polyester resins are mostly used in the auto body trade, internationally) Cleverley was able to identify fillers by spectra colours ranging from black through shades of brown, yellow and green, to silver and white.

A different application of spectrophotometry has enabled Britain's Dr J. B. F. Lloyd, of the Home Office Forensic Science Laboratory, Birmingham, to give world forensic workers a precise new technique – characterization of mineral oil traces.

Oil Drips

'The circumstances may be,' says Dr Lloyd, 'that oil and grease may be found on pedestrians struck by motor vehicles, oil drips left where vehicles have been parked, or oil carried on stolen engine parts. Waste oil is a widely-distributed material likely to be transferred at scenes of crime . . .'

Back in 1951 a continental worker characterized

petroleum products such as car oil by the fluorescence of a sample diffused on blotting paper, and in 1955 Dr A. D. Baynes-Cope disclosed his technique for examination of pitch (as from car-battery cases), mineral oil and grease.

A few years later, using a Baird Automatic SF 100E spectro-photofluorimeter at the Home Office Laboratory in Birmingham, England, Dr Lloyd made use of a completely new technique known as synchronous excitation of fluorescence emission. The spectra of minute samples of car oils and fuels were examined, and the fluorescence noted while the samples were excited at varying wave lengths.

Crashing Distance

In the crime laboratory graphs were plotted of the fluorescence spectra of hydrocarbons likely to be encountered in car-crime cases. Then it was the work of only a few minutes to check a new suspect sample against a known control.

In most accident and hit-and-run cases there are skid or brake marks left on the road, and forensic workers may have to interpret these. Few ordinary motorists even consider what enormous forces produce the familiar burn marks on the road. They are actually the result of the car's energy in being braked, changed into heat, and then burning the road.

Forensic workers need to determine stopping and 'crashing' distances from these marks, and a cross-section of them were told by Mr S. S.

Oldham (a consultant engineer specializing in this aspect of car-crime research) at a Forensic Science Society meeting in Great Britain.

'The energy stored up in a moving vehicle varies as the square of its speed: in other words, if you double the speed it has four times the energy stored in it, so that in reducing the speed from 40 to 20 m.p.h. the brakes have to convert to heat three times the work they would have to do in completing the stop from 20 m.p.h.

'As an example, a fully-laden vehicle weighing six tons, travelling at 30 m.p.h., has stored up a kinetic energy of 404,000 foot-pounds. If the brakes can stop it with even a 50 per cent reading on an efficiency meter, the dissipation is equal to 267 horsepower, in less than three seconds!

'When the wheels are locked during brake application, the tyre slips over the road surface and the heat generated is concentrated in this area. It can, and does, melt the tar on the road surface, producing the characteristic black marks.'

New Techniques

For forensic tests after a running-down accident, the police usually drive the vehicle over the same road surface at the scene, producing identical burn marks. This enables forensic experts to testify that, to produce the marks found, the vehicle had to be driven at such-and-such a speed, and the brakes applied until the wheels locked – when the vehicle slid to a standstill in so many feet.

Not all car accidents and car-crimes are deliberate, and a good deal is due to 'the nut at the wheel'. As Mr Oldham put it: 'I am sure that the average car driver has no conception of the tremendous power and kinetic-energy-potential that he is in charge of, or how ill-fitted he is by nature to drive a motorcar at all – when one considers the very slow reaction-time possessed by humans.

'It is about three-fifths of a second which, at 30 m.p.h. or 44 feet-per-second, means that he will travel roughly 27 feet before he can react to anything!'

Escaping criminals, drunken drivers, and almost every category of motorist driving crazily, depend upon tyres. It is not surprising, therefore, that forensic and allied workers in many countries are still building up a fund of new techniques – not always in agreement. Among world leaders in this forensic sphere are Mr R. J. Grogan of Fort Dunlop in association with Mr T. R. Watson of the Birmingham Home Office Forensic Science Laboratory, in Britain.

The Grogan-Watson team have found new facets quite apart from the obvious 'fingerprint' matching of tyres to treadmarks at a scene of crime. In most cases they can instantly identify patterns by tyre width and features such as knife-cuts (sipes), decorative trade pattern lines, and so on. It is often possible to identify a type of vehicle from its tyre mark.

'There is a very common tendency,' explains Mr Grogan, 'to believe that criminals reverse into the gateways to fields before discarding their wares: but examination of tyre prints in relation to gateways usually shows that the vehicle has been driven in forwards, and has either been reversed when out of sight or, more commonly, been driven in a circle inside the field.

'Oil spots will usually indicate the position of the engine, and when taken into conjunction with tyre marks show whether a front- or a rear-engined car has been used.'

Forensic investigation of car crime often produces startling results – but seldom more surprising than in the case of gang-leader Georgie Day who, in 1957, was taken terribly injured to St Leonard's Hospital, Hoxton, in East London.

'He's been the victim of a hit-and-run accident,' said the two men who brought Day to the Casualty Ward. But even before Day died in hospital, detectives of the Criminal Investigation Department were certain they were on a murder hunt.

There were no blood marks in the street where the two men said Day had been hit by a car. Then, less than twenty-four hours later, an abandoned truck was found in a Peckham (South London) street, and was discovered to have the rear wheels stained with blood of Group-B – the group of the dead gangster. Fibres from his blue serge suit were discovered adhering to an oily rear spring. And on the hub-caps of the truck there were smears of red brick dust.

At once the CID team began a hunt for a wall, possibly one which had been knocked down and hurriedly rebuilt. Local police reported such a wall in Brockley, South-east London, and when the detectives dug the soil at the base of the brickwork they found more Group-B bloodstains. Meanwhile the post-mortem examination revealed that Day had been hit by something heavier than a hit-and-run car blow.

A crime pattern was built up, and on December 11 at the Old Bailey, Mr Justice Glyn-Jones sentenced the two men who had 'rescued' Day to terms of imprisonment – one of four years, and one of three.

The truth was that Day had been involved in a big theft of lead, and the truck had crushed him against the wall while it was being unloaded.

Of his two confederates, the judge stated that they had acted 'with selfish cruelty' in finishing their theft before taking him to hospital.

Using techniques now routine in all cases of car crime, the London CID and the Metropolitan Police Forensic Laboratory had been able to reach the truth of the matter – thus ensuring that justice was done, and was seen to be done.

Today's computer technology enables criminal investigators to do more than anyone dreamed in the days of Holmes and Watson. They can devise a computerized model of the crime scene and probable sequence of events, making it easier to visualize precisely what happened. Computers can also translate physical evidence (for example, the tyre tracks) into useful numerical data. From skid lengths and other factors, the computer can even give a computation of the speed of the car.

Clues From Hair

Looking at a human hair under a microscope the forensic scientist can obtain information about the age, race and sex of its owner.

HAIR CAN provide crime investigators with important clues. Apart from burning, hair is virtually indestructible. It remains identifiable even on bodies in an advanced state of decomposition or attached to objects after a crime has been committed.

The forensic scientist using a microscope can make even a single head hair yield information about the race, sex and age of its owner, and while hair does not have the same individual character as a fingerprint, it can provide vital evidence.

For example, in August 1951, a woman's body was found in a rural spot near Nottingham. The victim, Mabel Tattershaw, a 48-year-old housewife, had been strangled. Minute inspection of her clothing revealed some hairs which were immediately sent to the forensic laboratory, where microscopic examination showed them to be identical with the head hair of Leonard Mills, an 18-year-old clerk and the chief suspect. Together with other damning evidence, these hairs helped to take a murderer to the scaffold.

Chemical Changes

Apart from the obvious characteristics of length, colour and texture, hair seen under a magnification of x200 has an amazing variety of properties. An individual hair is a solid, roughly cylindrical structure. It consists of an inner core or medulla containing colouring pigment, a middle layer – the cortex – made of a dense, horny substance known as keratin, and an outer layer, the cuticle, composed of tiny overlapping scales.

The cuticular scales, which vary in shape between individuals, are of great value when matching hairs; most importantly, the scales enable human hair to be readily distinguished from that of animals. The differences between animal hairs are quite marked and any hair discovered is quite easily matched to a particular creature. Dog hairs, for example, found on a suspect's clothing can place him at the scene of a crime.

The part of the body from which a hair has come is also determined by its shape. Head hairs, for instance, are usually square at the ends while eyebrow hairs are finely tapered. Moustache hairs tend to be triangular in section.

Sex is not as easily determined from head hair except by the now vanishing differences in length. Hair that is treated; bleached, dyed, lacquered, singed or curled may give additional help in sexing hair, but there are differences in the pubic hairs, which appear rather longer in men and somewhat coarser in women. Male pubic hairs are always looked for on alleged victims of rape.

It is possible to tell the age of hair, but only within fairly wide limits. Chemical changes occur with age, and laboratory tests can distinguish between hair from a child and an adult; hair also thickens slightly with age and this thickening can be measured.

Cross-section

When it is sent for examination to the Forensic Science Laboratory hair is normally dry mounted on a glass slide for viewing under a comparison microscope. To examine it in cross-section, the specimen is mounted in a wax block from which wafer-thin slices are cut and mounted on glass slides. The cross-sectional shape and appearance of the medulla is then viewed microscopically.

Impressions of the cuticular scales are sometimes made on cellulose acetate for detailed study; the forensic scientist also has a variety of tests available for dealing with dyed hair and examining for age.

The brilliance of the forensic laboratory cannot shine, however, without the most thorough and painstaking work of investigating officers at the scene of the crime; fortunately, in regard to hair, nature is on the side of the crime investigator. The hair of every part of the body has a definite period of growth and is continuously lost and replaced; minute examination of clothing and other articles can therefore pay dividends.

Decomposed Remains

Evidence provided by hair has played an important part in a number of murder investigations. In October 1942, the badly decomposed remains of a woman's body were found buried on a heath near Godalming, Surrey. It was estimated that the body had been lying in the heather for about five weeks. This was the so-called 'Wigwam' murder, in which the victim, who had been stabbed and beaten about the head, lived in a crude shelter made of branches and heather.

Police searching the heathland made several discoveries which enabled them to confirm the victim's identity as Joan Pearle Wolfe. They also found a heavy birch branch with hair adhering to it lying in long grass about 400 yards from the body. Laboratory examination identified this as the weapon responsible for the head injuries; nine head hairs sticking to the heavy end of the branch proved to be identical with the head hair of the victim. August Sangret, a French-Canadian soldier from a nearby camp, had been living with the girl in the 'Wigwam' for several months. He was tried for murder, found guilty and executed at Wandsworth.

Scraps of Paper

Probably the most famous murder featuring hair evidence was the Podmore Case. On January 10, 1929, a man's body was found behind some boxes in a locked garage in Southampton. The victim, Vivian Messiter, an oil company agent, had been dead for some time, and rats had attacked the body. A puncture wound over the left eye at first led the local police to think that the man had been shot, but the real cause of death was multiple fractures to the skull – Messiter had been battered to death with a heavy, blunt instrument.

Sir Bernard Spilsbury, the famous forensic expert, examined the body and described the terribly battered head as 'being fractured everywhere except on top'. Boxes near the body had been spattered with blood to a height of several feet. The pathologist concluded that a large hammer, wielded with great violence, would account for the injuries.

The dead man had been on the missing persons list for nine weeks and police had checked at the garage, but finding it locked, did not pursue the enquiry. It was only when another oil company representative came to take over the agency that the garage door was forced open and Messiter's body was discovered. Among papers found in the dead man's lodgings was a reply to an advertisement for local agents signed, 'William F. Thomas'. The police quickly got onto the trail of W. F. Thomas and discovered that a man of that name had worked for a Wiltshire building contractor. A large sum of money in wage packets had disappeared, and after being interviewed by the county police, Thomas had vanished.

Thomas's departure had been so hurried that he foolishly neglected to tidy up his lodgings thoroughly. There, detectives subsequently found some scraps of paper bearing the words, 'Podmore' and 'Manchester'. It did not take long to establish that a man called Podmore, a motor mechanic working in Manchester, had left that city three days before W. F. Thomas took lodgings in Southampton. Meanwhile, Scotland Yard turned up its files and the record of William Henry Podmore, a man who had been in the hands of the police several times, was brought to light. As a result of this careful routine police work Podmore was found and taken in for questioning. He had, it appeared, been Messiter's assistant, but his story about his movements and use of false names and addresses was very involved. The police did not have enough to make a murder charge stick, but Podmore got six months' imprisonment for a fraud committed in Manchester.

The detectives investigating Messiter's murder were convinced Podmore was their man. A bloodstained hammer had been found close to the murder scene – it was a heavy tool and one end of the head was sharply pointed. An engineer from another garage nearby told the police that he had lent the hammer to a stranger at the end of October. Podmore was included in an identity parade but the engineer failed to pick him out.

The breakthrough in the investigation came with a detailed examination of a receipt book for oil sale commissions. It was discovered that indentations between the lines of a genuine receipt had been made by pencilled writing on the sheet above, which had been torn out. The indentations when specially photographed revealed a fictitious receipt for commission made out by 'W. F. Thomas'.

Police theorized that Messiter had discovered that he was being swindled and tackled Podmore about it. Knowing that the Manchester police wanted him for fraud, Podmore lost his nerve and attacked his accuser with the hammer. Podmore was completely without sympathy at his trial, for it was obvious that as Messiter lay unconscious on the floor of the garage, his head had been smashed with blow after blow from the hammer.

The hammer was unquestionably the murder weapon. Spilsbury found on it a hair which corresponded with the eyebrow hair of the dead man. Podmore was tried at Winchester Assizes in March 1930 – it had taken the police over a year to accumulate sufficient evidence. But the prosecution was successful and Podmore was convicted and hanged. Public opinion was against Podmore and a great play was made on the hair found on the murder weapon. One newspaper carried a headline, 'Two hairs hanged this man!' and followed up with a sensational piece about 'the revealing lens' and 'the most vital clue of all'.

The hair evidence in the Podmore case was only part of a painstaking police investigation. It undeniably identified the murder weapon and while it helped, it did not of itself hang Podmore. This underlines the judgement which forensic scientists bring to their job. They know how much reliance to place on evidence and, in the case of hair, realize that its incriminating value has to be carefully evaluated.

It is not yet possible to identify individuals by hair with the same exactitude as by fingerprints, but new techniques such as neutron activation analysis are constantly being developed to aid forensic investigation. In activation analysis, hair is irradiated in a nuclear reactor and the subsequent rate of decay is calculated electronically. This increases the individuality of hair and is one means by which the gaps in forensic knowledge are bridged in this important and ever-widening sphere of criminal investigation.

One to five hair roots can contain sufficient tissue for analysis. Hairs contain only trace amounts of DNA, and are generally not suitable for testing by current methods in routine forensic use. However, a highly specialized method known as mitochondrial sequencing is beginning to be used more and more. It was this method that was recently used to identify one of Napoleon's hairs and members of the Romanoff family.

Post Mortem

Legal or 'forensic' medicine plays an increasingly important part in the battle against the violent criminal. The police pathologist begins his grim work at the scene of the crime.

LEGAL MEDICINE is an American term for something which, in Britain, is called medical jurisprudence by some and forensic medicine by others (the latter is the more usual term, but the differences are, largely, a matter of interpretation). Newspapers frequently refer to a 'medico-legal expert'. Most European countries follow, in their own languages, the French *médecine légale.*

In the United States legal medicine belongs, broadly, to the nineteenth and twentieth centuries. The former saw the official beginning, apart from isolated earlier instances which were largely indirect legal medicine. A Dr J. S. Stringham, an MD from Edinburgh, more or less initiated matters when he lectured on legal medicine in 1804. He was followed by a Dr Benjamin Rush in 1811 who was the author of a book which contained a chapter on the 'Study of Medical Jurisprudence' – he was also a stern opponent of capital punishment. Two years later a Dr Caldwell gave a course of lectures on legal medicine at the University of Pennsylvania (Britain had founded the first chair of forensic medicine in 1807 at the University of Edinburgh). The next important milestone was when a pupil of Dr Stringham, T. R. Beck, was appointed professor of physiology and lecturer in medical jurisprudence in the College of Physicians and Surgeons, New York state. His classic *Elements of Medical Jurisprudence* was published in 1823, and appeared in several European countries.

Office of Coroner

After this, various works of importance followed, but though many notable American books were published on the subject, progress was slow. Even doctors and lawyers were not generally impressed with the infant group of sciences which, collectively, did not impress the country at large. Legal medicine over the early years suffered from incompetents and self-elected 'experts' who tried to get on the band-wagon, tending to create prejudice. The medical examiner system – the basis of legal medicine in some ways – was introduced in Boston in 1877 (the state of Massachusetts followed later). New York abolished the coroner in 1918 in favour of the medical examiner system.

The first step in early legal medicine, was the coroner, an Office which went to the States with the first wave of settlers, though the coroner today does not have the same powers as his counterpart in England. Indeed, he could even be open to actions by irate relatives because a post-mortem on a dead body had taken place, or parts of it removed for laboratory examination – while medical examiners have powers over the dead body almost as great as their counterparts in England.

To get this quite clear it is as well to look at both offices as often in the United States – and certainly in other English-speaking countries – they can be genuine puzzles to laymen.

As stated, the first settlers brought English law with them and the official known as the coroner first sat at an inquest in the Colony of New Plymouth, 1635, when a dead body was 'searched' and it was found that the death was from natural causes. Today the coroner should be seen as an elective office, meaning that, usually, a country official gains the position by popular vote for a term of two or four years. Qualifications for the office are not usually required, but in England a lawyer or a doctor (generally the former) is coroner.

Unnatural Death

It is a fact that in America anyone can be elected as coroner – undertakers, grocers, bowling-alley operators have been given the position in the past. On one occasion, in Indiana, it proved impossible to find the right man in a small locality and the pool-room inmates, sitting on the question, appointed the village idiot to the post.

The coroner, once elected, in a fairly large state could well have one or more physicians on his pay-roll, together with a forensic pathologist. Depending on the amount of 'business', they could also appoint deputies or assistants.

In the case of an apparently unnatural death, it

is reported to the coroner by the police. The Coroner's Physician will view the body at a funeral parlour, or in a morgue. Usually a corpse that has suffered violent death is not always seen by the coroner or his assistants, but by a pathologist *after* it has been examined by the police and removed to a place of temporary rest. The pathologist is not always a man experienced in the forensic field, but may be a hospital pathologist or a physician, who would hold the part time appointment or office.

End Corruption

On the other hand the medical examiner system was introduced by law in its first state, Massachusetts, in 1877, a post concerned 'with dead bodies of such persons *only* as are supposed to have come to their deaths by violence'. The basic idea was to end corruption among coroners in that state, but not until after World War II did the system really become nationwide practice.

The medical examiner, unlike the coroner, is a trained man in legal medicine, appointed by the state and on a par with the permanent state officials. He is provided with a proper laboratory organization and staff, and he examines a dead body as a pathologist, but he is not concerned with the legal angles of the case.

The office by appointment varies from state to state. For example, in New York the choice is made by the Mayor, but the selected man must be taken from classified lists compiled by the

Municipal Civil Service (New York possesses one of the most famous of all medical examiners in Dr Milton Helpern, a 'grand old man' of legal medicine – he has performed or supervised some 60,000 autopsies).

In another state, Maryland, the procedure is more cumbersome but equally efficient. The selected man is chosen by a board consisting of the Professors of Pathology at two universities, the Commissioner of Health in the chief city, the State Director of Health, and the Superintendent of State Police.

Progress Required

There is one thing in common in every state – the medical examiner must be medically qualified. The nearest thing in England would be the police surgeon (who is first on the scene on police notification – he and the pathologist are integral members of a team, the head of which is the investigating officer).

The medical examiner system is preferred by many to the coroner system since it means that sudden or unnatural deaths are dealt with from the moment of official discovery by a man fully trained in legal medicine. Lack of money, or money insufficiently provided, tends to slow up the system in certain places – though, even when it exists, some homicide investigators have yet to see the importance of letting the pathologist view the body where it is found and before anyone, including the undertaker, has touched it.

Generally, after the two specifics of coroner and medical examiner, legal medicine in the States tends to follow broadly the rules in England, allowing for local and legal differences.

Progress, however, is more widely required: '. . . law schools and medical schools in the United States have fallen far short of their expected task in the education of law and medical students insofar as legal medicine is concerned' is the view of the Editor of the *Legal Medicine Annual* (Appleton-Century-Crofts, NYC, 1969). While there has been much progress since this statement, it is still to be improved.

Legal medicine, however much or little of it there may be, is generally of a high standard, and its practitioners are able men, thrusting hard in search of new and useful discoveries, working under difficulties, but admirable at their tasks.

In rape, for instance, nothing can present the medico-legal examiner, or the physician, with quite so many imponderables. Forcible rape in the United States in 1971 reached an estimated total of 41,890 cases – a figure which has increased by 55 per cent since 1966, and 10 per cent since 1970. It is regarded by the FBI as one of the most under-reported crimes because of fear or embarrassment on the part of the victims.

There is always modesty or shock on the victim's part which makes for difficulties, or a family 'closing ranks' to protect the female concerned, and false accusations are nearly as hard to sort out as the real thing.

An Autopsy

Medical examiners deal with numerous undistinguished deaths each year, and must provide the details of an autopsy. In forensics, this generally means handling the body with an awareness of significant evidential findings. If the victim was shot, then care must be taken not to damage the bullet trajectory path or to mess up entrance and exit wounds. If poisoning is suspected, then tissues from the organs will be sent to the toxicology section of the laboratory for thorough analysis. Even just paying attention to the odours around the body can help. Cyanide, for example, smells like bitter almonds.

An autopsy is done to examine the internal organs of a dead body. First there's a search for trace evidence on the body, and an identification is made (if possible). When the death is not from natural causes, the coroner or medical examiner records the circumstances surrounding the death on an official form, along with all available information about the deceased person. He also records the results of the external examination and lists all physical characteristics, including height and weight. When the examination is complete, he will include the cause of death and sign the form. This is presented as the official statement to families and to the court.

Before anything is done to it, the body gets tagged and photographed, both clothed (if it was clothed when found) and unclothed. Then it is X-rayed, weighed and measured, and any identifying marks are recorded. Old and new injuries are noted, along with tattoos and scars. Trace evidence, such as hair and fibres, is collected off the body and from under the fingernails before it is cleaned. Even the nails are clipped. The wrapping sheet, along with clothing and trace evidence, is sent for analysis. Fingerprints are taken, and if rape is suspected, a rape kit is used for evidence collection. In cases of suspected suicide by gunshot, hands are swabbed for gunpowder residue.

Once the body is clean, it is laid out on its back on a steel table, with a stabilizing block placed under the head. The surgeon then makes what is known as a 'Y' incision, which is a cut into the body from shoulder to shoulder, meeting at the sternum and then going straight down the abdomen into the pelvis. This exposes the internal organs and provides easy access. The pathologist cuts through the ribs and collarbone and lifts the rib cage away from the internal organs.

He then uses X-rays of injuries or a lodged bullet as a guide, because he might have to trace a trajectory path or avoid a knife wound. He takes a blood sample to determine blood type and removes the individual organs to weigh them. Samples are taken of fluid in the organs, and the stomach and intestines are opened to examine the contents.

The final step is to examine the head. The eyes are probed for haemorrhages that reveal strangulation. After that, an incision is made in the scalp behind the head and the skin is carefully peeled forward over the face to expose the skull. Using a high-speed oscillating power saw, the skull is opened and a chisel is used to pry off the skull-cap. Then the brain can be lifted out, examined, and weighed. All tissues and samples are sent to the lab for further analysis. Organs that need to be kept for the investigation are preserved and the rest are returned to the body cavity.

JFK Forensic Disaster

President John F. Kennedy was assassinated in Dallas, Texas, in 1963 while riding in an open-top car before a large crowd. A bullet went through him and wounded Governor Connally, while a second one slammed into his skull. Kennedy was rushed to a Dallas hospital, but was then illegally transported to Bethesda Naval Hospital in Washington. Unfortunately, as Dr Michael Baden later discovered, even a case as significant as this one can be mishandled by untrained people.

In 1977, Baden was appointed to take charge of the forensic pathology investigation for the congressional Select Committee on Assassinations, and he recruited eight other medical examiners. As he looked further into the incident to see what could be determined, he saw what he described as a 'forensic disaster'. He alleged that if the autopsy procedure had been done correctly, the many conspiracy theories would never have got off the ground. Yet as it turned out, Commander James J. Humes, the pathologist who performed it, had never worked on a body with a gunshot wound. He'd also been instructed not to perform a complete autopsy, but only to find the bullet, which was believed to be still lodged in the body. In his subsequent reports, his medical descriptions were non-existent, and he basically referred interested parties to the photographs, which were also badly done by an inexperienced photographer. Humes didn't even turn Kennedy over to look at the wound in the back of his neck, or call the receiving hospital in Dallas to discover that a tracheostomy had been performed. He erroneously assumed the bullet had fallen out the same hole it had entered. He also failed to shave the head wound to see it clearly, and it was photographed through the hair. In addition, Humes miscalculated the wound's location by an error of four inches.

After only two hours, he prepared the body for embalming. Then, because his notes were stained with blood, he burned them. After he found out about the procedure done in Dallas, he rewrote his notes based on what he recalled and what he could figure out. He ended up including material he himself never saw and failing to track the bullets properly. Thus his report was filled with errors, which put Baden's team at a serious disadvantage.

They looked at the crime scene and autopsy photographs, Kennedy's clothing, autopsy reports, and X-rays. It soon became clear that the people in charge had not realized that there was an important difference between a forensic autopsy and a regular autopsy. For example, no one had known the difference between an exit and entrance wound, and therefore they could not pinpoint the bullet's origin. They also couldn't tell how many shots had been fired.

Then Baden realized that Kennedy's brain was missing, along with slides of tissues, so with the help of the bullet holes through the clothing and their experience with exit and entrance wounds, his team managed to piece together the fact that two bullets had entered Kennedy. One had pierced his throat and gone into Governor Connally. The other had gone through the back of his head and ended up in the front of the car. Both had come from behind.

After that discovery, they wrote a two-volume report, and Dr Baden stressed how important it was that only professionally trained doctors should be allowed to do autopsies of such international importance.

Bullet Force

Under the microscope an expert can tell not only the make and calibre of a bullet but also the weapon from which it was fired.

Rifle wounds are distinguished by the high velocity of the weapon – a bullet from 3,000 yards away may still be travelling at 300 feet per second – on impact. Bullets frequently pass through the body and if no resistance is met, entry and exit will be almost identical. The only slight difference being that the former is inverted at the edge and the latter everted. Internal damage will be present as a result of 'tissue quake' and extensive damage will be caused if the bullet is diverted within the body.

Although it ignites instantaneously, the explosive charge of a cartridge is still burning when the bullet leaves the muzzle of the gun. Consequently, hot gases, flame, smoke and particles of unburnt powder are discharged with the bullet and their effects may be found around the wound.

Powder particles embedded or tattooed in the skin may indicate the range at which a weapon was fired, although this only applies to a maximum of three feet.

Traditional gunpowder is black and is composed of potassium nitrate, sulphur and charcoal, but is not used a great deal today except in the manufacture of shotgun cartridges. Most modern powders are smokeless and grey in colour, consisting of flakes of nitro-glycerine or nitro-cellulose which will be readily recognized by the expert. Smokeless powders are explosively more efficient and leave fewer traces of burning and tattooing even at close range. Infra-red photography is used to determine whether marks on clothing are due to powder. The resulting graphic representation of powder residues gives a clear indication of the range at which a weapon was fired.

Estimations of range at which rifle weapons have been fired can be made by examining the lead deposits around entry wounds. Saturated aqueous solution of sodium rhodizonate sprayed on the previously acidified wound area gives a blue reaction if lead is present. Distinction between the lead patterns thus revealed can be related to the distance at which the weapon was fired.

One of the first questions to be asked at the scene of a fatal wounding involving firearms is, 'Was the shooting homicide, suicide, or just an accident?' The answer given must take into consideration the probable type of weapon which caused the wound, the range and direction of the discharge and the site of the injury.

In a suspected suicide, the wound must be in an accessible place, that is, within the subject's arm reach. The classic sites selected for suicide are the temple (right side for the right-handed person), forehead, mouth and the area of the heart. The range is necessarily close unless some device such as a piece of string or a length of wood has been used to pull the trigger. This is often the case where a rifle is the elected weapon.

Self-inflicted wounds are almost inevitably contact injuries with signs of burning and tattooing. Entry wounds not situated at the classic sites are always subject to suspicion and wounds inflicted outside of normal arm's reach are almost certainly not suicidal. It is rare for a suicide to fire twice in any one of the classic sites, and two or more wounds are therefore almost certainly homicide.

The question of accessibility arose in a shooting incident at an army camp near Warminster in 1918. Corporal Dunkin was found dead on his bed; on the floor nearby lay a ·303 Lee Enfield rifle. Dunkin had been shot through the temple. One round had been fired from the rifle. The bullet had passed through his head, entering in front of the left ear and exiting behind the right ear.

The police were undecided whether it was a case of suicide or murder. Sir Bernard Spilsbury examined the wound and estimated that it had been caused by a shot fired at a distance of 5 inches or more. The dead man's arms were exceptionally short for a man of his height and this proved to be a deciding factor.

Spilsbury showed that the corporal lying full-length on his bed could only have reached the rifle's trigger by pressing the muzzle firmly against his cheek. Clearly, then, suicide was out of the question and the police set about a murder investigation. Eventually, another soldier at the camp was convicted of murdering Dunkin as he lay asleep.

There are no distinctive features governing accidental shooting. The accidental discharge of a firearm may result from an action of the victim or by another person. The circumstances must be carefully considered and suicide and homicide specifically ruled out. Examination of the victim and the scene of death is important. Body wounds are inspected to determine the direction of the bullet – especially important is the track within the body linking entry and exit wounds.

Any weapon found at the scene must be carefully handled. Contrary to the practice of detectives in popular fiction, it is not correct procedure to lift up a pistol by inserting a pencil down the barrel – this may preserve any fingerprints but it is likely to damage important evidence in the gun's barrel. Any spent cartridges or wads should also be treated with care. If the bullet is still inside the body it should be removed with extreme care. Forceps are padded with gauze or rubber in order to preserve any marks on the bullet which may help identify the weapon which fired it. The clothing of the victim is also examined for traces of powder and other explosion products.

Where suicide is suspected the victim's hands are swabbed for powder traces. This is the 'dermal nitrate test' which analyses for the presence of nitrate residues blown back onto the firing hand. The test is not conclusive as nitrates from other sources, such as cigarette smoking, may give a false picture. However, together with tests for lead, it may give useful confirmatory evidence of suicide.

The basis for identifying firearms lies with the bullets and cartridges they fire. When a bullet is fired from a rifled weapon it is impressed with marks made by the lands and grooves of the barrel. The land leaves a series of slanting, parallel scratches which vary in number and width according to the manufacture of the weapon. Grooves also leave marks, for although calibre is measured between lands, the bullet is slightly larger and when fired expands to make contact with both lands and grooves.

Fired cartridge cases are also impressed with identifying marks. The firing pin makes an indentation in the base of the cartridge and scratches are left by the action of the ejector mechanism. The explosion which fires the bullet from a gun barrel also forces the cartridge case back against the breech block with terrific pressure – some twenty tons in a rifle. The cartridge case is thereby imprinted with any defects of machining marks on the metal surface of the breech.

Because the metal of every gun barrel and breech has individual irregularities and characteristics of wear, each cartridge and bullet fired from it will be 'personalized'. The firearms expert, by examining the marks made on a bullet, will identify the kind of weapon which fired it. The number, width, depth, angle and direction of grooves will speak to him as if they were a fingerprint. The tell-tale marks on cartridge cases also speak for the weapon that fired them.

In a murder case, test rounds fired from the suspected weapon are compared microscopically with the crime bullet. If the marks on the test rounds match those on the crime bullet, the suspected weapon without doubt fired the killing shot. This work is the realm of the firearms expert working with analytical precision, for a man's freedom may depend on his findings.

Test rounds are fired into containers of cotton wool to ensure that the only marks on the bullets are those made by the weapon. Test and crime bullets are examined side-by-side on a comparison microscope. This is essentially a pair of matched microscopes with a common eyepiece enabling two objects to be compared in the same field of view. A camera attached to the eyepiece of the microscope is used to make photo-enlargements which constitute important evidence in criminal proceedings.

The Poacher

On the night of October 10, 1927, Enoch Dix, a 35-year-old labourer, was poaching in Whistling Copse, near Bath in Somerset. It was nearly midnight when he entered the wood with his single-barrelled ·410 shot gun; his intention was to pick off a few roosting pheasants, rightfully belonging to Lord Temple, with the aid of a moonlit sky.

Dix's first shots were heard about a mile away by his Lordship's gamekeepers. Head keeper William Walker, and under keeper George Rawlings, loaded their 12 bores and headed for

Whistling Copse. They found Dix and challenged him. Dix's shot gun went off and Walker fell dying from a wound in the throat. Rawlings fired twice at the poacher.

There was no difficulty in identifying Dix as the poacher. Rawlings told the police that Dix had shot Walker at point-blank range. Dix at first denied any knowledge of the affair but the police found the gun at his cottage. He was asked to strip so that he could be examined for shot wounds as Rawlings was sure that he had hit him. Incredibly, his back, neck and thighs were covered with shot holes. His wife had dressed the wounds and he carried on the pretence of not being hit. It was useless for him to deny that he had been in the copse but he said simply that his own gun discharged with the shock of his being hit by the blast.

There was no question as to who held the gun which fired the lethal charge – it was a matter of deciding who fired first and at what range. At this point the firearms expert was called in to assist the police. Robert Churchill, the famous gunmaker and ballistics expert, set about calculating the firing distance. He fired at a series of whitewashed metal plates, using the under keeper's gun and identical cartridges, and varying the range. The weapon fired consistently, which was important.

After considering these test patterns, together with the wounds in Dix's back, Churchill concluded that the shot which hit the poacher was fired at not less than 15 yards – luckily for Dix, most of the keeper's blast was stopped by a tree.

If Dix's gun had discharged accidentally when he was hit, it must have gone off at a distance of 15 yards from the two keepers. At that range, tests showed Dix's shot gun to have a spread of 27 to 30 inches. But the wound in the dead keeper's throat was only five inches in diameter. To produce such a wound the poacher's gun must have been fired at less than five yards – at point blank range. The jury at Bristol Assizes returned a verdict of manslaughter against Dix and he was sentenced to fifteen years.

DNA Fingerprinting

With the exception of identical twins, the complete DNA of each individual is unique – making it invaluable in crime detection.

DNA FINGERPRINTING is a method of identification that compares fragments of deoxyribonucleic acid (or DNA). DNA is the genetic material found within the cell nuclei of all living things

A DNA fingerprint is constructed by first extracting a DNA sample from body tissue or fluid such as hair, blood or saliva. The sample is then segmented using enzymes, and the segments are arranged by size using a process called electrophoresis. These segments are marked with probes and exposed on X-ray film, where they form a characteristic pattern of black bars – the DNA fingerprint. If the DNA fingerprints produced from two different samples match, the two samples probably came from the same person.

DNA fingerprinting was first developed as an identification technique in 1985. Originally used to detect the presence of genetic diseases, DNA fingerprinting soon came to be used in criminal investigations and forensic science. The first criminal conviction based on DNA evidence in the United States occurred in 1988. In criminal investigations, DNA fingerprints derived from evidence collected at the crime scene are compared to the DNA fingerprints of suspects. The DNA evidence can implicate or exonerate a suspect.

Generally, courts have accepted the reliability of DNA testing and admitted DNA test results into evidence. However, DNA fingerprinting is controversial in a number of areas: the accuracy of the results, the cost of testing, and the possible misuse of the technique.

The accuracy of DNA fingerprinting has been challenged for several reasons. First, because DNA segments rather than complete DNA strands are 'fingerprinted', a DNA fingerprint may not be unique. Large-scale research to confirm the uniqueness of DNA fingerprinting test results has not been conducted. In addition, DNA fingerprinting is often performed in private laboratories that may not follow uniform testing standards and quality controls. Also, since human beings must interpret the test, human error could lead to false results.

The fact that DNA fingerprinting is expensive, means that suspects who are unable to provide their own DNA experts may not be able to adequately defend themselves against charges based on DNA evidence.

In the United States, the FBI has created a national database of genetic information called the National DNA Index System. The database contains DNA obtained from convicted criminals and from evidence found at crime scenes. Some experts fear that this database might be used for unauthorized purposes.

DNA and O.J.

A barking dog alerted a neighbour to the crime scene. Sukru Boztepe followed the dog back to the Brentwood condominium, saw the horrendous bloodshed, and urged his wife to phone the police. That set into motion the initial events in a convoluted series that made up what many called 'the Crime of the Century'. It also brought DNA testing in criminal cases to public awareness.

Nicole Brown Simpson, former wife of football celebrity O. J. Simpson, went outside her home late in the evening of June 12, 1994, and was met by an assailant who slashed her to death. The killer also slaughtered the man who was with her, Ronald Goldman, age 25. He was returning the eyeglasses to Nicole, that her mother had left behind at the restaurant where he was a waiter. They were both found dead, covered in blood, just inside the front gate.

Although Nicole was no longer married to Simpson, the police contacted him right away. Going to his home, detectives noted a bloodstain on the door of his white Ford Bronco. A trail of blood also led up to the house, but Simpson appeared to be gone. It turned out that he had just flown to Chicago.

He returned to Los Angeles and agreed to answer questions. Investigators then noticed a cut on a finger of his left hand that would prove to be a problem for him when they eventually charged him with the crimes. First, he told several conflicting stories about how he had got the cut, and second, the crime scene indicated that the killer had been cut on his left hand and had trailed blood outside the gates. That hardly seemed coincidental. Nevertheless, another narrative eventually overshadowed these problems.

Several droplets of blood at the scene failed to show a match with either of the victims' blood types. Then Simpson's blood was drawn for testing and comparison between Simpson's DNA and that of the blood at the scene showed strong similarities. Contrary to what Simpson's defence team was to say after his arrest, this blood could not have been planted after Simpson's blood was drawn.

The tests indicated that the drops had three factors in common with Simpson's blood and only one person in 57 billion could produce an equivalent match. In addition, the blood was found near footprints made by a rare and expensive type of shoe – shoes that O. J. wore and that proved to be his size.

Next to the bodies was a bloodstained black leather glove that bore traces of fibre from Goldman's jeans. The glove's mate, stained with Simpson's blood, was found on his property. There were also traces of the blood of both victims lifted from inside Simpson's car and house, along with blood that contained his own DNA. In fact, his blood and Goldman's were found together on the car's console.

Forensic serologists at the California Department of Justice, along with a private contractor, did the sophisticated DNA testing. Then other evidence emerged, such as the testimony of the limousine driver who came to pick Simpson up for the ride to the airport. He saw a black man cross the driveway and go into the house. Then Simpson claimed that the driver had been unable to get him on the intercom because he had 'overslept'. There were also photographs of Nicole and diary entries that attested to Simpson's abusive and stalking behaviour. In addition, when Simpson was notified that he would be arrested for murder, he fled with his friend, Al Cowlings, and hinted in a note that he might kill himself. With him were a passport, fake beard, and thousands of dollars in cash. Nevertheless, he pleaded 'Not Guilty', offered a huge reward for information about the crime, and hired a defence team of celebrity lawyers. Barry Scheck and Peter Neufeld, from New York, were the DNA experts, renowned for their work on the Innocence Project, which used DNA analysis to defend the falsely accused.

The defence team was going to call for a pre-trial hearing on DNA evidence, to challenge it from every angle, but decided instead to drop it. They knew that whatever happened could set a dangerous precedent and they realized that prolonging the trial process could antagonize the jury. They wanted the jury on their side. So they waived the proceeding, which many defence strategists felt was a radical decision, and went on with the trial. Barry Scheck felt confident that they could produce challenges in court before the jury, to persuade them of O.J.'s innocence.

The reliability of this evidence came to be known as the 'DNA Wars' and three different crime laboratories performed the analysis. All three determined that the DNA in the drops of blood at the scene matched Simpson's. It was a 1 in 170 million match, using one type of analysis known as RFLP, and 1 in 240 million match using the PCR test.

Nevertheless, criminologist Dr. Henry Lee testified that there appeared to be something wrong with the way the blood was packaged, leading the defence to propose that the multiple samples had been switched. They also claimed that the blood had been severely degraded by being stored in a laboratory van, and that the control samples had been mishandled by the laboratory.

What damaged the prosecution's case more than anything else were the endless explanations of the complex procedures involved in DNA analysis. The defence kept it simple and thereby befriended the jury. They then intimated that Detective Mark Fuhrman, who had been at O. J.'s home the night of the murder, was a racist and had planted evidence, although they could offer no proof.

The evidence was damning, but the defence team managed to refocus the jury's attention on the corruption in the Los Angeles Police Department. Then Simpson made a clear statement of his innocence, though he was not on the stand, and the defence attorneys disputed the good reputation of the forensics laboratories, proving that the evidence had been carelessly handled.

Deliberating for less than four hours, the jury took all this on board and freed Simpson with a 'Not Guilty' verdict. They defended themselves in interviews after the fact by simply stating that the prosecution had not made its case. It may be that those attorneys made some serious errors, but the doubt by the defence about DNA was ludicrous and did some damage with the public to the credibility of this type of evidence.

However, when it was first used in England as a way to determine the guilt of an offender, it proved to be quite impressive.

Reconstructions

A woman's body plunges from the apartment building and crashes onto the street below. 'It was an accident,' says the husband. Or was it murder . . . ?

IRIS NINA SEAGAR plunged to her death 200 feet from a Baltimore penthouse. In the early newspaper editions it was headlined as the tragic suicide of a 48-year-old blonde whom all the neighbours in the apartment block liked about as much as they privately disliked her heavy-drinking, younger husband. Nearby neighbours, who continually overheard the couple fighting, had the deepest sympathy with the unfortunate Mrs Seagar, saying that, of course, the conduct of a man like that would drive any decent woman to suicide.

It soon became horribly clear that Iris Seagar had not jumped from her balcony in a suicide's despair, but had been thrown out by her husband who was the $100,000 beneficiary of her insurance policy. Naturally, there was a suicide clause in the policy. But the husband's explanation was that she was meddling with a faulty window-fitted air conditioner and accidentally tipped over the guardrail.

Iris Seagar's was not the first 'Did she fall or was she pushed?' tragedy to occupy the attention of the police, the insurance investigators and forensic workers, and the psychiatric reports and social reports on the couple led to the strong conclusion of murder rather than suicide or accident. But the course of factual events – after Iris Seagar hit the sidewalk 200 feet below in a mass of pulp, blood and distorted bone – is illuminating to those who wrongly imagine that most forensic work is concerned only with tissues and test-tubes, fingerprints and fibres.

This aspect of the final solution to the Seagar case involved, in addition to the Homicide Squad, a meteorologist, architectural photographers and a physicist. Repeated tests were made with lifelike dummies built to simulate Iris Seagar's 5 ft 3 in, 127 pounds, and a television production company assisted with a video tape recorder coupled to an RCA closed-circuit electronic camera with a zoom lens. This VTR recording of the test falls enabled the forensic team to get a visual record instantly, without delay of processing 16-mm film. The tapes were played over and over again on RCA monitors so that the various trajectories of the falling dummies could be studied.

The body fell 200 feet, landing 16 feet 8 inches from the building, and this was the first fact which caused suspicion. A body falling from such a height falls outwards for a second or two, and the curve for this part of the trajectory can be plotted from many tests. Then the body plummets straight down.

With the various architectural features of the building, it was demonstrated after repeated drop-tests with the video-recorded dummies that the body could have landed no further from the sidewalk edge of the building than 10½ feet.

In free air a person cannot jump farther than on the ground. Weak, middle-aged Iris Seagar could not possibly jump a distance of 16 feet 8 inches in life. She certainly did not do so when plunging to her death. This tragedy emphasizes the many details which must be observed in every death investigation, but of course the forensic procedures are not the same worldwide.

In the United States, for example, the chief medical investigator is required to be a pathologist, and to have a background in forensic pathology. He arranges the autopsies, which are done by him and ordered by the county medical investigator or the county district attorney. The investigator and the police team then follow certain procedures which always concern forensic workers and, strange as it may seem, the authors of detective fiction and motion picture or television scripts. Things like the time and place of notification of death (if an informant calls from some distant place as related to the body, this may arouse suspicion). Exact location of the body. (Did she fall or was she pushed?) Exact time of arrival of interested parties at the death scene. Identification of the victim . . . retain all possible witnesses, and record or audiotape even statements by bystanders . . . Find why the victim was at the scene. (If not found lying peacefully in his own bed, the place of death may be an important clue.) What was the conduct of the victim immediately prior to death? Who found the victim? Who last saw the victim alive?

What Tools?

What tools does the forensic pathologist need, as a preparation for autopsies in homicide cases and/ or suspected suicide attempts? Dr D. E. Price, M.B., B.S., a distinguished pathologist attached to the Home Office forensic laboratories in England, made no secret of the equipment he used for post mortems.

1. Sample bottles
2. Swabs for blood and semen
3. Pencil torch
4. Pliers for extracting teeth
5. Measuring tapes
6. Handcuffs
7. Fingerprint brushes and powder
8. Anal thermometer
9. Tweezers
10. Adhesive tape for picking up microscopic fibres
11. Tape recorder for taking quick notes.

While the forensic worker may decide 'she was pushed', a jury is free to come to the decision that 'she fell'. It was Dr Price who drew attention to the strange death of a 60-year-old woman, a manic-depressive with a 41-year history of mental illness. At her sudden, tragic death, the usual insurance questions arose. The correct decision was of great financial importance to the heirs.

Suicide by drowning had been attempted at least twice in the preceding three years. An adequate description was available, including that of an abdominal scar and foot deformities. Thirteen days after she absconded from the mental hospital the first portion of a dismembered body was recovered from a nearby canal in which there was heavy barge traffic. During the next fortnight other portions of the same body were recovered. Dismemberment was due to barge propellers. Organs were not found, and facial identity, whether direct or by superimposition photography, was not possible.

Exact Results

'Evidence of stature, scars, hair comparison, foot/shoe deformities agreement and fingerprint comparison failed to convince a jury in spite of HM Coroner's summing up.

'Subsequently the High Court (Probate Division) gave letters of administration to the relatives, to whom the estate represented definite financial advantage. It is pleasing to record that the police authorities took the initiative and advised the relatives, who were disconsolate, to seek legal advice with a view to have the verdict set aside.'

Edmond Locard of the University of Lyons (a lawyer, not a forensic scientist) first put into words the guiding principle of so much successful forensic investigation. 'Every contact leaves a trace,' he said. A great deal of laboratory work is therefore concerned with contact traces, with taking moulds and impressions of marks in the hope of being able to fit a tool or a weapon to them, and thus linking the criminal with the crime. This might seem to be science applied to the handling of physical evidence. Yet it is dangerous to disregard the mathematical consequences.

If the tool is a perfect (hundred per cent) fit to the mark, it is of course better than a fifty-fifty chance that the suspect was at the scene of the crime. If, however, he has a perfect (hundred per cent) alibi, then the forensic worker must wonder what is the use of mathematics?

The matching of marks, etc., is a revolutionary branch of criminalistics which has caused many to investigate, from Burd and Kirk (1942) to Hatcher, Jury and Weller (1967), leading on to the work of the Californian toxicologist J. W. Bracket, Jr – Instructor in Physical Evidence in the City College of San Francisco.

Bracket concentrated on the fact that striated tool marks, such as those made by a slipping tool on a cash register, or by a gun barrel on a bullet, could be very important as identification evidence in justifying the conclusion that the two marks (that is, specimen on site, and a controlled mark) were generated by the same tool or instrument.

Occasionally, however, comparison of two sets of tool marks by different criminalists elicits varying opinions as to degrees of similarity, and indeed even different conclusions as to identity or non-identity of evidence. Bracket decided to investigate this problem mathematically.

The first step was to reduce the tool or weapon mark to the ideal state. Models were made in wax, plastic and other materials, so that the striae could be seen. Each striation was considered to be an element of a set of striae, representing only a position in two-dimensional space between neighbouring elements. The position was then quantized. That is to say, a whole number of unit distances away from each neighbour.

Geometric, number-based and what he termed 'outcome' models were then produced, complex graphs showing the 'match' and 'non-match' characteristics. The mathematics of these tests were computerized, so that juries would have a more precise ratio of forensic probabilities to consider, instead of – for example – the baffling proposition: 'It's one hundred per cent certain she fell, and a fifty-fifty chance she was pushed.'

While the forensic worker does not have to concern himself with whether a jury accepts or rejects his evidence, but only it if it was 100 per cent true, he would be less than human were he not to be interested in the outcome. This may depend partly upon psychological techniques (in which the United States is greatly advanced), and also upon the application of law. As has been pointed out in the courts, the German Civil Code and the Code Napoléon 'both engender a different psychological approach to questions of guilt and innocence'. L. R. C. Haward of the Graylingwell Hospital, Chichester, Sussex, England, reported an interesting example for forensic psychologists to highlight sources of data and error.

The unpleasant case concerned a certain English town where the police had reports that a public toilet was being used for indecent purposes. To abate the nuisance, police officers were concealed in a shallow cupboard for several hours each day, their vision partly obscured by a piece of sacking screen and by iron bars.

Nevertheless, they reported observing two men committing an act of gross indecency. One man after using the urinal turned round and was handled by a second man. Immediately the two police officers sprang out of the cupboard and charged both men with committing an offence, which they denied.

Psychical Factors

There was no scientific evidence – no tests for semen, no fingerprint checks, no photographic evidence. The case rested on probabilities. Fifty-fifty? One man was already under suspicion, and of dubious character. The other had previously been charged, but not convicted, with a similar offence. In any layman's terms that brings the probability of conviction to better than fifty-fifty.

A psychologist was appointed to assess the reliability of the police evidence. It was outside his terms to investigate the reliability of the defendants' evidence. But, as in English law the onus is on the prosecution to prove the guilt of the accused, it was therefore fitting that the prosecution evidence only should be submitted to psychological scrutiny.

This investigation ranged from sources of error (in memory and in perception), from psychical factors such as available light (photometer tests were made), the duration of time of the alleged indecency after urination, to the positions of the two men.

The passive participant gave as his explanation that the tail end of his pink silk scarf tended to stick out when his coat was undone. A large blow-up coloured photograph was therefore taken of the man wearing these same clothes, and line and wash pictures were also produced in court, based on plans obtained from the Borough Engineer.

Statistical experience disclosed that there is a probability exceeding 0.25 – that is, greater than one in four – that a mistake in perception will occur. What was the truth? Did they, or didn't they? Was there more a forensic worker could have done, for prosecution or for defence?

'We can never know in this case,' says Haward, 'for the quantitative evidence was not presented. Rather than confound the jury with expert opinion, counsel widely introduced the main possible sources of perceptual and recall error in his own cross-examination and address, and succeeded in raising sufficient doubt about the reliability of the police evidence to secure a verdict of Not Guilty.'

Enter the Psychic

In 1967 a man called John Norman Collins was implicated superficially in fifteen murders. Characteristics of the murders were strangulation, beating about the head, articles of clothing missing, nude or semi-nude bodies, evidence of sexual assault, disappearance without a struggle, and disposal of bodies to ensure discovery. Most of the girls had long, brown hair and pierced ears, and several were having their periods.

In trying to decipher the personality traits of an unknown homicidal predator, many things have to be taken into consideration: including victim background, time and place of the murders, method of abduction, murder weapon used, degree of planning and evidence of overkill.

A relatively recent development in the profiling field is the analysis of a suspect's geographic patterns – victim selection area, where the crime was actually committed, travel route for body disposal, where and how he dumped the bodies, and the degree of isolation of the dump site. It tells something about the suspect's mobility, method of transportation, potential area of residence, and ability to traverse barriers, such as crossing state lines.

Familiarity is part of one's comfort zone and many murderers begin their crime spree in areas where they live, with victims with whom they feel relatively safe. In this case, it was likely – and proved to be the case – that the murderer lived near the university campus. Collins, in fact, resided in Ypsilanti, a few blocks from campus, and went to school there.

When it appeared that the police, despite all their resources, were getting nowhere with their investigations, a citizens group called the Psychedelic Rangers decided to act. The entire community was beginning to see some supernatural force behind the string of murders, although it wasn't clear whether it was God's divine plan or the devil at work. One mother was convinced that her daughter was sent to her fate to save others. A few amateur astrologers stepped in, but no one had an answer.

At that time, Peter Hurkos was one of the most famous psychics in the world. In 1941 at the age of thirty, he fell off a ladder in the Netherlands while painting a house and survived a four-storey plunge. Suddenly he found he had psychic powers, especially the ability to 'read' a person by being in close proximity or touching an object associated with that person. He visited the United States in 1956 under the sponsorship of a research society and decided to remain. He became a regular celebrity. Among his accomplishments by 1969, he listed his success in solving 27 murders in 17 different countries.

He had offered his assistance in the Boston Strangler case which had shown his powers to have certain potential. He did identify a shoe salesman as the multiple murderer, but police determined that this person was not who they sought. When DeSalvo confessed, Hurkos insisted that was not the man and that his suspect was still at large. Investigators ignored him, although the public perception that he was instrumental in the case remained intact.

Archie Allen led the Psychedelic Rangers into negotiations for Hurkos's services. The psychic had requested $2500, plus travelling expenses, so the group sent out a plea for money. They received only a few donations, which amounted to $1010. Hurkos was initially insulted, but then agreed to come for the cost of his travel – perhaps because it was a high profile case, and any success could only boost his newly-revived career. He arrived on July 21, 1969.

His method was to hold pictures of the murder scenes in closed envelopes, reciting reconstructions of the murders in remarkable detail. Several officers commented later that he had turned them into believers, particularly the one who was accurately told that he had a gas leak in his camper. However, many of the facts had already been published in newspapers. A clever person could have read up on all of that.

Several times, Hurkos insisted he could solve the case within the next day or two, but this was not to be the case. He gave them a name, but it was just one more suspect to investigate. He said the killer was a genius who was playing with the police. He also called him a sick homosexual, a transvestite, a member of a blood cult, a daytime salesman, and someone who hung around garbage dumps. He said the killer was about five feet seven, blond and baby-faced, 25 to 26 years old, and about 136 to 146 pounds. He drove a motorbike and went to school at night. He was also associated in some way with a trailer. Hurkos also thought the murder count would reach nineteen. It was now a battle between larger-than-life adversaries – the killer and Hurkos – and he assured the public that, as a representative of the good, he would triumph.

Two days after arriving, Hurkos received a call

warning him to leave or be responsible for another murder. There is some evidence, too, that John Norman Collins actually went to a restaurant where Hurkos was showcasing his abilities so he could eavesdrop. He told friends that Hurkos was a fraud. Hurkos then received a note that sent him on a wild goose chase and raised everyone's hopes, but indicated only that someone – possibly the killer – was taunting him.

On July 27, Hurkos went on television and predicted that an arrest was imminent. He hoped the killer was listening, because he was going to describe him. Now he changed the description to a man who was six feet tall and had dark brown hair. However, Collins was not watching. He was picking up his next victim on a motorcycle. Her disappearance put pressure on Hurkos to deliver. However, a photo of her gave off no vibrations, although he believed that something bad had happened to her. He predicted that her body would be found by a roadway named Riverview or River Drive, and in fact it was found several days later in a ditch alongside Huron River Drive. That was about one mile from where Hurkos was staying, as if in challenge.

Upon hearing of the body's discovery, he hit his face and said, 'Her face was beat, beat, beat. It was wrinkled, like a monkey face.' He described the disposal site accurately, but still could not name the killer. When taken to the site, he didn't experience much in the way of 'vibrations', but said the man he 'saw' was not an American and that he was associated in some way with a ladder. That was all he could envision.

One account holds that a girl came to Hurkos's hotel at 1:30 a.m. one night, and in the presence of three police officers, said that she felt her boyfriend fitted the description. She hesitated to give much information, but finally said that his name was John Collins and he rode a motorcycle. However, there is no indication that the investigation of Collins was prompted by such a report, although it could explain the dramatic change in Hurkos' description of the killer.

A book about Hurkos's feats claimed that he also led police to the wig shop where the last victim was seen getting on the motorcycle, but there was no mention of this by the police or newspapers. In fact, it was the missing girl's roommates, not Hurkos, who had alerted police to the fact that she had gone to pick up a wig.

The next day after the body's discovery Hurkos left the city, vowing to come back a week later to wrap up the investigation. Before he could return, Collins was arrested.

Solving Sexual Crimes

Rape, incest, sexual assault – these are the crimes police regard with the most revulsion and contempt. The men in the world's morals squads are now doing everything possible to win their tough battle.

Few criminals are regarded with greater fear and contempt, or dealt with more harshly, than sex offenders. Yet these people are a part of our criminal population and the public has every right to expect that proper measures are taken to provide a maximum of protection for potential victims.

Judge John Rossetti of Canton, Ohio, worked to reduce sex crimes for many years. Finally, after an eleven-year legal battle when he appeared six times before the Ohio Legislature, a bill requiring the registration of convicted sex offenders was enacted into law. This is known as the Habitual Sex Offenders Law. It became effective on October 4, 1963, and since then has set the pattern all over the United States. It has reduced the grim total of sex offences, and decreased the workload of the police and forensic scientists in this sordid branch of crime. This register demands that no habitual sex offender shall be or remain in any county for more than thirty days without registering either with the Chief of Police of that city, or the Sheriff of the county.

This was a great step forward, for a person so convicted, and who travels for business or pleasure, might well be under pressure so that he abandons his criminal sexual activity.

In another area of the United States progress was made to control and contain sexual crime by setting up what was dubbed the 'Morals Squad'. This was born one cold morning in September, 1962, when Rochester police started an investigation into the brutal murder of a thirteen-year-old girl. Her body had been brutally ravished and was discovered in a gravel pit.

With the aid of investigators of the New York State Police the murderer was apprehended within ten days. However, this case headlined the need for a different registration of sex offenders. Special Agent (FBI) Walter V. McLaughlin was called in to instruct a group of police bureau men and women in the FBI Sex Crimes Investigation Course. The probe began to log all persons arrested on charges of rape, carnal abuse, sodomy, indecent exposure and endangering the morals of minors.

A six-digit code for sex offenders was used: (1) white, (2) negro, (3) other, and after four more digits relating to age, height, build and hair description, a code digit as follows: (1) limp or gait, (2) eye-glasses, (3) visible scars, crooked, deformed or missing limbs, (4) tattoos, (5) speech, (6) moustache or beard, (7) retarded, (8) ears, hearing defects, (9) teeth, mouth, (10) complexion, moles and (11) left-handed.

Without further delay all past and current prowler files, carnal-abuse and car files were vetted and translated into a digital code. This meant that when a new sex crime was reported, all possible suspects could be checked.

Identi-Kit

Just by using teletype digits a typical police bureau report on an alleged sex attack could be transmitted, an example of which reads:

> 'R (recidivist), 1965 in park, whistled at children, dropped trousers below knees. 1972, in High School zone, sitting in car, no trousers, pulled across intersection blocking path of teenaged girls. Drives 69 yellow T-bird. Licence No. 3X 412. Blonde straight, glasses.'

Even to save minutes in this way helped the Morals Squad to apprehend sex criminals and recidivists – those who keep on repeating their crimes. For example, from the Rochester case-histories there was grave concern when over an eight-week period a young man molested girls after presenting himself as a police officer.

An Identi-Kit composite was built up from the children's reports, but this did not result in a positive identification. Then from a community seventy miles south of Rochester, New York, a young man was arrested on a sex charge. The

Morals Squad checked the details of his offence with their digital system and computer-like file cards showing sexual modus operandi. Over the wire service went photographs from the agency which had arrested the man, and immediately the young children in Rochester were able to identify their assailant. He was consequently sentenced on the felony charge of carnal abuse.

Prior to the introduction of the Identi-Kit system in the 1950s, there was no swift and reliable way in which the police investigating a sex crime could get a 'mug print', or even wire it to other police regions. The Identi-Kit technique was developed by the Californian company Townsend Company Inc.

By 1970, forensic expert Jacques Penry had developed a system which became known as the 'Penry Facial Identification Technique', abbreviated from its initials to the more convenient name 'Photo-FIT'. This was built up from a representation of white male faces normally encountered in the British and European zones. Subsequently this was extended by John Waddington Ltd to incorporate Afro-Asian and Caucasian basic facial types.

This is all of great forensic importance in sex cases, where victims and other witnesses need the most rapid means of creating a portrait of an offender. While some villains are international, sex criminals are generally 'local'. For urgent identification of alleged sex offenders, the police use a system which deals with full-face and profile (162 pairs of eyes, 151 noses, 159 mouths and so on), in 12,000 million possible combinations.

Picture Technique

In 1963, New Scotland Yard started using a special monochrome photographic technique which helped in identification of alleged sexual crimes, by superimposition of transparencies.

For example, in a particular case of sexual attack, when a girl was strangled, it was helpful if the forensic workers could state if the victim was strangled on the floor, or on a couch believed to carry sexual stains. Under close examination the couch was found to have saliva stains at the top, mixed seminal and urine stains in the centre, and small tears at the lower edge, which could have been caused by the heels of a woman's shoe.

A woman police officer of the same height as the victim was photographed on her back, and this transparency was superimposed on that of the couch with the stains and cuts marked in white. A combined print was then taken, which clearly supported the theory of strangulation on the couch.

Measurements of this sort can be important in sex cases. This was highlighted in a sex murder at Morecambe, Lancashire, in the late 1940s, when Dr F. B. Smith assisted at the post mortem of 28-year-old Elizabeth Smith found drowned in a small stream.

There were curious facets of this murder, for when Dr J. B. Firth of the North Western Forensic Science Laboratory was called in to investigate he found no signs of a struggle. Yet the victim's under-clothing was soiled and soaked, indicating a long immersion, indicating that she had not accidentally slipped into the water. Dr Smith took specimens from the lungs, and prepared microscope slides. These disclosed the presence of very small single-cell water plants known as diatoms. This proved that water had been drawn into the victim's lungs, and that she had attempted to breathe while her mouth and nose were under water.

Police enquiries led to a Royal Air Force man David Williams being interrogated, and this action was so prompt that in fact he was discovered trying to dry out his clothes worn on the night of the murder. Dr Firth found that the man's jacket was wet chiefly in triangular patches across the lower corners of the pockets, as if he had been bending down in water. The bottoms of the trousers were wet for about eighteen inches, and there was also blood and seminal staining. Williams was tried at Liverpool Assizes for murder, and sentenced to death.

Forensic Art

A major advancement in the identification of sex offenders is forensic art. Forensic art encompasses several disciplines including composite art, image modification, post-mortem reconstruction and demonstrative evidence. However, composite art is traditionally the most commonly known discipline of forensic art. The art of composite drawing has been used by police agencies throughout history. When one recalls the Old West, the classic wanted poster with a drawing of a 'Bad Guy' comes to mind. These drawings were composites.

Composite Art is an unusual marriage of two unlikely disciplines, police investigative work and art. The cop/artist possesses a combination of both skills. The artist can create a quality facial drawing with assured confidence. Though drawing skills are important parts of composite art, the real challenge is in the ability to interview and relate to a victim or witness. The purpose is to successfully gather, interpret and illustrate the information obtained from the victim's memory.

In the past fifteen years, the discipline of composite art has evolved into forensic art. The forensic artist possesses knowledge of victim psychology, post-mortem reconstruction and human ageing. These artists currently use new computer technologies and digital imagery to create more successful investigative images.

Use of Drugs

Morals Squads, murder squads and indeed all those likely to be given a heavy workload as the result of misdirected sexual impulses of others, would be less busy if it were possible effectively and legally to decrease sexual desires.

Drugs have been administered in jails to volunteers, but in their initial trials were not very successful. As is well known, a British slang term for being in jail is 'doing porridge', and this comes from the diet of porridge and other plain food intended to diminish virility. However, as more and more new drugs are discovered, it is being proved that oversexuality can be controlled by this method.

'Dirty Old Man'

A tragedy can arise, and indeed did, if unqualified people attempt to form their own Morals Squad. This was emphasized in the tragic death of a retired shopkeeper in Flint, North Wales, in August 1973.

Two eight-year-old girls had been molested in the neighbourhood, and when the elderly shopkeeper was seen giving sweets to other little girls, a local vigilante squad made the grave error of thinking he was responsible for the sex attacks. They beat him up, and the next day he was found dead in bed. Yet he was absolutely innocent of any sexual offence. The police were already interviewing another man in connection with the attacks on the little girls. 'He was a kind but lonely man,' an observer said. 'He was always glad to give sweets to the children.' That kindness cost him his life.

Acid-phosphatase tests can detect the presence of seminal fluid, and serology can help to identify body fluids other than blood. But forensic scientists had not reached a stage when the age of the secreter can be proved. Yet the 'dirty old man' complex is hard to eradicate from the minds of some investigators, no matter how untrue it may be.

This was shown by the Rochester Morals Squad in New York when, in one three-month period, it received from one district in the city twelve complaints of molesting. Four incidents were rape, and residents in the district were in a state of near hysteria. Victims were females, aged fourteen to twenty-one.

Special assignments were given to investigators, thousands of man-hours were consumed, and eventually a male was apprehended and identified by three of the victims. The attacker was not a 'dirty old man' but a youth of fourteen!

The Ultimate Ghoul

Ed Gein, a shy and outwardly ordinary man, inspired the characters of both Norman Bates in *Psycho* and Buffalo Bill in *The Silence of the Lambs.* During the 1940s and 50s, he lived on a secluded farm in Plainfield, Wisconsin. Within the isolation of his family, no one noticed how odd he was, but left to his own devices, his weird and deadly proclivities began to emerge.

Ed was devoted to his mother, who was quite demented and thoroughly disgusted with sex. She thought it the world's greatest evil so she preached to her two sons that they were to keep themselves pure. When her husband died, she had even more influence, and then Ed's brother died, leaving him alone with this delusional woman. Mildly retarded and mentally unstable, he was completely dependent on her. When she suffered a stroke that paralyzed her, he nursed her even as she verbally abused him. Sometimes he crawled into bed with her to cuddle.

Then when Ed was 39, his mother died. He

could hardly bear it. He kept to the farm and spent his time doing odd jobs and reading magazines about headhunters, human anatomy, and the Nazis. He also contemplated sex-change surgery so he could become his mother – to literally crawl into her skin.

Then one day he spotted a newspaper report about a woman who had just been buried not far from his mother's grave. He decided to go out and dig her up so he could have a look at a real body – a female one. He got a friend named Gus, a gravedigger, to help him open up the grave. Over the next decade, he continued to visit the cemetery for more bodies, usually under a full moon. Sometimes he took the entire corpse and sometimes just certain parts. He later claimed that he had dug up nine separate graves in three different cemeteries.

Ed apparently just loved bodies. He was a true necrophile (also called a necrophiliac). Body parts excited him and he had no trouble having them in his home, no matter what their state of decomposition. From the bodies he dug up, he cut off the heads and shrank them, putting some on his bedposts. He also formed lampshades from the skin. Storing the organs in the refrigerator, and possibly cooking them, he made things like soup bowls out of the bones for his own use. Sometimes he had sexual contact with these bodies, and eventually he just went ahead and dug up his own mother. Rather than get a sex-change operation, he simply made himself a female body suit and mask out of the skin, and he would wear this outfit to dance around outside. Sometimes he even donned it to dig up a grave.

Finally, when it was clear that the skin would harden and crack, he decided to get bodies that were more pliable. That meant someone really fresh. In 1954, Gein shot a woman, Mary Hogan, who resembled his mother in size and brought her to his farm. No one suspected a thing. Three years later, he did it again to Bernice Worden, and this time the police decided to have a look.

What they found was a house of horror. Inside, they discovered numerous body parts: four noses, several bone fragments, nine death masks, a heart in a pan on the stove, a bowl made from a skull, ten female heads with the tops sawn off, human skin covering several chair seats, pieces of salted genitalia in a box, skulls on his bedposts, organs in the refrigerator, a pair of lips on a string, and much more. It was estimated that he had mutilated some fifteen women and kept their remains around him. In the barn they found the corpse of Bernice Worden, hung from the ceiling feet first.

At his disposition hearing (since he was judged incompetent to stand trial), Ed Gein was found to be insane. He seemed not to be aware that what he had done was wrong, and he died in 1984 at the age of 78 in a psychiatric institution. Since he never had actually hunted for deer, neighbours wondered what had been in the packages of fresh venison that he'd so generously brought them.

While Gein fails to display the compulsive lust characteristic of many necrophiles, he does represent the type of person who enjoys the company of the dead, sexually-speaking. Of course not all necrophiles are violent. Not all go from one body to another. In a way, it is difficult to say whether Ed Gein was the ultimate ghoul.

Proving Rape

A judge's daughter is found brutally murdered. She has been stabbed 37 times and dumped near her home. But had she been sexually assaulted – how do scientists prove rape?

RAPE IS RAPE, nearly all the world over, bringing a moment of unimaginable terror to the poor victim and sometimes destroying her mind.

Only in the United States is rape split into two different categories by lawyers, police and criminalists. *Forcible* rape is the carnal knowledge of a female through the use or threat of force, while *statutory* rape is usually in a lesser category, implying unlawful sexual intercourse with a female without her consent, but with ravishment which does not involve excessive force or violence.

The difference is one which involves the courts in lengthy, costly, hair-splitting forensic debates, because almost all sexual intercourse involves force on the part of one or other of the parties. Very often it has to be left to the forensic pathologist to produce the evidence on which will hang the verdict:

Did she want it, or didn't she? Did she struggle violently or was she attacked? Was she the completely uncooperating and unwilling victim of forcible raping, or after a show of force did she acquiesce in an act described in the current permissive cynicism: 'When rape is inevitable, relax and enjoy it?'

One of the last official duties of L. Patrick Gray before he was politically ousted from his post as Acting Director of the FBI, was to give his Bureau's view on certain aspects of forcible rape. This caused forensic science laboratories in most countries to be extremely busy in close association with psychiatric investigators.

In Mr Gray's final year (1971) 72 per cent of all offences reported in this crime class were actual rapes by force, while the remainder were attempts or assaults to commit forcible rape. 'This offence,' he pointed out, 'is a violent crime against the person, and of all Crime Index offences, law-enforcement administrators recognize this is probably one of the most under-reported crimes – due primarily to fear and/or embarrassment on the part of the victims. As a national average 18 per cent of all forcible rapes reported to the police were determined by investigation to be unfounded. This is caused primarily due to the question of the use of force or the threat of force frequently complicated by a prior relationship between victim and offender . . .'

Human Passion

On the other hand the British forensic student might feel the position is legally less complex in the United Kingdom, where the law (the Sexual Offences Act, 1956) is stated bluntly: *'It is felony for a man to rape a woman.'*

This goes back to the Offences Against the Person Act of 1861, and might seem to stop any hair-splitting between statutory rape and forcible rape. But as every lawyer knows, there are dozens of additions and sub-sections. Human passions being what they are, there are many shades of rape – from violation of a girl by her half-brother, to rape of a wife by her husband when they are living apart under a legal separation order.

The 'forcible' part of the act is usually covered in English law by some allied act of 'GBH' (grievous bodily harm), and punishment for this may be additional to the imprisonment for the rape itself.

Patricia Curran

The case regarding the murder of Patricia, daughter of Lord Justice Curran, opened in 1952. It became a *cause célèbre* lasting for ten years, involving a long campaign by a Sunday newspaper and political appeals to the then Northern Ireland Minister of Home Affairs.

Patricia's body was found in the grounds of her home at Whiteabbey, with 37 stab wounds including superficial face and neck injuries. There were deep cuts penetrating to the liver, but the limited amount of blood on the leaves of bushes suggested that the body had been dragged to the spot after the attack, and perhaps after the cuts on the face. The positions of her handbag, books and shoes also led the forensic investigator to believe they had deliberately been put there near the body, and not discarded in a struggle.

The post mortem was conducted by Dr A. M. Wells of Queen's University, Belfast, and Alan Thompson, a senior member of the North Western forensic laboratory staff started the examination until Dr Firth could be flown across from Glasgow. It was decided that the attack was made with a narrow-bladed knife, and that face and neck injuries were received while the girl was standing up.

In his subsequent report, made in conjunction with T. Alstead Cooper and his colleague Arthur Brooks, Dr Firth talked of the girl's yellow wool cap.

'I removed a small tuft of fibres from the top of the outside of this . . . I found that it included a number of bright red fibres which, when put under the microscope, appeared to be composed of acetate rayon. Entwined in the red fibres were three wool fibres which were dyed an olive-green shade. There were a few wool fibres dyed bright yellow, which showed close agreement with the wool fibres of the cap, but the red and green fibres were not represented in the material of any garments worn by the girl . . .'

This kind of routine evidence, coupled with work by the Royal Air Force Special Investigation Branch, eventually led to the arrest, trial and conviction of Leading Aircraftsman Ian Hay Gordon. It took the jury only two hours to consider their verdict, and they found Gordon guilty but insane.

If there had been a sexual attack, what was the

gravity of it? In his report Dr Firth stated:

'I made copious notes on the condition of each garment, but the only facts of any significance concerned the girl's panties. I found recent tears all along the outer seam of the right leg, including the frilly edging in the region of the crutch. The back seam of the right leg was also torn for a distance of 4½ inches, beginning an inch below the waistband. There were heavy bloodstains on the lower portion of the panties, mainly at the back of the crutch. The dispersal of blood indicated that the seams were torn *before* any blood reached the blood-stained zone – in other words, the results were consistent with the panties having been torn before the bodily injuries were inflicted, or at least very shortly afterwards. The elastic waistband was intact. It could be deduced from these facts that a determined effort had been made to remove the panties, and that it had not been successful, partly because the elastic waistband had remained intact, assisted no doubt by the additional protection of the girl's underslip and outer garments . . .'

Under English law, penetration of the vagina by the penis has to be established, not necessarily the emission of semen. It was, of course, not necessary to establish this with Gordon, who was being tried for murder. The psychiatrist Dr Rossiter Lewis said that in his opinion Gordon had been suffering from the schizophrenia and hypoglycaemia on the night the girl was killed, and that he did not have the full sexual inclination – 'as we know it'.

There has been much research into the aspects of subnormality and crime, with relation to epilepsy and aggravated subnormality of the mind. This also involved probing the mental pressures which result in rape, grievous bodily harm, forcible rape and even sexual murder.

This is why males accused of, say, forcible rape, are not only invited to have their clothing and their person examined for seminal testing and blood grouping, but may be asked to take the Wechsler Adult Intelligence Scale tests. This involves arithmetical reasoning, digit symbol tests, perceptual ability and memory-span.

Mental Illness

It may affect a subsequent verdict of Diminished Responsibility on the grounds of subnormality and/or mental illness in the form of reactive depression, and is not so isolated from forcible rape as it may seem.

While the layman might take it for granted that an essential element of forcible rape is the male attacker's overwhelming desire for an orgasm, this is not always the case. Indeed, it might be said to be one essential forensic difference between statutory and forcible rape. The male's natural desire for intercourse is kept normally within bounds by self-pride, affection and our many social disciplines. Only where extreme temptations and circumstances allow does an irresistible erection and desire for orgasm take place.

Forcible rape by subnormals presents far more

complex problems, and there may even be schizoid elements in the attacker's personality urging him to derive a perverted satisfaction from the knowledge that he has a new *power* – the power that he alone can decide how much the victim is to suffer in injury, or even in death, quite apart from the sexual assault.

Grave injuries may be inflicted before penetration, and the struggles may actually prevent emission and complete orgasm, because most women struggle frenziedly. Whichever way it goes, the forensic worker is likely to be faced with identifying seminal stains. One assumed it is now almost common knowledge that in the majority of cases such stains are as identifiable as blood groups.

Laboratory Methods

As the stains dry out on a victim's clothing they tend to desiccate, and it becomes harder to find intact sperms. With current laboratory methods this is not always important, and we have certainly advanced since the early work of Alfred Swaine Taylor, one of the fathers of forensic research.

Citing a case of forcible rape tried at Edinburgh, Scotland, on November 27, 1843, Dr Taylor recorded: 'A man labouring at that time under gonorrhoea was charged with a criminal assault on a child. The shift worn by the prosecutix, with other articles belonging to the prisoner, were submitted for examination. Some of the stains on the linen were of a yellow colour, and were believed to be those of gonorrhoea; others, characterized by a faint colour and a peculiar odour, were considered to be stains caused by the spermatic secretion. Digested in water, they yielded a turbid solution of a peculiar odour, and when submitted to a powerful microscope, spermatozoa were detected. The stains were similar on the linen of the prisoner and the prosecutix. I believe this to be a solitary instance of the use of the microscope for such a purpose in this country . . .'

Some seventy-five years after Taylor, forensic laboratories all the way from those of the FBI and the British Home Office were making an initial quick check – as one must in cases of alleged forcible rape – by taking garments of both parties and fluorescing them under filtered ultra-violet light. Speed is essential, for stains tend to dry out and it becomes increasingly difficult to separate vaginal discharge, semen, urine, soil staining and grass (chlorophyll) likely to be found when a victim alleges forcible rape in the open.

Fortunately the AP reaction can now be used as a routine in semen tests. Chemists discovered in the 1950s, that in certain substances acid-phosphatase occurs. The acid-phosphatase found in the human body is an acid medium, and in forensic tests for semen a complex substance is broken down into parts and a test solution produced which, if semen is present, exhibits a bright purple colour. The stain itself is not destroyed, and as several tests may need to be made by interested legal parties in cases of alleged forcible rape, this is most helpful.

The clinical work in the forensic laboratory is,

of course, almost at the end of the evidence-getting story. But the criminalist would not be human if he were not moved to pity by the sight he sometimes faces at the start of a rape case.

Canine Forensics

Dogs involved in forensic work are required to know basic skills aside from specific scent identification. They must pass obedience tests, swim proficiently, be sociable with other dogs and humans, travel with other dogs in vehicles and helicopters, and do agility type exercises as directed.

WHILE MANY people think that all dogs used in law enforcement basically do the same job, in fact some have distinctly different jobs from others. Dogs used for arson detection, for example, are trained differently from dogs used to track a suspect or to find someone lost in the wilderness, and they may have to prove themselves under different conditions. They all share certain specific traits, however. Working dogs in law enforcement need to be:

Healthy
Alert
Trainable
Manageable
Eager to hunt
High in stamina
Not easily bored
Focused
Responsive to reward

Since they work as part of a team, the handler, too, needs to have certain traits, such as physical fitness, ability to cope with what is found, ability to 'read' the dog, ability to work with a forensics team and a willingness to keep learning and training.

The dog's job is to find clues for the handler to interpret. Most importantly, they rely on their noses as the chief means of detection. Humans have around five million olfactory receptor cells, while a bloodhound has one hundred million. In other words, they're useful in this line of work because of their superior sense of smell. Dogs can make distinctions between recent and older scents, and can detect a variety of odours under many different types of conditions. Since scent is invisible, they can track and find things that no human could ever detect.

Because we leave a trail of minute particles of hair and skin, as well as sweat and other body oils, dogs can pick up our scent. Dogs also make distinctions among scents, so they can focus on one even though others are present. They get a 'scent picture' or 'scent print'.

Tracking Dogs

Bloodhounds are the most famous type of tracking dog. Having been the first dog bred specifically for their scent capabilities, they've been used to track humans since the sixteenth century. These days, most bloodhound handlers are volunteers, and some teams might get called on several times in any given week. Yet even as volunteers, they must keep their dogs in top shape.

There is no single breed that works best under every condition, and sometimes a good detector dog is a crossbreed, but all have in common the ability to follow a scent and to stick with it until the job gets done. When they come upon the substance or odour they're trained to find, they alert their handlers with a specific type of trained behaviour, such as a bark or a certain position.

There are eight different kinds of jobs that dogs are used for in the pursuit of crime:

Narcotics dogs (NDD): These dogs are used to find illegal drugs, quite often at airport customs. The dogs sniff at luggage, boxes and even at people carrying illegal narcotics. Their handlers train them by placing narcotics in rags that the dog learns to fetch or find in a hidden place. The narcotics dogs associate the drug with the 'game', and eventually just look for the drugs. They learn to search persistently in all kinds of places, and even to detect the scent of drugs overtly masked by other odours.

Tracking dog: In the case of a known fugitive or a recent crime scene where the suspect may not be far away, a tracking dog like a bloodhound may be used. If there's a piece of clothing, a car seat, or an item on which the subject left a scent, it's given to the dog and the dog then follows that scent, if it's present. (There are even cases where the scent was picked up from the air.)

Bomb detection dog (EDD): This dog is trained to search specifically for substances used in explosive devices. The dog knows not to disturb the area, since the bomb might detonate. Instead, it will just alert its handler to the bomb's presence. In cases when this job needs to be done in a hurry, such a dog is indispensable.
Arson detection dogs: They're trained to indicate the presence of the types of accelerants used to start and spread fires, such as gasoline or kerosene. When fire damages a large area and leaves a heavy smell of smoke, it's difficult for humans to detect the fumes, but specially trained dogs have little difficulty indicating that a fire was purposely caused.
Search and Rescue dog (SAR): People lost in the wilderness require teams that can work in many different types of rough terrain, such as rushing water and deep snow. Dogs like this must have agility and confidence, as well as the ability to be in a boat. They are also strong swimmers and have plenty of stamina.
Body detector dogs: They may be brought to an area of mass disaster, such as an earthquake or building collapse where bodies are buried, or taken to hunt for a missing person. They're trained with odours that smell like people, and they often find living victims. Some dogs respond best to the living and get upset when they encounter a body. In certain cases when it is suspected

that the missing person is dead, a more specialized dog may have to be brought in.

Cadaver dogs: These animals are trained to detect decomposition, so they're taken out to hunt for missing people presumed dead, such as when a murderer confesses but cannot recall where he put the body. Some are trained in special situations, such as hanging victims, submerged bodies, and swift water drowning. Essentially, they're trained to 'possess' the scent the way a hunting dog would possess game.

Human remains specialist dogs: They start as cadaver dogs but work at a more refined level, in that they only alert handlers to the presence of some type of human remains.

The Scent Pad

In 1977 in Cheektowaga, New York, a police officer was shot and killed at a Holiday Inn. An article containing the fugitive killer's odour was found, and eleven different law enforcement agencies responded with German shepherds and trailing bloodhounds to join the ensuing manhunt. However, the first dog had contaminated the article, which rendered it useless. William Tolhurst, a member of the Niagara County Sheriff's Department and an authority on man trailing bloodhounds, was among those who showed up to help. The incident inspired him to develop a way to preserve the scent and keep it away from contact with the dogs.

He invented the 'scent sleeve' in which scented material could be placed for protection. This device operated by pumping air over the scented article to push the scent into a receptacle. The receptacle captured and contained the odour, making the scent not only usable for multiple dogs but also quite portable.

A decade later, Tolhurst developed the 'Big T Trainer', where a scented item was placed in a container through which pressured air blew to deliver the scent wherever he needed it. Any kind of scent, from accelerant to cadaver, could be used. That, too, proved effective, but Tolhurst didn't stop there. He then developed a vacuum process to collect the scent into a sterile gauze pad, which could be stored indefinitely and transported to different locations. Finally he made the device itself portable, calling it the STU100 or Scent Transfer Unit.

With this invention, scent can be picked up even from arson and explosives scenes, and can be freeze-dried for long periods of time. That means the pads can be used several years later in the event they are needed in a court case. Scent can also be removed from water, metal fragments, and fingerprints, leaving everything at the crime scene intact. Even more surprising, it can be collected from the air in a building where someone broke in. The key is to give it to the dog and let the dog follow it or pick out the suspect in what's come to be known as 'scent line-ups'.

In one case, as reported by Bill Clede, Tolhurst was on an arson team that was trying to crack a series of crimes in which fires had been deliberately set around Niagara County. When they found a suspect, they surreptitiously acquired an article with his scent on it. Tolhurst made a scent pad, and with this he eventually linked three of the fires to the suspect. The officers confronted the man and he confessed.

Tolhurst calls scent 'the forgotten evidence', because investigators just don't think about it. It's delicate, can't be detected well by humans, and isn't visible. However, it can be powerful and in some cases, it might be the only available evidence. There is always a scent.

Perhaps one of the more demanding jobs of a dog handler is that of a human remains specialist.

Hunting Bodies

Locating the remains of a missing person can be one of the biggest challenges a forensic investigator may face. Sometimes the death was particularly brutal, the discovered body is that of a child, or the victim has been missing a long time and the remains are in bad condition. Occasionally the terrain to be searched is difficult to navigate or the corpse has been carefully hidden.

In fact, it was the presence of decomposition odour that led cadaver dogs in Philadelphia in August 2001 to the body of Kimberly Szumski, 36, a woman missing from her home three months earlier. She had been wrapped in plastic and duct tape, buried under cinder blocks, and cemented into a wall reinforced with steel bars. Nevertheless some scent escaped, throwing suspicion on the estranged husband, who had done construction work in that building. The dogs gave the signal, the walls were torn down and the body was located.

Unlike trailing scent dogs that stick with an odour on the ground, cadaver dogs find the scent in the air as well. The use of such dogs in police work began in 1974 for victims that had been buried in a forest. A dog was brought from Texas to New York for the task, and her first find was a college student buried under four feet of dirt. Now police agencies train dogs for this and there are numerous volunteer search dog teams as well.

Sandra Anderson from central Michigan handles *Eagle*, the dog in the Kupaza case. Eagle was also featured in an episode of *Unsolved Mysteries* in which he was taken into the home of Azizul Islam, a physician suspected of killing his wife. The woman went missing on December 20, 1999. Two days later, parts of a woman's body were found in a dumpster and a field. Apparently feeling confident, Islam allowed a search of his home. Anderson noticed strong bleach odours everywhere and she feared that this would hinder Eagle's work. However, the dog immediately gave the signal on a paint roller and soon indicated that there was something associated with human decomposition on the floor that the doctor had been painting. It turned out that there was blood in the paint and it matched the DNA found on the missing woman's toothbrush. Islam was arrested and convicted of murder.

A dog can scent a body in water because the oils from the cadaver come to the surface. As it decomposes, there's a great deal of odour that comes up, and at some point the decomposition gases begin to rise. If there's been a stabbing, there will even be a blood odour.

No matter what line of work these dogs are trained for, it's clear that they've become essential to forensic investigation.

PART FOUR

CASES OF SCIENTIFIC DEDUCTION

Saint Edward the Martyr

A thousand-year-old pile of bones huddled at the bottom of a lead casket was all that remained of Saint Edward the Martyr. Until his death at eighteen he had been England's King Edward. The legends told of treachery, assassination in ambush . . . then the scientists got to work.

THE CONSIDERABLE advances made by forensic medicine in the past half-century have led to the solving of literally thousands of violent crimes. Given a body – however badly disfigured or fragmented – medical detectives can build up a highly accurate picture of the victim and the manner of his death.

One of the most spectacular examples of this kind of forensic work occurred in Britain during the 1930s, when a pathologist working from a little pile of bones confirmed the details of a Saxon King's murder – a thousand years after the murder occurred.

During the reign of King Edgar – AD 959 to AD 975 – in England, the established Church was split into two factions. On the one hand were the monks of the great abbeys and religious houses, dedicated to improving the quality of life; on the other were the 'secular' clergy, bishops and priests who made fortunes from the administration of their parishes and spent their time drinking, feasting and womanizing. Many of the nobles supported the latter faction for their own ends, though at least two – the Northern King Oswald and Bishop Dunstan, later to become saints – fought for the reformation and unification of the Church.

Profligate Lifestyle

King Edgar himself, despite his own wildly extravagant lifestyle, supported the monks and built forty great monasteries during his reign. When he died his fifteen-year-old son Edward took up the cause, aided by Oswald and Dunstan. But Edward was to reign for only four years. In his eighteenth summer, while on a visit to his young brother Aethelred – later dubbed 'The Unready' – Edward was ambushed and murdered.

An account of the killing is given in the *Life of St. Oswald*, written about the year AD 1000 by a monk who was in Edward's entourage at the time of the attack: 'Soldiers were therefore holding him, one drew him (the King) to the right towards himself as though to give him a kiss (of welcome), another seized his left hand violently and wounded him, but he cried as loud as he could. "What are you doing, breaking my right arm?" and he fell from his horse and died.'

Piecing the details together from the rather complicated report – it was, of course, written in

Latin – a fairly clear picture emerges. Two soldiers approached the King, one on his left, the other on his right. The latter, while pretending to give him a kiss of peace, grasped Edward's left shoulder with his own right arm, at the same time getting a grip on the King's right forearm – the sword arm – with his left hand.

While Edward was pinioned in this fashion, the man on the left grasped his left arm and stabbed him with a knife. The King's horse, frightened, reared up and forced its royal rider back onto the high cantle of the saddle. With the soldier on the right still gripping the King, Edward's thigh was pressed across the cantle with enormous force.

Caught in the Stirrup

The horse then bolted, Edward fell from the saddle and was dragged along the ground by his left foot, which was caught in the stirrup. The breakages thus incurred, coupled with the stab wound, finished the King off. Within a few days his younger brother Aethelred, who appears to have instigated the ambush, had begun his own disastrous reign.

Some years went by, and the unfortunate young King was canonized as 'Saint Edward the Martyr'. His shrine at Shaftesbury in the south of England was a place of pilgrimage up until the early sixteenth century, when King Henry VIII finally dissolved the monastic system.

After the dissolution of the monasteries, Edward's relics, like those of many another early

English saint, appeared to be lost for ever. But on January 2, 1931, an archaeologist named J. Wilson Claridge discovered a lead casket containing bones on the site of the Abbey Church at Shaftesbury.

The casket was 21 inches long, 11 inches wide, and about 9 inches deep. The bones had been neatly arranged, the small ones at the bottom, long ones at one side, and part of a skull on top. Certain clues, coupled with legends of the place, indicated to Claridge that the remains might be those of Edward the Martyr.

It was, said the scholastic world, a 'tremendous discovery' – if, that is, the identity of the bones could be proved.

It was at this point that forensic science stepped in, in the person of Thomas E. A. Stowell, MD, a Fellow of the Royal College of Surgeons and a distinguished pathologist. Stowell met Claridge, heard of his discovery, and asked to see the bones. After the first brief examination he announced that they were those of a young man who had sustained a remarkable number of 'greenstick fractures' – fractures which occur in the pliable bones of the young. But he would need considerably more time to reach a complete conclusion. The British Museum Department of Anthropology saturated the remains with synthetic resin to strengthen them, and then handed the bones over to Stowell for his 1,000-year-late post mortem.

Stowell began by establishing the height of the dead man. By measuring the long bones of his arms and legs, making obvious allowances for scalp and heel pad thickness, and estimating various other factors from the other bones available, he was able to say that the deceased had been between five feet six and five feet eight inches in height.

'Sexing' the Skeleton

He had already guessed that the bones were those of a male, and he now set out to prove it. There are several methods of 'sexing' a skeleton. The pelvis is generally most informative, but the sacrum – the wedge-shaped bone at the bottom of the spine – or the femur or thigh bone are also informative. The skull too can be used as a guide and there are what might be called 'mathematical' methods for sexing a skeleton by measuring the 'heads' of the humerus – upper arm bone – or femur.

Having established the height and sex of the remains, Stowell now began to investigate his age. An American report, *Skeletal Changes in the Young*, sets out various guidelines, and from these Stowell deduced that the dead man was between 17 and 21 years of age. He plumped for the lower age because of the characteristic green-stick fractures.

Stowell then set out to establish the race of the deceased. The skull, he decided, was *dolichocephalic*, or long-headed. The Saxons were typically long-headed, whereas the 'ancient' Britons and the Celts, the two predominant races in the England of King Edward, were among the 'round-headed' races. So almost certainly the remains were those of a Saxon.

After examining the sutures, or bone-joins of

the skull vault, Stowell went on to the vertebrae of the spine – the small bones which carry the spinal cord from the skull to the pelvis. In the neck there are normally seven of these bones, but the 'Edward' casket contained only portions of the first, second and seventh. The missing third, fourth, fifth and sixth cervical, or neck, vertebrae may have disintegrated, and by following up further clues Stowell concluded that the four missing bones tallied with the dead person having suffered a severely broken neck.

An investigation of the thoracic vertebrae – which run down the middle of the back – showed that the 'laminal spurs' or projections from the main bone were very small. These laminal spurs grow with age, and through them Stowell was able accurately to pinpoint the age of the dead man: he had died in his eighteenth year.

An examination of the lumbar vertebrae, or lower backbone, clinched this finding.

Assault Victims

Stowell then came to the forearm bones. The left radius, which along with the ulna supports the arm from elbow to wrist, had been broken in at least four places, while the ulna itself showed the beginning of a transverse fracture. Going by the *Life of St. Oswald* and these bones, Stowell was satisfied that the left forearm had been forcibly twisted inwards, the arm probably being bent behind the back – the surgeon had seen such injuries on assault victims.

Perhaps most impressive of all was the left thigh bone, which had suffered a transverse, or greenstick, fracture – a splitting of the bone upwards and downwards, which is comparatively rare. According to the *Life of St. Oswald*, the King's body had been forced backwards over the saddle cantle and then dragged along the ground by the left foot. Some time previously, Stowell had conducted a post mortem on a boy who had been dragged, feet upwards, along the ground by the driving belt of a lathe. He had sustained precisely the same type of fracture as that under examination.

Tibia Fracture

The left tibia – the larger and stouter of the two leg bones – had also sustained a greenstick fracture of the type to be expected after a pressure such as the King was said to have undergone.

Finally, Stowell examined the right shoulder-blade or scapula, the right humerus or elbow bone, and the right haunch bone, all of which bore fractures which were consistent with the body having fallen from the saddle and hitting the ground on the right side – the force being taken by the shoulder, elbow and protuberant part of the hip.

Stowell was satisfied. In his report he wrote that the bones were those of a male of the age of King Edward, and that they showed 'a concatenation of fractures which precisely fit the story of the murder . . . the attack on the left upper limb, the drawing of the body to the right . . .' Stowell could not think of any other series of violences which would have produced exactly the same results. In conclusion he stated: 'I cannot escape the conviction that, on historical, anatomical, and surgical grounds, beyond reasonable doubt we have here the bones of Saint Edward, King and Martyr'.

A Trace of Arsenic

The arsenic Dr Taylor found in 'bottle no. 21' almost ruined his reputation . . . and may have allowed an inept killer to escape.

THE MEDICAL MAN who takes to murder has, perhaps, oddly, never been very successful. Palmer, Pritchard, Lamson, Cross, Cream, Crippen, Ruxton and Smethurst were all dealt with by the law, and of them only Cross, Lamson and Ruxton had any real professional qualifications, and none of them, except perhaps Crippen, showed real expertise.

One of the most curious cases was that of Thomas Smethurst, a 'doctor' who obtained his degree through what would today be called 'a diplomatic mill', in this case the University of Erlangen in Bavaria. It is certain Smethurst practised and, from somewhere, acquired a quite respectable medical knowledge.

He was born, according to some sources, in Lincolnshire in 1805. It is believed his father was a herbalist, and that he had two brothers and a sister. In 1827 he married a lady twenty years his senior, said to be a patient of his at the time. Mary Smethurst brought to him a very modest fortune, and this he put to good use for six years by running a hydropathic establishment at Moor Park in Surrey, where Swift wrote *A Tale of a Tub*. This was a successful and profitable venture, for in 1852 Smethurst became a 'gentleman of leisure'.

The Smethursts seemed a pleasant and contented couple without any real roots, or children. In appearance he was a rather small and insignificant man, with thick reddish hair and a not very commanding presence which he managed to overcome with a slight pomposity, and the authority usual to medical men. In the autumn of 1858 the Smethursts were living in a boarding house in the better part of Bayswater, London, at 4 Rifle Terrace which was at the top of what is now Queensway, not far from Whiteley's Store.

In October a new lodger arrived at the house, Miss Isabella Bankes, a 43-year-old spinster of some means. She possessed £1,800 in property and lived on the life interest of £5,000 which, on her death, would revert to her family. There was an immediate attraction between Miss Bankes and the doctor. Smethurst managed to spend little time with his semi-invalid wife, but a great deal with Miss Bankes, and the affair became so marked to everyone except Mrs Smethurst that the landlady, appalled at the boarding-house gossip, told Miss Bankes at the end of the first week in November that she would probably be more comfortable 'elsewhere'.

There was a quick exodus. Miss Bankes set up house in rooms at 37 Kildare Terrace, not far from Rifle Terrace, and there the 'star cross'd lovers' – as a newspaper was to call them – were so enamoured of each other that they came together, Thomas Smethurst having calmly left his wife.

The picture of Isabella Bankes that has survived does not suggest that she was a Victorian Helen of Troy, for she was 'a gentle lady of quiet aspect, a bright eye and a kindly manner'.

'United Illegally'

She was sufficiently attractive, however, for Smethurst to bigamously 'marry' her at Battersea Parish Church on December 9, 1858 – at his trial he was to excuse this action by claiming '. . . we united ourselves illegally, but it was for a permanency, and the marriage took place this way: at the request of Miss Bankes . . . she knew I was married – and in order that she should be protected from reproach hereafter, this marriage was preliminary to one at a future period, in the event of my wife dying – she is now 74 years of age.'

'Dr and Mrs' Smethurst now settled in rooms at 27 Old Palace Gardens, between The Green and the River Thames at Richmond. Here they lived peacefully – or, anyway, without attracting notice – until March 28, 1859, when Isabella was suddenly taken ill with symptoms resembling those of dysentery.

The illness did not clear up quickly and on April 3 Isabella was still so unwell that her lover did something that has always puzzled believers in his guilt. He sent for medical help, seeking the co-operation of Dr Julius and Dr Bird, who were at that time the most prominent medical men in Richmond. Dr Julius, as the senior physician, obtained all his information about the medical history from Smethurst and from the patient.

Smethurst was always present at every visit to the sick-room, though neither of the doctors found any fault with his medical knowledge. The patient was diagnosed as suffering from diarrhoea and was given medicines which, however, failed to help. It was felt that healthier quarters, above river level, might help, and the couple moved to 10 Alma Villas, on Richmond Hill. The move was made on April 15, when the doctor supported his weak spouse in a cab which took them and their possessions to the new quarters on the first floor of a very charming house.

Smethurst wrote to Louisa Bankes, sister of Isabella, at her home in Maida Vale. She came at once to Richmond on April 19, but did not stay very long. The doctors now diagnosed poison of some sort, but certainly Smethurst did not act like a poisoner. He treated the invalid with the greatest kindness and patience, and her genuine affection for him was obvious, yet he never permitted anyone to see her unless he was also in the room.

Smethurst called in a third, very prominent, doctor to see what could be done, and then on April 30 summoned a solicitor. The solicitor was shown the draft of a will drawn up 'by a London barrister' – despite the fact it was wholly in Smethurst's handwriting. It left all Isabella's property to her 'friend'. A final will was drawn up by the solicitor, in haste, and was signed quite willingly by Miss Bankes.

Nevertheless this last action disturbed the two local physicians. They now became very suspicious, and decided to test the bodily evacuations of the patient. As a result of what they found they called the police, and Thomas Smethurst was promptly arrested. Over twenty bottles and containers holding, or having held, various medicines were removed from 10 Alma Villas. The unfortunate Miss Bankes appeared to have been only dimly aware of what was happening. Her doctors and her sister attended her, but in spite of every care she died on May 3.

The manifest suspicions of three well-known medical men, the arrest, and police evidence were not, just the same, sufficient to impress the Richmond magistrates. It was decided that Smethurst should be discharged on the basis of insufficient evidence. He went free, but only for a brief time.

The local coroner was less inclined to see the evidence and the suspicions in the same light. He considered the available facts and after various questions to witnesses issued a warrant for the re-arrest of Smethurst. It was not long before one of the greatest medical jurists of the time entered into the picture. This was Dr Alfred Swaine Taylor, Professor of Chemistry at Guy's Hospital, who is remembered today as author of the classic *Taylor's Principles and Practice of Medical Jurisprudence* which, under succeeding editors, remains a cornerstone of forensic medicine.

As Government analyst, he gave evidence at the preliminary hearings to the effect that he found arsenic in vomit from the deceased. In one bottle of medicine – 'No. 21' in the list of articles taken from Alma Villas – he also found arsenic. This naturally increased suspicion of Smethurst.

Dr Taylor had arrived at his conclusions by using the analytical method known as the Reinsch Test, devised by a German chemist, Hugo Reinsch, in 1842 as a new method of detection of arsenic poisoning. The test was reasonably simple. Solutions suspected of containing arsenic were strongly acidified by the addition of hydrochloric acid. Pieces of copper foil were then introduced, and the liquid was heated to near boiling point. The presence of arsenic was shown by deposits on the copper. If present in any quantity, the poison showed as a lustrous black deposit, while a steel-grey coating indicated smaller quantities.

Remarkable Contrasts

Dr Taylor was satisfied after his investigations that arsenic was indeed present, but in the medicine bottle he examined he calculated that there must have been less than a quarter of a grain of arsenic mixed with the four ounces of matter in the bottle. Arsenic, he noted, presents remarkable contrasts, which tend to depend on the human body – adults have died from the ingestion of 0.12 grain, while others have tolerated, and overcome with medical help, as much as eight grains. However, Dr Taylor's evidence at the preliminary hearing clinched the committal for trial.

Thomas Smethurst – still described as 'Dr' in the newspapers – was taken to the Old Bailey's Central Criminal Court for his trial. Three years before, the

Central Criminal Court Act of 1856 had been passed; Palmer, the Rugeley Poisoner, had been tried there through this Act by which an accused person could be tried for an offence outside the jurisidiction of the court, instead of at the local assizes, in order that he could receive a fair trial.

The hearing was held on July 7, 1859, before the Lord Chief Justice Baron Pollock with the great Mr Serjeant Ballantine prosecuting. One of the great sensations of that bitter legal contest was the evidence of Dr Taylor, for though he stated that he had received no less than 28 articles from Alma Villas through the police for examination, only bottle No. 21 was of any importance, plus the vomit. He had to make an admission which more or less turned the case upside down.

He stated that though he had found arsenic according to the Reinsch Test, he came up against a factor that was to fault his findings, and this was the presence of possible impurities in the reagents used. In other words, both hydrochloric acid and metallic copper invariably contained minute quantities of arsenic, with the hydrochloric acid often containing the larger quantity of the impurity.

The copper had shown the steel-grey of minute quantity, but Dr Taylor's unhappy position in court was that he had to admit the arsenic may well have been in the reagents – the process of ensuring absolute purity is not a difficult one, but it is possible that either the doctor or, more probably, one of his assistants did not take the proper prior steps.

But medical opinion was on his side, in the

shape of Professor Odling of Guy's Hospital, the Professor of Practical Chemistry, and others. The overall opinion was that there had been a continuous administration of some irritant poison, such as arsenic or antimony. Against this the defence put forth its own medical experts, who claimed that the dead woman had died not by slow arsenic poisoning, but by idiopathic dysentery. Just to play safe, it was also suggested that ordinary bismuth, which Miss Bankes had been given from time to time, almost always contained arsenic.

It was revealed in court that the deceased had been nearly two months pregnant. It was also suggested that she might have died from 'gastric complications' following her condition, while Dr Taylor proposed that the accused might have given the woman potassium chlorate after the arsenic, to eliminate its traces.

The judge in his summing-up clearly indicated that he thought Smethurst guilty. This the jury obviously accepted, for they took only twenty minutes to return a verdict of guilty. The sentence of death was passed, but as so often happens, the public, which had been anti-Smethurst, promptly switched sides on hearing the verdict, and there was a great outcry against it. Experts in law, medicine, toxicology and other spheres began to join the passionate discussion.

Hard Labour

A medical journal venomously suggested that 'we must now look upon Professor Taylor as having ended his career, and hope he will immediately withdraw into the obscurity of private life, not forgetting to carry with him his favourite arsenic copper'. This tasteless attack was quite without result. Dr Taylor went on from success to success, and in 1865 he published the book on medical jurisprudence that immortalized his name.

The Home Office was disturbed by the raging controversy and directed a leading London surgeon, Sir Benjamin Collins Brodie, to look into the matter and study the trial record, to the surprise of the medical profession and the irate fury of Lord Chief Justice Baron Pollock.

Brodie offered as his opinion that there was 'not absolute and complete evidence' of Thomas Smethurst's guilt. The Home Secretary did not intervene until two days before the execution date, when the condemned man was reprieved and freed, to be at once arrested for bigamy. He served a year's hard labour, an unduly harsh sentence when he should have received penal servitude.

After his release he went to live in a house off Vauxhall Bridge Road and, though still a comfortably situated man, aroused sensation by suing for the legacy left to him by Isabella Bankes and, to the distress of her family, winning his case. Nothing is known of him after that except an item in a local paper referred to 'Dr and Mrs Smethurst', which suggests that, after all his troubles, he at last returned to his true wife.

The Girl in Pyjamas

The body is charred, the features battered, but the dead woman is easily recognizable. Preserved in formaldehyde and studied for ten years, the corpse finally yields an identity and a conviction. But doubts linger. The experts have botched the job . . .

MOST FORENSIC scientists would confidently claim that given a body they should be able to identify it beyond reasonable doubt. In the last decade fragmented bones have been conclusively identified as belonging to a particular person.

But in the strange case of the Australian 'pyjama girl' no such positive identification was forthcoming; and the fault was at least partly due to the over-enthusiasm of forensic experts. In a word, they botched the job, and this despite the fact that they had had the body pickled in a special coffin and available for examination over a period of ten years.

The township of Albury lies on the borders of New South Wales and Victoria, between the cities of Melbourne and Sydney. On the fine, bright morning of September 1, 1934, a farmer was cleaning a culvert some six miles from Albury when, stuffed inside, he found the body of a young woman. She was clothed only in ragged pyjamas. The head was covered with a bag, the body was charred, and alongside it were patches of oil, which suggested deliberate burning.

The farmer contacted the police, and the corpse was taken to the mortuary at Albury, where a post mortem was performed. It was immediately obvious that the girl had been subjected to considerable violence. There were extensive burns on the body's left side and a wound, roughly the area of an ordinary matchbox, had exposed the brain above the left eye. Another wound under the left eye had almost driven the eyeball into the skull, the left temple was battered, and below the right eye was the entrance hole of a bullet. Death appeared to have taken place anything from one to four days before the discovery of the body, the three major wounds having been delivered with a 'blunt instrument'.

The only other immediate point of note was that the bag in which the head had been wrapped had also contained a towel which bore traces of what appeared to be laundry marks – in the normal process of things a vital clue, but in this case one which seems to have been ignored.

While police published details of the dead woman in an attempt to identify her, the body was moved to Sydney University, where a second post mortem was held. Here, pathologists confirmed that the wounds around the left eye and temple had been caused before death, the bullet having finally killed the terribly injured woman.

They concluded that the victim had been between 22 and 28, and noted that her hands and feet were large, her breasts small and firm, the body well shaped, and the ears unusual and highly individual in formation. The eyes, according to the Sydney experts, were blue-grey, and the race Anglo-Saxon. The second autopsy over, the body was placed in a special metal coffin which was then filled with formalin – an aqueous solution of formaldehyde which preserves organic tissues indefinitely.

Strangely Shaped Ears

By this time, reconstructed photographs of the girl's face had been printed in all the newspapers. A Mrs M. Presley saw them and went to the police. The dead woman, said Mrs Presley, was her granddaughter, Mrs Anna Philomena Coots, whose maiden name had been Morgan. She had lived in a Sydney flat with her husband, a writer. After seeing the body, Mrs Presley 'positively' identified her because of the strangely shaped ears and blue eyes.

From this point on all should have been straightforward enough, but in fact it was the beginning of a 'search for identity' which was to last for ten years. For the first four of those years, a stream of witnesses viewed the grisly remains, lying suspended in their preserving fluid. Mrs Callow, Anna Morgan's landlady, agreed with Mrs Presley that this was her former lodger, and John Morgan, Mrs Presley's first husband, also swore that the body was Anna's.

But one important witness disagreed with the

others. Mrs Jeannette Routledge, Anna's mother, looked long and hard at the battered corpse, and then told police officers: 'I am certain that this is not my daughter.' She seemed calm and rational at the time, and when police asked her to make a statement to this effect she did so.

Despite this, her testimony might have been disregarded, if a police sergeant named King had not seen the body in June 1938. He had known the dead woman, he said. Even allowing for the wounds and the crinkling of the skin which was the result of steeping in preservative, he swore that this was Linda Agostini, a girl well known to King and his wife, but whom they had not seen since 1931.

Shortly after King had made this statement a coroner's court was finally convened. Five witnesses testified that the body was that of Anna Philomena Morgan, while Mrs Routledge and Sergeant King disagreed. The coroner accepted the majority opinion, and the verdict was that Anna Morgan had been murdered by a person or persons unknown.

The inquest revived public interest and the 'pyjama girl' case hit the headlines once again. This time, the publicity caught the eye of Dr Palmer Benbow, who, like a number of medical men before him, took a keen interest in criminology and had a reputation as an amateur investigator. His full methods were never revealed, but he gained access to the body and the other relics of the case – the tattered pyjamas, the bag, and the piece of towelling. Unlike the police, Benbow examined the 'laundry marks' on the towel minutely, and these somehow led to a shack on a piece of common ground near Albury.

At the hut he found an old painted bedstead which, he alleged, matched up with flecks of paint found on the corpse, and some woollen material in the hut that corresponded with fibres found in the dead girl's hair. Proceeding with his investigations, the doctor traced an alcoholic who had known Anna Morgan. This person named a man who, he told Benbow, had beaten Anna up with a piece of the bedstead.

And here the doctor's investigations virtually came to an end. He later stated that he had been 'obstructed' and the clear implication was that he had been obstructed by the police. Later he was to allege that the man – who was never publicly named by Palmer Benbow – said to have 'beaten up' Anna Morgan had been an intimate of an Australian Commissioner of Police; had, in fact, been a member of the same social circle as both the Commissioner and the Commissioner's mother.

Whatever the cause, Dr Benbow felt unable to continue with the inquiry. In an attempt to have his full findings published, Mrs Routledge's lawyers applied to get legal control of Anna Morgan's estate – a token gesture as the estate was worthless – which was calculated to start a re-examination of all the facts. The attempt failed, and once again the 'pyjama girl' lapsed into obscurity.

No Decent Burial

For a further six years the pickled corpse lay in a corner of the medical laboratory at Sydney University. The files on the case were, of course, still open, and no one in authority seemed inclined to give the body a decent burial. Then, in March 1944, the assertions made by Police Sergeant King seemed to receive collaboration. An Italian waiter named Tony Agostini appeared at police headquarters, and made a statement before the same Commissioner who was alleged to have 'covered up' Palmer Benbow's investigations. Agostini confessed to the murder of his wife Linda.

Linda Platt, an Englishwoman, had married Agostini in 1930. She was an attractive woman, similar in height and build to the corpse in the formalin-filled coffin. She was even said to have had the same unusually shaped ears. The only positive difference between her and Anna Morgan was that Linda's breasts were 'large and drooping'.

Agostini told police that the marriage had not been successful, for Linda was a jealous neurotic who drank too much. In an attempt to patch things up, the couple had moved from Sydney to Melbourne. Linda had, the police knew, been alive in August 1934, when she was seen by a friend who knew her well but after that she had vanished, and Agostini had subsequently reported her as a missing person, claiming that she had run off with a lover.

During much of the Second World War Tony Agostini had been interned as an alien and it was after his release, while working as a waiter in Melbourne, that he had come forward with his confession. A rather short, balding and bespectacled man, Agostini appears to have given his long, rambling confession to the Commissioner quite freely.

Despite the move to Melbourne, he claimed, the couple just could not get along. One morning, after quarrelling the night before, they woke up in bed: Linda was pointing a gun at Tony. Agostini struggled with her, and the gun went off close to her right cheekbone and killed her. Panic stricken, he carried the body to the top of the stairs, but he was not a strong man and he dropped it. It bounced three times on the stairs, causing the three head wounds.

Next day, Agostini continued, he had driven out of Melbourne with the body, dumped it in the culvert where it was found, and then set fire to it in an attempt to prevent identification. To those who were familiar with the case there was an obvious discrepancy here. Forensic experts at the second post mortem had affirmed that the battering injuries to the head had been caused *prior* to death, and they certainly did not tally with the body having fallen down a flight of wooden stairs.

But the authorities decided to make an effort to solve the mystery once and for all, or at least to arrive at some sort of truth. The pathetic, ten-year-old corpse again came under the hands of experts, this time embalmers and morticians, who were hired to 'make the body more acceptable to lay viewers'.

They had a formidable task, for the formalin, despite its many excellent qualities, had worked changes on the once-pretty features of the dead girl. The wounds had puckered slightly, the skin was wrinkled and fish-white, and the very outline of the features had become blurred. In spite of these difficulties the morticians, using wax, cosmetics and special hair cleanser, had the corpse prepared for viewing in record time, and on March 4, 1944, six friends of Linda Agostini, plus Police Sergeant King, were ushered into the mortuary to view the result. All of them 'positively identified' the body as that of Linda Agostini.

On March 23 a second inquest was opened. This time the coroner was faced with a battery of lawyers – one for the police, one for Agostini, and two for Mrs Routledge, Anna Morgan's mother. From the start there were violent arguments among the three legal teams. First an exchange, complicated and inconclusive, took place over whether or not the teeth of the corpse had been interfered with, and this was followed by a disagreement over the length of time which had elapsed since the witnesses had seen the living and the dead woman.

One woman witness introduced an important point when she claimed that the breasts of the corpse were not those of Linda – Linda had large breasts, and those of the corpse were small and firm. In answer to this the police contended that long immersion in the preservative liquid had caused the breasts to shrink, although experts counter-claimed that, though formalin would cause skin-shrinkage, it would not cause radical changes in the size and shape of the breasts.

A Clumsy Technique

Then came confusion about the colour of the eyes. Anna Philomena Morgan had had blue-grey eyes, while those of the corpse were brownish. But an expert stated that the dead woman's eyes were either blue or grey but neither brown nor hazel. The eyes had, like the rest of the body, suffered from the pickling process. To get a positive ruling on this, a pathological examination was put under way, but the technique was clumsy, and the eyeballs were destroyed during the experiment.

After further argument, the coroner somewhat wearily accepted the view that the corpse was that of Linda Agostini, a belief largely supported by the husband's confession and several moles found on the body which were said to be conclusive. Agostini was duly tried and convicted of manslaughter. He got six years' hard labour, and was released in 1950.

To some extent, the curious 'pyjama girl' case remains a mystery. Over the ten-year period between the finding of the body and the last inquest a great deal of confusion had crept in. Scientists had bungled, and the police had been obstructive, whether deliberately or not. Some experts still claim that the pickled corpse was that of Anna Philomena Morgan. But it was as Linda Agostini that it was finally buried in Preston Cemetery, Melbourne, in July 1944.

Injection of Insulin

As a loving husband, he was naturally distraught after finding his wife Elizabeth dead in the bath. But why did Kenneth Barlow's dry clothes show no trace of his efforts to revive her? And what accounted for the strangely dilated pupils in the staring eyes of the drowned woman?

On the evening of May 3, 1957, 38-year-old Kenneth Barlow and his wife Elizabeth decided to stay home and watch television. After tea, Elizabeth said she felt unwell and went to the bedroom to lie down. She told her husband to call her at 7.30 p.m. as there was a television programme that she particularly wanted to see.

Barlow called his wife at the requested time, but she decided to miss the programme and stay where she was. At about 9.20 Barlow heard her calling for him; she had been sick. Barlow changed the bedclothes and prepared to retire to bed himself. Elizabeth said she would have a bath. Barlow dozed off to sleep, and when he woke up at about 11.00 p.m. his wife was not in bed beside him.

He hurried into the bathroom, where he found his wife drowned in the bath. He tried to pull her out but could not manage it, so he pulled out the plug to let the bath-water drain away and then tried artificial respiration, but his efforts were of no avail.

Overcome by Weakness

A neighbour called the doctor, who arrived just before midnight. He was met at the house in Thornbury Crescent, Bradford, by Barlow, and together they went up to the bathroom. Barlow's wife, aged about 30, lay on her right side in the empty bath. She had apparently vomited while in the bath and, overcome by weakness, had slipped down into the water and drowned. Her body bore no signs of violence, but the doctor noticed immediately that the pupils of her eyes were widely dilated. He called the police.

A detective-sergeant from Bradford CID was sent to the house. He had a quick conference with the doctor and then questioned Barlow, who said he was a male nurse at Bradford Royal Infirmary. Barlow was quite calm and related the story of how he found his wife. The police called in forensic experts. They were quick to note various suspicious signs. The dead woman's dilated pupils indicated the possibility of drugs having been administered.

Kenneth Barlow's pyjamas were quite dry, despite the efforts he said he had made to get his wife out of the bath. Moreover, there were no signs of splashing in the bathroom which would have been expected in the circumstances, but there was water in the crooks of the dead woman's elbows which threw doubt on the attempt to revive her by artificial respiration.

Two hypodermic syringes were found in the kitchen. Barlow explained their presence by saying that he was giving himself injections of penicillin for a carbuncle. He pointed out that he was a nurse and often had syringes in the house. He denied giving his wife any injections.

The forensic examiners took the syringes away with them, and Mrs Barlow's body was removed for post mortem examination. The doctors were at a loss to explain the sudden attack of weakness which apparently led to the woman's death. Her organs were sound and free of disease. She was two months pregnant, but that in itself offered no explanation of her death. No injection marks could be found anywhere on her body.

Traces of penicillin were found on the syringes taken from the house, which seemed to support Barlow's explanation of their use. But the doctors were still puzzled by the dilated pupils. Comprehensive tests were made of the body fluids and organs, but no traces of any poison or drug were found.

Baffled by these negative findings, the doctors suggested a further minute examination of the dead woman's body. They were looking for marks of an injection. This examination was made difficult by the proliferation of freckles over the dead woman's skin. But, with the aid of a hand lens, their persistence was rewarded. Two tell-tale needle marks were found on the right buttock and then another two, more recently made, in the fold of skin under the left buttock.

The skin and tissue around the second set of marks as cut into, revealing unmistakable signs of inflammation – clear evidence of a needle having been pushed through the flesh. The appearance of the marks suggested that an injection had been made only a matter of hours before death. An injection had undoubtedly been given, but what substance had been administered? There was no ready answer, so a meeting of doctors, forensic experts and chemists was called to consider the facts of the case.

Blood Sugar Deficiency

Specifically they were asked to suggest what agent or drug might have caused the symptoms which preceded Mrs Barlow's death. Her husband, a male nurse, had described them – vomiting, sweating and weakness. Added to these was the dilation of the pupils. The view of the experts was that these symptoms described hypoglycaemia – a deficiency of blood sugar and the opposite of diabetes.

Insulin treatment of diabetes had been practised for thirty years or more. It was well known that diabetic patients could die as a result of taking too much insulin. It was equally recognized that healthy persons given insulin by accident could also die from shock. The insulin deprived the blood of the sugar it needed and hypoglycaemia resulted.

Mrs Barlow was not diabetic: that had been checked. It had also been found that blood taken from the heart contained an above-average level of sugar – the opposite of what would be expected had she been given insulin.

Again the doctors had come up against an obstacle to their theories, but good police work confirmed that they were on the right track. Inquiries about Kenneth Barlow revealed that he was often given the duty of administering the insulin injections to patients at the hospital where he worked.

Perfect Murder

A patient who had been treated by Barlow recalled a conversation he had with him. Talking about insulin, Barlow had said, 'If anybody gets a real dose of it, he's on his way to the next world'. Barlow apparently had also boasted to a fellow nurse that the perfect murder could be committed using insulin. The police also discovered that his first wife had died in 1956, aged 33. No firm cause of death was found.

This was still circumstantial, however, unless insulin could be positively identified in the dead woman's body. The problem facing the experts was that there were no prescribed tests for detecting insulin. There was also the contrary evidence regarding the high sugar level found in the heart blood. The experts in this case were working at the frontiers of existing knowledge, and perhaps this made them conscious of the possibility of making forensic history. At any rate, they found in medical literature an explanation for the high blood sugar level in the heart.

The phenomenon of high blood sugar had been

observed in several incidents where a person had died a violent death, and research on this biochemical change showed that in the moments before death the liver assisted the struggle to survive by delivering a heavy charge of sugar to the bloodstream. This reached as far as the heart before the circulation stopped. Consequently, the heart blood was disproportionately high in blood sugar.

In the case of Mrs Barlow, therefore, the high blood sugar level did not contradict the possibility that she might have been given insulin. With this obstacle out of the way, the experts prepared to make extracts from the tissues excised from the dead woman's buttocks.

A number of mice were injected with various quantities of insulin and their reactions observed. In this controlled experiment the small creatures twitched and trembled and became very weak. They then went into a coma and died. Now, other mice were injected with some of the tissue extracted from the dead woman. They showed exactly the same reaction – they went into a coma and died.

Some of the extracts were stronger than others. Those made from the injection sites in the left buttock had a more rapid effect on the mice and confirmed the doctors' belief that this injection had been made only a few hours before Mrs Barlow died, for the injection was so recent that much of the insulin had remained unabsorbed in the tissues. The estimate of the quantity in the body was 84 Units. But the actual quantity injected must have been a great deal higher than this.

The experiments were repeated with other laboratory animals. The results were the same. One doubt still had to be resolved in order to satisfy the doctors completely. It was current medical opinion – and that of Kenneth Barlow too – that, once injected into the bloodstream, insulin disappeared very quickly. If this were correct it would not have been possible to find any in the tissues of the dead woman.

Once again new research came to the aid of the forensic experts. It had been reported that acidic conditions preserved insulin. In Mrs Barlow's case, the formation of lactic acid in the muscles after death prevented the breakdown of the insulin. Chemical changes in the muscles after death were known to produce lactic acid, but it had never been necessary to relate this to the injection of insulin. At least, not until the death of Mrs Barlow.

On July 29, 1957, Barlow was arrested and charged with murdering his wife with insulin. He continued to deny giving his wife an injection of any kind for a while, but then admitted to giving her an injection of ergonovine to abort her pregnancy. He said that she had agreed to this. He had stolen the ergonovine from the hospital where he worked and gave the injection on the day that his wife died.

Abortion Drugs

The forensic experts had made a routine check for abortion drugs when they analyzed the dead woman's body fluids. None were found. Barlow's confessed use of an injection appeared to be a move to escape the charge of premeditated murder. But it cut no ice with the police. Barlow's trial, which began in December 1957, created considerable interest on account of the scientific evidence involved. The work of the forensic experts had been thorough and their evidence was virtually unshakable.

A medical expert called by the defence suggested that there might be another, natural, cause of Mrs Barlow's death. His thesis was that Mrs Barlow might have had a fit of weakness which caused her to slide down into the bathwater. And, in a moment of fear when she thought she was drowning, her body reacted by discharging a massive dose of insulin into the bloodstream. The insulin induced coma and death. This shock reaction accounted for the insulin found in the body after death.

This theory contrasted sharply with the carefully presented scientific evidence of the prosecution. If it could be said to have offered a flickering hope of acquittal for the accused it was soon snuffed out. The theory was quickly and efficiently demolished by one of the prosecution's expert witnesses. He calculated that to account for the 84 Units of insulin found in Mrs Barlow's body her pancreas would have to have secreted the unheard of quantity of 15,000 Units.

Kenneth Barlow maintained that the remarks made to a colleague about murder by insulin were only a joke. It was a bad joke. The judge, who commended the forensic scientists for their work, sentenced Barlow to life imprisonment.

INSULIN

Insulin is a hormone secreted into the bloodstream by the pancreas. Its main action is to regulate the amount of sugar in the blood. When insufficient insulin is secreted, an excess of sugar builds up in the body – this is diabetes or hypoglycaemia. Until the discovery of insulin in 1921, diabetes resulted in death.

Treatment of diabetes with insulin can lead to an excessive lowering of the blood sugar – hypoglycaemia. Unless quickly corrected by giving sugar by mouth, hypoglycaemia can also lead to death.

Symptoms of hypoglycaemia

Weakness, giddiness, pallor, sweating, irritability, tremor, lack of judgement and self-control, dilated pupils and coma. These symptoms are likely to appear when the blood sugar level falls below 60 to 70 mg/100 ml.

Smoke Without Fire

'Hot money' was given a whole new meaning by his gang. For, wherever there were flames, there was Leopold Harris. Inevitably, people began to talk. And could there, so to speak, be smoke without fire?

IF INSURANCE companies in the 1930s had possessed any degree of mutual cooperation, Leopold Harris – whose very name became synonymous with arson – could never have operated his successful business at all. The old-established firm of Harris & Company, Fire Assessors of Finsbury Pavement, in the heart of the City of London, was eminently respectable when it was run by its founder, Harris's father, but when tall, bulky Leopold took over he was to find he had too little patience for the slow profits of legitimate commerce.

Harris & Co., under its shrewd and fast-moving new owner, had a way of maintaining contacts in the most unlikely places, and it began to get a reputation for 'fire chasing'. When a fire broke out, the firm's representative – usually Leo Harris – was quickly on the spot, having got authority from the policy owner, and hard at work assessing damage and preparing to negotiate with the insurance company concerned.

Fire claims have to be settled between the

parties concerned by adjustment. Only too often the vital books, invoices and records of a business go up in the fire itself, and assessment of actual loss becomes extremely difficult.

Leo Harris was perhaps a normal and decent-enough man, but his lifestyle was expensive and money in large quantities was needed. His daily contact with the insurance companies and Lloyd's underwriters, and the vast sums they handled, must have set his mind working. There seemed to be an easier, quicker way of making a living than by the daily grind of regular fire assessments on behalf of other people, who would get most of the money concerned.

In what must have been a moment of mental aberration, Harris made his first attempt to adjust the balance in his favour by faking a 'burglary' at his home in Southend, Essex, and putting in a claim for £1,500. Something about the claim – never yet explained – must have made the insurers suspicious, for they refused to pay. Harris brought suit, and lost. The judge said quite frankly that the claim 'looked bogus to him'.

Remarkable Carelessness

It reveals the arm's-length attitude of insurance companies that they did not get together and, as it were, warn Harris 'off the turf' – he was, later, to deal with individual companies, staying strictly in their own furrows, which is why he was able to succeed so long and survive so well. But his burglary claim had made him cautious, and he went to extreme lengths to make absolutely sure that no hint of his presence, other than as a simple assessor, was ever revealed in the arson cases he contrived.

To say he began on such-and-such a date is impossible. He may have tried mock runs, of which nothing is known; certainly his foolproof and *mentally* astute plans must have required a great deal of forward-planning. His ideas were excellent, and he could well have pulled off undocumented fires, only beginning his road to success and then failure when he brought in partners to assist him.

The case seems to begin with a man named Capsoni who, in 1926, was an agent for Continental silk-makers. Capsoni heard that a customer and friend, Louis Jarvis of West London, had lost his business in a fire. On attempting to console Jarvis, Capsoni was astonished at his gaiety. It seemed, he learned on questioning, that the fire had brought Jarvis £21,500 insurance compensation of which, he explained with remarkable carelessness, only £3,000 had gone to Leo Harris and his brother David for 'services rendered'.

Capsoni, hard-pressed by government duties imposed on imported silk, agreed to ally himself with Jarvis, in his real name of Jacobs. They formed a firm known as Fabriques de Soieries Ltd., of 196 Deansgate, Manchester, and brought a large quantity of bankrupt stock and 'old soldiers' – salvaged goods from other fires, or damaged goods tastefully rewrapped – all of which made a fine display in the firm's showroom. The cost of setting up this superficially attractive and tasteful collection of goods was met in utter secrecy by Leo and David Harris. Capsoni, who possessed an artistic soul, put together what he called a 'Confirmations Book', containing samples of the goods belonging to the firm, the quantities bought, and the low prices paid, which, if he had only known it, was to act as 'a sword of retribution'.

Policies for £60,000 were taken out; elegant lengths of silk were displayed in the Deansgate premises, exposed so that they would burn quickly. The fire arrangement was simple. Two photographic developing trays made of celluloid (a then popular and enormously inflammable material) were obtained. One was wedged inside the other, and a taper stuck in between. The taper, which had been timed, burned for fifteen minutes before it touched and ignited the trays, a cheap and infallible device for arson which the 'gang' was to use all the time. Between lighting the taper and the fire there was time for the arsonist, Capsoni, to get away and establish his alibi. By sheer 'coincidence' Leo Harris was staying that night at the neighbouring Midland Hotel.

When the Fabriques de Soieries fire began one of Harris's many contacts advised him, and in his capacity of assessor he was on the spot almost before the firemen had unrolled their hoses. The fire was put out far too soon for Harris, but the firemen had worked hard, using enormous quantities of water, which did the required amount of damage. Harris put in a 'reasonable' claim for £32,000, which was settled for £29,000. This was divided, after costs had been allowed, by giving £1,000 to Capsoni, £12,000 to Jarvis, £8,000 to Harris and £1,000 to David Harris. It was, Capsoni said, 'money for old rope'.

In the meantime the legitimate and slow business of Harris & Company went ahead assessing fires, something in which it had an enviable reputation, while the proprietor's mind concentrated on further aspects of fire-raising. An ingenious plan for future operations presented itself. Harry Gould was married to Harris's sister. His business, in which Leo Harris was a sleeping partner, was that of a buyer of salvage. Gould bought salvage from perfectly 'respectable' fires – to which he was guided by Harris & Company.

When Harris brought Gould into the 'arson' side of the firm, Gould was able to supply Leo Harris's nominees, who were setting up businesses for firing, with a few hundred pounds' worth of damaged but re-wrapped goods, and invoice them at huge prices. After the bogus fire claim was settled, Gould, who never missed a trick, was able to buy back his own now even more damaged goods for use in future fires. It was like printing his own money.

The next fire, in Leeds, was stocked with goods largely bought by Capsoni in Italy for the firm, Continental Showrooms, which was insured for £15,000, but certain insurance companies backed out for their own reasons. One being that the final insurance figure with another firm was £6,300. The fire was a success but the assessor for the insurance company was a tough, sceptical Yorkshireman who did not like Harris's assessment at all. The settlement was finally agreed at £3,350.

Paid Without Argument

Nor was Harris's next effort very successful. This involved Alfred Alton Ltd., a cloak and mantle business which had begun life as Cohen and Company, before being bought out by Harris. A branch was opened in Manchester, handsomely stocked with singed material and 'old soldiers', and was duly fired with the reliable system of photographic trays and taper by Capsoni. Payment of the claim presented no difficulties as the assessor for the insurance company accepted Harris's assessment of the damage, and £9,000 was paid without argument. In current values this was a considerable amount of money.

So far all had gone well, and the London end of Alfred Alton Ltd. was allowed to run down quietly into routine liquidation. Unfortunately the official liquidator was typical of his kind, an inquisitive and diligent man who wanted answers to a lot of facts – more, indeed, than Leo Harris could give with safety. The liquidator wanted books, invoices, records and details which would have resulted in showing the secrets of the Manchester branch and the bogus insurance claim.

Through a pliable nominee he made an offer to buy up Alfred Alton Ltd. at a rate that would give 15 shillings in the pound to the liquidator, something he could scarcely refuse. The offer was accepted and even though it galled Harris to pay out the money, he gained a period of time to carry on his activities.

Almost Routine

Next came the Franco-Italian Silk Company, of 185 Oxford Street. By now the procedure had become almost routine, for the new firm was packed with 'old soldiers' and damaged stock, and insured for £30,000. When, after various organizational delays, the place went up with the help of the inevitable photographic trays, the assessor, a Mr Loughborough Ball, and Leo Harris seemed to get along like twin souls. A cheque for £21,966 18s. 4d. was eventually received.

In 1930 Leo Harris was the head of a veritable organization. He, Gould and Capsoni were joined by the friendly Mr Loughborough Ball. But their major recruit was Captain Eric Miles, Chief Officer of the London Salvage Corps, which acted for the insurance community. Miles had come into the organization by allowing Harris to guarantee a bank overdraft for him: the Corps, by nature of its duties, got news of every fire in London within seconds of a fire brigade being called. This information, it seemed, would be invaluable to Harris, and in connection with fires to which there was attached any hint of suspicion, since it would be more than possible for Miles's report, sent via the Corps to the insurance office concerned, to lean favourably in the direction of Harris, or his clients.

The Harris Fire Raising Organization, fully manned and highly efficient, was now set on a prosperous course, and might have gone endlessly about its business of profitable fires, had not the human element put an end to it all. One of the prime factors in keeping the scheme working was a supply of nominees, or dummies, who posed as the owners of respectable businesses and obtained insurance; Harris took over from there.

The man who found most of the dummies was a Harris employee named Harry Priest. Unfortunately Priest drank, and one day drunkenly approached a very respectable man named Cornock, suggesting he might like to be set up in a business, which would be capitalized by 'a friend', and receive a share after the subsequent fire. Cornock was horrified, and went for advice to a friend, George Mathews, who had once been employed in the Intelligence Department of Lloyds.

Audience of Fire-bugs

This was the end. Mathews took Cornock to see a brilliant London solicitor, William Charles Crocker, who had been quietly solidifying his suspicions about Leo Harris. With this new information, and its contents of facts and names, Crocker was able to move into top-gear, and laid plans enabling Mathews and Cornock to play the parts of greedy but fearful businessmen anxious to make money but apparently scared of anything to do with arson, although not beyond persuasion.

It was an outstanding performance that should have been played to a better audience than a collection of fire-bugs. Soon the plan yielded fruits, news of a *coming* fire. From that moment on Crocker could not be faulted, using his staff and laying plans which caused Harris to tie himself up in a tangle of his own making.

At the trial Gould and another man instantly pleaded guilty. Harris and a band of thirteen men faced the judge in No. 1 Court in a heatwave that did not add to comfort. Up to that time it was the longest trial in the history of the Old Bailey, running for thirty-three days and involving literally tons of documents, exhibits and relics, including Capsoni's famous 'Confirmations Book' with its pieces of silk and the prices paid which, when laid against the insurance claim, was damning in itself.

The front pages of British newspapers were packed, day after day, with the constant sensations springing out of this notable *cause célèbre*. The hard work done by Crocker was the Crown's chief weapon, the more deadly because of the solicitor's remarkable talent for tying up seemingly unconnected facts, the careful probing which produced forensic support for the facts of arson, and a total achievement of personal detective work that could not have been bettered by a leading professional from New Scotland Yard.

Crocker had made sure that not a single error appeared in his testimony, and it had to be strong, for the fire-raisers had among their legal defenders some of the finest talent in the British courts, such names as Sir Henry Curtis Bennett, KC, Mr Norman Birkett, KC, Mr G. D. Roberts and Mr T. Christmas Humphreys.

It was a remarkable fight but near the end Leopold Harris gave in and admitted his guilt. He went to prison for fourteen years, his brother for five, and Gould for six. The rest of the conspirators shared jail sentences totalling twenty-two years.

Dead Giveaways

One little clue would bring mystery man Pierre Voirbo to the guillotine . . . straight from the room in which he had perpetrated his horrible crime and washed away (or so he thought) every last trace.

EDGAR WALLACE wrote a novel called *The Clue of the Twisted Candle*, in which an ingenious murderer succeeds in sealing a room by wedging a candle under the heavy latch of the door. As the candle gradually bends in the warmth of the room, the latch – inaccessible from outside – falls into its groove. Wallace was writing in the early days of forensic science, but, even so, his stratagem would have given little trouble to most experienced police officers. To begin with, some of the soft candle wax would inevitably have scraped off on the underside of the heavy latch, and the most stupid detective would have worked out the truth within minutes.

In real life, most 'vital clues' are altogether less obvious. In the two hundred years or so since its beginnings, scientific crime detection has reached a high degree of efficiency. Even so, the kind of brilliant deduction practised by Sherlock Holmes plays little part in the solution of modern crimes. It is a matter of hard work, patience and luck.

We can see all three of these elements in the classic case of the demob suit, recounted by Superintendent Bob Fabian of the Yard. In the summer of 1946, Police Constable Arthur Collins attempted to detail five men who were trying to enter a building in Warwick. He was so badly beaten and kicked that for a time it was feared that he might die. The five men escaped, and the only clue was a small piece of cloth torn from the jacket of one of the men by the constable's wife – who had tried to come to the rescue of her unconscious husband. The Warwick police decided to ask the help of Scotland Yard, and Fabian was put onto the case.

The cloth was photographed, and the photographs sent off to tailors all over England. Then it was exhibited in the window of a local newspaper office. An ex-army officer was able to tell Fabian that it was undoubtedly from a demob suit. Fabian plodded to the nearest Ministry of Supply Depot in Birmingham. There, a check with a register showed that this pattern had been manufactured by a firm in Wellington, Somerset.

The police drove through the night – only to be told, at the factory, that this cloth had been enough for no less than five thousand suits. Moreover, soldiers often sold them to 'wide boys' at the gates of the camp. However, they were able to give Fabian the address of two factories in Birmingham and one in Glasgow who had bought the cloth. Fabian drove back to Birmingham. Neither of the two factories had started using their consignment yet.

Fabian went on to Glasgow. There a supervisor looked at the torn fragment, and was able to tell, from the stitching, the name of the man who had made it into a suit. 'Stitching is as distinct as handwriting,' he said. Finally, the long-shot paid off. The workman looked at the cloth, and was able to recall that the suit was made for an exceptionally tall and broad man – it had had to be specially made, so he remembered it.

Foul Well-water

The Ordnance Depot at Branston, near Burton-on-Trent, was able to give Fabian the name of the ex-soldier for whose demob they had ordered the suit, and the police found him at the Birmingham address to which the suit had been posted. When the police constable's wife identified him as her husband's assailant, the big Irishman (6 feet 2½ inches tall) broke down and admitted his part in the robbery. He received four years' penal servitude.

This same quality of incredible patience can be found in a case that certainly ranks among the epics of classic detection. It took place in 1869. During the January of that year, a restaurant owner in the Rue Princesse, Paris, noticed that the water from the well tasted foul. He investigated, and found a parcel floating in the water. When it was opened it proved to contain the lower half of a human leg. The horrified restaurateur sent for the police. A young detective named Gustave Macé was placed in charge of the case. He looked down the well and found another parcel. In it was another leg, encased in a stocking.

Doctors told Macé the legs were almost certainly a woman's. Acting on this assumption, Macé obtained the files of 122 missing women and set about tracking them. It took him months, and finally there were only three left. Shortly after Macé had finally succeeded in tracing these remaining three, the doctors admitted that they could have been wrong. The legs were womanish, but could have belonged to a man. Macé heaved a sigh and started all over again.

He had two leads. On December 22 of the previous year, a policeman had met a man wandering along the Rue de Seine carrying a hamper. Because of the late hour, he asked the man what was in it. The man said he had just arrived in Paris from the country by train; unable to find a cab, he had been forced to walk with his hamper of country products.

He looked so honest that the policeman let him go, but his description – short, round-faced with a black moustache – led Macé to suspect that this was the same man who had been seen a few days earlier throwing lumps of meat into the River Seine. Someone asked him what he was doing, and he said he was baiting the river because he intended to fish the next day. Since then, large gobbets of meat had been fished out of the river – too big for the average fish to swallow.

The stitches on the parcel in which the first leg had been sewn had a professional look about them. Moreover, why had the murderer chosen the restaurant to dump the leg? It might, of course, be a dissatisfied customer who wanted to spoil the trade. Or it might be someone who had lived in the upstairs part of the house at some time. He asked the concierge if there was a tailor in the house. No. Had there *ever* been one? No. But there *had* been a tailoress. That sounded a long-shot, but Macé had no other lead. He interviewed the girl, who told him that she often did jobs for other tailors. Did any of them ever visit her at the house? Many of them did, she said. One in particular, M. Voirbo, was very kind and helpful. He often fetched water up from the well for her.

Strange Habits

Voirbo was a tailor, and he knew the well. Macé asked the girl if this Voirbo had any special friends. There *was* one old man, she said, a M. Bodasse. She didn't know where he lived, but he had an aunt who lived in the Rue de Nesle. Macé didn't know the aunt's exact address, but compared to tracing a hundred or so missing women it was child's play to locate her, Madame Bodasse was able to tell Macé that her nephew lived in the Rue Dauphine. He was a retired craftsman who had been a tapestry manufacturer. Oddly enough, he hadn't been seen for some weeks now, but that wasn't unlike him. His habits were strange.

The concierge at old Bodasse's apartment startled Macé by telling him Bodasse was at home. She had seen the light in his flat the night before. But he wouldn't answer the door. He was an eccentric. Macé felt he had now discovered the identity of the victim. His guess was confirmed when Madame Bodasse identified the stocking – made of white cotton, with a man's sock sewn on the bottom – as belonging to her nephew. She also thought the legs were his.

As to the mystery man, Pierre Voirbo, he was a police spy, a man who pretended to be a rapid anarchist and attended left-wing meetings – only to make reports to the police, Macé broke into Bodasse's apartment. Everything looked neat, and an eight-day clock was still ticking. Macé decided to have the place watched, and borrowed a couple of men from the secret police. This proved to be a mistake; they knew Voirbo as a colleague, and when they saw him entering the building, they accosted him and asked him why they were supposed to watch him. Macé's quarry was alerted.

But Macé already had much valuable evidence. Bodasse's strong box was empty. But in the back of a watch Macé found a piece of paper with numbers of various securities written on it. Probing Voirbo's background, Macé discovered that, until a few months ago, he had lived in fairly cheap lodgings and had seemed to be poor. Then he had married and moved elsewhere, paying his rent with a five-hundred-franc share that could be cashed by anyone.

Macé hastened to the money-changer. He had kept the counterfoil of the share. The number tallied with one of those in the watch. Macé decided it was time to interview Voirbo. Now began the cat and mouse game. Voirbo was a plump, cheerful young man of thirty, and he appeared to be a man of resourcefulness and character. Treating Macé as a friend – since they both worked for the police – he admitted that he had been worried about Bodasse's non-appearance.

He suspected that he might have been killed – in which case the murderer was an alcoholic butcher named Rifer, a petty crook, who had almost certainly been aided by three criminal acquaintances, whom Voirbo also helpfully pointed out. When Macé checked, he discovered that two of the three had perfect alibis; they had been in jail throughout December. And not long after, the alcoholic butcher had a fit of DT's and was taken to an asylum.

Macé decided he had to arrest Voirbo. It proved to be a wise decision, for Voirbo had a ticket to Havre in his wallet, and other indications showed he intended to embark for America. Voirbo seemed surprised and offended. What had he done that Macé should suspect him? They both knew there was no evidence.

Empty Strong Box

This, unfortunately, was true. Macé went to talk to Voirbo's wife, a quiet girl who obviously knew little of her husband's character and still less of his activities. Macé learned from her that she had brought her husband a dowry of 15,000 francs – about £600. Voirbo had gained the consent of her parents by telling them that he had 10,000 francs in securities. In fact, he had produced them before the wedding, but where were they now? The strong box was empty. Macé searched the house. Finally, in the cellar, he found Bodasse's securities. They had been soldered into a tin box, and suspended in a cask of wine.

Even that did not *prove* Voirbo a murderer. Macé now returned to Voirbo's old flat. A young couple had moved in, but they showed Macé precisely where the table had been when they first arrived. Macé was convinced this was where Bodasse had been killed; the cleaning woman had told him that Voirbo was notoriously untidy; yet on the morning of December 17 – the day after Bodasse was last seen alive – his room had been polished and scrubbed. If Bodasse had been killed at the table, then he had probably also been dismembered there, and his blood must have run on the floor. This was perfectly clean; but it sloped a little towards the bed.

Macé staged his final scene with all the dramatic flair of a fictional detective. Voirbo was taken to his old room in the Rue Mazarin. He seemed calm and indifferent. Macé took a jug of water, poised it over the spot where the table used to stand, and poured it. The water flowed slowly across the floor, and formed a pool under the bed. Voirbo suddenly became restive. Macé sent for a mason, and ordered him to take up the floor tiles under the bed. The dark undersides were found to be coated with dried blood. Suddenly, Voirbo's nerve broke, and he made his confession.

A Scoundrel in Love

He had been tired of being a scoundrel, a petty crook, he said. He decided he wanted to settle down as a married man. He was in love with the gentle Mademoiselle Rémondé, but it was necessary to impress her parents that he also had money. He begged his friend Bodasse to lend it to him. When Bodasse refused, Voirbo decided he had to die.

He invited him to his room for tea, one day after they had dined together. Voirbo moved casually behind him, picked up a flat iron, and struck Bodasse on the head. Later, he dismembered the body and distributed the pieces around Paris, mostly in the river. After meeting the policeman who wanted to look into his basket – which contained bones and flesh – he decided to get rid of the legs by dumping them in the nearby well.

Voirbo was guillotined for the murder of Desiré Bodasse. But for one tiny mistake – sewing the leg into a piece of calico – he would have avoided suspicion. What is more, if he had kept his wits about him, he could have avoided detection even when the underside of the tiles showed traces of blood. He only had to deny that he knew where it came from, or declare that it was animal blood from a joint. In 1869 there was still no way of testing blood to determine whether it came from a man or an animal.

The story of how blood analysis was perfected is one of the great epics of scientific detection. Great scientists like Pasteur and Koch had discovered that if a human body is injected with *dead* germs, the blood will develop a resistance to living forms of the same germs; thus immunization was discovered. Twenty years later, in the 1890s, a German, von Behring, discovered that if a horse is injected with dead diphtheria germs, the serum from its blood – the clear liquid that separates out when blood is allowed to stand – will actually help children who are suffering from diphtheria to recover: the serum develops 'fighting' properties.

Around the turn of the 20th century a chemist named Paul Uhlenhuth discovered that this same serum has even more remarkable properties. If a rabbit is injected with human blood, its blood serum develops a *resistance* to human blood. And if the serum is placed in a test tube, and the tiniest drop of human blood is introduced into it, it turns cloudy. It will not react at all to animal blood.

In 1901, shortly after Uhlenhuth had made this discovery, a travelling carpenter named Ludwig Tessnow was arrested on the Baltic island of Rügen, suspected of a particularly atrocious murder. Two small boys had been found in the woods, hacked and torn to pieces, scattered over a wide area. Three years earlier, Tessnow had been arrested on suspicion of killing two schoolgirls near the village of Lechtingen, near Osnabruck.

He had protested that certain stains on his clothes were of woodstain, not blood, and the police had to release him for lack of evidence. Now he was questioned about a recently washed suit that showed slight traces of blood. Tessnow said that some of the almost obliterated stains were cattle blood, and the others were woodstain. When the examining magistrate received the information from Osnabruck, he realized he was dealing with a man possessed of some insane desire to batter living creatures and tear them to pieces. A month before the two boys had been murdered, someone had attacked seven sheep in a field, cut them open and scattered the entrails all over the field. The shepherd had seen the man running away; he now identified Tessnow as the sheep butcher. But Tessnow denied everything.

Human Bloodstains

Fortunately, the prosecutor had kept abreast of new developments in legal medicine, and had heard about Uhlenhuth's discovery. He sent Uhlenhuth the bloodstained clothing, and also the stone that had been used to batter the children. Uhlenhuth dissolved dozens of small stains in salt water and tested them all. He found 22 human bloodstains and half a dozen stains of sheep's blood. His evidence convicted Tessnow, who was sentenced to death.

Not only would the serum distinguish human blood from animal blood; it would also distinguish different *types* of human blood: the groups A, B, O and AB. This discovery did not provide sufficient evidence to hang a suspect in Gladbeck, Germany, in 1928, but a jury of sceptical burghers declined to convict on purely scientific evidence. The accused was 20-year-old Karl Hussmann, a dominant and violent student.

In the early hours of March 23, 1928, a youth named Helmut Daube was found dying in the street. His throat had been cut and his genitals slashed off. The police soon discovered that Daube's closest friend was his fellow-student Hussmann. When they went to Hussmann's house, they discovered that his shoes had been recently washed, and showed traces of blood. His clothes were also bloodstained. Hussmann had completely dominated Daube, and the two had been lovers. Recently, however, Daube had realized that he preferred girls and had tried to break away.

At first Hussmann claimed the blood was that of a cat he had killed, but Uhlenhuth's test quickly revealed that it was human blood. Hussmann then changed his story and said he had had a nosebleed. The forensic laboratory at Bonn demonstrated that this was also impossible, for the blood on the shoes was type A – Daube's group – while Hussmann was type O.

The feeling of the court was that, while they were not convinced of Hussmann's innocence, they were by no means happy about convicting him on what, to them, amounted to purely circumstantial evidence, so Hussmann was acquitted. But the case drew wide attention to the use of testing for blood groups in criminal cases. Since that time, many criminals have been hanged on the evidence of a dried blood-spot on a wooden floor.

On humane grounds, perhaps the jury was right to disregard circumstantial evidence, for there is also the danger of hanging an innocent man. The case of Burton Abbott provides a thought-provoking illustration. Abbott was known to his neighbours in Alameda, California, as a quiet, rather intellectual man. He had never been known to be violent and had no police record.

On July 15, 1955, Abbott's wife was looking through old clothes in the basement when she found a wallet. It contained the identification card of 14-year-old Stephanie Bryan, some photographs, and an unfinished letter dated April 28, 1955. That had been the day when Stephanie had disappeared after coming out of school in Berkeley. She had never been seen since.

Georgia Abbott took the wallet upstairs and asked her husband how it had got there. He seemed as puzzled as she was, and they called the police. The next day, the police dug up Abbott's basement and found Stephanie's schoolbooks and her bra. Abbott pointed out that his garage had recently been used as a polling place, and that dozens of people had been in and out. However, a newsman went up to Abbott's summer cabin on Trinity Mountain with two dogs. The dogs led him to a shallow grave. Stephanie Bryan's body was found in it. She had been strangled with her own panties, and the circumstances pointed to sexual assault.

Abbott was arrested and tried. He insisted that he knew nothing whatever about Stephanie or her clothes – and there was certainly no definite evidence to connect him with her disappearance. But the jury convicted him. There were several stays of execution. The last one came just after

11.15 a.m. on March 14, 1947, but it arrived a few minutes too late. The cyanide gas pellets had been dropped under the execution chair at 11.15 precisely. Abbott persisted in denying his guilt to the end, although he is said to have told a doctor: 'I can't admit it. Think of what it would do to my mother.'

All the evidence suggests that Abbott was the killer of Stephanie Bryan. Yet there is an element of doubt. For example, he *could* have been framed by her real killer. The brilliant triumphs of scientific crime detection should never blind us to the fact that the word 'clue' means an *indication*, and that, forensically, there is a vital difference between an indication and a final proof.

Exonerated by Science

The cases listed in this chapter could be just the tip of an iceberg – since there are still certain places that do not accept DNA evidence. Also many authorities routinely destroy all evidence after appeals have been exhausted.

ONE OF THE main problems facing the authorities, is the credibility of eye-witness testimony. In case after case, the rape victim makes a firm identification of the assailant, and the evidence seems bulletproof. Yet DNA testing results in that defendant not only being freed from prison, but in some cases successfully suing for wrongful imprisonment. It is quite astonishing that 20 per cent of all DNA tests conducted reveal that the person charged with the crime was 'excluded' by the test – meaning the blood of the defendant did not match with the semen, blood, hair or other body cells found on the victim or at the scene of the crime.

One of the cases involved a forensic chemist who testified at 130 criminal trials before it was learned he had lied about his credentials and training. In some cases he had committed outright perjury concerning his actual findings. All of those cases were reviewed, and the chemist was prosecuted for perjury.

Gilbert Alejandro

On the evening of April 27, 1990, a woman in her fifties came home and was attacked from behind by a man. The man placed a pillow over her head and sexually assaulted her. He then fled the house. The woman could not describe the man except for basic physical size. She also noted that the man was wearing some kind of cap, a grey T-shirt, and dark-coloured shorts. The police canvassed the area and questioned three men, one of whom was wearing clothes matching the victim's description. The suspect, Alejandro, was picked out from his photograph in police records.

In October 1990 Gilbert Alejandro was convicted of aggravated sexual assault and was sentenced to twelve years in prison.

The prosecution based its case on several points:

- The victim identified Alejandro from a police photograph.

- The victim identified Alejandro in court (although she stated that she had a pillow over her head during the assault).

- Fred Zain, the chief forensic expert testified that a DNA test of Alejandro's sample matched DNA found on the victim's clothing 'and could only have originated from him [Alejandro]'.

- Alejandro's only alibi was from his mother, who testified that he was at home at the time of the assault.

It came to light that the State's forensic expert in this case, Fred Zain, had falsified results and lied about his credentials when he was employed as a State police serologist in West Virginia. When Alejandro's lawyers were informed of this, they filed a writ of *habeas corpus.* Alejandro was subsequently released to his parents and placed on electronic monitoring.

On July 26, 1994 the Court heard Alejandro's petition. Present at this hearing were an original trial juror, the original jury foreman, and a Bexar County forensic DNA analyst. The two jurors testified that they based their guilty verdict solely on Zain's testimony and without his testimony the jury would have acquitted on the basis of reasonable doubt. The DNA analyst testified that results from at least one other DNA test had excluded Alejandro. He also testified that the test to which Zain testified was inconclusive and could not have been the basis of a conviction.

In July 1990 the original DNA tests done in this case proved to be inconclusive. It proved that the source of semen left on the victim's nightgown did not come from Alejandro. The district court also reported that an additional test was done on December 19, 1990, after the trial, and it too excluded Alejandro. According to the district court's findings of fact, Fred Zain knew of these exculpatory results and failed to report them to anyone.

As a result of the findings the court of criminal appeals overturned Alejandro's conviction and released him to stand trial again without Zain's testimony. The district attorney, however, declined to prosecute the case. On September 21, 1994, Alejandro was released from electronic monitoring and all charges were dismissed

Kirk Bloodsworth

On July 25, 1984, a nine-year-old girl was found dead in a wooded area. She had been beaten with a rock, sexually assaulted and strangled.

Kirk Bloodsworth was convicted on March 8, 1985, of sexual assault, rape, and first-degree premeditated murder. A Baltimore County judge sentenced Bloodsworth to death.

The prosecution based its case on several points:

- An anonymous caller tipped police that Bloodsworth had been seen with the girl earlier in the day.

- A witness identified Bloodsworth from a police sketch compiled by five witnesses.

- The five witnesses testified that they had seen Bloodsworth with the little girl.

- Bloodsworth had told acquaintances he had done something 'terrible' that day that would affect his marriage.

- In his first police interrogation, Bloodsworth mentioned a 'bloody rock', even though no weapons were known of at the time.

- Testimony was given that a shoe impression found near the victim's body was made by a shoe that matched Bloodsworth's size.

The following came to light when the case went to appeal: Bloodsworth said he had mentioned the bloody rock because the police had one on the table next to him while they interrogated him. The terrible thing mentioned to friends was that he had failed to buy his wife a taco salad as he had promised. Finally, police withheld information from defence attorneys relating to the possibility of another suspect. The Maryland Court of Appeals overturned Bloodsworth's conviction in July 1986 because of the withheld information. He was retried, and a jury convicted him a second time. This time Bloodsworth was sentenced to two consecutive life terms.

After an appeal of the second conviction was denied, Bloodsworth's lawyer moved to have the evidence released for more sophisticated testing than was available at the time of trial. The prosecution agreed, and in April 1992 the victim's panties and shorts, a stick found near the murder scene, reference blood samples from Bloodsworth and the victim, and an autopsy slide were sent to Forensic Science Associates for Polymerase Chain Reaction (PCR) testing.

The FSA report, issued on May 17, 1993, stated that semen on the autopsy slide was insufficient for testing. It also stated that a small semen stain had been found on the panties. The report also concluded that Bloodsworth's DNA did not match any of the evidence received for testing. FSA did, however, request a fresh sample of Bloodsworth's blood for retesting in accord with questions about proper labelling on the original sample.

On June 3, 1993, FSA issued a second report that stated its findings regarding Bloodsworth's DNA were replicated and that he could not be responsible for the stain on the victim's underwear.

In conclusion, on June 25, 1993, the FBI conducted its own test of the evidence and discovered the same results as FSA. In Maryland, new evidence can be presented no later than one year after the final appeal. Prosecutors joined a petition with Bloodsworth's attorneys to grant Bloodsworth a pardon. A Baltimore County circuit judge ordered Bloodsworth's release from prison on June 28, 1993. Maryland's governor pardoned Bloodsworth in December 1993. Bloodsworth served almost nine years of the second sentence, including two years on death row.

Mark Diaz Bravo

On February 20, 1990, a patient at the psychiatric

hospital where Bravo worked claimed she had been raped in an alcove earlier that afternoon. During the course of police interviews, she named several different people as her assailant. One of those she named was Bravo. She later stated she was sure Bravo was the attacker.

A Los Angeles County jury found Mark Diaz Bravo guilty of rape in 1990. He was sentenced by the court to a prison term of eight years.

The prosecution based its case on several points:

- The victim named Bravo as the assailant and made an in-court identification.

- Bravo had misrepresented himself in the past on applications and on his business card.

- Blood tests done on a blanket near the crime scene showed a blood type consistent with Bravo's blood type, which is found in only 3 per cent of the population.

- Bravo's alibi defence was not aggressively pursued.

Bravo's appeal to the intermediate court of appeals was denied. Before his appeal was decided in 1992, he filed a post-conviction motion in the Superior Court of Los Angeles County. In 1993 a superior court judge granted Bravo's motion to release a blanket, a sheet, and a pair of panties to the defence for DNA testing.

Prosecutors received a report from Cellmark Diagnostics on December 24, 1993, stating that none of the tested semen had DNA that matched Bravo's. On January 4, 1994, Bravo's lawyer filed a writ of *habeas corpus.* A Los Angeles County Superior Court judge ordered Bravo to be released on January 6, 1994. The judge stated that Bravo had not received a fair trial, that the victim had recanted her testimony, that Bravo's alibi was unimpeachable, and that the DNA tests were irrefutable. On January 7, 1994, Bravo was released from prison after serving three years of his sentence.

Dale Brison

On the evening of July 14, 1990, the victim was walking from a convenience store to her home when an assailant came from behind her, put one hand on her throat and one on her waist, and forced her to walk with him. The assailant stabbed her in the side as they walked, and the victim lost consciousness. When she awoke, the assailant was walking her to some bushes near an apartment complex. The assailant then repeatedly assaulted the victim sexually.

Dale Brison was convicted of rape, kidnapping, aggravated assault, carrying a prohibited offensive weapon, and three counts of involuntary deviate sexual intercourse. Brison sought DNA testing during the trial, but his request was denied.

The prosecution based its case on several points:

- There were two separate victim identifications of Brison near the victim's apartment building.
- A hair sample from the scene of the crime was consistent with Brison's.
- Brison's alibi, sleeping on the couch of his home, was corroborated only by his mother.

Following his conviction the Superior Court ruled that DNA testing must be performed if the evidence had been kept and the semen stain from the victim's underwear was not badly degraded. The report showed that no result was discernible from the vaginal swab, but the semen stain from the victim's panties yielded results that absolved Brison as the assailant. After the DNA tests were performed, the district attorney's office conducted its own. The results matched those of the first one, and Brison was freed after serving three years of his sentence.

Leonard Callace

In January 1985 a teenage girl was walking to her car in the parking lot of a shopping centre. She was accosted by two men at knife point and forced into a nearby car. One man, allegedly Callace, sexually assaulted the victim repeatedly while the other man watched from the front seat. The second man was never identified.

A Suffolk County jury took one hour to convict Leonard Callace of sodomy, sexual abuse, wrongful imprisonment and criminal possession of a weapon. Callace rejected a plea bargain that would have given him 4 months in prison if he pled to a lesser charge. On March 24, 1987, Callace was sentenced to 25 to 50 years in prison.

The prosecution based its case on several points:

- A sketch by police artists resembled Callace.
- The victim identified Callace from a photo array and made an in-court identification.
- The blood group of the semen was type A, the same as Callace's.
- Callace's alibi was uncorroborated.

Callace's case went to the court of appeals but was denied. While in prison, Callace learned about DNA testing and how it was used to free a former inmate. He asked his attorney about the original trial evidence.

Callace's attorney remembered two things from the original trial record. First, the victim had just picked up her jeans from the cleaners. Second, the victim spit out semen onto the jeans after one of the assaults. Therefore, any semen on those jeans would have come from the assailant. If it did not match Callace's, he could be freed. The defence used this information to secure the jeans from the prosecution for DNA testing. On June 27, 1991, a Suffolk County Court judge granted

Callace's motion to consider DNA tests as 'new evidence'. The judge also ruled that if the samples did not match, he would hold a hearing to consider post-conviction relief for Callace.

The analysis performed on the victim's jeans showed that DNA in the semen stains did not match Callace's. On October 5, 1992, Callace was released from prison. The prosecution dismissed all charges against Callace and declined to prosecute in a new trial because of the DNA evidence and the reluctance of the victim to endure another trial. Callace served almost six years of his sentence.

Rolando Cruz and Alejandro Hernandez

On February 25, 1983, a 10-year-old girl was kidnapped from her home, raped, and bludgeoned to death. Her body was found several days later in a wooded area. An autopsy showed she had died from several blows to the head, and her body evidenced a broken nose, post mortem scratches and sexual assault. Two weeks later an anonymous tip led sheriff's detectives to Hernandez. He allegedly made statements that he knew the men involved in the crime but that he was not one of the perpetrators. On the basis of his statements, Hernandez was arrested on March 6, 1984.

Several days later, the detectives spoke with Cruz, who was an acquaintance of Hernandez. Cruz allegedly reported 'visions' to the police – visions whose details were similar to those associated with the crime. Cruz was indicted on March 9, 1984, on the basis of those statements.

In 1985, Rolando Cruz and Alejandro Hernandez were jointly tried, convicted and sentenced to death for kidnapping, rape and murder.

The prosecution based its case on several points:

- Several law enforcement officers testified that Cruz and Hernandez made incriminating statements.
- Several witnesses testified that Cruz and Hernandez admitted to having intimate knowledge of the crime.
- Cruz's alleged 'dream visions' of the murder, though not tape recorded, were admitted into evidence on the basis of the testimony of sheriff's detectives.
- The alibi defences of the two men were not aggressively pursued.
- The Hernandez defence also contended that any incriminating statements by him against others were made to collect a $10,000 reward.

Following an appeal by Cruz, the Illinois Supreme Court ruled that Cruz was 'denied a fair trial by reason of introduction of admissions of codefendants'. The court ruled on January 19, 1988, that the men should have been tried separately when it was clear that the prosecution was going to use incriminating statements by defendants as evidence against one another. The case was reversed and remanded to the DuPage Circuit Court. Cruz was again convicted by a jury and he appealed. The Illinois Supreme Court initially affirmed the circuit court's decision, but, agreed to look at Cruz's conviction again. This time, on July 14, 1994, the court reversed the decision of the circuit court. The reversal was largely based on statements made by another man, Brian Dugan, a convicted rapist-murderer, who claimed to have committed the crime alone. Dugan's confession was made through hypothetical statements during a plea bargain for other crimes, so the confession could not be used against him.

Hernandez's second conviction, in a separate appeal, was also reversed and remanded. He was convicted a third time by a jury, and this conviction, too, was overturned.

In September 1995 DNA tests showed that neither Cruz nor Hernandez were the contributors of the semen found at the crime scene. Tests also determined that Brian Dugan could not be eliminated as a potential contributor. Prosecutors contended that the DNA evidence showed only that Cruz and Hernandez were not the rapists, but they could still have been present at the crime. Cruz's new defence team decided on a bench trial.

Hernandez awaited a fourth jury trial.

Conclusion. Before the judge gave a directed verdict in the Cruz case, a sheriff's department lieutenant denied a testimony he had provided in previous trials. In the earlier trials, the lieutenant provided corroborating testimony that two of his detectives told him immediately about Cruz's dream-vision statements. At Cruz's latest trial, however, the lieutenant said he was in Florida on the day of the supposed conversations and could not have spoken to anyone about Cruz's statements. On November 3, 1995, a DuPage County judge acquitted Cruz on the basis of the recanted testimony, the DNA evidence, and the lack of any substantiated evidence against Cruz. Rolando Cruz served eleven years on death row.

Hernandez's case was also dismissed, and he was set free. He served eleven years on death row. Brian Dugan has not been charged with the murder. He has refused to testify about the case unless he is granted death-penalty immunity.

David Vasquez

In the early morning of January 24, 1984, a woman was sexually assaulted and murdered in her home by an assailant who had entered the home through the victim's basement window. The woman died from asphyxiation by hanging.

David Vasquez pleaded guilty to second-degree homicide and burglary on February 4, 1985. He was sentenced to 35 years in prison. He had pleaded guilty to the crime after allegedly confessing to the crime and reporting details that were not released to the public. Vasquez, who is borderline retarded, later reported that he had only dreamed the crime.

In addition to Vasquez's guilty plea, the prosecution proffered the following evidence to the court:

- Two witnesses placed Vasquez near the victim's house on the day of the crime.

- Vasquez could not provide an alibi.

- Hair analysis of pubic hairs found at the scene were consistent with Vasquez's hair.

- A guilty plea meant that Vasquez would not be subject to the death penalty upon conviction.

Vasquez's defence attorneys filed for a suppression of two of his confessions. Following DNA tests on the evidence from several rape/murders, all the tests incriminated a man named Timothy Spencer as the assailant in rape-murders that were identical in *modus operandi* to the Vasquez incident. However, attempts to compare hair found at the scene with Vasquez's blood sample were inconclusive.

The Commonwealth's attorney and Vasquez's defence attorneys filed motions with the governor to grant Vasquez an unconditional pardon. The motions were based on the DNA tests of Spencer and an FBI report that indicated the Vasquez crime and the Spencer crimes were committed by the same person. The report also stated that the crimes 'were not perpetrated by someone who was mentally deficient'. The governor granted the pardon, and Vasquez was released on January 4,

1989. Vasquez had served five years of his sentence.

Timothy Spencer was arrested, tried and convicted for two other rape-murders. He was never formally prosecuted in the Vasquez incident because he had already been sentenced to death.

The Black Widow

The case involving Marie Hilley is still a mystery. In the true tradition of 'black widows' Marie murdered her husband – but it didn't stop there!

THE STORY OF Marie Hilley is a study in deceit, pathological obsession and serial murder. Marie Hilley was not the only 'black widow' of note from the tiny mill town of Blue Mountain, Alabama. In the 1950s Americans were shocked at the criminal exploits of Nannie Hazle Doss. She was a sweet-looking woman whose jovial manner during her confessions earned her the nickname 'The Giggling Grandma'. Nannie, who was raised in Blue Mountain and later moved to Oklahoma, killed eleven people, including five husbands, two of her children, and her mother. Although Marie Hilley's tally of victims wasn't nearly as staggering as Nannie Doss's, her dark shadow loomed larger over Blue Mountain than Doss's ever had.

Huey Frazier and Lucille Meads were hard workers and came from families whose lives were centred on the local mills. When they married in January, 1932, they were already accustomed to the long hours of work required just to make a living in Depression-era Alabama. When her daughter Audrey Marie was born on June 4, 1933,

Lucille Frazier was not able to stay at home to care for the child; she had to return to her job at the Linen Thread Company as soon as she could. The task of caring for Marie was left to her relatives. There was never any doubt that the Fraziers loved Marie, but times were hard and a single income didn't stretch far enough to meet the needs of a family of three. Huey and Lucille loved and trusted their families and were grateful for their help. And they tried to make up for the lost time with Marie by spoiling her. Marie's clothes weren't the best money could buy, but they were pretty and neat, and better than those of a lot of the kids around her. Even from an early age Marie got her own way – the slightest correction or denial was likely to provoke a loud tantrum. The Fraziers, perhaps out of guilt, never saw fit to administer any real discipline.

A Brighter Future

The Fraziers saw a brighter future for Marie, they didn't want her to have to spend countless years breathing the linty, stifling air of the mills. She would graduate high school and be a secretary, a humble ambition that seemed, in the context of the Fraziers' times and surroundings, the loftiest of dreams. Blue Mountain girls usually got no more than a grade school education before they began working at Linen Thread. Marie would be different – she was special, and her parents told her so.

In 1945 the Fraziers moved from Blue Mountain

to Anniston, and Marie began 7th grade at Quintard Junior High School. Though Anniston was close to Blue Mountain geographically, socially it was worlds apart. Anniston had its own upper class, comprised chiefly of the owners of the various mills and factories where Marie's relatives had always worked. At Quintard, Marie found herself among children of privilege, and she made friends with them. She became a member of the student council and was serious about her studies. She earned herself a reputation for maturity and intelligence. She was pretty, well-dressed, and by the end of her 7th grade year had been chosen Prettiest Girl at Quintard by the Anniston High School yearbook staff.

Her successes continued at Anniston High. Marie joined the Future Teachers of America and the Commercial Club, an organization for girls who planned secretarial careers. Her seriousness established her among her peers as a girl with depth and dependability. Her looks and style made the boys look twice, and while she enjoyed their attention, she was already spoken for. Marie was Frank Hilley's girl.

Frank Hilley

Frank Hilley was from an Anniston family whose men worked in the area's other big industry, pipe making. Clarence and Carrie Hilley had a close, warm family, and Frank and his two sisters, Freeda and Jewel, never lacked love and attention. Although Frank had a bit of a temper, he was loyal and reliable. He met Marie when she was twelve and he was a junior in high school, and by the time he graduated he was smitten with her.

Against her parents' wishes, Marie returned his affection. Though Frank wasn't from one of Anniston's moneyed families, he treated her like royalty. He was jealous of other boys' attentions towards her and did his best to keep his temperamental girl happy. Like most young couples they had intense, dramatic arguments, but they always made up. When Frank went into the Navy after high school, he pined for Marie and counted the days until they could be together again. He had been assigned to Guam, and the distance and time away were unbearable. Afraid of losing Marie, he married her while he was on leave in May, 1951.

Marie stayed behind in Anniston to finish high school while Frank went to Long Beach, California to finish his spell in the Navy. Marie joined him there after her graduation and later accompanied him when he was reassigned to Boston in 1952. At the end of his tour of duty they discovered Marie was pregnant, and when he was discharged they moved back home to Anniston, where they bought a small home. Frank got a job in the shipping department of Standard Foundry while Marie worked as a secretary. Their first child, Michael Hilley, was born on November 11, 1952.

Stirrings of Trouble

To all appearances the Hilleys seemed happy and settled, but the first stirrings of trouble had already begun. Marie loved to spend money – when Frank had sent home his paychecks from California Marie had spent them with astonishing speed. When the time came for her to join him out West, she had no money with which to make the trip and her in-laws had to pay her way. These habits didn't abate, and though Frank liked to keep Marie happy, he found it increasingly difficult to keep pace with her constant spending. There were arguments, but Frank didn't like to fight and found it easier to go along with Marie.

By the time Carol Hilley was born in 1960, Frank had been appointed foreman of the shipping department at Standard Foundry. Marie had gained a reputation as an excellent executive secretary. Though the family's collective income had increased, it still barely kept pace with Marie's spending. Marie was also starting to develop a disturbing work pattern – though her employers always found her professional and effective at her duties, but her co-workers thought otherwise. Marie judged and put on airs and played power games, but was always careful to remain respectful to the boss. At each job, she eventually became unpopular with those around her and left, telling friends and family that she'd been ganged up on by her fellow employees. Her references were always excellent, though, and she never had trouble getting another job.

Marie worked for some of the most powerful men in Anniston, all of whom spoke very highly of her. Later, Frank Hilley would find out one of the reasons why.

As the years passed, Anniston's inhabitants grew to know the Hilleys. Frank was a member of the Elks Club and the Veterans of Foreign Wars and was well liked around town. Marie was active in the First Christian Church and volunteered at her kids' schools. Some found her peculiar, and some noted that she reacted badly when she didn't get her own way. Mostly, however, people dismissed her little quirks, attributing them to a highly-strung nature.

Their children Mike and Carol wanted for nothing except, perhaps, their mother's attention. Like her own parents, Marie showered her children with material possessions but remained emotionally remote. She administered little discipline, leaving that task to Frank's mother Carrie, who cared for the children while Marie and Frank worked. Marie favoured Mike and allowed him to grow into a little hellion, brushing off his behaviour with a casual 'boys will be boys' attitude. As for Carol, she always seemed to stay somewhat in the background. Carol was a tomboy, nothing like the demure, proper daughter Marie wanted, and they clashed continually. Frank Hilley, noticing the effect Marie's treatment was having, took a special interest in Carol, taking her for ice cream and to football games. Their close relationship was starting to get to Marie.

Frank started to worry about his wife.

Sometimes she would be awake all night, and he would hold her while she shook in nameless fear. She was restless and he was unable to soothe her. She taunted him with love letters she said she received from local men, and then there was her spending. Marie's refined tastes kept the bills coming to the Hilley home year after year. Sometimes Frank would reprimand her, but to no avail. Marie wanted the best, and she wanted it now. She rented a post office box and began having some bills diverted there so that Frank wouldn't know what she was spending. She also began to take out loans. In Anniston, a town of less than 30,000 people, Frank Hilley was respected, and businesses extended credit to his wife out of courtesy to him. Frank had always paid every bill on time, so when his wife's accounts weren't settled they started to worry – this wasn't like Frank.

By the end of 1974 Frank couldn't ignore the troubles in his home any longer. Word of his wife's credit arrangements leaked back to him through the grapevine. Worse still, he came home sick from work one day to find Marie in bed with her employer, Walter Clinton. Frank told his son, who was married by now and attending Atlanta Christian College, of these latest developments. He didn't mention, however, about his own increasingly failing health.

Frank was sick a lot during 1974. At first he attributed his weariness and periodic bouts of nausea and vomiting to something he'd eaten, or to exposure to chemicals at the foundry. He took

Alka-Seltzer and bore his symptoms as best he could. But his illness persisted, and by May of 1975, he had to consult a doctor. Dr. Jones, the family's physician, first prescribed fluids, then Kaopectate and Maalox, then an antispasmodic medication. Nothing helped, however. When Frank's sister Freeda Adcock visited him on May 22, he told her he was sicker than he'd ever been and that he feared he would die. He also told her that Marie had, on Dr. Jones's orders, given him an injection. At the time, Freeda thought nothing of it.

At 3:30 the following morning Marie found Frank wandering round the garden in his underwear. She took him to the hospital, where tests showed that his liver had failed. Dr. Jones changed his diagnosis to one of infectious hepatitis and prescribed new medications. Frank's condition worsened; he was jaundiced, hallucinating and very agitated. It was all Mike Hilley could do to keep his father from jumping out the window. At around 4:00 a.m. on May 25, Mike left the hospital to pick up his grandmothers and bring them to see Frank. When he returned about an hour later he found his mother asleep and his father dead. The official cause of death was infectious hepatitis, and Frank Hilley was buried on May 27, 1975. Mike Hilley preached the sermon at his father's funeral.

Marie, the Widow

Frank Hilley's autopsy report stated that he'd died of natural causes, so Marie had no trouble collecting on the life insurance he'd bought through Standard Foundry. The total of Frank's policies was around $31,000, not enough to make a woman wealthy, but still a nice windfall. Marie began spending – a car, clothes and jewellery for herself; a diamond ring for her mother. Mike and his wife Teri received appliances and clothes, while Carol Hilley got a car, a stereo, furniture and countless other gifts. However, those closest to Marie noticed that this did nothing to quiet her increasing restlessness. She complained to several people that no one in her family loved her, least of all Carol. She complained about her boss and her job, and about a string of petty thefts at her home which she said began before Frank's death.

Marie gathered her family about her – Lucille had been diagnosed with cancer soon after Frank died, and Marie brought her into her home to care for her. She also invited Mike and Teri to live with her. Mike had a job as assistant pastor at Indian Oaks Church and appreciated his mother's offer. He relished the thought of having his family close while he began his career in the ministry. They accepted, but were soon to regret their decision. Marie and Carol fought constantly, and his mother's demands for his time and attention wore Mike down. On top of that, Teri was often ill with stomach trouble. During the time she and Mike lived with Marie, Teri was in the hospital four different times and had a miscarriage, which only added to the tension in the Hilley home.

When the pressure became too great, Mike and Teri found an apartment. But the night before they were set to move out, Marie's house caught fire. Marie, Lucille and Carol moved into the new apartment until repairs could be completed. When the time came for them to move back home, the apartment next door to Mike and Teri's caught fire, forcing the couple to move back in with Marie until they could find new housing. When they finally succeeded in moving away from Marie, a strange new series of events began.

Lucille Frazier died in January, 1977. In the following months, the Anniston Police were to become increasingly familiar with Marie Hilley. The petty thefts had continued, she told police. She reported gas leaks, and claimed she found a small fire in her closet late one night. Neighbour Doris Troy, to whose house Marie had a key, found a similar fire in her own hall closet, but had no idea who could've set it. Both Marie and Doris Ford reported harassing phone calls. Police responded to dozens of complaints from both Marie Hilley and Doris Ford. Every officer was familiar with Marie and at least one took that familiarity a few steps further. Officer Billy Atherton fell for the beleaguered but charming widow and the two began a sexual relationship.

Becoming more and more restless, Marie, with Carol in tow, moved in with Mike and Teri in their new home in Pompano Beach, Florida. It was now 1978 and Carol had just graduated from high school. Marie got an office job and returned home late most nights, but her nervous presence and well-established spending habits made life difficult in the Hilley home. Upon her arrival in

Pompano Beach, she had run up $600 worth of charges on Mike's Visa Card, saying she would pay him back later. She still constantly fought with Carol, and Mike and Teri were very relieved when she and Carol moved back to Anniston after a few months.

Carol Becomes Ill

Unbeknown to the family, Marie had been buying insurance. There were several policies, including fire insurance, cancer coverage, and life insurance coverage on herself. But Marie had also insured the lives of her children – Mike for $25,000, while Carol, through two policies, was insured for $39,000.

When they first returned to Anniston, Marie and Carol moved in with Frank's sister Freeda, then with his mother Carrie Hilley. The strange occurrences started all over again. Small fires, cut phone lines and, increasingly, a tendency in Carrie Hilley toward nausea and vomiting. Marie got a job at Dresser Industries and also worked nights for Harold Dillard, the owner of a local construction company. She started a manipulative, twisted affair which was designed to bring Dillard under her spell and make him leave his wife. At the same time she began another affair with Calvin Robertson, an old school friend who had long since relocated to San Francisco. She told Robertson that she had cancer and couldn't afford the treatments she needed. He sent money, and she soon returned news that she had been cured.

When he came to visit her in Anniston he was like a schoolboy, and by the time he left he was convinced he would die for Marie Hilley. However, he wasn't quite ready to leave his wife just yet.

Carol Hilley first became ill in April, 1979. Now nineteen and a freshman at a nearby college, she returned to her high school for its annual Junior-Senior Prom. The night's festivities included food, drink, a little marijuana – and as the party wore on Carol became nauseated. It wasn't serious enough to spoil her fun, so she ignored it, concentrating on having a good time. The following day, though, the nausea returned with a vengeance. Carol left church services early and vomited in the parking lot. On returning home she discovered that her grandmother, Carrie Hilley, was in the hospital after fainting at church. Carol accompanied Marie to the hospital, where she was sick all afternoon.

Over the summer Carol grew sicker and weaker. Although she was becoming increasingly dependent on Marie's care, she still insisted on moving into her own apartment. Marie was a constant presence there, expressing concern and acting as Carol's caretaker. She administered Carol's various medicines and often cooked for her. She took her to several doctors, none of whom was able to explain with any certainty what was exactly wrong with Carol. The nausea and vomiting, now almost constant, were accompanied by tingling sensations in her hands and feet and ever-worsening muscle weakness.

In August Carol was admitted to Regional Medical Center in Anniston for the fourth time since April, and Dr. Warren Sarrell was baffled and concerned. He suggested to Marie that she should take Carol to Birmingham to see Dr. John Elmore, a psychiatrist. Marie did just that, telling the doctor that Carol was despondent and had said several times that she wanted to die. On Dr. Elmore's recommendation, Carol was admitted to the psychiatric ward at Carraway Methodist Hospital in Birmingham.

Carol, confined to the hospital, could not know that her mother was rapidly becoming entangled in her own web of lies and misdeeds. The cheques Marie had written for the furniture for Carol's apartment had bounced, as had many others, including some written for premiums on the policy on Carol's life. The bank filed charges, and Marie was arrested, and then released on bail. In Florida, Mike Hilley was slowly coming to the conclusion that his father had not died of natural causes. He placed a call to the Calhoun County coroner asking about the possibility of an exhumation, and was told that he would need lots of solid evidence for one to take place.

The final alarm was sounded by Eve Cole, a friend of Carol's. She had been present at Carol's apartment one night during the summer when Marie had given Carol an injection. When she called Carol at Carraway Methodist, Carol mentioned offhandedly that Marie had given her more injections during her hospitalization. Concerned, Eve told Carol's Aunt Freeda, who called Mike Hilley, who in turn called his sister to find out the truth. Yes, she told him, Marie had given her shots. Mike then called Dr. John Elmore, who, although he did not believe that Marie was poisoning Carol, thought she might be part of the overall problem. He asked Marie not to visit Carol for a while.

Marie became frantic. The day after Dr. Elmore told her of his wishes, she removed Carol from Carraway Methodist, saying she was taking her daughter to the Mayo Clinic or to Ochsner Hospital in New Orleans. Carol had been at Carraway Methodist for three weeks, she said, and hadn't improved. She was taking her where she could get better care. Mother and daughter spent that night at a motel, and the next day Carol was admitted to University of Alabama Hospital in Birmingham. Dr. Brian Thompson was assigned to her case.

On September 20, 1979, Marie was arrested again on more cheque charges and the rest of Carol's family took the opportunity to reveal their suspicions to Carol's doctor. Though the story was fantastic, Dr. Thompson took it seriously. He checked Carol's fingernails and toenails for Aldridge-Mees lines, white deposits clearly visible in the nails of those who've been dosed with arsenic. The lines appeared on every nail. Dr. Thompson felt sure that further tests would reveal that Carol Hilley was loaded with arsenic, and had been so for a long time.

Upon hearing his sister's diagnosis, Mike Hilley wrote a long letter to Ralph Phillips, the Calhoun

County Coroner. He recounted his father's rapid decline and death, Lucille Frazier's death, Marie's various banking troubles, and finally Carol's illness. His mother was mentally ill, he asserted, and he wanted to help her. Marie, still in jail on cheque charges, was now officially under suspicion of murder and attempted murder.

Mounting Evidence

Lieutenant Gary Carroll had grown familiar, even friendly, with Marie Hilley in 1977 when she'd been in almost constant contact with the Anniston Police Department with reports of suspicious fires and phone calls. On September 26, he conducted and taped a two-hour interview with Marie, when she tried to dodge accusations and to lay blame elsewhere. With careful questioning, however, Carroll got her to admit that she'd given Carol injections both at home and in the hospital, and that she'd also given her mother injections. All of these, she claimed, were actually medicine.

Subsequent developments were as stunningly rapid as Carol's poisoning had been agonizingly slow. Frank Hilley's body was exhumed on October 3, 1979. Three days later, Freeda Adcock searched the house where Marie and Carol had lived with Carrie Hilley and found a pill bottle half full of liquid, which proved to be arsenic. Arsenic was also found in a pill bottle Marie had had in her purse when she was arrested. The evidence mounted and Marie was charged with the attempted murder of her daughter.

Meanwhile, the toxicology reports from Frank Hilley's exhumation came back – arsenic was present in his tissues at many times the normal level. It was too soon, however, to tell conclusively if the poison had been the cause of his death. The day after the toxicology reports were released, Lucille Frazier's body was exhumed – arsenic in her tissues ranged from four to ten times the normal level, although it was cancer that finally killed her.

Marie's bail was remarkably low, considering the seriousness of the main charge against her. Five local residents, at the ambivalent request of Mike Hilley, put up $10,000 bail for the attempted murder charge and $2,000 for each of the cheque charges, for a total of $14,000. Marie was released on bail on November 11, 1979, and Wilford Lane, her attorney, took her to Birmingham to stay at a motel. In the coming days she claimed she was afraid of reprisals from Frank's sisters and asked to be moved to another motel, from which she made numerous phone calls to Mike and other relatives asking for money.

On November 18, when Wilford Lane and his wife came to the motel to visit Marie, they discovered she was missing. Her clothes were strewn about the room, her suitcase lay on the floor and her purse had been emptied onto a bed. The only things that were missing were her wallet, credit cards and chequebook. A scrawled note on motel stationery read, 'Lane, you led me straight to her. You will hear from me'.

On that very day Carrie Hilley died of cancer in

Anniston – tests done on strands of her hair in the previous weeks had indicated elevated arsenic levels. Marie Hilley was now suspected of poisoning at least four people.

Marie's trail went cold almost immediately. On November 19 Margaret Key, Marie's Aunt, found that her house had been broken into, her car was missing, as were some clothes and a suitcase. A note at the scene said the car could be found in nearby Gadsden, and that the burglars would not bother Margaret Key any more. The car was discovered a few days later in Marietta, Georgia. The FBI then joined the pursuit, tracking Marie from Marietta through Georgia to Savannah, where she was reported to have left a motel with a man. After that, there was nothing – she simply disappeared.

Back in Anniston, the final toxicology reports from Frank Hilley's exhumation had come in – Marie was indicted on January 11, 1980 for the murder of her husband.

John Homan

It is not clear whether Marie Hilley knew John Homan before she claimed to have met him in Fort Lauderdale in 1980. Carol remembered that her mother had mentioned a John Ronin who taught at Emory University in Decatur, Georgia. But according to both Marie and John, they met in Fort Lauderdale, Florida in February of 1980. Marie was now going by an alias, Lindsay Robbi Hannon, and she hinted to John, the 33-year-old owner of a boat building business, that her past was tragic. She told him she was 35, from Texas, and had lost both her children in a car accident. John Homan's own life was no picnic – his alcoholic mother died when he was young, and he was an awkward, shy man. He was recently divorced and he found Marie's attentions soothing. By March they had started living together. Using a fictitious resumé, Marie got a job as a secretary at an accounting firm in West Palm Beach. She didn't stay long, though – in October she and John left Florida for New Hampshire, where John's brother Peter lived.

Marie and John rented a tiny house in Marlow, New Hampshire. John found work at Findings, Inc., which made small parts for jewellery. Marie got a customer service job at Central Screw Corporation in nearby Keene, New Hampshire, where her efficiency and Southern charm enabled her to excel. Her co-workers found her fascinating. Posing as Robbi, she told them of her children's tragic death, of life in a wealthy Texas family, and of an inheritance which she would eventually claim. It was about this time that she started to complain of severe headaches and said she'd been to many doctors to try and find relief, but to no avail. Though some of her co-workers found her abrasive and pushy, most considered her a sympathetic figure. The men, especially, found the woman they knew as Robbi Homan to be earthy and fun to be with.

Marie's stories grew more and more involved. She was dying, she told those around her, of a rare blood disease that caused her body to make too many red blood cells. Though she and John were now married, she left her husband alone from time to time, telling her co-workers she was seeking treatment out of town from various specialists. She began to speak in detail of a sister, her twin whom she called Teri Martin. Sometimes she would shut herself into an office at work, saying she was phoning Teri, who was having marriage problems and needed her. It was Teri, she said, who would take care of her during her upcoming trip to Texas. She was making one last attempt to find a treatment for the illness that appeared to be making her increasingly more ill.

Marie left Marlow in September, 1982 and only stayed in Texas a few days. On September 23 she arrived in Pompano Beach, Florida. That day she had her hair bleached, then went to an employment agency seeking work under the name Teri Martin. By the end of the day she had secured a secretarial position at Solar Testing Service. She worked there for six weeks, telling her new boss Jack McKenzie about her twin sister Robbi, who was gravely ill. Her sister had recently suffered a stroke and developed cancer, she claimed, and Teri felt responsible for her. When McKenzie received a call in mid-November from his secretary claiming that she was in New Hampshire and her sister had died, he wasn't surprised. She told him she'd be staying in New Hampshire and thanked him for his kindness. On November 10, Marie (now assuming the role of Teri) called John Homan to break the news that his wife Robbi had died. The following day she flew to New Hampshire.

John Homan claims to have believed Marie Hilley's new ruse until the moment she was apprehended. Her hair was still bleached, and during her stay in Florida she had lost quite a lot of weight. As Teri, she carried herself differently, so it is at least somewhat believable that John, insecure and highly suggestible, was fooled. The day after her arrival she and John went to the office of the Keene Sentinel to place Robbi Homan's obituary. This short piece contained several fabricated details which would finally be Marie's undoing.

Teri moved in with John Homan, and got a job just across the state line in Brattleboro, Vermont at Book Press, a book printing company. Like her sister Robbi, Teri was a competent secretary. She settled into her new job comfortably, and for a while things seemed quiet. A group of doubters at Robbi's old workplace, however, decided to focus on the obituary. They first discovered that the hospital to which Robbi's body had supposedly been left – Medical Research Institute of Texas – did not exist. Then they found that the church to which the obituary stated Robbi had belonged in Texas was fictitious as well. A check of obituaries and coroner's records in the Dallas area around the date of November 10, 1982 yielded nothing. The doubting Central Screw employees took their findings to manager Ron Oja, who began some checking of his own. The gossip about this amateur investigation spread, and it wasn't long before local police were informed that something wasn't right about the woman who claimed to be Teri Martin.

Detective Bob Hardy of the Keene Police Department started by interviewing the workers from Central Screw, then made some phone calls of his own. Again, nothing in the obituary added up. Hardy began making inquiries with other law enforcement agencies. The New Hampshire State Police told him something interesting – a woman named Carol Manning who fitted Teri Martin's description was wanted for bank robbery. The authorities began watching Teri. They soon decided she was not Carol Manning, but thought she must be Terry Lynn Clifton, another fugitive.

The Arrest

On January 12, 1983, they apprehended her at Book Press. When they asked her name, her answer puzzled them. She was Audrey Marie Hilley, she claimed, and she was wanted in Alabama on bad cheque charges. When police put her name out on the wire the word came back quickly – she was indeed Audrey Marie Hilley, but she had more than just cheque charges to face back in Alabama.

Marie was taken back to Anniston on January 19, 1983. By now another charge had been added – the murder of Frank Hilley – and Marie's bail was set at $320,000. This time no one stepped forward to pay it. Carol Hilley, now physically recovered from her ordeal, had conflicting emotions but was anxious to see her mother. When Carol visited the jail, Marie cried and hugged her and professed to love her. She had missed her terribly, she claimed. However, she offered no explanation for the poisoning. After that first visit, Marie and Carol saw each other often and spoke on the phone frequently. Carol badly wanted to believe that her mother had never meant to poison her, which worried prosecutors. They needed Carol's testimony.

Judge Sam Monk presided over the trial. Assistant District Attorney Joe Hubbard was the prosecutor, and Wilford Lane and Thomas Harmon defended Marie. Right from the start it was obvious that the defence was going to soil Carol's reputation, to make her seem unstable enough to poison herself. 'We expect,' Harmon said, 'the evidence to show that Carol Hilley has used drugs extensively,' and that 'Carol Hilley is, in fact, either a homosexual or has engaged in homosexuality. In addition, we expect the evidence to show that Carol Hilley has, on at least three occasions, attempted suicide.' Carol's performance under cross-examination, though, was admirable. She admitted she had smoked pot, but no, she wasn't a drug addict. She also admitted to having engaged in homosexual acts, but no, she wasn't mentally unbalanced because of it. She had tried to kill herself, but the attempt before her mother was arrested was almost laughable – she'd taken a total of five Tylenol. The other attempts occurred as she was trying to deal with the physical and emotional torment caused by the poisoning. Prosecutors needn't have worried – Carol's testimony that her mother had given her mysterious injections during her illness rang lucid and true.

Freeda Adcock's testimony served to establish that arsenic had been found among Marie's possessions. In addition to the pill bottle she had found at Carrie Hilley's home, Freeda later found a bag containing jars of baby food, a spoon and a bottle of rat poison that contained arsenic. Defence attorneys objected that these items, as well as the bottle Gary Carroll had found in Marie's purse after her arrest, had been seized illegally and should not be presented as evidence. Judge Monk overruled them. Freeda also testified that Frank Hilley told her that Marie had given him an injection. Eve Cole corroborated Carol's claim that her mother had given her injections. Still, Marie's attorneys claimed that Carol had poisoned herself, and that Freeda Adcock's testimony was false. Freeda had always hated Marie, the defence claimed, and she would say anything to see her put away for good. But Wilford Lane and Thomas Harmon were in for a shock.

Marie had told her attorneys that Gary Carroll had interviewed her after her 1979 arrest, but she hadn't told them that the interview had been taped. In that recording Marie admitted to giving Carol two injections, saying they were anti-nausea medicine, and claiming to have obtained one from a woman she had met at the hospital. She also admitted that she might be mentally ill, that she might need some help. Marie could not claim she'd never said such things – they were all there on the tape. From that point her defence crumbled. It took the jury just three hours to come to its verdict – Marie Hilley was guilty of the murder of Frank Hilley and of the attempted murder of Carol Hilley. The following day she received a life sentence for the murder and twenty years for the poisoning. At the sentencing hearing, she again professed her innocence.

The Speculation

On June 9, 1983, Marie entered Tutwiler State Women's Prison in Wetumpka, Alabama. She was assigned a job as a data processor and was classified as a medium security prisoner. Despite reports that she talked constantly of escape and had reportedly made plans for a break out, she was reclassified in 1985 as a minimum security prisoner, which made her eligible for passes and leaves from the prison. In late 1986 her first eight-hour pass was approved. That pass and three others came and went with no trouble; Marie returned to Tutwiler promptly each time, and by February, 1987 she had qualified for a three-day furlough. On February 19, she left Tutwiler Prison for the last time.

John Homan had relocated to Anniston, and he and Marie spent the weekend in a hotel room there. On Sunday morning she told John that she wanted to visit her parents' graves and would meet him at 10:00 a.m. at a local restaurant. She wasn't there. Returning to the hotel room, John found a note: 'I hope you will be able to forgive me,' it read. 'I'm getting ready to leave. It will be best for everybody. We'll be together again. Please give me an hour to get out of town.' Marie wrote that a man named Walter was taking her out of town and that she would fly to Canada and contact John later. John called the sheriff. Given Marie's history, authorities assumed she had a well-crafted plan of escape and had left the state quickly, but no one expected what happened next!

On February 26 police were called to a house near Blue Mountain. A strange, delirious woman was on Sue Craft's porch and she needed help. She said her name was Sellers and that her car had broken down. She was suffering from hypothermia. Sue Craft did not recognize the woman as Marie Hilley, though she had known Marie years before. Within a few minutes Marie lost consciousness and began convulsing, and her heart stopped in the ambulance on the way to the hospital. No one knew how long she'd been wandering, but her body temperature had fallen to 81 degrees. Marie Hilley, who had always aspired to wealth and position, died an ugly, lonely death very near her childhood home. On February 28, 1987 Marie Hilley's children buried her beside Frank Hilley, the husband she had murdered.

Doctor Death

His patients – mainly elderly women – were living alone and vulnerable. They adored their doctor – Harold 'Fred' Shipman – but no film director could plan a grislier scene . . .

EVEN WHEN their contemporaries began dying in unusually high numbers, patients remained loyal to the murderous doctor. It seemed as long as he spared them, his victims loved their doctor – to death.

In the dead of a black August night, relentless rains and driving winds formed the perfect backdrop for an exhumation. But this was no psychological thriller – the Manchester police were observing a real-life drama, the raising of the mud-streaked coffin of wealthy Kathleen Grundy.

She had been interned just five weeks earlier in the Hyde cemetery. This 81-year-old ex-mayoress held, in death, the key to solving nearly 400 murders. This would give killer Dr Harold Shipman the dubious distinction of being the greatest serial murderer the world has ever known.

How could this prolific serial killer go undetected for so long? And what made him the monster he became? The answers lie in a story that started over fifty years ago – in a red brick terrace house in the north of England.

Far From Normal Childhood

Shipman was born into a working-class family on June 14, 1946, but his childhood was far from normal. He kept a distance between himself and his contemporaries, mainly due to the influence of his mother, Vera. Apparently his mother was friendly enough, but she really did see her family as superior to the rest of the human race. Also 'Freddy' was her favourite – the one she saw as the most promising of her three children. As a student, Shipman was comparatively bright in his early school years, but rather mediocre when he reached upper school level. Nonetheless, he was a plodder determined to succeed, even when it meant re-sitting his entrance examinations for medical school.

He had every opportunity to be part of the group – he was an accomplished athlete on the football field and the running track. In spite of this, his belief in his superiority appears to have stopped him from forming any meaningful friendships. And there was something else that isolated him from the group. His beloved mother had terminal lung cancer. As she wasted away, Fred willingly played a major supportive role.

Every day after classes, he would hurry home, to make his mother a cup of tea and chat with her. She counted the minutes as she waited, and found great solace in his company. This is probably where he learned the endearing bedside manner he would adopt later in his practice as a family physician. Fred watched in fascination as his mother's pain subsided whenever the family doctor injected her with morphine. Her fight for life finally ended on June 21, 1963.

Vera's death left her son with a tremendous sense of loss.

Two years after his mother died, Harold Shipman was finally admitted to Leeds University medical school, although getting in had proved to be a struggle. Most of his friends from his earlier years remember him as a loner. They also remember the one place where his personality changed – the football field. Here, his aggression was unleashed, his dedication to win intense. But Shipman finally found companionship in a girl called Primrose, three years his junior. Shipman married her when she was seventeen and five months pregnant.

By 1974 he was a father of two and had joined a medical practice in the Yorkshire town of Todmorden. In this North England setting, Fred's personality began to blossom – he became an outgoing, respected member of the community both in the eyes of his fellow medics and patients.

But the staff in the medical offices where he worked saw a different side of the young practitioner – not yet thirty, Shipman had become a control freak.

The Darker Side

Hard working, and enthusiastic, Shipman fitted well into the medical practice. But his career in Todmorden came to a sudden halt when he began having blackouts. His partners were devastated when he gave them the reason. He suffered, he said, with epilepsy – but this was only a cover-up. The truth soon emerged, when practice receptionist Marjorie Walker stumbled upon some disturbing entries in a narcotics ledger. The records showed how Shipman had been prescribing large and frequent amounts of pethidine in the names of several patients. Moreover, he'd written numerous prescriptions for the drug on behalf of the practice. Although this was not unusual, the prescribed amounts were.

Following the discovery of Shipman's over-prescribing, an investigation by the practice followed. To their alarm, they discovered many patients on the prescription list had neither required nor received the drug. Fred was challenged in a staff meeting and was accused of using the pethidine for his own purposes.

Shipman's way of dealing with the problem was to provide an insight into his true personality. Realizing his career was on the line, he first begged for a second chance. When this was denied, he became enraged and stormed out, hurled a medical bag to the ground and threatened to resign. The partners were dumbfounded by this violent – and seemingly uncharacteristic – behaviour. He was ultimately forced out of the practice and into a drug rehabilitation centre in 1975.

Two years later, his many convictions for drug offences, prescription fraud and forgery cost him a surprisingly low fine – just over £600.

Back in Business

It is unlikely, today, that Harold Shipman would be allowed to handle drugs unsupervised, given his previous track record. However, within two years, he was back in business as a general practitioner. He was accepted into the Donneybrook Medical Centre in Hyde in the north of England. Again, he played the role of a dedicated, hard-working and community-minded doctor. He gained his patients' absolute trust and earned his colleagues' respect. In Hyde it appeared, Harold Shipman was free to kill.

Many of Shipman's former patients undoubtedly owe their lives to a determined and intelligent woman named Angela Woodruff. Her dogged determination to solve a mystery helped ensure that, on Monday, January 31, 2000, the jury at Preston Crown Court found Shipman guilty of murdering fifteen of his patients and forging the will of Angela's beloved mother, Katherine Grundy. Ms. Woodruff, however, was not the first to realize something was very wrong where Dr. Shipman was involved.

Local undertaker Alan Massey began noticing a strange pattern: not only did Shipman's patients seem to be dying at an unusually high rate; their dead bodies had a similarity when he called to collect them. "Anybody can die in a chair," he observed, "But there's no set pattern, and Dr. Shipman's always seem to be the same, or very similar. Could be sat in a chair, could be laid on the settee, but I would say 90 per cent were always fully clothed. There was never anything in the house that I saw that indicated the person had been ill. It just seems the person, where they were, had died. There was something that didn't quite fit."

Massey decided to confront Shipman, and paid the doctor a visit. Reassured by Shipman's ease at being questioned, the undertaker took no further action. But his daughter, Debbie Brambroffe – also a funeral director – was not so readily appeased. She found an ally in Dr. Susan Booth.

From a nearby practice, Dr. Booth had gone to the funeral directors to examine a body. British law requires a doctor from an unrelated practice to countersign cremation forms issued by the original doctor. They are paid a fee for this service which some medics cynically call 'cash for ash'. Debbie was concerned about the number of deaths of Dr. Shipman's patients that they'd attended recently. She was also puzzled by the way in which the patients were found. They were mostly female, living on their own, and found dead sitting in a chair fully dressed. Dr. Booth spoke to her colleagues and one of them, Dr. Linda Reynolds, contacted coroner John Pollard. He in turn alerted the police. In a virtually covert operation, Shipman's records were examined and given a clean bill of health because the causes of death and treatments matched perfectly.

What the police did not discover was that Shipman had re-written patient records after he killed. The quality of that investigation has been questioned because the police failed to check for a previous criminal record. Nor did they make inquiries with the General Medical Council. Had they done so, Shipman's past record of drug abuse and forgery might well have led to a more thorough approach.

Kathleen Grundy

The sudden death of Kathleen Grundy on June 24, 1998, came as a terrible shock to all who knew her. A very active 81-year-old, she was well known to the people of Hyde. A wealthy ex-mayor, and a tireless worker for local charities until the day of her death. Her absence was noted when she failed to show at the Age Concern club. There, she helped serve meals to elderly pensioners. Because the wealthy widow was noted for her punctuality and reliability, her friends suspected something was wrong. When they went to her home to check up on her, they found her lying on a sofa. She was fully dressed, and dead.

They immediately called Dr Shipman. He had apparently visited the house a few hours earlier, and was the last person to see her alive. He claimed the purpose of his visit had been to take blood samples for studies on ageing. Shipman pronounced her dead and the news was conveyed to her daughter, Angela Woodruff.

The doctor told the daughter a post mortem was unnecessary because he had seen her shortly before her death.

After her mother's funeral Angela returned home, where she received a phone call from a company of solicitors. They claimed to have a copy of Ms. Grundy's will. A solicitor herself, Angela's own firm had always handled her mother's affairs. The original document lodged in 1986, was still held by her firm. The moment she saw the badly typed, poorly worded paper, Angela Woodruff knew it was a fake. It left £386,000 pounds to Dr Shipman. She reluctantly concluded the doctor had murdered her mother for profit, and it was at this point that she went to her local police. Her investigation results ultimately reached Detective Superintendent Bernard Postles.

His own investigation convinced him Angela Woodruff's conclusions were accurate. To get solid proof of Kathleen Grundy's murder, a post mortem was required which, in turn, required an exhumation order from the coroner. This was a rare occurrence for any British police force, but by the time the Shipman trial had begun, his team had become uncomfortably familiar with the process. Of the fifteen killed, nine were buried and six cremated. Katherine Grundy's was the first grave opened. Her body was the first of the ongoing post mortems.

Samples of her tissue and hair were sent to different labs for analysis, and the wait for results began. At the same time, police raided the doctor's home and offices. It was a low-key exercise, but timed so Shipman had no chance of learning a body had been exhumed for a post mortem. Police had to be certain no evidence could be destroyed or concealed before their search. When the police arrived, Shipman showed no surprise.

Rather, his approach was one of arrogance and contempt as the search warrant was read out.

One item crucial to police investigations was the typewriter used to type the bogus will. Shipman produced an old Brother manual portable, telling an improbable tale of how Ms Grundy sometimes borrowed it. This unbelievable story was to work against Shipman – especially when forensic scientists confirmed it was the machine used to type the counterfeit will and other fraudulent documents.

Further searching of his house yielded medical records, some mysterious jewellery and a surprise. The Shipman home was littered with filthy clothes, old newspapers and, for a doctor's home, it was nothing short of unsanitary.

Morphine

The toxicologist's report showed that the morphine level in the dead woman's body was the cause of death. Not only that, her death would have occurred within three hours of having received the fatal overdose. Shipman claimed that the stylish and conservative old lady was a junkie. Even today psychologists speculate on the possibility that he wanted to be caught. Otherwise, why would he hand them the typewriter and use a drug so easily traced back to him? Others believe he saw himself as invincible, believing that, as a doctor, his word would never be questioned. The detective realized the case went far beyond one death, and the scope of the investigation was broadened immediately.

The problem which the police faced now, was which deaths to investigate. It was decided that those who had not been cremated and had died following a Shipman 'house call' took precedence. Obviously only uncremated bodies could yield tissue samples for examination. All the bodies that had been cremated were investigated, mainly, on the basis of known pre-existing conditions, recorded causes of death, and Shipman's presence before they died. It became clear that, whenever he could, the doctor had urged families to cremate their dead and had also stressed no further investigation was necessary. It may seem strange now that no relatives found this peculiar, but people typically trust their doctors, especially in times of great stress. Even if they had questioned the doctor, he had the computerized medical notes to prove patients had seen him for the very symptoms he cited as leading to causes of death. Police were later to learn that he had altered computer records to make everything match. Callously, Shipman made most of these changes within hours of his patients' deaths. Often, immediately after killing, he would hurry to his office and adjust his records.

In the case of 82-year-old Kathleen Grundy, he reinforced his later statement that she was a morphine junkie by inventing and backdating several entries.

His sheer audacity in suggesting this highly respected woman had been scoring hits from drug dealers was overwhelmingly stupid. The moment he made the statement, his credibility crumbled.

The Trial and the Verdict

It took the judge – Mr. Justice Forbes – two weeks to meticulously dissect the evidence heard by the jury. He urged caution, noting that no witness had actually seen Shipman kill, and also urged the jurors to use common sense in arriving at their verdict.

In summing up, he said, in part:

> "The allegations could not be more serious – a doctor accused of murdering 15 patients . . . You will have heard evidence which may have aroused feelings of anger, strong disapproval, disgust, profound dismay or deep sympathy."

At 4:43 p.m. on Monday January 31, 2000, the foreman declared all the jury's verdicts were unanimous – they found Shipman guilty on fifteen counts of murder and one of forgery. The disgraced doctor stood motionless and betrayed no sign of emotion as he heard the jurors' verdicts read. Shipman's wife Primrose, who was wearing black, also remained impassive. Her boys – one beside her and the other seated behind – looked down and seemed to diminish on hearing the results.

The judge passed fifteen life sentences for the murders and a four-year sentence for forgery. Then he broke with the tradition that usually involves writing to the Home Secretary about his recommendations on length of the sentence:

> 'In the ordinary way, I would not do this in open court, but in your case I am satisfied justice demands that I make my views known at the conclusion of this trial . . . My recommendation will be that you spend the remainder of your days in prison.'

Fifteen murders had been dealt with and the fifty-seven day trial was over. But the extent of the killing was yet to be revealed . . .

Horrifying Statistics

British police are so convinced that Shipman's killing 'antics' started so long ago, that a special helpline has been set up for those concerned about how friends and relatives died while under the killer's care. A report about the case is filled with chilling statistics.

When Shipman's patient list was compared with those of doctors with similar lists, it was concluded that Shipman had 236 more in-home patient deaths than would normally be expected. Most of these deaths involved women over the age of seventy-five.

The reason Harold Shipman killed may never be known. As long as he professes his innocence, the mystery will remain, for this serial killer is unique. There were no signs of violence, no sexual overtones, no known motive – except for the one exception – the money. Some psychoanalysts speculate he hated older women, citing comments he made about the elderly being a drain on the health system. Others feel he was re-creating his mother's death scene, in order to satisfy some deep masochistic need. His belief in his own superiority makes this questionable.

The fact that he left so many indelible clues indicates, some say, that Shipman desperately wanted to be discovered and stopped; that he was fighting a compulsion he simply could not control.

Conclusive Evidence

An eight-year-old girl goes off to play with her brothers and sister in a secluded wheatfield close to her grandparents' home . . . but she fails to return home.

ON SATURDAY July 1, 2001 at 7 p.m. little Sarah Payne goes off with her two brothers and sister to play in a secluded wheatfield only 150 metres from her grandparents' home near East Preston, West Sussex.

While they are playing Sarah hurts herself and decides to walk home. Her 13-year-old brother Lee follows but loses sight of his sister. He later told the police that he saw a white van and a Ford Mondeo on the lane. Sarah did not return home and is reported to the police as a missing person. Many local people helped the officers to search the area.

On the Sunday a full-scale search is launched involving 300 people, among them police officers with sniffer dogs, soldiers and volunteers. Members of the public are urged to check their gardens, and a total of 150 officers are assigned to the job.

Meanwhile, 250 miles away in Cheshire, a woman helps a 'distressed' little girl matching Sarah's description – and answering to her name. This was in a motorway services toilet at Knutsford on the M6 in Cheshire. However, the police did not release details of this 'sighting' for another week for operational reasons.

That same evening a man in his forties is arrested at a flat in Littlehampton, West Sussex, and a white van is towed away.

The next day another man, in his thirties, from the Crawley, West Sussex, area, is arrested. Meanwhile, Sussex Under Water Search Unit scoured storm drains leading to the sea and 600 members of the public called giving information. The police continued to question the two men for another day. Finally, officers are granted an extra 36 hours to question the man in his forties. Meanwhile Sarah's parents make an emotional TV appeal.

On Wednesday July 5, Sarah's brother Lee takes part in an identity parade in Brighton involving the man in his forties, but police later release both men on bail because of insufficient evidence.

The hunt now turns nationwide, and the police ask other forces to check their known sex offenders. Convinced that she is still alive, Sarah's parents make another tearful TV appeal directly addressing their daughter, holding up cards from well-wishers and telling her to 'hang in there'.

On Friday, July 7, a reconstruction of Sarah's last-known movements is filmed with the help of four local children who agree to play the parts of the missing eight-year-old and her brothers and sister. Following this police received more than 500 calls in response. Police mount a stop-and-question operation to question day-trippers to the area exactly a week after Sarah disappeared.

One week later the Payne family visit the centre of the police operation at the Littlehampton incident room and thank officers for their tireless work in the search for Sarah. Police now release details of the possible sighting made at Knutsford eight days earlier, and call for other people who may also have seen Sarah to get in touch. This time more than 800 people responded. Meanwhile, a second possible sighting is made, in Scotland, but police do not disclose this for another two days.

Detectives now have an e-fit picture of the man seen with the girl in Knutsford, and this is published on the covers of several national newspapers. Police release the possible second sighting of Sarah at a service station on the A80 near Glasgow. However, the description of the man 'she' was with does not fit the individual in their e-fit picture. CCTV footage from the service station is flown down to Sussex for closer scrutiny.

At this stage in the investigations, the police have had more than 10,000 calls from members of the public. This was more than 20 times the usual response to an appeal on BBC1's *Crimewatch UK*. Police announce that a man, thought to be in his thirties, was arrested on the Wirral in connection with Sarah's disappearance. But it turned out that the arrest was not a 'significant' development and he was released after a fairly short time.

On Monday July 17, detectives hunting for missing Sarah find the body of a young girl north of Littlehampton. The discovery was immediately given top priority by the Forensic Science Service who sealed off the surrounding area for a fingertip search for clues – including the slightest scrap of DNA evidence.

Evidence

The breakthrough came after a woman telephoned detectives in October to say that she had driven over a child's dress in a lane within hours of the abduction. It was only a later appeal that led her to make the link with Sarah. A search team was immediately dispatched to the Goose Green crossroads south of Coolham in West Sussex, but no trace was found of the dress.

They did, however, find a girl's black shoe and a fragment of a dress. They were found in a hedge about a mile from Pulborough where the eight-year-old's body was retrieved from a shallow grave. This was a very important discovery as these items could provide valuable DNA evidence. Forensic scientists carried out very thorough tests on the fragment of dress and the child's shoe, which they believed belonged to murdered schoolgirl Sarah Payne. Police believed that the items were thrown from a moving vehicle by her killer some time on July 2 – the day after Sarah was abducted. Both items, which were covered in mud and well camouflaged, had been badly damaged, possibly by a hedge cutter. It had been established that the hedge had been trimmed on July 15, two weeks after Sarah disappeared, and two days before her body was found.

Detective Superintendent Peter Kennett said: 'If they do turn out to belong to Sarah it is an extremely significant find.' Police said it could be up to two weeks before scientists have completed tests which will show whether there are traces of DNA on the clothing that could lead to Sarah's killer.

At Last a Conviction

On Wednesday, 7 February, 2001 a man appeared in court charged with the kidnap and murder of eight-year-old Sarah Payne. His name was Roy Whiting, a 42-year-old mechanic from Littlehampton, West Sussex. He had been arrested in Kent the day before and taken for questioning by murder squad detectives.

Whiting had been taken into police custody three times for questioning over Sarah's disappearance and murder. Whiting was first arrested 24 hours after Sarah disappeared but was released without charge. He was rearrested on July 31 but again freed after questioning by officers working on the inquiry. But the final conviction was due to the hard work of the forensic scientists once again.

The Oklahoma Bomber

It was April 19, 1995 – a lovely spring morning in Oklahoma. A yellow Ryder Rental truck carefully made its way through the streets of downtown Oklahoma City carrying a deadly cargo.

JUST AFTER 9 a.m. on April 19, 1995, a yellow Ryder Rental truck pulled into a parking area outside the Alfred P. Murrah Building. The driver stepped down from the truck's cab and casually walked away. A few minutes later, at 9:02, all hell broke loose as the truck's deadly 4000-pound cargo blasted the government building with enough force to shatter one third of the seven-storey structure to bits. Concrete, steel and glass rained down everywhere. In the smouldering rubble were adults and children alike – alive and dead.

Timothy James McVeigh saw himself as a crusader, a warrior, an avenger – and last, but not least, a hero. In reality, he was little more than a misguided coward. He never even heard clearly the sound of the initial sirens of emergency vehicles rushing to the scene. Because, blocks away, he was wearing earplugs to protect himself from the roar of a blast so powerful it lifted pedestrians off the ground.

A massive ball of fire momentarily outshone the sun and the north side of the building disintegrated. Traffic signs and parking metres were ripped from the pavement. Glass shattered and flew like bullets, targeting – and maiming – pedestrians blocks away.

Some of the lucky ones had left their usual posts to get a coffee, deliver documents or simply visit nearby offices. As they did, their offices and fellow workers were blown away. In the children's day-care centre directly above the mobile bomb, devastation was horrific. Upper floors collapsed on those beneath them, setting up a chain reaction that crushed everything and everyone below.

Rescue workers were at the scene almost immediately. Professionals and volunteers alike clawed their way through the rubble to help dig out the wounded and remove the dead. Temporary silences were observed so listening devices that can detect even human heartbeats were employed to locate anyone still living. In one case, sounding devices located a buried woman – Dana Bradley – as she cried for help. The twenty-year-old lay bleeding in a foot of water. For five hours, her leg had been pinned under a pile of cement. The massive pile of rubble trapping her could not be shifted, so the rescue team's only hope of getting her out alive was to amputate her crushed limb. She pleaded with them to try another way, but to delay posed a double threat. She could bleed to death, or the building could collapse on Dana and the rescue team – the rescuers had been driven out once before when the building had begun to shake.

On returning, volunteer Dr. Gary Massad faced one of the hardest decisions of his career. Because anaesthetic could trigger a fatal coma, the operation would have to be done while the patient was fully conscious. There was just no other way. Once the operation was done, she was finally dragged from the ruins and hospitalized. Dana Bradley lost more than part of her leg in the bombing; she also lost her mother and two young children.

No Licence Plate

Oklahoma Patrol Officer, Trooper Charlie Hanger, had been dispatched to Oklahoma City. Like many law enforcement officers, he'd been summoned to provide whatever assistance he could. He was about 75 miles from the disaster area when he noticed a beat-up 1977 Mercury Grand Marquis. What caught his attention was the yellow car's lack of a licence plate. He pulled the driver over and got out of his patrol car. Timothy McVeigh got out of the yellow truck and went to meet him.

Hangar wanted to know why McVeigh had no licence plate. McVeigh explained he'd just bought the car. When Hangar asked if he had insurance, registration, or a bill of sale McVeigh explained everything was being mailed to his address. Then he handed over his driver's licence.

It was then Hangar noticed a bulge under

McVeigh's jacket. "What's that?" the cop asked. When McVeigh said it was a gun, the trooper held his own weapon to McVeigh's head. Then Hangar confiscated the 9-mm Glock, as well as an ammunition clip and a knife. McVeigh pointed out he had a legal right to carry a gun. Hangar cuffed McVeigh, put him in the police car and phoned his base. He asked his dispatcher to run a computer check on McVeigh's Michigan driver's licence and the Glock.

After confirming McVeigh had no record, he explained that his New York concealed-weapon permit was not legal in Oklahoma. With McVeigh's permission, he searched the Mercury and found nothing but a baseball cap, some tools and a plain white envelope. The prisoner was told to leave everything in the car, which the trooper locked before taking McVeigh to the Noble County Jail in Perry, Oklahoma.

On the way there, McVeigh managed to hide a business card in the police car. The card was to cause problems for the man who'd supplied it – military supply dealer Dave Paulson. On the card, McVeigh had written 'TNT $5/stick need more' and 'Call after 01 May, see if I can get some more'. He left the card as payback for the way Paulson had dishonoured a dynamite and blasting caps transaction, assuming the FBI would eventually interrogate the weapons dealer on his connection with the bombing. And of course he was right.

At the jail, McVeigh was booked on four misdemeanour charges – unlawfully carrying a weapon, transporting a loaded firearm in a motor vehicle, failing to display a current licence plate, and failing to maintain proof of insurance.

McVeigh had also been carrying various miscellaneous items including earplugs, four .45-calibre bullets and $255. He was fingerprinted and photographed, and identified as prisoner number 95-057. It was the first time McVeigh had been charged with anything – and his first time in a jail. As McVeigh quietly waited in a cell, events were moving rapidly in other parts of the country.

In Virginia, at the FBI's behavioural science unit, profiling was underway. Whereas most investigators were convinced the bombing was the work of foreign terrorists, Clinton R. Van Zandt had other ideas. A psychological profiler who had worked as chief FBI negotiator at Waco, Texas – site of The Branch Davidian siege, Van Zandt noted the date of the attack. April 19, 1993 was exactly two years to the day when the deaths at Waco had occurred. He believed the perpetrator to be white, male and in his twenties. Furthermore, he theorized the suspect would be a military man and possibly a member of a fringe militia group. His assessment would be proven correct as the investigation progressed. Terrorism expert Louis R Mizell Jr. noticed that the date coincided with that of Patriot's Day, the anniversary of the Revolutionary War Battle of Concord, revered by the militia movement.

The rear axle of the Ryder truck had an identifying number on it, which had been blasted through the air and landed on a Ford Festiva. Also found was the rear bumper from the same truck – its licence plate number still legible. Both truck parts were rapidly traced to the name of the renter – Robert Kling, an alias McVeigh used on the rental agreement.

Agents raced to the Ryder Rental agency in Junction City. There, owner Eldon Elliot and his employees assisted an FBI artist who created two pictures: one of the man who rented the truck, as well as another who'd been in the office about the same time. Labelled John Doe 1 and John Doe 2, the suspects' portraits were shown throughout the rental agency's area. By the evening after the bombing, manager Lea McGown of the Dreamland Motel said she recognized the man federal agents called Kling.

Ms. McGown said the man had registered under the name of Timothy McVeigh, and that he had parked a large Ryder truck in the motel parking lot. It was yellow, she said, the same colour as the old Marquis he arrived in. Furthermore, when he signed in he gave Nichols farm in Decker, Michigan as his address. This matched the one on his driver's licence – and on the charge sheet at the Perry Police Station.

Time was running out for Timothy James McVeigh.

'Red Dawn'

It was after McVeigh had graduated that he developed an intense interest in the rights of gun owners. At his father's insistence, he did a stint at business college, but found it too monotonous.

His days of formal education were over. It was at this time that he discovered *The Turner Diaries.* He obsessed over this novel by former American Nazi Party official William Pierce. Writing under the name Andrew Macdonald, Pierce pumps out a litany of hate through the main character – Earl Turner. This 'hero' demonstrates his contempt for gun control laws by truck-bombing the Washington FBI headquarters.

About the same time, the movie *Red Dawn* helped convince McVeigh it was time to become a survivalist like Jedd – the film's hero played by Patrick Swayze. In the movie, Jedd leads his band of followers into the woods with seemingly endless rounds of ammunition and supplies they'll need to survive. Their mission is to destroy an invading Communist army.

Now needing funds to finance his growing fantasies, McVeigh went back to work for Burger King while he looked for a better paying job. Soon he was employed as an armed security guard with the Burke Armoured Car Service, where he's remembered as a diligent employee.

By now, he was twenty years old. He had a uniform, a gun and an armoured vehicle to drive around in. But he longed for better targets, bigger guns and real tanks. So, on May 24, 1988 Tim McVeigh joined the Army. There, he'd meet two men who would join him on his trip to terrorism.

It seemed that McVeigh had finally found his calling. The Army was everything he wanted in life, and more. When he joined, he was no leader, but an eager follower. There was discipline, a sense of order, and all the training a man could want in survival techniques. But, most of all, there was an endless supply of weapons, and instructions on how to use and maintain them.

While in basic training, he met two other soldiers who were to support his obsessive journey into crime: Terry Lynn Nichols and Michael Fortier.

Terry Nichols joined the army at a relatively mature age. He was nicknamed 'the old man' by the other recruits, and was twelve years older than McVeigh. They connected on the rifle range at Fort Benning and quickly formed a bond. Initially, McVeigh looked up to Nichols, but the balance shifted as their friendship grew. Nichols, who was married with a son did not warm to the strict Army routine, although he liked the weaponry. In fact the only reason he joined the army was because his other attempts at holding down a job had failed. He didn't last, he left to raise his son after his wife had left him.

Fortier, like McVeigh, was young. He was a very different character favouring pill-popping and pot-smoking. He probably only signed up because of his family's military background. Fortier and McVeigh became even closer after Nichols had left the service.

The three went from basic training to Fort Riley, Kansas. There, McVeigh became a gunner on the Bradley fighting vehicle. He'd already shown an extreme skill in marksmanship and he showed an unusually high level of skill with every weapon he used. As a result, he quickly advanced and was remembered as 'an excellent soldier'.

His military prowess earned him an invitation to try out for the Special Forces and he trained hard on his own time to ensure his chance to wear the Green Beret. But before he was due to be evaluated, Saddam Hussein cast a shadow over his plans. In 1991, the Gulf War broke out and McVeigh's First Infantry Division was dispatched to the Persian Gulf to serve in Desert Storm. Again, McVeigh excelled as a soldier and served with distinction. He became lead gunner on the Bradley Fighting Vehicle in the first platoon. In the army, Tim had become a VIP, and returned home with a fistful of decorations including the coveted Bronze Star.

He once again attempted to gain acceptance into the Special Forces. But he had lost a lot of stamina in Desert Storm, and was simply not fit enough to make the grade. This failure triggered a waning interest in military life and he left the army.

Life as a civilian was disillusioning. He felt nobody was interested in welcoming a war hero back into the workforce, and he became increasingly embittered with the system. He'd traded his army uniform for that of security guard.

Now, *The Turner Diaries* assumed an even greater importance. Without the army – and its discipline – he'd lost his identity, and his hatred for government festered. Then, early in 1993, he left his job and took off with everything he owned, and began driving around America, hoping to bring some meaning into his life. But he started by looking in all the wrong places. He decided to seek out his old army friends. He wanted to spend some time with Michael Fortier in Kingman Arizona, then visit Michigan to see Terry Nichols – now staying on a farm owned by his brother James Nichols. With the prospect of Fortier and Nichols back in his life, McVeigh felt like he could belong again. They were kindred spirits who supported his anti-government views.

One of the events that triggered his final drastic act started on February 28, 1993 when federal agents raided the property of the religious group called the Branch Davidians, headed by David Koresh. When the agents charged the Branch, lives were lost and many were wounded.

Sensing that the rights of the group to bear arms were being violated, McVeigh headed for Waco to lend support. In an interview he said to a student reporter: 'The government is continually growing bigger and more powerful, and the people need to prepare to defend themselves against government control.'

He left Waco a few days later and went to stay with Michael Fortier and his wife Lori in their mobile home in Kingman. But although they agreed on politics, Fortier's drug habits bored McVeigh to the point where he soon moved on to Tulsa, Oklahoma and Wanenmacher's World's largest Gun and Knife Show – just one of many gun shows he visited on his travels.

These events lifted McVeigh's spirits enormously. Gun show people seemed to think the way he did. One in particular – Roger Moore – had invited McVeigh to visit his Arkansas ranch. Moore often went by the name 'Bob Miller' at the shows. He didn't want people to know too much about him, and when McVeigh arrived at the ranch, he understood why. When Moore showed McVeigh around, it was obvious the place was loaded with weapons, explosive materials and other valuables. The security surrounding the ranch was almost non-existent and both Moore and Nichols would come to regret this visit.

When McVeigh arrived at the Nichols' Decker, Michigan farm, the reports coming out of Waco dominated the airwaves. In between watching the standoff on TV, the Nichols brothers introduced McVeigh to the art of making explosives out of readily-available materials. Tim was interested, but not yet ready to act on the information. Then, on April 19, 1993 they watched in horror as the Branch Davidians' compound was battered and burned into oblivion. This so outraged McVeigh and Nichols that they decided they had to put a stop to it, just like the heroes in *Red Dawn.*

In Preparation

McVeigh and Nichols started to build up knowledge from various bomb-building manuals. They followed the recipe and stockpiled their materials – bought under the alias Mike Havens – in rented storage sheds. The recipe also called for other ingredients like blasting caps and liquid nitro methane, which they stole.

They also stole to pay for their despicable

enterprise, and Nichols robbed gun collector Roger Moore at gunpoint. Moore claimed the thief had taken a variety of guns, gold, silver and jewels – about $60,000 worth. Nichols also stole Moore's van to haul away the loot. When police made a list of visitors to the ranch, McVeigh's name was on it. Earlier, McVeigh and Nichols travelled to the Fortier's Kingman home and stashed the stolen explosives in a nearby storage shed McVeigh had rented. When Fortier saw the explosives, McVeigh explained his plan. He stayed with the Fortiers, and while there, he designed his bomb. He showed Lori – using soup cans – how the drums he planned on using could be arranged for maximum impact.

A fuel McVeigh wanted for his bomb was the rocket fuel anhydrous hydrazine, but its expense made it impossible to obtain. Instead he settled on a satisfactory equivalent – nitro methane. In the course of trying to locate volatile fuels, McVeigh had phoned from the Fortiers, knowing full well his calls could be traced to the Fortier's telephone number – and the calling card he bought under the alias, Darel Bridges.

In mid-October 1994, McVeigh's grandfather died and his plans were thwarted. He headed home to Pendleton, New York. There, he helped sort out his grandfather's estate and further poisoned his young sister against the government. After watching a TV programme on WACO, he advised his sister that he had moved from the propaganda to 'action' stage. He also used her word processor to compose a letter titled 'ATF

Read'. It denounced government agents as 'fascist tyrants' and 'storm troopers' who had better be ready to pay for their actions at Waco. It warned the ATF: 'all you tyrannical mother fuckers will swing in the wind one day for your treasonous actions against the Constitution of the United States'.

While McVeigh was in Pendleton, he was unable to reach Terry Nichols. The co-conspirator had gone to the Philippines to see his current wife and baby daughter. Before he left, however, he paid a visit to his son and first wife Lana Padilla. While there he left her a few items including a sealed package, telling her it was to be opened only in the event he never returned. She opened it anyway. Inside the package was a letter detailing the location of a plastic bag he'd secreted in Padilla's home. It contained a letter to McVeigh telling him he was now on his own – and $20,000. There was also a combination to Nichols's storage locker, and when she opened the shed, she found some of the spoils of the Moore robbery.

In mid-December 1994, McVeigh and the Fortiers met in McVeigh's room at the Mojave Motel in Kingman, Arizona. There, he had Lori gift-wrap boxes containing blasting caps in Christmas paper. He then promised Fortier a cache of weapons from the Moore robbery if he would accompany McVeigh back to Kansas. On the way, McVeigh drove through Oklahoma City to show Fortier the building he intended to bomb, and the route he would take to walk away from the building before the blast. At this stage they parted.

The getaway car would be his 1977 yellow Marquis since his other car had been damaged in an accident. The plan was for Nichols to follow the car in his truck. After McVeigh parked it away from the bombsite, they would drive back to Kansas. The night before the bombing, they left the Marquis after McVeigh removed the licence plate and left a note on it saying it needed a battery. Then, they drove away and Nichols dropped him off at his motel.

The following afternoon, McVeigh picked up the Ryder truck and parked it at the Dreamland Motel for the night. The next morning he drove it to the Herington storage unit. When Nichols finally arrived – rather late – they piled the bomb components in the truck and drove to Geary Lake to mix the bomb. On completion, Nichols went home and McVeigh stayed with the Ryder truck. He parked in a gravel lot for the night and waited for dawn. He was wearing his favourite T-shirt, on the front of which was a picture of Abraham Lincoln with the motto *sic semper tyrannis*, the words Booth shouted before he shot Lincoln – 'Thus ever to tyrants'. While on the back of the T-shirt was a tree with blood dripping from the branches. This read, 'The tree of liberty must be refreshed from time to time with the blood of patriots and tyrants'.

Once again, like his role model in *The Turner Diaries*, he headed for a federal building where he was convinced ATF agents were working. But it was the people of Oklahoma City who would pay a terrible price for McVeigh's compulsive and irrational paranoia.

The Trial

The trial of Tim McVeigh opened on April 24, 1997. The lead defence attorney, Stephen Jones, had represented many unpopular clients in his time, but McVeigh was probably the most loathed individual he ever defended. Valiantly, he worked against overwhelming odds and damning evidence. He would need all the powerful cross-examination skills for which he was famous.

But the lead government lawyer, Joseph Hartzler, would easily overwhelm the defence team. A natural choice for the prosecution, he had previously won convictions against terrorists who plotted the bombing of a Chicago building. His reputation for building powerful cases on circumstantial evidence would be crucial – after all, no witness had actually placed McVeigh at the crime scene. The defence, however, had a mountain of facts to present.

Judge Robert Matsch, chief district judge for the District of Colorado, decreed McVeigh and Nichols would have separate trials – to ensure they were treated fairly. Because of this the trial was moved from Oklahoma, where public sentiment could have made a fair trial impossible, to Colorado. Nonetheless, sheer numbers were on the side of the prosecution – and ultimately, justice. There were 141 witnesses for the prosecution, opposed to just 27 for the defence.

Prosecutor Hartzler's opening statement summarized the events of the day – the explosion that destroyed the Murrah Building and the loss of innocent lives. He honed in on the Ryder truck and its deadly purpose: 'The truck was there also to impose the will of Timothy McVeigh on the rest of America in the hopes of seeing blood flow in the streets of America'. He also pointed out the message on the T-shirt that McVeigh had worn on that day. Having laid out the motive in further detail, it was Jones's turn to speak for the defence. In McVeigh's defence, Jones concentrated on mistaken identities and tried to negate the credibility of witnesses for the prosecution – among them three people McVeigh had trusted most – his sister Jennifer and friends Lori and Michael Fortier. The Fortiers had been so close that McVeigh had even been best man at their wedding. But as it turned out their testimonies were to be the most damning.

Lori Fortier told how McVeigh had arranged cans of soup to show how he could construct a truck bomb. And she told how she had laminated a fake driver's licence for McVeigh – the one in the name of Robert Kling McVeigh which was used to rent the Ryder truck. Lori even said when cross-examined by Hartzler: 'We turned the news on early that morning . . . we saw that the building had been blown up, and I knew right away that it was Tim'.

When Jones cross-examined the Fortiers, he showed them in the worst possible light. Their credibility was indeed suspect – after all, they had betrayed Tim in the hope that Michael Fortier would receive a lighter sentence.

When McVeigh's sister Jennifer appeared, she did so under the same terms as Lori Fortier – as a government witness, nothing she told the court could be used against her. Jennifer admitted under cross-examination that she had not been coerced into lying by the FBI in an earlier interview, and that every negative thing she'd told them about Tim was true.

Most damaging of all to McVeigh at the trial was Michael Fortier. Out of his cell for the occasion, he told in detail of events leading up to the bombing. His appearance was emotional, and full of contrition. When reminded that all the Fortiers had to do to stop the carnage was to lift the phone and warn authorities, Michael agreed. Fortier's hero-worship of McVeigh was evident when he told the court: 'If you don't consider what happened in Oklahoma, Tim is a good person'.

That statement probably did more to diminish Fortier than Jones could ever do. On his side, Jones had FBI wiretaps and phone recordings where Fortier exposed himself as a buffoon and liar. No doubt Jones hoped to have the jury think, 'Well, if this guy lied to the FBI and so many others, why believe him now?' In any case, Fortier's testimony had effectively nailed McVeigh.

Less dramatic events during the trial had already shown how phone cards consistently tracked McVeigh's location. Fingerprints on receipts proved his purchase of bomb ingredients. Explosives residue on his clothing and earplugs confirmed his involvement.

The jury took three days to decide – Timothy James McVeigh had indeed bombed the Murrah Building.

Final Execution

Timothy McVeigh was finally executed on June 12, 2001 by lethal injection. McVeigh made no final statement, but gave prison officials a handwritten copy of a nineteenth century poem which ends, 'I am the master of my fate, I am the captain of my soul'. McVeigh's execution was the first lethal injection by the U.S. government ever, and the first federal execution in 38 years.

Over 1400 journalists gathered outside the federal prison in Indiana but less than 200 protesters attended.

In a report on June 11, Timothy McVeigh is described as confronting death in good spirits. He is also reportedly convinced that he is the 'victor' in his personal war against the government. McVeigh still maintains he planted the bomb to 'teach the government a lesson', in retaliation for federal raids at Ruby Ridge, Idaho, and the Branch Davidian compound in Waco, Texas. In an excerpt from letters sent to *The Buffalo News*, McVeigh called the bombing 'a legit tactic'.

Forensic Science Today

Modern forensic science has a broad range of applications . . .

MODERN FORENSIC science is used in civil cases such as forgeries, fraud, or negligence. It can help law-enforcement officials determine whether any laws or regulations have been violated in the marketing of foods and drinks, the manufacture of medicines, or the use of pesticides on crops. It can also determine whether automobile emissions are within a permissible level and whether drinking water meets legal purity requirements. Forensic science can also be used to help us learn whether a country is developing a secret nuclear programme. However, forensic science is most commonly used to investigate criminal cases involving a victim, such as assault, robbery, kidnapping, rape, or murder.

Forensic science as practiced today is a high-technology field using electron microscopes, lasers, ultraviolet and infrared light, advanced analytical chemical techniques, and computerized databanks to analyze and research evidence. As shown in some of the cases documented in this book, forensic science has proved time and time again whether the person on trial is guilty or innocent . . .